Principles of the Common Law

# Principles of the Common Law

Michael Arnheim

Of Lincoln's Inn and King's Inns, Dublin
Barrister at Law
Sometime Fellow of St John's College, Cambridge

Duckworth

In memory of my beloved parents

First published in 2004 by
Gerald Duckworth & Co. Ltd.
90-93 Cowcross Street, London EC1M 6BF
Tel: 020 7490 7300
Fax: 020 7490 0080
inquiries@duckworth-publishers.co.uk
www.ducknet.co.uk



A catalogue record for this book is available from the British Library

ISBN 0 7156 3270 1

Typeset by Ray Davies
Printed in Great Britain by
CPI Bath

# Contents

# Preface

There is no shortage of books entitled 'Principles of Hog Law' or the like, but the word 'principles' in such contexts has come to mean no more than 'introduction to'. Such books often do not even set out the principles of the branch of law in question, nor (with a few notable exceptions) is this a feature generally to be found in more 'advanced' law texts. Most lawyers would probably be hard pressed to enunciate many, if any, of the basic principles of the common law. This is hardly surprising, as the last time any attempt was made to publish them was in Herbert Broom's *Legal Maxims*, of which the first edition appeared in 1845 and the tenth and last nearly a century later, in 1939. But this is a symptom rather than a cause. The real problem is that, as adherence to principle inhibits judge-made law, the old principles have increasingly fallen victim to judicial activism.

The present work makes no pretence to being a comprehensive compilation of the principles of the common law but offers instead an explanation, analysis and discussion of some of the most important and controversial of them. The period since 1939 has been a time of rapid change for the common law and there is now less agreement than ever about what those principles are, their nature and status, or even whether the common law is based on principle at all – and what is meant by 'principles' as against 'rules' or 'policies'.

But, if the common law is not based on principle, then what is its basis? Precedent? The doctrine of binding precedent, or *stare decisis*, is honoured increasingly in the breach rather than in the observance. Since 1966 the House of Lords has allowed itself to overrule its own past decisions. It has used this power sparingly, however, preferring instead simply to distinguish cases from which it wishes to distance itself. No two cases are ever fully 'on all fours' with each other in any event. But, where a judge or court follows a previous decision as a precedent it is on the basis of the *ratio decidendi* of the earlier case. Whatever definition is adopted of this much-debated term, it is hard to deny that it is essentially the *principle* informing the case that is being followed.

Principle and precedent, therefore, far from being two distinct alternative bases, are in fact the twin bulwarks upon which the majesty of the common law rests. Both are equally essential. A particular set of material facts may well cry out for a particular principle, and once that principle is applied to those facts a precedent is created.

Principles coupled with precedents make law predictable, and their absence make it unpredictable. Law which is unpredictable is uncertain, and uncertainty leads to injustice because it is unfair if essentially similar cases are not decided on the same basis. Vague and amorphous concepts such as the 'fair, just and reasonable' test proposed in recent years should not, however, be confused with real principles.

The common law originated in England but spread under the British flag to the four corners of the earth. The USA and most other former British colonies and dominions still retain a common law system. While concentrating on English common law, this book has a good deal to say about the use of common law principles in America and to a lesser extent in Australia and elsewhere. Where there is a difference between English common law and that to be found elsewhere it is often because the English judiciary has moved away from traditional principles. Even the language of English law has started to diverge from tradition. Thus the old term 'plaintiff' has recently been replaced in England alone with 'claimant'. More serious is the fact that the way the English courts now interpret the maxim 'No one should be a judge in his own cause' makes it harder to have a judge disqualified from sitting than it is in either the USA or Australia. Likewise, the old legal adage that 'An Englishman's home is his castle' is now less true of England than America, especially if the householder has the temerity to kill a burglar who is in the process of breaking into his home.

The fundamental principle that 'No one should be a judge in his own cause' is a timeless axiom, another such being 'Nobody shall profit from his own wrongdoing', and it is less than reassuring to find that they are not always applied with the rigour that they deserve.

Universal principles like these can often be traced back to the Romans and before. A principle of particular interest to the ancient Greeks was that of obedience to the law, which is discussed below with the aid of a little known dialogue quoted by Xenophon. Unless otherwise indicated all translations from Latin and Greek are my own.

It gives me little pleasure to say 'I told you so', but several decisions which are criticised in the main body of this book have now been reversed, notably *Naomi Campbell v Mirror Group Newspapers* [2004] UKHL 22, discussed on pages 177ff. Michael Douglas and Catherine Zeta-Jones won an unlikely victory at trial: [2003] EWHC 786 (Ch); see p. 180f. and my recently published *Handbook of Human Rights Law*. I should also mention one small new weapon in the arsenal of the weak and uninfluential defamation claimant, namely a Conditional Fee Agreement, i.e. 'no-win-no-fee' (see p. 188ff.), with the caveat that it may backfire.

I wish to thank my research assistants, Jan Dormann and Toran Shaw, especially for doing some of the routine work that is always such a chore. I am also indebted to my friend Jane Maple for her proofreading. All remaining errors are of course entirely my responsibility.

My publisher Deborah Blake of Duckworth is owed a special word of gratitude for her support and her long-suffering cheerfulness through several extensions of the deadline.

Dr Michael Arnheim
Holborn Chambers
6 Gate Street
Lincoln's Inn Fields
London WC2A 3HP

# Table of Cases

## *Table of Cases*

# Table of Statutes

# I

# Principles, Rules and Policies

This book is about the principles of the common law. But, it may pertinently be asked, are there really any such principles? Is the common law not simply made up of a succession of individual judgments linked by precedent – if at all?

There has been a good deal of debate within the judiciary itself about the relationship between principle and precedent. In theory these two concepts should be complementary and not opposed to each other at all. Lord Denning appeared to be adopting this inclusive view when he made an impassioned plea for what he called 'a science of law':

> Just as the scientist takes his instances and from them builds up his general propositions, so the lawyer should take his precedents and from them build up his general principles.[1]

The first problem with this formulation is that Lord Denning here treats the principles as emerging from the precedents and not the other way around. In other words, the process of thought described here is inductive rather than deductive reasoning, which is what one might expect where principles are concerned. For, if the principles of law are derived from judicial decisions, where do these decisions come from? The conventional answer would be that they in turn are based on precedent, i.e. previous cases. But, what makes a case a precedent? The conventional answer is that it is its *ratio decidendi* which determines this, which has been variously termed the 'principle' of the case or the 'rule of law' inherent in it. In his *Introduction to Legal Reasoning* E.H. Levi identified the thinking involved as a three-step process:

> The steps are these: similarity is seen between cases; next the rule of law inherent in the first case is announced; then the rule of law is made applicable to the second case.[2]

Lord Denning's view of legal reasoning as inductive rather than deductive – as starting from the cases rather than from rules or principles of law – formed part of his judicial activism. Going hand in hand with this was his belief that the principles of the law were not fixed in the heavenly firmament but could be changed by the judges as they saw fit:

> Just as the propositions of the scientist fall to be modified when shown not to fit all instances, or even discarded when shown to be in error, so the principles of the lawyer should be modified when found to be unsuited to the times or discarded when found to work injustice.[3]

The argument here is somewhat disingenuous. The scientific theory that the earth was flat, for example, could be disproved by objective evidence. The same cannot be said for the criteria that Lord Denning selected for deciding on the validity of legal principles. They are inherently subjective. How is it to be decided whether a particular principle is 'unsuited to the times' or whether it 'works injustice'? Lord Denning does not tell us. In fact, what we are talking about here is, to put it at its simplest, the judges' gut instinct, which is usually dignified by the label of 'public policy'. This theory allows judges to ride roughshod over time-honoured principles.

### *Is the common law based on principles?*

This brings us back to our starting point: Is the common law based on principle at all? This is still a matter of debate as far as English law is concerned. Scots law is plainly based on principles largely drawn from Roman Law rather than on precedent. These principles have been systematised and set out in orderly fashion in a succession of 'institutional writings', which have long been accorded the status of authorities which may be relied upon by the courts. The most notable of these are Viscount Stair's *Institutions of the Law of Scotland* (1681), Erskine's *Institute of the Law of Scotland* (1773) and Bell's *Commentaries on the Law of Scotland* (1800) and *Principles of the Law of Scotland* (1829). The way these texts are used by the Scottish courts is well illustrated by the judgments in *Burmah Oil v Lord Advocate*.[4]

But what about English law? Can it also be said to be based on principles? If so, what are they, where do they come from and how are they to be ascertained? Above all, what do they mean and how are they to be interpreted and applied?

### *Blackstone*

Sir William Blackstone (1723-80) identified the source of the common law as 'established rules and maxims', whose authority he attributed to custom, or 'general reception and usage':[5]

## I. Principles, Rules and Policies

> Some have divided the common law into two principal grounds or foundations: 1. established customs; such as that where there are three brothers, the eldest brother shall be heir to the second, in exclusion of the youngest: and 2. established rules and maxims; as, 'that the king can do no wrong, that 'no man shall be bound to accuse himself,' and the like. But I take these to be one and the same thing. For the authority of these maxims rests entirely upon general reception and usage; and the only method of proving, that this or that maxim is a rule of the common law, is by shewing that it hath been always the custom to observe it.

According to this, custom and the common law are 'one and the same thing'. What about rules and maxims (i.e. principles)? Blackstone appears to regard these terms also as interchangeable, as he refers first to 'rules and maxims' and then merely to maxims'. In short, for Blackstone the principles of the common law derive from custom.

This presents quite a contrast to the more modern view which traces the origin of principles to judicial decision-making. For Blackstone, 'judicial decisions are the principal and most authoritative *evidence* that can be given of the existence of such a custom as shall form a part of the common law' (italics supplied). The key word here is 'evidence': judicial decisions do not *make* law but only reflect what the law is. What then is the relationship between principle and precedent? For Blackstone –

> ... it is an established rule to abide by former precedents, where the same points come again in litigation; as well to keep the scale of justice even and steady, and not liable to waver with every new judge's opinion; as also because the law in that case being solemnly declared and determined, what before was uncertain, and perhaps indifferent, is now become a permanent rule, which is not in the breast of any subsequent judge to alter or vary from, according to his private sentiments; he being sworn to determine, not according to his own private judgment, but according to the known laws and customs of the land; not delegated to pronounce a new law, but to maintain and expound the old one.[6]

A judge may depart from a previous judicial decision which is 'most evidently contrary to reason, much more if it be contrary to the divine law'. 'But even in such cases', adds Blackstone, 'the subsequent judges do not pretend to make a new law but to vindicate the old one from misrepresentation.' He sums up his position as follows:

> The doctrine of the law then is this: that precedents and rules must be followed, unless flatly absurd or unjust: for though their reason be not obvious at first view, yet we owe such a deference to former times as not to suppose they acted wholly without consideration.[7]

Is this still the law today? For Blackstone wrote over two centuries ago. There are those who would pooh-pooh Blackstone's formulation as either hopelessly obsolete or hopelessly naive, or both. The cynic would say that judges work backwards: they first decide which party in a particular case they want to win, and only then do they try to justify their decision by reference to authority, rules and principles. Activist judges and their acolytes, on the other hand, maintain the need to keep the law abreast of modern needs and are not slow to cast themselves in the role of the saviours of the law from the dead hand of the past.

In a celebrated paper on 'The Judge as Lawmaker' published in 1972, Lord Reid frankly admitted the existence and inevitability of judge-made law. But, he concluded, 'in order to prevent the law from becoming a jungle you must give our young men some unifying principles which they can understand and use'.[8]

Lip-service is still regularly paid by judges to 'principles', sometimes even at their colleagues' expense. So, for example, in *Murphy v Brentwood District Council* decided in 1990 Lord Keith of Kinkel gave the ultimate quietus to the hitherto celebrated House of Lords decision in *Anns v Merton*:[9] 'I think it must now be recognised' that *Anns* 'did not proceed on any basis of principle at all, but constituted a remarkable example of judicial legislation.'

Whatever else we may say about this attack, it clearly commends 'principle' and condemns 'judicial legislation'. And this is no isolated text. There is no shortage of similar praise for 'principles' in judicial decisions down to the present day. We can only assume therefore that the common law of England *is* based on principles – whatever that may mean.

### *Principles and rules*

The words 'principle' and 'rule' are often used by lawyers and laymen alike as if they were synonyms. So, for example, we find references sometimes to the 'principle of ultra vires' and sometimes to the 'rule of ultra vires'. Is there a difference between a rule and a principle, and, if so, what is it?

Ronald Dworkin, a legal academic, has suggested that 'Principles have a dimension that rules do not – the dimension of weight or importance ... Rules do not have this dimension.'[10] If two principles 'intersect', the 'weightier' principle will prevail. But, 'If two rules conflict, one of them cannot be a valid rule.' No examples are given. But, what if there is conflict not between two principles or between two rules but between a principle and a rule? Which one takes precedence? As one of them *has* to take precedence over the other, rules must presumably also have 'weight'. Indeed, the old New York case of

*Riggs v Palmer*[11] which Dworkin cites is actually an example of this, the question before the court being whether a murderer could inherit under the will of his grandfather, who was his victim. Here the rule that a will should be honoured came into conflict with the principle that no one should profit from his own crime. The principle trumped the rule, from which we should presumably conclude that the principle was 'weightier' than the rule.

Or was the law honouring wills also a principle? It is hard to tell. Even Dworkin admits: 'It is not always clear from the form of a standard whether it is a rule or a principle.' And: 'Sometimes a rule and a principle can play much the same role, and the difference between them is almost a matter of form alone.' If this means anything at all, it presumably indicates that principles and rules may sometimes appear indistinguishable and at other times differ only in superficial appearance.

It may perhaps be more useful to say that both terms, 'principles' and 'rules', refer to obligatory standards but that a principle is more fundamental and therefore more important than a mere rule. It is the *rule* of the road in Britain that you must drive on the left, but it is a *principle* of the common law that every user of the public highway owes a duty of care to every other user of the public highway. What this means is that where there is a clash between a principle and a rule the principle should prevail. If a motorist could prevent an accident merely by crossing over to the wrong side of the road, what should he do? Should he refuse to cross over because he would be in breach of the rule of the road? Or should he make every effort to prevent an accident even if it means breaking a rule? The latter choice is likely to be viewed by a court as the lesser of two evils and therefore the less culpable. Why? Because the duty to drive on the left is outweighed by the duty of care to others on the road. Why? Because the latter is by its very nature a higher, more important obligation than the former. We could refer to both of them as rules, differentiating them simply as 'higher' or 'lower' rules, or we could characterise the higher rule as a principle and the other as merely a rule.

This classification is further justified by the fact that, while principles tend to have a moral content, rules are often quite arbitrary. So, although it is the rule of the road in Britain, most Commonwealth countries and Japan that you must drive on the left, in the USA and the rest of the world the rule is exactly the opposite. Until the time of the French Revolution the universal rule was to ride on the left. This made sense on the assumption that most people were right-handed and therefore wore their sword on the left. If you rode on the left you would draw your sword with your right hand and be able to protect yourself against anyone who came alongside you on the right. Because riding on the left was traditional, Revolutionary France rode on the right – just to be different. It is clear from this that 'the rule of the road' is just that, a rule rather than a principle. But, if we look at the French origin of the obligation to drive on the right we might perhaps label it a 'policy', as it was politically motivated. This just shows how fluid all these labels are.

One approach may be to see principles as a sub-set or sub-category of rules - on the basis that all principles are rules but not all rules are principles. In this sense principles may be regarded as higher rules or general rules. Alternatively, rules and principles may both be viewed as belonging to another larger category, which we might label 'standards', 'obligatory standards' or 'legal doctrines'.

The broad category of rules includes rules and standards which clearly stand well outside the sphere of law altogether. So, for example, the game of cricket is governed by a set of rules, but not even the most fervent cricket enthusiast would claim that these rules form part of the law of England or any other country. Similarly, spitting in public is an anti-social and unhygienic practice which is now generally regarded as unacceptable. But, it is a moral standard of behaviour, not a legal rule. However, if Parliament were to pass a law prohibiting spitting in public, then it would become a legal rule - as indeed it once was in certain countries. Adultery is another example of conduct which is generally disapproved of in most societies. In some countries adultery is also a criminal offence, sometimes even punishable by death; in others, like the United Kingdom for example, it used to be against the law but is not any longer.

But, to return to law, let us take a few simple hypothetical examples to illustrate the difference between rules and principles.

(1) 'Householders must paint their front doors blue.' This is clearly a rule and not a principle. It is a specific and detailed order with no obvious justification.

(2) 'Householders must clear snow from the pavement in front of their property.' The phrasing here is very similar in style to that of the previous rule, but it is quite easy to justify. Does that make this a principle? Probably not. It is still a little too specific for that.

(3) 'Householders are liable for any injury caused to anyone slipping or falling on snow in the pavement in front of their property.' Though phrased in a style which might appear more appropriate for a principle, this is essentially a restatement of (2) from a different perspective. Is that enough to convert it from a rule to a principle? It is probably still a bit too specific and arbitrary, as it begs the question: what about injuries unconnected with snow?

(4) 'Householders are responsible for keeping the pavement in front of

their property clean and safe, and they are liable for any injuries resulting from their failure to do so.' This is more general and less arbitrary than any of the previous statements. Is that enough to make it a principle? Possibly. However, it lacks the quality of timelessness, which is something we tend to associate with the highest of principles. For, why should householders be responsible for anything that happens outside the boundaries of their property? Should this not be a matter for the local authority which owns the pavement in question? In other words, what we have here could more accurately be described as a policy than as a principle.

(5) 'Everyone is liable for any injury resulting from any act or omission of his.' Here at last we are in the presence of something that is indisputably a principle. How do we know? First, it is a general obligation. Secondly, it has a definite moral content. Thirdly, it is reasonable. Moreover, it has a timeless quality.

### *Principles, rules and policies*

Instead of a clearcut distinction between rules and principles what we find is a continuum extending from petty rules to general rules to principles and ultimately to high principles or to axioms, namely self-evident rules such as 'No one should be a judge in his own cause' or 'Nobody shall profit from his own wrongdoing', both of which are considered later in this book. The more specific, detailed or arbitrary a standard is the more likely it is to be regarded as a rule, the term 'principle' being reserved for more general standards of a higher order or with a moral content. Does it matter whether a particular standard is regarded as a rule or a principle? No. In the event of a conflict between a principle and a rule we should no doubt expect the principle to prevail, though that is by no means always the case.

In *Malcolm v University of Oxford*,[12] for example, an author who had been invited to submit a book to a publishing house was asked to make major revisions and resubmit it. The author balked at the prospect of virtually rewriting the book. He eventually agreed but only on condition that the publishers gave him a firm commitment to publish the work once revised. This was done, with the extremely unusual proviso that the revisions did not make the book any worse than before! On this basis the author rewrote the book. That the revised version was an improvement was not disputed, but the publishers still refused to publish it, claiming that there was no contractual obligation on them to do so. The judge at first instance agreed with them, albeit 'with considerable regret'. There had indeed been 'a firm commitment' on the part of the Oxford University Press to publish the work, it was held, but the court felt unable to find a binding contract because of the vagueness of that commitment. Too many questions were left unanswered: 'for example, how many copies were to be printed, in hardback or paperback or both, at what price and yielding what royalty?' As pointed out by the present author shortly afterwards, this should not have got in the way of the fact that there was an *agreement* to publish with enough *certainty* to constitute a binding contract. The Court of Appeal found that there was indeed a contract. Here the *principle* of contract as agreement overrode the technical rule-bound approach adopted at first instance which expected formal agreement to have been reached on numerous points of detail. However, principle does not always prevail over rules, and it would not have done so in *Malcolm* either had the author not appealed.[13]

What is more likely to get the better of principles, however, are not rules but policies. The chief identifying mark of a principle as against a policy is the element of timelessness. By contrast, a standard based on political or social considerations or economic convenience is better characterised as a policy rather than a principle. But it is not always easy to distinguish the two categories.

### *Marital rape*

The issue of rape in marriage is a good example of this problem. The traditional position as stated in 1736 was:

> But the husband cannot be guilty of a rape committed by himself upon his lawful wife, for by their lawful matrimonial consent and contract the wife hath given herself up in this kind unto her husband which she cannot retract.[14]

Was this a principle, a rule or a matter of policy? As an extrapolation from what was then seen as the fundamental basis of the marriage contract, it was probably a principle. Rape was defined by the Sexual Offences (Amendment) Act 1976 as follows: 'A man commits rape if – *(a)* he has unlawful sexual intercourse with a woman who at the time of the intercourse does not consent to it; and *(b)* at the time he knows that she does not consent to the intercourse or he is reckless as to whether she consents to it ....' *In R v J – (rape: marital exemption)*[15] it was held that the word 'unlawful' in this definition meant 'illicit', i.e. outside marriage. It was therefore held that the traditional exemption had been preserved by the modern statute. However, in *R v R – (rape: marital exemption)*[16] the House of Lords unanimously answered in the affirmative the certified question of law of general public importance submitted to it by the Court of Appeal: 'Is a husband criminally liable for raping his wife?' Did this signify a change in the law or was the implication that this had always been the law?

Because judges are not supposed to make law but only to declare what the law has always been, any change in the law made by the courts is treated as if the law had never been any different. If the judges came out and admitted that they were changing the law that would be tantamount to claiming the power to legislate and would challenge the doctrine of the legislative supremacy of Parliament. The fact that this doctrine is itself a legal fiction because Parliament is in reality controlled by the executive would not affect the significance of the legal fiction that only Parliament has the power to change the law.

So, if the House of Lords was admitting that it had changed the law about marital rape then that would have been an admission that it had overstepped the proper limits of its authority. On the other hand, if the law had always been what it is now said to be, then generations of judges had obviously got it wrong.

Related to this is the classification of the doctrine about rape in marriage. If it is a principle we would expect it to have been there all along, but if it has only recently been changed then it is more likely to be a policy decision. To confuse matters further, it was actually referred to by the House of Lords as an 'exception to a general rule'.

The basis of the change in the law was that the role of women had changed in recent years and that marriage now represented a partnership of equals rather than control of the husband over the wife, so that consent to sexual intercourse was required just as much within marriage as outside it.

The leading speech given by Lord Keith of Kinkel concluded as follows:

> I am therefore of the opinion that section I (I) of the 1976 Act presents no obstacle to this House declaring that in modern times the supposed marital exception in rape forms no part of the law of England.[17]

The use of the phrase 'in modern times' is tantamount to an admission that this was a policy change. But Lord Keith then went on to quote an extract from the judgment of Lord Chief Justice Lane in the Court of Appeal, whom he described as taking 'a similar view'. This is what Lord Lane said:

> The remaining and no less difficult question is whether, despite that view, this is an area where the court should step aside to leave the matter to the parliamentary process. This is not the creation of a new offence, it is the removal

> of a common law fiction which has become anachronistic and offensive and we we consider that it is our duty having reached that conclusion to act upon it.[18]

Upon examination it is clear that Lord Lane's was a much more cautious approach than that subsequently adopted by the House of Lords. First, Lord Lane made a point of raising the possibility of leaving the problem to be cured by Parliament – the only proper course where a change in the law is called for. By stressing that 'this is not the creation of a new offence' he was trying to avoid the possibility of any accusation that the judges were legislating.

Perhaps the most useful way of looking at this issue is as a clash between two principles: the general principle of the need for consent to sexual intercourse and, what is really an exception to that general principle, the principle of the wife's automatic consent to sexual intercourse in marriage. It would not be difficult to conclude that in the event of a clash the general principle of consent is to be preferred to the marital exception.

### *Public policy*

Alternatively, the change in the law may be seen as a matter of public policy, as was practically admitted by Lord Keith. It was Lord Chief Justice Hobart (died 1625) who described public policy as 'an unruly horse', by which he meant that once mounted it was difficult to control. Needless to say, that great judicial activist Lord Denning disagreed:

> With a good man in the saddle, the unruly horse can be kept in control. It can jump over obstacles. It can leap the fences put up by fictions and come down on the side of justice, as indeed was done in *Nagle v Feilden*.[19] It can hold a rule to be invalid even though it is contained in a contract.[20]

But some of Lord Denning's own judgments, many of which were reversed on appeal in his own lifetime and others overruled later, point up the problems inherent in policy-based decisions, in particular their subjective and sometimes even arbitrary nature.

In recent times there have been many, undoubtedly far too many, examples of judicial policy decisions. The modern history of the law of negligence, for example, is one long series of policy decisions, starting with *Donoghue v Stevenson*[21] and culminating in the current doctrine of 'pure economic loss'.[22] Judicial review,[23] with its shifting criteria, is another area rich in policy decisions, and so is crime. Indeed, there are few areas of law not affected by it.

Principles and policies overlap, but in general it can be said that while principles are more likely to be timeless, based on reason and reflected in a line of decided cases, policy decisions are essentially reactions to current events and are therefore likely to be contrary to precedent and sometimes to reason as well. The opportunity to make policy decisions tends to be welcomed by activist judges, as they can then break with time-honoured principles and precedents in the name of progress. It also enables them to strike a blow for judicial supremacy over the other branches of government.

### *Compilations of principles*

Despite the lip-service which is still paid to the importance of principles in the common law, it is significant that there is no modern compilation of these doctrines.

There has however been a succession of such works in the past. Indeed, the two most venerable texts on English law fall into this category, namely the *Tractatus de Legibus et Consuetudinibus Angliae* (*Treatise on the Laws and Customs of England*) commonly attributed to and indeed referred to simply as Glanvill, dating from between 1187 and 1189 in the reign of Henry II, and Bracton's treatise written under the same title between 1250 and 1259 in the reign of Henry III. Much of Glanvill is concerned with procedure, but it also includes a brief résumé of the principles of substantive law. Bracton is more ambitious. Modelled to some extent on Justinian's *Institutes* and *Digest*, this remarkable work is an attempt to set out the basic principles of English law, which are often strangely familiar. So, for example, in the section 'On acquiring dominion by purchase' Bracton states that 'there can be no purchase without a fixed price', a principle derived from Roman law but one which, with certain exceptions, is still applicable in the common law today.[24]

The next landmark in English juristic scholarship is occupied by the writings of Sir John Fortescue (c. 1394 - c. 1476), which focus specifically on constitutional and political matters: *De Laudibus Legum Angliae* (*In Praise of the Laws of England*), written in about 1470, and *The Governance of England*, first published posthumously, in 1714. But these books are discussions of the law rather than attempts to set out its principles and they contain more than a trace of political propaganda.

Sir Thomas Littleton's *Tenures*, written in about 1481, a masterpiece of legal exegesis, sets out the principles of English land law as it had grown up over the years. Compiled quite independently of any Roman law source, it has been hailed as the first real textbook of English law. Because of the fundamental changes that have affected this area of the law since that time, notably the introduction of a whole statutory regime in 1925, Littleton is not of much practical importance any more. Its greatest relevance probably lies in constitutional law through Sir Edward Coke's diffuse commentary on it in *Coke on Littleton*, published as the first volume of his *Institutes*. The fact that Coke gave his magnum opus this Latin title, borrowed from the compilations bearing the names of the Roman jurist Gaius and the Emperor Justinian, is itself significant. Coke's intention was to produce a comprehensive account of the leading principles of English law. The work is certainly conceived on a grand scale, covering as it does land law, the Constitution, statute law in general, crime and procedural law. Only the first book was published in Coke's lifetime, the rest appearing in 1641, on the very eve of the Civil War.

Sir Edward Coke (1552-1634) was a leading player in the run-up to the English Civil War. As Attorney-General from 1594 to 1606, covering the last years of the reign of Elizabeth I (1558-1603) and the first of James I (1603-25), Coke was an ardent champion of the Crown and the royal prerogative. He showed himself an enthusiastic, not to say savage, prosecutor in the leading trials of the day, including those of the Earl of Essex in 1600-01, Sir Walter Raleigh in 1603 and Guy Fawkes and his co-conspirators in 1605. Then, appointed Chief Justice of Common Pleas in 1606, he suddenly changed into a scourge of the Crown. Translated to King's Bench in 1613 in the hope that his sympathies would revert to the Crown, he continued his opposition to the prerogative. Dismissed by James I in 1616, it was not long before Coke re-emerged in a new guise, this time as a leader of the parliamentary opposition to the Crown. So much so that he was briefly lodged in the Tower for his pains, but in the Parliament of 1628 he was in the forefront of the opposition once again, inspiring and participating in the drafting of the Petition of Right passed by both Houses of Parliament in that year.

Coke was one of the most colourful characters ever to sit on the English bench. Uniquely qualified by his sharp intellect and scholarly bent to compile an authoritative and comprehensive restatement of the principles of English law, his polemical nature impelled him to twist the law to suit his purposes. The reliability of his *Institutes* as a source of law is therefore sometimes questionable. There is a similar problem with his *Reports*, a record of his own decisions on the bench with interspersed comments. These are nevertheless a valuable source not only of Coke's own judgments but also of earlier decisions which are cited and often discussed, sometimes in considerable detail. Coke was an antiquarian by inclination, and his writings are a veritable treasure trove of earlier decisions and laws, many of which do not survive in any other form.

Coke's great antagonist, Francis Bacon (1561-1626), was not only a distinguished lawyer but also a prolific writer and probably one of the greatest intellects in English history (not to mention the claim advanced by some that it was he who was the true author of the works of Shakespeare!). A believer in codification, he, together with one or two others, actually embarked on an abortive attempt to codify the law of England. But what does survive and is perhaps Bacon's most valuable contribution to law is his *Maxims of the Law*, a brief and very incomplete attempt to identify the principles underlying the whole of English law. Had Bacon persisted with this work it might perhaps have come to enjoy the status of a major source of law. As it is, the principles assembled are largely concerned with land law, though there are some of more general applicability and greater relevance to the modern world.

It was left to Herbert Broom to compile *A Selection of Legal Maxims* (first published in 1845) based on Bacon's writings among others. The word 'maxim', which has now rather fallen out of use as a term of art, gives a very inadequate impression of the importance of these statements of fundamental principles. This is how Broom put it in the Preface to his first edition:

> The frequency with which Maxims are not only referred to by the Bench, but cited and relied upon by Counsel in their arguments; the importance which has, in many decided cases, been attached to them; the caution which is always exercised in applying, and the subtlety and ingenuity which have been displayed in distinguishing between them, seem to afford reasonable grounds for hoping that the mere Selection of Maxims here given may prove useful to the Profession, and that the examples adduced, and the authorities referred to by way of illustration, qualification, or exception, may, in some limited degree, add to their utility.[25]

Broom's confidence was justified at the time. In Britain alone his *Maxims* went through no fewer than ten editions in the space of almost a century, the last appearing in 1939. Yet today, not only is Broom's book largely forgotten but, what is rather more disquieting, the Maxims themselves are all too often ignored as well.

Probably the biggest name in authoritative legal texts is that of Sir William Blackstone (1723-80), an academic lawyer turned judge, whose views on the common law were discussed earlier in this chapter. He has frequently been cited in the English courts, though not perhaps with quite the same fervour as across the Atlantic. Blackstone's *Commentaries on the Laws of England*, which first appeared in 1765-70, were based on his lectures as Vinerian Professor at Oxford, the first lectures on English law ever given at any English university (only Roman law having been taught up to that time).

Blackstone's value as an authority depends less on his own views than on the old authorities which he cites and, not least, on the clarity of Blackstone's arrangement of his material and his pellucid exposition of the principles in all the main branches of the law.

Though Blackstone has often been cited in court, his arch-critic Jeremy Bentham (1748-1832) is rarely, if ever, accorded that distinction. This is because, besides his convoluted and opaque prose style, he was more interested in what the law should be than what it actually was. In his earliest writings, *A Fragment on Government* and *A Comment on the Commentaries* published in 1776, Bentham launched an out-and-out attack on Blackstone's whole approach to law. One of Bentham's pet projects was the codification of the law. He devised a new methodology for an all-encompassing code covering all aspects of human behaviour, which, having been adopted in one country, would eventually become universal, so that Bentham himself would become 'legislator of the world'. Though this ambitious project never came to fruition, Bentham did produce one volume of a *Constitutional Code*, which was published towards the end of his life.

'The greatest happiness of the greatest number' was for Bentham the bedrock principle not only of his political and economic theories but also of his view of the law. As each individual was the best judge of what was in his own interest, Bentham argued, the role of the state should be restricted. This led to another fundamental principle, namely that laws should be made by a duly elected legislature and not by unelected judges.

So, ironically, on this fundamental point, which is now so much under attack, Bentham agreed with his bête noire, Blackstone. Coming from diametrically opposite standpoints these two great jurists agreed that judges should not make law.[26]

II

# Law and Logic

*Est quidem vera lex recta ratio naturae congruens.*
(True law is right reason in conformity with nature.)

Cicero (106-43 BC)[1]

Nothing is law that is not reason.

Powell J in *Coggs v Bernard* (1703)[2]

**Are logic and reason still fundamental principles of the law? The answer must be Yes in order to achieve intelligibility, certainty and predictability, without which the law becomes arbitrary, inequitable and unjust.**

## *Oliver Wendell Holmes*

'The life of the law has not been logic: it has been experience.' This famous remark made by Oliver Wendell Holmes Jr comes from the beginning of his book on *The Common Law*.[3] What is meant by this is that, as he put it, law 'cannot be dealt with as if it contained only the axioms and corollaries of a book of mathematics.' As Holmes put it elsewhere, 'the whole outline of the law is the resultant of a conflict at every point between logic and good sense – the one striving to work fiction out to consistent results, the other restraining and at last overcoming that effort when the results become too manifestly unjust.'[4] This ties in with another oft-quoted aphorism of his, that the principles of the law are not a 'brooding omnipresence in the sky.' In other words, rules and principles are not abstract concepts but must be tied to reality. But perhaps it is yet another of Holmes's dicta that explains his attitude to the common law best of all: 'The prophecies of what the courts will do in fact, and nothing more pretentious, are what I mean by the law.'[5] Here we have the same emphasis on the practical, but predictability of the outcome of a case presupposes certainty of the law, and certainty can only be based on principle, reason and logic. Unless cases with similar material facts are consistently decided on the same reasoned and logical basis, predictions or 'prophecies' will be impossible.

## *II. Law and Logic*

### *Comparative thinking*

Most people think they can think – and none more so than lawyers. But all too often what passes for thought is in reality merely feeling, sentiment, prejudice or wishful thinking, which is not thinking at all. Everyday speech is full of examples: 'I think it's a lovely day'; 'He thinks of her all the time'; 'We think the world of you'; 'I think I'll try'; 'I really can't think how you manage!'

One cardinal feature which is present in all real thinking is the element of comparison. This is not always obvious, but there is a tacit comparison involved even in such simple and straightforward thoughts as: '(I think) this table is big enough'; '(I think) City is going to win the cup'; or '(I think) there'll be another bus along soon.'

How much is 'enough'? It will of course vary according to the question in hand, but it will always involve a comparison of one kind or another. To decide whether the table is 'big enough' you have to compare its size with that of, say, the flower-arrangement that you want to put on it or the space occupied by the people that you wish to seat around it. Likewise, to conclude that City is going to win the cup you will have to have studied the team's form by comparison with that of its rivals'. And, unless your remark about the bus is pure wishful thinking, you will have to have compared an entry on the timetable with your watch. If you wanted to test the reliability of the timetable you would have to compare what the timetable said on past occasions with the actual performance of the buses.

In fact, even when you simply describe something as 'big', 'small', 'old', 'new', 'cheap' or 'expensive', you are actually making a tacit comparison. A 'big' dog is invariably a lot smaller than, say, a 'big' elephant, but it is not confusing to use the word just the same, because when we say 'Brutus is a big dog' we are comparing his size not with that of an elephant, a hippopotamus or a mouse but with other dogs we have seen. The point is that 'big', though it does not appear to be a comparative term, is practically meaningless unless we think about it in a comparative way.

### *Donoghue v Stevenson*

Law likewise has a comparative basis. When, for example, a certain Mrs Donoghue was served a bottle of ginger beer with a semi-decomposed snail floating in it, she sued the manufacturers for the shock and gastroenteritis she had suffered as a result of her novel experience. When the case reached the House of Lords two of the judges were for throwing Mrs Donoghue's complaint out, on the ground that even if everything she said was true the manufacturers could not be held liable as there was no contract between her and them – because she had not actually bought the ginger beer herself but had been 'treated' to it by a friend. Lord Atkin, however, in what is now one of the best known judgments in English law, found for Mrs Donoghue by extending the concept of the duty of care. Thanks to the support of two Scottish judges Lord Atkin's view prevailed and permanently changed the law. But the point is that both diametrically opposed views applied a comparative approach. The two English law lords compared the facts of Mrs Donoghue's case with contract cases while Lord Atkin compared it with cases in tort.

*Donoghue v Stevenson*[6] is now generally regarded as establishing a new principle as the basis for the tort of negligence. But Lord Atkin could hardly put it like that at the time. For, a judge is supposed to interpret and apply the law, not to make it. So he was at pains to find some precedent which he could fasten on to. One of the few cases which he prayed in aid was *George v Skivington.*[7] Mr George bought a bottle of hairwash for his wife from a chemist who had made up the preparation himself. Mrs George used the hairwash and developed a rash as a result. The action against the chemist was brought by both Mr and Mrs George. On what basis could the wife claim, as she had not bought the preparation and therefore had no contractual relationship with anyone? It was held that the chemist owed a duty of care not only to the husband as purchaser but also to the wife as 'the person for whose use the vendor knew the compound was purchased'.

Did Mrs George's success depend on the fact that the chemist knew that the hairwash, though bought by her husband, was intended for her use? Lord Buckmaster, one of the dissenting judges in *Donoghue v Stevenson*, certainly thought so. Indeed, he went further and roundly condemned Lord Atkin's doctrine as simply wrong. 'This conception is simply to misapply to tort doctrines applicable to sale and purchase. The principle of tort lies completely outside the region where such considerations apply ....'

Lord Buckmaster's robust dissenting speech repays careful study, embodying as it does the traditional position of the English judiciary as upholders of time-honoured principles encapsulated in precedent. So incensed was he at Lord Atkin's radical departure from this norm that he did not even bother to attend the formal speech-reading ceremony. (It was read out instead by his fellow-dissenter Lord Tomlin.)

The language of Lord Buckmaster's speech reveals his disquiet. 'If one step, why not fifty?' This challenge echoes down the years. What Lord Buckmaster meant was that an apparently slight deviation from established principle was likely to lead to more major shifts. This turned out to be prophetic: the half-century that followed *Donoghue v Stevenson* saw such an expansion of the scope of the tort of negligence that the House of Lords has spent the past two decades reining it in.

A practically unknown case of a few years after Mrs Donoghue's encounter with the phantom snail illustrates how a logical extension of contract principles could be applied in a very similar case. In *Lockett v Charles*[8] a husband and wife had lunch together in a restaurant. Both had whitebait. The husband paid for both. So far nothing out of the ordinary. The wife got food poisoning. Both husband and wife sued the restaurant, but the claim was framed purely in contract. As neither husband nor wife was 'in charge of the proceedings' the judge had no difficulty in finding that the restaurant proprietor had a contract with both of them and that there had been a breach of an implied warranty that the food was fit for human consumption. The husband was awarded damages of £99.40 and the wife £100.

Was Mrs Lockett's food poisoning really caused by the whitebait? After all, her husband, who had had the same dish, did not suffer any adverse after-effects. This point was not mentioned in the judgment, though it may be reflected in the fact that the wife was awarded only 60 pence (12 shillings) more than her husband. Above all, were both husband and wife parties to the contract with the restaurant? And, if so, as was all too readily assumed by the court in *Lockett v Charles*, why was it not possible for Mrs Donoghue to be regarded as a party to a contract in her case? The joint assumption of responsibility and family connection between the Locketts would probably have served to distinguish their case from Mrs Donoghue's. But, had the same approach been adopted in *Donoghue v Stevenson* as in *Lockett v Charles*, no one would ever have heard about the snail in the bottle and Lord Atkin would have had to find some other vehicle for his new-fangled theory.

### *Argument by analogy*

The reason this is of interest is that it demonstrates the importance of comparisons in law. Indeed, argument by analogy, which is really just another way of putting it, lies at the very heart of legal thinking. It is of particular relevance to the common law with its emphasis on binding precedent or the doctrine of *stare decisis*.

The trouble is that an argument by analogy is only as good as the analogy on which it rests. An argument by false analogy is no argument at all. Even the great Leonardo da Vinci fell into this trap. Observing birds in flight he concluded that man too could fly with the aid of flapping wings. The false analogy here was that a man with strapped-on wings was essentially the same as a bird. In fact, of course, with their very light and hollow bones and other aerodynamic features birds are adapted to flight in a way that human beings are not. It was only when this false analogy was abandoned that air travel became possible.

Leonardo fell victim to his own argument by false analogy. But false analogies can also be used deliberately to mislead others or at least to lead them to reach a conclusion which they would not accept if they recognised the weakness of the analogy on which it is based.

### *Marbury v Madison*

*Marbury v Madison,*[9] one of the most famous of all decisions of the US Supreme Court, can also be justly celebrated for its clever and not entirely honest logic. William Marbury was appointed a Justice of the Peace in the District of Columbia by President John Adams just as the reins of power were about to be transferred to his longtime political foe, Thomas Jefferson. Marbury's commission had been duly signed and sealed, but in the bustle at the end of the Adams administration it had inadvertently not been delivered. Marbury asked the new Secretary of State, James Madison, to complete the formalities to allow Marbury to take up his post. Not surprisingly, this request fell on deaf ears. So Marbury went to court seeking a writ of mandamus to compel Madison to deliver the commission.

In a masterly judgment Chief Justice John Marshall argued that:

(a) Madison's refusal to deliver the commission to Marbury was unlawful.

(b) Madison could therefore be compelled by court order to deliver the commission to Marbury.

(c) But the Supreme Court was not the proper tribunal to make such an order.

(d) Because the statute which purportedly gave the Supreme Court this power (section 13 of the Judiciary Act 1789) was itself invalid.

(e) Because that section was effectively an attempt to amend the Constitution without going through the proper procedure for constitutional amendment.

(f) So, although Marbury had right on his side, he must seek redress elsewhere.

Those unfamiliar with the intricacies of *Marbury v Madison* may be surprised at its apparent negativity. After all, is this not the decision which established the right of the US Supreme Court to judicial review?

## II. *Law and Logic*

The issue fastened on at the time was whether the Supreme Court had the power to order the Secretary of State to do something by means of mandamus. This was resolved in a manner which did not offend anyone too badly. Marbury and the Federalists to whom he owed his appointment as Justice of the Peace were mollified by the fact that he was held to be in the right, while the Jeffersonians could take comfort from the fact that no order was made against the Government.

The whole thing was nicely calculated by Marshall, himself a staunch Federalist, who while determined not to find in favour of the Jeffersonians was equally afraid of issuing an order which would be disobeyed, thus exposing the weakness of his court.

While Marshall appeared to be renouncing jurisdiction he was actually laying claim to a whole new swathe of law. This was the claim of the Supreme Court to be able to set aside legislation as unconstitutional - a claim which was introduced by the back-door but which became the mainstay of the subsequent power of the court: namely judicial review.

Marshall's fancy footwork was at its best in arguing in favour of this power of judicial review. Not surprisingly, it is an argument by analogy, which goes something like this:

(a) Article I section 9 of the Constitution prohibits the passing of bills of attainder (i.e. legislation prosecuting named individuals for treason).

(b) If such a bill is passed and a person is condemned under it, 'must the court condemn to death those victims whom the Constitution endeavours to preserve?' Obviously not.

(c) Likewise, therefore, if any other law is passed which is repugnant to the Constitution, the court must have the power to declare such a law void.

The example of bills of attainder was a master stroke on Marshall's part. How could the court possibly pronounce a sentence of death over someone condemned under a law specifically prohibited by the Constitution? This draconian example makes it easy for Marshall to extend the analogy to any law, state or federal, which is adjudged by the court to be unconstitutional.

But the analogy is so strained as to be almost invalid. The point about bills of attainder is that they are specifically and expressly forbidden by the US Constitution. If Congress were to pass such a bill it would be flouting the Constitution in a very deliberate way; and so would any court which recognised or enforced such a bill.

All that this means is that the judiciary is just as subject to the Constitution as the legislature and the executive. How does one get from there to the proposition that the Supreme Court has the right to determine that a law passed by Congress is 'unconstitutional' and therefore void? The answer is: by way of a false analogy. The steps in the argument, which were carefully left unexpressed by Chief Justice Marshall, may be set out as follows:

(a) The US Constitution says that bills of attainder shall not be passed.

(b) Therefore, any law which is incompatible with the Constitution must be void.

(c) 'It is emphatically the province and duty of the judicial department to say what the law is.'

(d) So, it is for the Supreme Court to determine whether a particular law is or is not in conformity with the Constitution.

(e) Therefore, any law which the Supreme Court declares unconstitutional is automatically void.

There is an imperceptible logical drift from bills of attainder - which are expressly prohibited by the Constitution - to any other laws which the Supreme Court may decide are 'unconstitutional'. This is what may be called 'argument by drift'.

### *Syllogisms*

Marshall's argument may be formally restated in the form of a syllogism:

(a) Any law incompatible with the Constitution is void.
(b) The Supreme Court has the right to say what the law is.
(c) Therefore, any law which the Supreme Court says is incompatible with the Constitution is void.

This type of argument goes back to the ancient Greeks:

A.
All horses have tails;
Pegasus is a horse;
Therefore Pegasus has a tail.

Unfortunately, however, it is not always obvious whether a particular argument is valid. Let us try rearranging our Pegasus syllogism:

B.
All horses have tails;
Pegasus has a tail;
Therefore Pegasus is a horse.

A syllogism is made up of two factual statements, known respectively as the major premise and the minor premise, from which a conclusion naturally follows. It is important to realise that for an argument to be valid it needs to be judged in terms of two quite distinct and independent criteria. First, is it based on true facts? And secondly, is it logical?

To the untrained eye our two Pegasus syllogisms may appear almost indistinguishable. In fact, however, one is true and the other false. How can we test this? In A. both premises are factually correct and the logic of the syllogism is sound as well. The facts in B. are unimpeachable, but it fails the second test, as will quickly be apparent from common sense. In terms of the information given in the two premises in B. Pegasus need not be a horse at all. He could equally well be a pig, a mouse, an elephant or a giraffe. The point of course is that although horses have tails they are not the only animals who are so endowed. If we were to represent all tailed animals by means of a circle, horses would occupy a smaller circle within it. So far the diagram would apply equally to both A. and B. Pegasus (in the form of a dot) should now be placed in the diagram. In A. his position is clear: inside the inner circle (i.e. the circle of horses). But in B. we cannot be sure: Pegasus could be anywhere inside or outside the inner circle. All we know is that he is somewhere within the outer circle (i.e. the circle representing all tailed animals).

Not all arguments based on syllogistic reasoning are set out fully. It can sometimes be useful to restate such an argument in order to test its validity, as we did with *Marbury v Madison* above.

Sometimes both sides of an argument may be reduced to syllogistic form. Thus:

Murder is wrong;
Abortion is murder;
Therefore abortion is wrong.

But:
Every woman has the right to control her own body;
A foetus is inside a woman's body;
Therefore a woman has the right to choose what to do with a foetus.

## *II. Law and Logic*

Which of these arguments is right? The problem is not with the logic but with the factual accuracy of the minor premise in each. The statement that 'Abortion is murder' is itself the conclusion of an argument by analogy, which could also be expressed as a separate syllogism:

Killing a human being is murder;
A foetus is a human being;
Therefore killing a foetus is murder,

The problem lying at the heart of the whole abortion debate is clearly therefore the question: Is a foetus a human being or not? Although ostensibly a factual question there is no clearcut answer to it but shades of opinion ranging from those who believe that an embryo is a human being from the moment of conception to those who regard birth as the decisive point.

### *Logic in interpretation*

Logical thought is – or should be – one of the principal foundations of law. In dealing with any case it is necessary, first, to identify which area of law and what legal provisions are applicable. The relevant law must then be interpreted and applied. Each of these processes is an exercise in logical thought. Take, for example, the case of someone who has a meal in a restaurant and then absconds without paying. The applicable area of law is clearly crime, and more particularly the law of theft. But does the legal definition of 'theft' cover the sort of situation that we are considering here? It seems obvious that it should. For, are not the four ingredients of theft present here? Namely, (a) a dishonest (b) appropriation (c) of property belonging to another (d) with the intention of permanently depriving the other of it. Yet the English courts adopted a narrow interpretation of these criteria, so that restaurant bill-dodgers, hotel guests leaving without paying and passengers doing a 'runner' from a taxi cab were not caught by the Theft Act 1968. A separate Act, the Theft Act 1978, had to be enacted to criminalise these obviously dishonest forms of conduct. Computer hackers were another category of criminals for whom a special law had to be passed, the Computer Misuse Act 1990. Yet all these examples could easily have been accommodated within the pre-existing Theft Act 1968. The fact that they were not would be more understandable if the courts consistently adopted a narrow, literalistic approach to legislation. However, there is in practice no single approach, and it is by no means unheard of for a single statutory provision to be subjected to totally divergent interpretations.

A good example of this occurred in a recent case involving a challenge to the detention of nine foreign nationals detained under the Anti-Terrorism, Crime and Security Act 2001, which allows foreign suspected terrorists to be detained indefinitely without trial or charge.[10] The Special Immigration Appeals Commission held that this provision was discriminatory and so breached Article 14 of the European Convention of Human Rights, which had been incorporated into English law by the Human Rights Act 1998. The Commission therefore declared the provision in question to be incompatible with the Convention. However, this decision was reversed by a unanimous Court of Appeal. In the words of Brooke LJ: 'If the security of the nation may be at risk from terrorist violence, and if the lives of informers may be at risk, or the flow of valuable information they represent may dry up if sources of intelligence have to be revealed, there comes a stage when judicial scrutiny can go no further.'

Both the Commission and the Court of Appeal accepted that it was for the Government, not the courts, to decide whether the country was in 'an emergency threatening the life of the nation', which was the basis of the detention orders. But the Court of Appeal did not ask the Home Secretary to disclose the grounds for his suspicion that the people concerned were involved in terrorism, nor was there even a challenge to the provision that suspicion alone was enough to allow them to be detained. The court concluded that the detention powers were not discriminatory, did not infringe the Convention and were also not a disproportionate response to the public emergency threatening the country. Lord Woolf CJ, presiding, did however sound a note of warning that the courts should be mindful of the dangers of unjustified discrimination against foreigners. 'This is especially the case if, as here, non-nationals are being detained based on conduct which has not been proved but is only suspected. The mistakes which have been made in the past, in relation to internment of aliens at the outbreak of war, should not be forgotten.'

This is presumably a reference to the famous case of *Liversidge v Anderson*, which, surprisingly, however, was not specifically cited. Mr Liversidge (not his original name) had been interned during World War II on the basis that the Secretary of State had 'reasonable cause to believe' that he was 'of hostile origin or associations'. Liversidge sought a declaration that his detention was unlawful together with damages for false imprisonment. The case went all the way to the House of Lords, which by four votes to one upheld his detention as lawful. The sole dissenting voice was that of Lord Atkin, noted as a radical judge, who mercilessly attacked his fellow law lords:[11]

> I view with apprehension the attitude of judges who, on a mere question of construction, when face to face with claims involving the liberty of the subject, show themselves more executive-minded than the executive.

Then comes the famous passage which has echoed down the years:

> In England amidst the clash of arms the laws are not silent. They may be changed, but they speak the same language in war as in peace. It has always been one of the pillars of freedom, one of the principles of liberty for which, on recent authority, we are now fighting, that the judges are no respecters of persons, and stand between the subject and any attempted encroachments on his liberty by the executive, alert to see that any coercive action is justified in law. In this case, I have listened to arguments which might have been addressed acceptably to the Court of King's Bench in the time of Charles I.
>
> … in English law every imprisonment is prima facie unlawful, and … it is for a person directing imprisonment to justify his act. The only exception is in respect of imprisonment ordered by a judge, who, from the nature of his office, cannot be sued, and the validity of whose judicial decisions cannot, in such proceedings as the present, be questioned.

Though Lord Atkin's was a lone voice it is his dissenting opinion which has come to be treated as representing the law. The Court of Appeal's decision in the Anti-Terrorism case may possibly have dented the authority of Lord Atkin's powerful plea.

The real problem here, in both *Liversidge v Anderson* and in the recent Anti-Terrorism Act case, is the inconsistency of the different views adopted by different judges in interpreting the same statute. Consistency of thought is demanded by logic. Even more important, without consistency the law becomes unpredictable and therefore uncertain, which inevitably leads to injustice.

### *Argument from authority*

Another type of thought which may fly in the face of logic is argument from authority, which is the mainstay of so much legal thinking. It is by no means confined to law, though. 'Contraception is a sin because the Bible says so' is an example of this kind of thinking. To the sceptic this in itself can never be conclusive. He will want to ask:

(a) What exactly does the Bible say about contraception?
(b) How is it to be interpreted?
(c) Is it applicable to modern methods of contraception?
(d) And why should we accept what the Bible says anyway?

Similarly, when a lawyer argues from the authority of a precedent, a statute or possibly some academic opinion, it is necessary to ask:

(a) What is the relevance of the authority?
(b) What is the status of the authority?
(c) How is the authority to be interpreted?
(d) How, if at all, is the authority to be applied?

This may all seem pretty obvious, except, unfortunately, for the fact that this methodical approach is by no means always adopted by the courts, which sometimes even try to make up the law as they go along.

This is termed 'judicial activism' by those who favour it and 'judicial supremacism' by its critics. Some of the objectionable features of this approach were listed in a less than flattering study of that masterly judicial activist, Lord Denning:

> Authorities are cited for propositions which they do not support, inconvenient precedents are glossed over or pronounced as outdated, inequitable or unjust, legal principles are put forward for which there is no authoritative support, speeches of law lords are misconstrued or quoted out of context, and support for value decisions are sought from history, poetry and literature.[12]

Lord Denning is variously disparaged or commended for inventing the doctrine of promissory or equitable estoppel in *Central London Property Trust v High Trees House*,[13] but a close reading of his judgment will reveal just how great a master he was of law and logic alike. It is commonly supposed that the case of *Hughes v Metropolitan Railway Co*,[14] upon which Denning J, as he then was, chiefly relied, was something of a red herring. It is certainly true that the word 'estoppel' does not appear anywhere in that case, but Lord Denning was able to show that the principle upon which it was decided was not as remote from that contended for by himself as might have been thought. Moreover, in *Salisbury v Gilmore*,[15] heard a few years before *High Trees*, Denning KC, as he was then, successfully invoked a remarkably similar principle drawn from *Birmingham & District Land Co v London & North Western Railway Co.* as expressed by that great commercial jurist, Bowen LJ:[16]

> If persons who have contractual rights against others induce by their conduct those against whom they have such rights to believe that such rights will not be enforced or will be kept in abeyance for some particular time, those persons will not be allowed by a court of equity to enforce the rights until such time has elapsed, without at all events placing the parties in the same position as they were before.

## *II. Law and Logic*

Such was Lord Denning's finesse and fancy footwork that it enabled him to weave a merry dance around his opponents. Throughout his long career on the bench he often fell foul of the House of Lords, where his most formidable opponent was the doughty former Lord Chancellor, Viscount Simonds, who ably parried Lord Denning's nimble assaults on conventional views and counter-attacked from an impregnable fastness built on tradition, precedent and logic coupled with a clarity of language second only to that of Lord Denning himself.

### *Statutory interpretation*

The famous rebukes hurled by Lord Simonds at Lord Denning half a century ago over his approach to statutory interpretation have reverberated down the years. The best known example occurred in *Magor & St Mellons Rural District Council v Newport Corporation.*[17] By the Newport Extension Act 1934 the boundaries of Newport were to be expanded so as to take in the richest parts of two neighbouring rural districts, each of which had its own council. These two district councils were to be compensated for their loss of rates. That was provided for by ss 151 and 152 of the Local Government Act 1933. The matter was complicated by the County of Monmouth Review Order 1935 (made by the Minister of Health under powers given to him by section 46 of the Local Government Act 1929). This Order amalgamated what was left of the two rural district councils into one, the Magor & St Mellons Rural District Council. The appointed date for the extension of Newport and for the amalgamation of the two district councils was the same, namely (and, as it turned out, appropriately) 1 April 1935. But Newport argued that, as the two district councils to which Newport was obliged to pay compensation ceased to exist at the very moment when the compensation was due, no compensation was payable! This was an unworthy legalistic argument which would clearly result in injustice.

The question before the court here, as always when interpreting statutes, was: What was the intention of Parliament? Lord Denning's answer was that, whatever the legal niceties, it was obviously the intention of Parliament in this case that the new rural district council should be able to claim the compensation owing to its two predecessors: 'The effect of the Minister's Order was, if I may use a metaphor, not the death of the two councils, but their marriage.'[18] The intention of Parliament was, he held, quite clear:

> This was so obviously the intention of the Minister's Order that I have no patience with an ultra-legalistic interpretation which would deprive them of

> their rights altogether ... We do not sit here to pull the language of Parliament and of Ministers to pieces and make nonsense of it. That is an easy thing to do, and it is a thing to which lawyers are too often prone. We sit here to find out the intention of Parliament and of Ministers and carry it out, and we do this better by filling in the gaps and making sense of the enactment than by opening it up to destructive analysis.[19]

Lord Denning's was a dissenting judgment in the Court of Appeal, and it met with even less of a welcome in the House of Lords, which unanimously upheld the majority decision of the Court of Appeal, which in turn had upheld the trial judge.

A week before being appointed Lord Chancellor Lord Simonds devoted the whole of his short speech in the House of Lords to reprimanding Denning LJ's approach to statutory interpretation:

> It is sufficient to say that the general proposition that it is the duty of the court to find out the intention of Parliament - and not only of Parliament but of Ministers also - cannot by any means be supported. The duty of the court is to interpret the words that the legislature has used. Those words may be ambiguous, but, even if they are, the power and duty of the court to travel outside them on a voyage of discovery are strictly limited ....
>
> The second part of the passage that I have cited from the judgment of the learned lord justice is, no doubt, the logical sequel of the first. The court, having discovered the intention of Parliament and of Ministers too, must proceed to fill in the gaps. What the legislature has not written, the court must write. This proposition which restates in a new form the view expressed by the lord justice in the earlier case of *Seaford Court Estates Ltd v Asher*[20] (to which the lord justice himself refers), cannot be supported. It appears to me to be a naked usurpation of the legislative function under the thin disguise of interpretation, and it is the less justifiable when it is guesswork with what materials the legislature would, if it had discovered the gap, have filled it. If a gap is disclosed, the remedy lies in an amending Act.[21]

What we have here are two diametrically opposed approaches to statutory interpretation: Lord Denning's 'purposive' approach on the one hand and Viscount Simonds's more literal approach on the other. The difference is not merely technical but goes to the role of the judiciary in its relations with the other branches of government.

Lord Simonds cited with approval Lord Wright's speech in *Assam Railways v Inland Revenue Commissioners*,[22] in which the question arose whether it was permissible for the court to consider a Royal Commission Report in order to discover the 'intention of Parliament' in interpreting a statute based on that Report. Lord Wright declared forthrightly that 'on principle no such evidence for the purpose of showing the intention, that is the purpose or object, of an Act is admissible; the intention of the legislature must be ascertained from the words of the statute with such extraneous assistance as is legitimate.'

What assistance is 'legitimate'? According to the purists, this is limited to 'such external or historical facts as we may find necessary to enable us to understand the subject-matter to which the instruments relate and the meaning of the words employed'.[23]

Perhaps the best and most concise statement of the literal approach is that made by Lord Reid in *Black-Clawson International Ltd v Papierwerke Waldhof-Aschaffenburg AG*:[24]

> We often say that we are looking for the intention of Parliament, but that is not quite accurate. We are seeking not what Parliament meant but the true meaning of what they said.

### *Pepper v Hart*

In *Pepper v Hart*, decided in 1993, the House of Lords broke with the time-honoured rule that the courts could not look behind the actual words of an Act of Parliament in order to determine its meaning. It is now permissible in certain circumstances for a court to refer to 'parliamentary materials', notably speeches made by the minister steering the legislation through Parliament. But this would be allowed only where:

> (a) the legislation is ambiguous or obscure, or leads to an absurdity;
> (b) the material relied on consists of one or more statements by a minister or other promoter of the Bill together if necessary with such other parliamentary material as is necessary to understand such statements and their effect;
> (c) the [parliamentary] statements relied on are clear.[25]

Did this infringe parliamentary privilege as enshrined in section 1 art 9 of the Bill of Rights 1688 which provides 'That the freedome of speech and debates or proceedings in Parlyament ought not to be impeached or questioned in any court or place out of Parlyament'?

The House of Lords held that the radical change in the law which they were introducing did not offend against this fundamental principle. But it certainly does give the courts discretion to look behind the wording of legislation in a way which they never had before. In particular, it is now open to the courts to decide that a provision in an Act of Parliament is 'ambiguous or obscure, or leads to an absurdity' – presumably in that respect disagreeing with all those parliamentarians (not to mention the professional parliamentary draftsmen) through whose hands those words have come through all the stages in the elaborate process required for the passing of legislation.

This change in the law is itself a major piece of judge-made law. Ought Parliament as the legislature not to have had the right to decide whether it wished to allow the courts to look behind the face of Acts of Parliament in this manner? Yet the voice of Parliament was not heard, thus yielding yet further ground to the advancing forces of the judiciary. The long battle between legislature and judiciary is still unresolved: In the words of Erskine May's *Treatise on the Law, Privileges, Proceedings and Usage of Parliament*, compiled by the Clerk of the House of Commons and other parliamentary officials:[26]

> After some three and a half centuries, the boundary between the competence of the law courts and the jurisdiction of either House in matters of privilege is still not entirely determined.

### *Conclusion*

*Pepper v Hart* represents a major victory for the purposive approach, though the literal approach has by no means been eliminated and often puts in an appearance when least expected.[27] Consistency on the part of the judges would make decisions more predictable and so promote clarity and therefore justice. Unfortunately, however, this has not happened, and the trend is towards ever greater judicial independence, even to the stage where a statute has effectively been rewritten[28] and new principles invented.[29]

## Excursus A

## 'Ministers are no more elected than Judges'

A lecture published by a senior English judge provides us with a good example of a type of logic that has become increasingly prevalent in recent years. The lecture, entitled 'The Common Law and the Constitution', is by Sir Stephen Sedley, now a Lord Justice of Appeal.[1]

The main thrust of the lecture in question is a defence of activist judges against accusations of 'judicial supremacism'. The lecture strongly defends what is there termed the 'continued judicial invigilation of executive government' and rejects the characterisation of this trend as 'a comprehensive judicial assault on the foundations of democracy'.[2]

Sir Stephen states the premise which he seeks to rebut as follows:

> The premise is that executive government, since it derives its authority from a

> majority in the House of Commons and is in turn answerable through ministers to Parliament, speaks for the people, so that those who challenge government are challenging democracy.[3]

This premise Sir Stephen vigorously rejects as 'entirely misleading', and the rest of the lecture is devoted to marshalling 'a series of reasons both of practice and of principle' to prove this. The first of these reasons may be identified as follows:

**(1) The British Constitution is based on a system of 'dual sovereignty' shared between Parliament and the courts. By contrast, the executive lacks any claim to sovereignty.**

*Comment*: Is sovereignty indivisible or can it be shared? The conventional British doctrine of 'the sovereignty of Parliament' creates more problems than it solves. The alternative doctrine of 'the separation of powers' is hardly more satisfactory. Sir Stephen Sedley's 'dual sovereignty' of legislature and judiciary marks a radical departure from both of these doctrines. What is the basis for it? The only authority cited by Sir Stephen is a single sentence from Lord Bridge's speech in *X Ltd v Morgan-Grampian*:[4]

> The maintenance of the rule of law is in every way as important in a free society as the democratic franchise. In our society the rule of law rests upon twin foundations: the sovereignty of the Queen in Parliament in making the law and the sovereignty of the Queen's courts in interpreting and applying the law.

What is the constitutional status of this quotation? Did Lord Bridge (who, incidentally, is not normally thought of as a particularly radical judge) have the authority single-handedly to change one of the most fundamental principles of the British Constitution? Of course not. Nor indeed was he making any attempt to do so. In *X Ltd v Morgan-Grampian* the court had to balance two rights: confidentiality and freedom of expression. A company's confidential business plan had been leaked to a magazine, which intended to publish it. The company took out an injunction to stop publication and also asked the court to order the magazine journalist concerned to disclose his source. The company succeeded on both points. However, the journalist made it clear that he he was going to disobey the court order to disclose his source. *That* is what Lord Bridge is referring to in the extract quoted by Sir Stephen Sedley. The point Lord Bridge was making was simply that, important as freedom of speech was, there were certain circumstances where it had to give way to other considerations. In the instant case, Lord Bridge stressed, the journalist was effectively 'setting himself above the law' by refusing to disclose his source as he had been ordered to do by the court applying an Act of Parliament (the Contempt of Court Act 1981, section 10). In adopting this attitude the journalist was mounting a 'serious challenge to the rule of law' as expressed by both the legislature and the judiciary. It can be seen from this that Lord Bridge's omission of any mention of the executive was not because Lord Bridge regarded it as not sharing in sovereignty but simply because it was not relevant to the case in hand. Lord Bridge was not seeking to identify the whereabouts of sovereignty in the British Constitution but merely to emphasise the seriousness of the journalist's refusal to obey the law. Lord Bridge was clearly not trying to recast the British Constitution – nor did he have any authority to do so had he wished to!

The fact that Sir Stephen Sedley found it necessary to base a whole new view of a fundamental constitutional doctrine on a single obiter dictum quoted out of context from a recent case is less than reassuring. The type of argument used here by Sir Stephen belongs to a well-known category which might be termed 'argument from authority', a classic example of which is: 'The world was created in seven days because the Bible says so'. The trouble with this type of argument is that it is only as strong as the authority on which it claims to rest.

One can only wonder why Sir Stephen Sedley is so concerned to show that there is 'dual sovereignty' in the British Constitution, shared between legislature and judiciary. Sir Stephen's declared aim is to combat the view that judicial attacks on executive decisions amount to an attack on democracy itself. Sir Stephen Sedley counters this by means of a comparison between judges and Government ministers in an attempt to show that judges have as much of a claim to democratic legitimacy as ministers:

> Ministers are no more elected than judges: both are appointed to office by the Sovereign on the advice of the Government of the day. It is judicial independence, an essential component of any democracy, which dictates that judges are not answerable to Parliament, just as parliamentary sovereignty dictates Parliament's immunity from judicial adjudication. But while ministers are accountable legally to the courts and politically to Parliament, there is no constitutional requirement that ministers must be accountable to the representatives of the electorate. Those who are peers answer only to the unelected chamber. Moreover neither law nor convention requires them to be members of either House: in recent decades at least two persons have held ministerial office when they were neither MP nor peer.
>
> Others must say why, in spite of these elementary constitutional facts, much of the press has in recent times insistently suggested that executive government is the pinnacle of the democratic structure and that judges who overset

ministerial decisions are overstepping their powers and jeopardising democracy.[5]

Are these really 'elementary constitutional facts', as Sir Stephen claims? The trouble is that by labelling them in this way Sir Stephen exempts himself from the need to prove them. For, what they really are is a series of assertions. This represents yet another all too common mode of argument, what may be termed 'argument by assertion', which is not really a form of argument at all. Sir Stephen's assertions are intended to counter the following frequently expressed views:

(a) Ministers are democratically elected; judges are unelected.

(b) Ministers are accountable to Parliament, a democratically elected body; judges are not accountable to anybody.

(c) Ministers have to be members of one or other house of Parliament; (except for the law lords, who also sit in the House of Lords as a Parliament) judges are not members of either house of Parliament.

Sir Stephen's reply to these points follows on from his 'dual sovereignty' point discussed above and is as follows:

**(2) 'Ministers are no more elected than judges: both are appointed to office by the Sovereign on the advice of the Government of the day.'**

There is some truth in this, but only on a superficial formal level. Like judges, ministers are formally appointed by the Crown. In the case of ministers this is done on the advice of the Prime Minister, and in the case of judges on the advice of the Lord Chancellor. But once we penetrate beneath this very superficial level we find big differences:

(a) The great majority of ministers actually *are* elected – as Members of Parliament. (See more on this under point 3, below.)

(b) But, perhaps even more important, the function of general elections in modern Britain is no longer primarily to elect individual members of Parliament but to elect a Government. By casting their vote for a Labour or Conservative candidate voters are really hoping to elect a Labour Government or a Conservative Government. That is one of the main reasons why third and smaller parties tend to do so badly in Britain: because, under the voting system that we have, such parties are most unlikely to be able to form a Government. So voting for such a party is seen by many as a wasted vote. Seen against this background it soon becomes apparent that ministers as members of a Government or prospective Government depend on the electorate. And this applies even to those ministers who are members of the House of Lords. True, they do not have to stand for election to that Chamber. But, if their party loses the election they will be out of office.

(c) This ties in with collective ministerial responsibility, one of the chief principles of cabinet government. The key to this is Government unity or solidarity. The Government stands or falls together, and each minister has to toe the line. If a Government introduces unpopular policies or mismanages the economy, the electorate will be likely to turn them out at the next general election – and this means all of them, including the peers among them.

(d) In addition, there is individual ministerial responsibility, another basic principle. Although there has been a certain amount of criticism of ministers for not resigning in certain circumstances, it is now accepted that a minister should resign for mistakes or failings in his department only where he has had knowledge of the relevant facts and personal involvement in the decisions concerned. That however does not mean that ministers who do not resign are not likely to suffer some other penalty. Indeed, the reluctance of ministers to resign and the perception of mistakes and failures occurring without anyone to blame is undoubtedly one of the reasons for the fall of John Major's Government in the general election of 1997.

*Conclusion*: So, to say that 'Ministers are no more elected than judges' is at best misleading.

**(3) 'It is judicial independence, an essential component of any democracy, which dictates that judges are not answerable to Parliament, just as parliamentary sovereignty dictates Parliament's immunity from judicial adjudication.'**

This is an admission that judges are not answerable to Parliament. It is interesting that Sir Stephen Sedley accepts that Parliament should be 'immune from judicial adjudication' – on the fundamental ground of parliamentary sovereignty, which he suddenly here appears to accept: whatever happened to 'dual sovereignty'? But, is Parliament actually 'immune from judicial adjudication'? In fact, serious inroads have been made by the judges on parliamentary legislative supremacy, not only in the field of EU law, where this change has been thrust upon them by Luxembourg, but also more generally. In the way that the courts interpret Acts of Parliament they are less concerned than ever to avoid usurping the legislative role.

Indeed, in *M v Home Office*[6] it has been truly said that 'an established statute was virtually re-written' by the judges.[7] Yet, in the statement quoted above, Sir Stephen Sedley is essentially saying that the judges must be independent of Parliament in return for the fact that Parliament is independent of them. Now that this latter statement no longer holds completely true, then presumably the former statement should no longer be religiously observed either.

This is not quite so fanciful as might be thought. For judges are subject to impeachment by the legislature in the USA, where the doctrine of separation of powers has always given the judges far more power than in Britain. And, unlike Presidents, American judges have often been successfully impeached, a form of control that is still very much alive in America today but has not been exercised in Britain for over three hundred years.

**(4) 'But while ministers are accountable legally to the courts and politically to Parliament, there is no constitutional requirement that ministers must be accountable to the representatives of the electorate.'**

This sweeping generalisation is evidently dependent for proof upon the two following sentences:

(a) **'Those who are peers answer only to the unelected chamber.'**

The point being made here is that, as ministers who sit in the House of Lords are obviously not elected, they are not accountable to the electorate. This was true up to about two hundred years ago, but now only in the most formal of senses. For example, Lord Carrington resigned as Foreign Secretary in 1982 because of his misjudgment of Argentine intentions over the Falklands. Yet he was a member of the House of Lords. The point is that a Government stands or falls as a unit and the weakening of the power of Parliament as an institution over the past two hundred years has increased the power of the electorate. So, though a minister who happens to be in the Lords is not accountable to 'the representatives of the electorate', he is indirectly accountable to the electorate itself. In this regard public scrutiny should not be lost sight of. For, the fact that a minister is in the Lords rather than the Commons will make no difference to the amount of press and media attention which he attracts. The media often have their own political agenda which may or may not coincide with the interests of the public, but this still places ministers of every variety under close scrutiny.

The distinction drawn by Sir Stephen Sedley between the democratic accountability of ministers who are MPs and those who are either peers or not in Parliament at all is a superficial one, as may be seen in other respects as well. For example, the fact that a minister is not a member of the Commons does not prevent a Commons Select Committee from summoning him to attend and testify before it. These Committees, which are made up exclusively of backbenchers, jealously preserve their right to decide on their own agenda, and can investigate any matter within their purview. They then publish reports of their findings. Although they contain a majority of MPs of the governing party, they are by no means subservient to the Government, as has been made clear on more than one occasion, under both Conservative and Labour administrations. These reports can be hard-hitting, and will 'name and shame' ministers and civil servants alike. So, whether a minister is an MP, a member of the House of Lords or neither will make no difference.

In addition, the House of Lords has committees of its own. Select Committees have no power to punish or discipline. Their power lies in being able to investigate and report, thereby naming and shaming ministers. Although ministers who are members of the House of Lords are not themselves subject to election, if they embarrass the Government they cannot expect to hold their posts for very long. Moreover, if the Government falls they will certainly be out of a job. So, a minister in the Lords – or one without a seat in either House – who ignores public opinion is a very short-sighted minister indeed.

(b) **'Moreover neither law nor convention requires them [viz. ministers] to be members of either House: in recent decades at least two persons have held ministerial office when they were neither MP nor peer.'**

This is Sir Stephen's *pièce de résistance*, which flies in the face of all conventional wisdom on the subject.

Gerald Kaufman, a former minister himself, opens his book on *How to be A Minister* with the words: 'Before you begin the process of learning how to be a minister, you first have to become one. An obligatory first step is to become a Member of Parliament or – in the case of the Conservative Party – a peer.'[8] The obligation for Ministers to have a seat in Parliament is likewise characterised by a contemporary academic author as 'an axiom of the British Constitution'.[9] It would hardly be necessary to labour the point, were it not for Sir Stephen Sedley's bald rejection of this 'axiom'.

Sir Stephen bases his whole argument on this point on two people who 'held ministerial office when they were neither MP nor peer', the two ministers in question being named in a footnote as Patrick Gordon Walker and Frank Cousins.[10]

In fact, Sedley's argument might appear to be backed by stronger evidence than he indicates, as there were quite a few earlier cases of non-parliamentary ministerial appointments, especially in wartime. During the First World War no fewer than four ministers were brought in from outside Parliament, and in World War II there were five. All these ministers were elected to Parliament unopposed. In peacetime there have been fewer cases, only 12 throughout the twentieth century, none of them being uncontested.[11] Four of these ministers failed to win a parliamentary seat and at once resigned their ministerial office.

But let us look a little more closely at the two examples cited by Sedley. Frank Cousins and Patrick Gordon Walker were both appointed as ministers by Harold Wilson in 1964, at a time when neither of them had a seat in either House of Parliament. Gordon Walker's appointment as Foreign Secretary was announced by the new Prime Minister on 16 October 1964, the day after the general election which had given Labour a slender majority in the Commons. The reason Gordon Walker did not have a seat was that he had just lost the seat at Smethwick that he had previously occupied. Frank Cousins, who was appointed to the new post of Minister of Technology a few days later, had not held a parliamentary seat before as he was General Secretary of the Transport and General Workers' Union, which had given him leave of absence to serve in the Wilson Government.

Harold Wilson not only recognised the need for these two Ministers to have seats in Parliament but went to great lengths to regularise the situation for them, as he explained in his memoirs written a few years later:

> Seats had to be found for Patrick Gordon Walker and Frank Cousins. Two senior MPs, Frank Bowles and Reg Sorensen, with some reluctance on their part, were persuaded by the whips to go to the Lords. Frank Cousins was adopted for Nuneaton, and Patrick Gordon Walker for Leyton.[12]

A similar but more colourful account is given by Richard Crossman, Minister of Housing and Local Government in Wilson's first cabinet:

> It wasn't so easy to find two constituencies whose Members were even willing to consider going to the House of Lords in order to make room for Frank Cousins and Patrick Gordon Walker. Finally two old stalwarts, Sorensen of Leyton and Frank Bowles of Nuneaton, were put under tremendous pressure. Both of them are loyal Members and both are rather on the Left. Each in his own slightly sulky way finally agreed to go to the Lords and leave room for the two Cabinet Ministers.[13]

## *II. Law and Logic*

In the event, in the by-elections held on 21 January 1965, three months after the general election of 15 October 1964, Cousins managed to win Nuneaton with a much reduced majority, but Gordon Walker was narrowly defeated in Leyton. One of the reasons Crossman gave to explain these poor results was 'the resentment in the constituencies at having a Cabinet Minister foisted on them and a respected senior Member turned out'.[14]

In the words of Harold Wilson:

> Patrick telephoned me at once to offer his inevitable resignation. Knowing what he was going through, I said, having expressed my commiseration, 'Let's not talk about that: come and have a chat in the morning, when you've had some sleep.' There could be no question of his going on, though I undertook to bring him back into the Administration at some future time when he was back in the House.[15]

This episode raises the following issues:

(a) If it was not essential for a minister to have a seat in Parliament, then why did the Prime Minister go to such lengths to secure seats for these two ministers – causing offence to two senior backbenchers and to the constituency electorates? For, it is clear that Messrs Sorensen and Bowles had to have their arms twisted before they agreed effectively to retire from active politics. And the verdict of the voters was clear enough, though, as Crossman believed, the attempt to foist a cabinet minister on them was probably only one of several reasons for their disaffection.

(b) Why was it necessary to adopt such high-risk tactics to get ministers elected to Parliament unless it was required?

(c) If he was not in breach of any constitutional rule, why did Gordon Walker not simply carry on as Foreign Secretary notwithstanding his defeat in the Leyton by-election? Had he done so without provoking a constitutional and political crisis for the Government, then we *might* indeed have been able to say that there was no rule about a minister having to have a seat in Parliament – or, more accurately perhaps, that that convention did not exist *any longer*. But, Gordon Walker did not even make the slightest attempt to challenge the convention. He resigned as soon as he knew that he had lost the by-election. In reality, had he tried to brazen it out, Wilson would probably have dismissed him.

(d) And, again, if there was no rule about parliamentary membership, why did Wilson make Gordon Walker's return to Government dependent upon his return to Parliament? (In fact, Gordon Walker did succeed in winning Leyton back for Labour in the 1966 general election - and he was then given a ministerial appointment again).

*The need for ministers to have a seat in Parliament: conclusion*

For a three-month period Cousins and Gordon Walker clearly were ministers without being members of either House of Parliament. But, does that prove, as Sedley maintains, that 'neither law nor convention' requires ministers to be members of one or other House of Parliament? There is certainly no rule of *law* to that effect, but what about convention? Do these examples prove that there is no such rule? That is one possible explanation, but there are two others, which, as we shall see, are far more likely:

(i) that these two ministers were in *breach* of a rule requiring them to be members of one or other House of Parliament; or

(ii) that there *is* a rule but the rule has a certain amount of flexibility built into it.

The whole approach of Harold Wilson and his Government indicates that they recognised only too well the obligation of a minister to have a seat in Parliament. Not only did they anxiously try to find seats for the two ministers concerned, but when one such attempt was unsuccessful the minister in question promptly resigned.

The language used by Harold Wilson is likewise indicative of his recognition of the force of the convention:

(1) 'Seats *had* to be found for Patrick Gordon Walker and Frank Cousins.'[16]

(2) 'Patrick telephoned me at once to offer his *inevitable* resignation.'[17]

(3) '... I undertook to bring him back into the Administration at some future time *when he was back in the House*.'[18] (Italics supplied.)

Alternative (ii) is probably preferable, namely that the convention has a certain amount of flexibility built into it. The convention as acted upon in practice would state that a minister either had to be a member of one of the Houses of Parliament when appointed or become one within a short period thereafter, failing which he must resign his ministerial office forthwith.

On this basis, the appointment of a minister from outside Parliament does not constitute a breach of the convention, provided a parliamentary seat is secured within a reasonable time, failing which the minister must resign his appointment. In fact, there is not a single case on record where a minister refused to resign after failing to secure a parliamentary seat.

What then about such oddities as the situation in John Major's last administration and in the first Blair administration, where the Solicitor-General for Scotland (Colin Boyd) was outside Parliament and no attempt was ever made to secure a seat for him either in the Commons or in the Lords? This curiosity in fact belongs to a tiny sub-class made up of the law officers for Scotland, i.e. Lord Advocate and Solicitor-General for Scotland, who, though generally regarded as members of the executive, are primarily legal advisers to the Government on matters of Scots law and, in addition, officers of the law requiring them to be involved in the impartial administration of justice. That is why they are not always members of the ruling party and are sometimes outside Parliament. But this is much more likely to be found in the case of the Scottish Solicitor-General than in that of Lord Advocate, who (as in the Blair Administration) is often in the Lords. This is a recognised exception to the general rule that ministers must be in Parliament. In such a case the law officer concerned would not really be part of the executive at all.

Another oddity, now most unlikely to recur, is the appointment of Commonwealth leaders as British ministers without their being members of either House of Parliament. The best-known case is that of the South African leader General Jan Smuts, who served in Lloyd George's War Cabinet between 1917 and 1919. The only other example also comes from wartime, when R.G. Casey of Australia was appointed by Churchill to the unusual post of Minister of State and Minister Resident in the Middle East during World War II. The wartime crisis is undoubtedly one reason for this, another being the fact that, in Smuts's case, he was a Member of Parliament and a Minister of the Crown in South Africa, holding the combined portfolios of Defence, Mines and the Interior. This was before the Statute of Westminster 1931, which conferred Dominion status on Canada, Australia, New Zealand and South Africa and made the Sovereign the King of each Dominion separately. So, in 1917, by virtue of his South Africa appointment, Smuts could have been regarded as already a Minister not just of the Crown but of the British Crown. And he was answerable to Parliament – albeit the one sitting in Cape Town, not in Westminster.

The real point about the rule that, with these few anomalous exceptions, ministers must have a seat in Parliament, is that this convention goes to the heart of the Constitution as a whole, as it concerns the accountability of ministers to Parliament. Had Harold Wilson simply ignored the rule and allowed Patrick Gordon Walker to remain Foreign Secretary without a seat in either House of Parliament, this would probably have provoked a constitutional crisis, with the Government's position being attacked as undemocratic, which it would have been, as a cabinet minister outside Parliament would be answerable neither to the electorate nor to Parliament.

In conclusion on this point, then, had Sir Stephen Sedley said that though there was no *law* which required a minister to have a seat in Parliament, *convention* demanded that (with a very few anomalies) he must either have a seat when appointed or must obtain one as soon as possible, it would have been impossible to disagree with him. But Sedley LJ expressly states, as quoted above, that 'neither law nor convention requires them [viz. ministers] to be members of either House'.[19] This is at best misleading.

### *Conclusion*

One of the main arguments against judicial activism is that judges are unelected. Hence Sedley's concern to show that ministers are not elected *qua* ministers, and that even though most ministers *are* elected as Members of Parliament, there is no need for them to be. In this way Sedley seeks to undermine the democratic legitimacy of the executive. This paves the way for concluding that the democratic credentials of the judiciary are as good as if not better than those of the executive government.

The true rule about ministers as members of Parliament, as we have seen, is that, with the exception of the two Scottish Law Officers, a minister must either be a member of one or other House of Parliament when appointed or become one as soon as possible. This is why, as we have seen, Harold Wilson went to such lengths to find seats in the Commons for Frank Cousins and Gordon Walker, and, when the latter failed to obtain a seat at the first opportunity, he immediately resigned from the cabinet.

If Sedley is right, why did Harold Wilson actually go to the great trouble of creating vacancies in the Commons merely to enable his two extra-parliamentary ministers to contest them in by-elections? Indeed, if Sedley is right there would have been no need for Gordon Walker to resign at all - and we might have expected quite a few more extra-parliamentary ministers than there actually are. In fact, the overwhelming majority of ministers are already MPs when appointed to ministerial office, and the rest are very largely members of the House of Lords, also at the time of their appointment to office. These are powerful precedents with a long pedigree which have been faithfully followed with the few exceptions mentioned above.

## *II. Law and Logic*

How are we to characterise these apparent exceptions? There are essentially three ways of doing so:

(i) We can regard these exceptions as *breaches* of the rule that ministers must have a seat in one or other house of Parliament. This is quite acceptable. After all, every rule or law is broken at some time or other. Is there a law against theft? Of course there is. Yet thousands of thefts take place every year, most of which go unpunished. Does the fact that there are all these thefts mean that theft is legal? Not at all. The thefts are merely *breaches* of the law.

(ii) Another way of looking at the apparent exceptions to the rule about ministers is as exceptions built in to the rule itself. If the rule is stated as requiring ministers *either* to have a seat in Parliament *or* to find one within a short period, and as exempting the Scottish law officers from this requirement altogether, then there are no breaches of the rule and the exceptions are exception only to the main rule but are themselves part of a more elaborate rule. The rule is then similar to many other rules of law, as, for example, the need in the law of contract for the acceptance of an offer to be communicated to the offeror *except* in the case of a so-called unilateral contract. The fact that a rule contains exceptions does not invalidate the main rule itself.

(iii) The third way of classifying the apparent exceptions is to regard the exceptions as cancelling the rule or as evidence that the rule does not actually exist at all. This of course is Sedley's approach. If the exceptions were numerous or overwhelming enough, this might be a possible argument. So, to revert to the example of theft, if theft became so widespread that the police and the courts turned a blind eye to it and did not even try to prosecute its perpetrators, then we might be able to say that the Theft Acts were now a dead letter and did not really exist. Yet, although theft actually *is* endemic in most societies and most thieves are not caught, let alone punished, we are still a very long way from saying that theft is legal. Similarly in regard to extra-parliamentary ministers. If the situation was reached where most ministers were appointed from outside Parliament and remained indefinitely outside Parliament without resigning their ministerial office, then we could say with Sedley that neither law nor convention required ministers to be members of either House. But, as we have seen, the evidence does not support this position.

To put no finer point upon it, Sir Stephen Sedley's categorical assertion that 'neither law nor convention requires them [viz. ministers] to be members of either House' is simply wrong. And the collapse of this assertion brings the whole of Sedley's argument crashing down with it. The argument appears to run something like this:

*Excursus A. 'Ministers are no more elected than Judges'*

(i) Ministers do not have to have a seat in either house of Parliament.

(ii) Therefore ministers are not democratically accountable.

(iii) The judges, by contrast, serve the interests of democracy by being independent.

(iv) Therefore the judges are more democratic than ministers.

This whole edifice rests on the first premise (statement (i)), which as we have seen will not stand up to scrutiny. As a result the whole edifice crumbles to dust.

III

# Obedience to the Law

**Is there an obligation to obey the law? The concept of law, however defined, contains within it the element of command and the requirement of obedience or compliance. Does this mean that everyone is obliged to comply with any law regardless of its content? No. But the basis for non-compliance is by no means clearcut.**

Is there an obligation to obey the law? The debate over this question has been raging longer than any other, going back to the time of Socrates nearly two and a half millennia ago.

On one level it might seem obvious that such an obligation must exist in any legal system. For, however we define 'law', it invariably has overtones of compulsion. This is so even when we speak of such 'laws' as the law of gravity or the law of averages, the implication being that we are in the presence of a rule which has to be obeyed in any circumstances. The same applies to such mock 'laws' as 'Parkinson's law' or 'Murphy's law'. The reason why the label 'law' was attached to these spoof rules was to suggest jocularly that they too are dictates of science or nature which must invariably be obeyed.

There is, however, a very big difference between scientific laws and man-made laws. The law of gravity is beyond the power of man or beast. Whether we like it or not, apples will continue to drop off trees on to the ground as they have done since the beginning of time. But man-made laws, such as those against murder, assault and theft, are disobeyed every day. That does not mean that there is no obligation to obey these laws, but it raises some queries about the whole concept of obedience to law.

Let us now look at some of the most commonly expressed objections to the concept of obedience to the law.

**Objection 1: Obedience to the law cannot logically be a principle of law.**

This may be referred to as the internal/external argument, which is not unrelated to 'Catch 22'. For, is not the command 'You must obey the law' part of the law itself? If so, then what is it that obliges anyone to obey *that* command? The command will only become obligatory once the law as a whole is accepted as obligatory. This brings us back full circle to the question: then what obliges us to obey the law? The only satisfactory logical answer is to be found in something separate, something outside the law itself, something higher than the law, or a higher form of law.

The trouble with that is that it can easily lead to a vicious circle or eternally swirling spiral. For, if there is a higher law that commands us to obey the ordinary law, then what is it that gives the higher law that special status? There must be a *yet* higher law. And so we end up in perpetual pursuit of an ever higher authority.

The same type of logical conundrum is also found in constitutional law where the question is: 'To what does a constitution owe its validity?' In his *Constitutionalism and the Changing World*, published in 1939, McIlwain drew a fundamental distinction, as he put it, 'between those laws which a government makes and may therefore change, and the ones which make the government itself'.[1] This latter type of law is what H.L.A. Hart in *The Concept of Law* calls a 'rule of recognition', and in the language of Hans Kelsen in The *General Theory of Law and State* and *The Pure Theory of Law* it is a 'Grundnorm'.

The writings of legal theorists such as these have made it appear necessary for there to be a fundamental law transcending what may appear to be even the most supreme of laws in any given system. Such distinguished British academic writers as E.C.S. Wade and Sir Ivor Jennings identified this fundamental law, 'rule of recognition' or 'Grundnorm' in the British Constitution with the common law. This type of thinking can be traced back much further. Theophilus Parsons, later Chief Justice of the Supreme Judicial Court of Massachusetts, made the point during the ratification of the Massachusetts Constitution in 1778, that it was no use incorporating a Bill of Rights embodying 'the unalienable rights of mankind' in the Constitution itself. As it was to be a higher form of law than the Constitution, the Bill of Rights should be enacted 'previous to the ratification of any constitution'.[2] The US Constitution *does* however include a Bill of Rights, which, though added after the ratification of the rest of the constitution, forms an integral part of the Constitution itself.

The wording of Article VI of the US Constitution is particularly telling:

> This constitution, and the laws of the United States which shall be made in pursuance thereof; and all treaties made, or which shall be made, under the authority of the United States, shall be the supreme law of the land; and the

> judges in every state shall be bound thereby, any thing in the constitution or laws of any state to the contrary notwithstanding.

What this purports to do is to establish the Constitution as 'the supreme law of the land', together with the laws made 'in pursuance' of the Constitution and treaties made under the authority of the new state. It is clear from this wording that the laws and treaties are subordinate to the Constitution. Likewise, Article V lays down the formula for amending the Constitution, showing that the whole document is deeply entrenched.

But how can the Constitution establish itself as supreme and control its own fate? Hart and Kelsen, following the same reasoning as Theophilus Parsons, would say that it cannot do so. There must be some more fundamental rule above and beyond the Constitution itself. The US Constitution opens with the words: 'We the People of the United States ... do ordain and establish this Constitution for the United States of America.' Could the people of the United States then be the ultimate source of the power of the Constitution? The objection, once again, is that these words are actually to be found in the Constitution itself. Historically speaking, however, the US Constitution can be traced back to a constitutional convention made up of delegates from the thirteen original states. But the right of the electorate to amend the Constitution is strictly circumscribed by Article V. In reality the US Supreme Court undoubtedly has more power over the Constitution than anyone else. But, in theory at any rate, they decide constitutional questions in terms of the Constitution itself, not in terms of some law higher then the Constitution. In practice, in interpreting the constitution each Supreme Court justice brings to bear upon it his own ideas, beliefs, background and personality. This results in the springing up not of one set of fundamental laws but of as many as there are different opinions in the Supreme Court. How different is this from there not being any 'rule of recognition' at all?

But is there really any necessity to posit a fundamental rule or higher law? Several British jurists have rejected the concept of a 'rule of recognition' altogether:

> All rules of law have historical sources. As a matter of fact and history they have their origin somewhere, though we may not know what it is. But not all of them have legal sources. Were this so, it would be necessary for the law to proceed *ad infinitum* in tracing the descent of its principles. It is requisite that the law should postulate one or more first causes, whose operation is ultimate and whose authority is underived ... The rule that a man may not ride a bicycle on a footpath may have its source in the by-laws of a municipal council; the rule that these by-laws have the force of law has its source in an Act of Parliament. But whence comes the rule that Acts of Parliament have the force of law? This is

> legally ultimate; its source is historical only, not legal ... It is the law because it is the law, and for no other reason that it is possible for the law itself to take notice of. *No statute can confer this power upon Parliament, for this would be to assume and act on the very power that is to be conferred.*[3] (Italics supplied.)

This commonsense approach brings us down to earth with a thud. On this basis, it is clear that, though the doctrine of obedience to the law cannot strictly speaking be regarded as forming part of the law itself, the importance of that concession should not be exaggerated. It leads us back to the simple question with which we began: Is there an obligation to obey the law?

This fundamental question can be asked and answered quite independently of the question whether such an obligation is characterised as a 'Grundnorm', a 'rule of recognition' or some other kind of overarching principle. The answer must be Yes, for the simple reason that, as was mentioned above, the concepts of obligation and obedience lie at the very heart of the definition of what law is.

Can *all* laws be seen in terms of obligation and obedience? This is the second objection to the idea that law has to be obeyed.

**Objection 2: There are some laws to which the concept of obedience is inapplicable.**

This objection was originally directed at John Austin, the nineteenth-century British legal philosopher who famously defined law as command:

> Every *law* or *rule* (taken with the largest signification which can be given to the term *properly*) is a *command*. Or, rather, laws or rules, properly so called, are a species of commands.
>
> ...
>
> A command ... is a signification of desire. But a command is distinguished from other significations of desire by this peculiarity: that the party to whom it is directed is liable to evil from the other, in case he comply not with the desire.
>
> Being liable to evil from you if I comply not with a wish which you signify, I am *bound* or *obliged* by your command, or I lie under a *duty* to obey it. If, in spite of that evil in prospect, I comply not with the wish which you signify, I am said to disobey your command, or to violate the duty which it imposes.
>
> ...
>
> The evil which will probably be incurred in case a command be disobeyed or (to use an equivalent expression) in case a duty be broken, is frequently called a *sanction*, or an *enforcement of obedience*.[4]

This, say Austin's detractors, may be all very well and good when it comes to criminal law, but it can hardly apply to all other branches of law. The Biblical injunction 'Thou shalt not kill' is obviously a command. Modern laws are not usually couched in such direct language, yet it would be hard nevertheless to find any society in which there was not a law against murder. But what about constitutional law, contract or the law of property, to take just a few basic examples? In what sense can these be regarded as being made up of 'commands'? Clearly, not in a literal sense.

In order for a valid contract to come into existence there must be an offer and an acceptance of that offer. That is a basic tenet of the Anglo-American common law of contract. What relevance does the concept of obedience have to this? Apparently none at all. No one is ordered or commanded by the law to make an offer, nor is anyone under any legal obligation to accept an offer made to him. Yet, upon examination, it will be seen that the concept of obedience is not too far below the surface. For what contract law is saying is essentially: 'These are the requirements for a valid contract, which you must satisfy if you want your transaction to be recognised as legally binding.' Once a legally binding contract has come into existence, the law says: 'You must now carry out your obligations under the contract. If you fail to do so, you will have to pay the other side compensation in the form of damages.' In other words, contract law comprises certain rules which have to be obeyed in certain circumstances.

What about a law which says 'The age of majority is eighteen'? Surely there is nothing here which can possibly be obeyed or disobeyed? Once again, upon closer inspection, the concept of obedience is found to be lurking just beneath the surface. For what this law does is to vouchsafe certain rights to persons over the relevant age. In so doing, it forbids people younger than eighteen from claiming those rights. So, someone aged sixteen would be breaking the law if he pretended to be eighteen in order to be enrolled on the electoral register. Likewise, refusal on the part of a returning officer to allow someone to vote who was genuinely eighteen would be an unlawful act on the part of the official.

In this broader sense, then, the concept of obedience *can* be seen as relevant to law as a whole. Perhaps, though, the word 'obedience' should be replaced by something a little more general. So, instead of saying that there is an obligation to *obey* the law we might say that everyone is required to act *in accordance* with the law, or, better still, that everyone is prohibited from acting *contrary* to the law. Or, even better, instead of talking about *obedience* perhaps we should rather think in terms of *compliance*. It makes perfect sense to ask, for example: Does this document *comply* with the legal requirements for a valid contract/deed/will? Or, has the claimant in this case *complied* with the procedure laid down by the Civil Procedure Rules?

**Objection 3: Everyone has the right to disobey a law which he considers invalid.**

This third argument is the most modern and at the same time the most ancient objection of all to the principle of obedience to the law. It is also the most far-reaching objection. Its advocates include all those who justify disobedience to laws which they characterise as 'immoral', 'unjust' or simply as 'doubtful'. Thus Ronald Dworkin in an essay entitled 'Civil Disobedience':

> If the law is doubtful, [everyone] may follow his own judgment, even after a contrary decision by the highest competent court.[5]

Dworkin explains his position with reference to the US judicial system:

> Sometimes, even after a contrary Supreme Court decision, an individual may still reasonably believe that the law is on his side ... We cannot assume, in other words, that the Constitution is always what the Supreme Court says it is.[6]

The original article from which these quotations are taken first appeared in 1968, when young American men called up to serve in Vietnam burnt their draft cards in protest. In so doing they were breaking a federal statute making such conduct a criminal offence.

American young men were obliged to serve in the armed forces if drafted. Dworkin's point is that 'draft-dodgers' who disobeyed the law should not have been prosecuted, as the law was 'doubtful'. In what sense does Dworkin maintain that this was the case? 'In the United States, at least', says Dworkin, 'almost any law which a significant number of people would be tempted to disobey on moral grounds would be doubtful - if not clearly invalid - on constitutional grounds as well.'[7]

This raises more questions than it answers:

(a) What is meant by 'a significant number of people'? A million, a thousand, a hundred, ten? Dworkin offers no guidance.

(b) How is one to *know* how many people are 'tempted to disobey'? This too is uncertain.

(c) What is meant by 'tempted to disobey'? Dworkin is careful not to require actual disobedience for a law to be labelled as 'doubtful'. But being 'tempted' to disobey is a peculiarly private matter. There are probably many people who at one time or another are *tempted* to disobey the law against murder but who get no further than sticking pins in their intended victim's effigy, if that.

(d) However, according to Dworkin, the temptation to disobey has to be based 'on moral grounds'. What exactly does this mean? 'Moral grounds' presumably means on the basis that the law in question is in some sense 'wrong'. This sounds straightforward enough – until one starts looking at actual examples. Was opposition to Prohibition in the 1920s based on moral grounds? Most people who objected to the Eighteenth Amendment to the US Constitution were probably motivated by a desire to be able to buy alcohol as and when they liked, but such opposition could be couched in moral terms too. For, was Prohibition not an infringement of individual liberty? If this is accepted, then what about the laws against the possession of drugs? Is it not a similar curtailment of individual freedom to stop people from smoking cannabis (marijuana) if they feel like it? And if so, on Dworkin's argument, are the drug laws not 'doubtful' as well?

(e) Not content to talk about laws which are 'doubtful' on moral grounds, Dworkin goes further by saying that such laws would be doubtful 'if not clearly invalid' on constitutional grounds as well! And what if the 'doubtful' or 'clearly invalid' law itself forms part of the US Constitution? Does this mean that even a provision of the US Constitution can be disobeyed if a 'significant number' of people object to it on moral grounds? Taxation would be a good example. If it was felt by a 'significant number' of people that taxes were being applied to immoral purposes, then would they be entitled to refuse to pay?

(f) Perhaps the key word in the whole of Dworkin's formulation is the word 'almost'. Dworkin does not suggest that *any* law would be 'doubtful' if 'a significant number of people' were 'tempted to disobey' it 'on moral grounds' – but only *almost* any law! Who decides which ones qualify and which do not? Or on what basis those that qualify do so? Nothing is said about this, but the cynical answer is that Dworkin has formulated it in this way so that he himself can determine which ones qualify and which do not. The example he chooses is the draft law at the time of the Vietnam War. But what about, say, a law obliging employers to ensure that at least 30% of their employees are black? There would very likely be a 'significant number of people' who would be 'tempted to disobey' such a law. Would their opposition be 'on moral grounds'? As the law would be a form of compulsory discrimination against the majority of the population, opposition to it could well be based on the belief that the law was wrong, i.e. there would be a moral basis for the opposition to it. In those circumstances, would Dworkin be prepared to treat this law as 'doubtful' too? The point is that the decision whether a law would qualify as 'doubtful' is essentially a political question. The US draft laws may in broad terms be characterised as 'right wing', while affirmative action may generally be thought of as 'left wing'. One's choice of 'doubtful' laws will therefore be likely to depend on one's political standpoint. In short, the whole exercise is highly subjective.

Is Dworkin's approach really a logical or even a sensible attitude to adopt to the question of obedience to the law? Or is it essentially an anarchical approach allowing people to disobey laws with which they happen to disagree? If so, then, far from bolstering the rule of law, Dworkin's approach must be seen as essentially subverting that fundamental principle.

### *Socrates*

A very different attitude to Dworkin's was adopted nearly two and a half millennia ago by someone who actually went so far as to sacrifice his own life to the principle that the law must be obeyed. The person in question was of course Socrates (469-399 BC), arguably the most famous philosopher of all time.

Socrates was convicted on a trumped up charge of 'impiety', the chief count being one of 'corrupting the youth' of Athens. The accusation was brought by Socrates' political enemies. Not only was his conviction not supported by the evidence but the law under which he was indicted was itself passed specially with him in mind. Nevertheless, when sentenced to die by drinking hemlock poison, Socrates cheerfully accepted his fate. While in prison awaiting execution he was urged by his friends to escape, which he could easily have done, and even the guards did their best to facilitate the escape of their respected prisoner. Yet Socrates doggedly refused to avail himself of this opportunity. Instead, he went to his death protesting his innocence while at the same time exhorting obedience to the law. The argument advanced by Socrates, as reflected in the dialogue known as the *Crito* written by his disciple, Plato, runs as follows:

(a) Living a virtuous life (literally, 'living justly') is of prime importance.

(b) This means that one should never deliberately act wrongly (literally, 'unjustly').

(c) It is even wrong to requite one wrong with another, as two wrongs do not make a right.

(d) There is a tacit agreement on the part of every citizen to obey the laws of his state.

There are two separate strands to the argument, which are then neatly tied together at the end of the dialogue. The first is based on the belief that it is wrong for the virtuous man to act wrongly himself, even in response to a wrongful act by another. So, however wrong it may have been for the Athenian court to convict Socrates, it would have been equally wrong of him to try to evade his sentence. The second strand of the argument then examines the citizen's duties towards the state. The position attributed to Socrates here is based on what is essentially a precursor of the concept of the 'social contract'. He argues that in return for the benefits conferred on its citizens by a state the citizens must obey the laws: and failure to do so will subvert (literally 'destroy') the laws and the structure of civilised society supported by them.

Does this mean that one should always obey any Government order? No: only lawful orders. Socrates himself had previously risked his life by *disobeying* a patently illegal order from Critias, a leading figure in the Athenian Government of the day.

There is a fine line to be drawn here. By disobeying Critias' order Socrates was not impugning the laws of Athens in any way, as Critias' order was itself at variance with those laws. However, escape from his death-cell was seen by Socrates as an attack not only on the false verdict which had condemned him but also on the law under which he had been tried. In the words that Plato puts into Socrates' mouth in the *Crito*, Socrates had been wronged by men, not by the laws, which he would be attacking if he escaped. The counter-argument to this would be that a legal system which allowed such a patently unjust verdict to be handed down was itself unworthy of respect, much less self-sacrifice.

### *The Nuremberg Trials*

This problem came to a head in the Nuremberg war crimes trials held in the wake of World War II. Most defendants pleaded not guilty on the ground that they had merely been obeying 'superior orders'. The German Nazi regime was based more than practically any other on obedience, which was elevated into the so-called 'Führer Principle' (*Führerprinzip*). This is spelt out in the SS Manual, starting with the SS oath:

> We take the oath of allegiance and valour to you, Adolf Hitler, as our Führer and Chancellor. We swear obedience unto death to you and the superiors appointed by you, so help us God.

This is then explained:

> Obedience is the foundation of the Army (*Wehrmacht*), trust is the foundation of obedience.

This is further backed up by a citation from Hitler's *Mein Kampf*:

> In the school of the army, the youth is to learn not only obedience but, by doing so, is to acquire the prerequisite qualities to take command later on. He must learn to keep silence, not only when justly reprimanded but must also learn, if necessary, to bear injustice in silence.

The *Führerprinzip* is then starkly summed up as:

> Obedience without asking the reason why. Faith in leaders must be so strong that every man is convinced that the leadership is the right one.

So far the doctrine appears to be one of blind and unquestioning obedience, but this is expressly qualified in the SS Manual itself:

> Therefore blind and trusting obedience, so long as nothing obviously illegal or immoral is demanded. Not slavish obedience, but the compliance of a free man based on his own free resolution.[8]

Even the *Führerprinzip* itself therefore stopped short of requiring obedience to orders to kill unarmed and defenceless civilians, as for example in the concentration camps. Such conduct was not required by any law or official order – nor indeed could it conceivably have been. That is no doubt why the Nazi leaders coined euphemisms such as 'the final solution' and why Nazi sympathisers down to the present day tend to deny that the Holocaust ever happened.

Murder, rape and torture were as unlawful in Germany – even under the Nazis – as anywhere else. The fact that the Nazi regime not only turned a blind eye to the perpetration of such crimes but that its leaders were instrumental in ordering their subordinates to commit them could not exculpate those subordinates – as even the *Führerprinzip* recognised.

Why then were those who either gave or carried out such orders not simply tried under German law after the war? The reason is that the Allied authorities decided to try those responsible not only for generally recognised criminal offences but also for a broader category of what now came to be called 'war crimes'. As the war drew to a close there was much debate as to how this was to be done. Winston Churchill suggested that the Nazi leaders should be 'hunted down and shot'. But, once the war was well and truly over, cooler counsels prevailed. In August 1945 an International Military Tribunal was set up by the Allies to try those charged with 'war crimes'. What system of law was to apply? A hybrid form of supranational law was compiled in the so-called London Charter, which was described neither as a 'code' nor even as 'law' at all.

This was done deliberately in order to get around two problems. First, there was the problem that not all charges brought were strictly a matter of law at all. One such charge was that of being responsible for the War, which had previously been regarded as a political rather than as a judicial matter. This count was included only in the indictments of the Nazi leaders.

But a charge which was levelled against much lowlier defendants was that of belonging to a 'criminal organisation'. The London Charter listed six Nazi organisations under this head but contained no definition of the term.

This raised the spectre of the so-called 'ex post facto' problem. Membership of the SS, for example, had not of course been unlawful during the Nazi regime but suddenly became a criminal offence after the war. This raised a fundamental legal question: How could it be right to convict someone for doing something that was not unlawful at the time when it was done?

The Allies adopted a practical strategy to get around this problem. Though mere membership of the SS was now a criminal offence in itself, it was not treated as such in practice. The relevant count of the indictment was framed in very broad terms, stating simply that a named defendant was 'charged with membership, subsequent to September 1, 1939, in the Schutzstaffel der Nationalsozialistischen Deutschen Arbeiterpartei (commonly known as the 'SS'), declared to be criminal by the International Military Tribunal and paragraph 1(*d*) Article II of Control Council Law No. 10.' On the face of it, membership of the SS should have been enough to secure a conviction on this count. In practice, however, more was needed. For example, Josef Vogt, one of the more obscure Nuremberg defendants, who had been a member of the SS since at least 1936, was acquitted of being a member of a criminal organisation: 'The most that can be said is that he knew that there were concentration camps and that there were inmates.'[9]

As we have seen, the Nazis themselves were unwilling to appear to be acting unlawfully. Indeed, in the early days of the Nazi regime the Minister of the Interior, Wilhelm Frick, found it necessary to restrain some judges whose anti-semitic zeal outstripped the new regime's legislation discriminating against Jews. This was not done out of any love for the Jews on the part of Frick but simply because he thought it preferable to keep such actions on a legal footing.[10]

Not surprisingly, the 'ex post facto' problem has attracted the attention of academic commentators. One case which has been much discussed is that of a woman who in 1944, while Germany was still under Nazi rule, had reported her soldier husband to the authorities for making derogatory remarks about Hitler, which was a criminal offence under two German laws passed in 1934 and 1938. The husband was duly arrested, charged, convicted and sentenced to death, though in view of Germany's critical military plight he was sent to the front instead, where he apparently lost his life. After the war the wife was charged in a West German court with 'illegally depriving a person of his freedom' (*rechtswidrige Freiheitsberaubung*), an offence under the German Criminal Code of 1871, which had remained in force throughout the Nazi period. The wife's defence was that, though she had been under no obligation to denounce her husband to the Nazi authorities, he had been rightly convicted under the law in force at the time, so that she could not possibly be said to have done anything illegal herself. She was however convicted under the 1871 Code.

The discussion of this case has not been assisted by disagreement among the commentators as to what the basis was of the wife's conviction. The 1949 court was caught on the horns of a dilemma in regard to the Nazi statutes of 1934 and 1938:

(a) it could accept them as valid;
(b) it could declare them null and void; or
(c) it could accept them as nominally valid but refuse to apply them.

Was the 1934 statute under which the husband had been condemned good law? If so, the wife could hardly have been guilty of *illegally* depriving him of his liberty. Should the wife then have been acquitted? That would have looked like a condonation of the Nazi past by the judiciary of the German Federal Republic. Alternatively, could the 1949 court have declared the Nazi statute of 1934 to be invalid? This would have amounted to arrogating to the judiciary a power which they did not possess. A third possibility would have been for the court to say of the 1934 statute, not 'This is not law' but 'This is law but it is so evil that we will refuse to apply it.' Though apparently less sweeping than simply declaring the statute not to have the force of law at all, this approach gives the court the power to decide which laws to apply on the basis of some standard of their own. In other words, we are here in the presence of some indeterminate and undefined Higher Law (see Chapter IV). From another point of view, Lon Fuller's comment is apt: 'Surely moral confusion reaches its height when a court refuses to apply something it admits to be law.'

On what ground could the Nazi statute of 1934 have been set aside in any event? H.L.A. Hart was under the impression that this was done by the 1949 court on the basis that the Nazi law was 'contrary to the sound conscience and sense of justice of all decent human beings'.

However, contrary to Hart and also to Lon Fuller, who also believed that the 1949 court had effectively set aside the 1934 Nazi statute, the wife was actually found guilty under the 1871 Criminal Code without challenging the validity of the Nazi statute of 1934.[11]

### *Pericles and Alcibiades*

The problem of 'good' and 'bad' laws was most vividly discussed in an ancient work which has not been cited in any of the modern treatments of the subject. This is the so-called *Memorabilia of Socrates* by the historian Xenophon (c. 430 – c. 354 BC), a younger contemporary and friend of the great philosopher. Embedded in this strangely neglected work is a brief dialogue between Pericles (c. 495-429 BC), the Athenian general and statesman, and his young ward, Alcibiades (c. 450-404 BC), who was to combine a reputation for military expertise with that of a rake. Xenophon was no philosopher, so it is quite likely that this little gem of a dialogue reflects an actual historical exchange. But its significance does not depend on that. Whether truth or fiction, it encapsulates the essential dilemma underlying the question of obedience to the law. It is worth quoting in full.[12]

*Alcibiades*: Say, Pericles, could you teach me what a law is?

*Pericles*: Of course.

*Alcibiades*: Then, by the gods, please instruct me. For, whenever I hear certain people praised for being law-abiding I think to myself that nobody deserves such praise unless he knows what a law is.

*Pericles*: Your request, Alcibiades, is not at all difficult. You want to know what a law is. Well, laws are whatever are promulgated after being passed by the people meeting together in the assembly, laying down what ought and what ought not to be done.

*Alcibiades*: And do their resolutions make it obligatory to do good things or bad?

*Pericles*: Good things, of course, my young man, certainly not bad.

*Alcibiades*: But what if the decisions about what should and should not be done are taken not by the people as a whole but, as in an oligarchy, by only a few men meeting together? How are such resolutions to be characterised?

*Pericles*: Everything that is duly promulgated after deliberation by the sovereign power in a state is known as a law.

*Alcibiades*: So, then, in a state ruled by a dictator (literally, 'tyrant') who prescribes to the citizens what they ought to do, is this law as well?

*Pericles*: Yes, even the decrees of a dictator in power are to be regarded as law.

*Alcibiades*: What then is violence and lawlessness, Pericles? Is it not whenever the stronger compels the weaker to do his bidding not by persuasion but by force?

*Pericles*: I think so.

*Alcibiades*: Then whatever a dictator compels the citizenry to do by decree and without their consent is unlawful?

*Pericles*: I believe so; and I withdraw my previous remark that whatever a dictator decrees without consent is law.

*Alcibiades*: And when a ruling oligarchy makes decrees without the consent of the many, should that be regarded as violence or not?

*Pericles*: It seems to me that anything that anyone compels someone else to do without his consent, whether by decree or not, is violence rather than law.

*Alcibiades*: So, the decrees enacted by the ruling masses against property owners without their consent are also violence rather than law?

*Pericles*: Certainly. When I was your age, Alcibiades, I too was a dab hand at this kind of game; for the conundrums on which I used to test my wits and score clever points were just the same as the ones that appear to interest you now.

*Alcibiades*: What a pity I did not know you, Pericles, when your mental powers were at their height!

Alcibiades plays the innocent throughout, pretending to sit at Pericles' feet while actually leading him into a trap – twice. The great statesman at first adopts a high-handed attitude and treats the whole question with contempt. His initial answer is couched in terms of the democratic constitution of the Athens of his day: whatever is decreed by the people in Assembly is law. Pericles makes it clear that he regards such laws as good rather than bad. But this is not a decision he takes on the basis of their contents. On the contrary, his position is that *all* laws passed by the Assembly are good by definition.

But what about non-democratic states? In response to Alcibiades' skilful probing, Pericles admits that he does not treat oligarchies or even dictatorships ('tyrannies') any differently from his own beloved Athenian democracy. By relentless logical pressure Pericles is forced into a matter-of-fact positivist conclusion: whatever the Government in power decrees is law. It makes no difference what the content or moral tone of such legislation may be, nor whether sovereign power is exercised by the citizenry as a whole, by an oligarchy or by a single man. Pericles sums up his position at this stage of the dialogue quite succinctly: 'Everything that is duly promulgated after deliberation by the sovereign power in a state is known as a law.'

Having led Pericles up the garden path, Alcibiades now leads him down again. Against Pericles' unabashedly amoral positivist structure Alcibiades brings to bear a powerful moral battering ram in the form of the concept of consent. 'If anything enacted by the sovereign power in a state is automatically lawful,' says Alcibiades in effect, 'then what is the definition of unlawfulness? Is it not where those in power impose their will on their subjects without their consent?'

In view of his arrogant, self-assured attitude up to this point, Pericles might have been expected to stand his ground. His clearly articulated position makes up in objective logical cohesiveness what it lacks in morality and flexibility. But it rests on the same fundamental principles that has characterised positivism for over two thousand years down to the present day and has the same practical implication: namely, that the law must be obeyed simply because it is the law.

But, instead of reasserting this view, Pericles immediately capitulates in the face of Alcibiades' moralistic onslaught and concedes that his original position was wrong. The new definition of law is one based on consent: No one is obliged to obey any order to which he has not given his consent. This means that the purported laws of dictators ('tyrants') or oligarchs which have been imposed on the majority against their will do not have the force of law. Alcibiades then comes in for the kill by asking Pericles about statutes passed by the Athenian masses against the property-owning classes. This would have been a sore point with the historical Pericles, who, though himself an aristocrat, was a politician who supported the masses against his own class. The Athenian Constitution of the day was a direct democracy, with the most important decisions being taken by the citizenry meeting together in the Assembly ('ecclesia'). Dominated as it was by the poor, this body adopted radical measures against the rich. It is to such measures that Alcibiades refers in his challenge to Pericles, who is content to accept that such radical legislation is invalid against the rich if it is passed without their consent.

This places Pericles in an even more untenable position than before, as he has now conceded that no law is valid without the consent of those that it affects. A modern democratic politician would have sought to extricate himself from Alcibiades' trap by distinguishing Athenian legislation from that of a dictatorship or oligarchy. The difference, he would point out, is that in the Athenian case the legislation in question was passed by the majority, whereas in the other cases it had only minority support. Why does Pericles not make this obvious point? The answer is that, though the Athenian democracy did operate on majoritarian principles for vote-taking, there was no belief in 'majority rule'. The sanctity attached to this principle is a comparatively recent development, which rests squarely on a belief in equality. The ancient Greeks, by contrast, believed in the intrinsic inequality of people, thus precluding them from treating majority voting as anything more than a convenient arithmetical device for reaching a decision.

What then does Xenophon's little dialogue teach us about obedience to the law? In the end Alcibiades' consensual definition of law is shown to be ludicrous, as it makes it virtually impossible for any law ever to command unquestioned obedience. This sends us back to Pericles' matter-of-fact positivist definition at the beginning of the dialogue, which of course accords with Socrates' self-sacrificing principle that obedience to the law is paramount.

### *Conclusion*

The concept of law, however defined, contains within it the element of command and the requirement of obedience. Does this mean that everyone is obliged to obey any law regardless of its content? No. That is something that not even the Nazi *Führerprinzip* demanded. For, as we have seen, this principle stopped short of requiring obedience to anything 'obviously illegal or immoral'. The key word here is 'obviously'. An order to commit murder would be obviously illegal and equally obviously immoral. That is why the Nazis never tried to legalise genocide: the orders to kill the concentration camp inmates were always couched in veiled terms. For even the Nazis recognised that such conduct could never be justified in terms of any system of laws.

But what about, say, a court ordering Siamese twins to be separated against the will of their parents - where it is known that this will inevitably kill the weaker sibling? This is not a hypothetical example: these are the facts of a case which recently came before the English Court of Appeal. On the basis that both twins would otherwise have died within a few months, the Court ordered them to be forcibly separated, thus effectively killing one of them. These particular Siamese twins were joined at the abdomen and shared a single heart and pair of lungs. Did this court order in fact amount to an unlawful killing, or possibly even to an incitement to murder? The parents (who subsequently allowed the court order to be carried into effect) opposed it on the ground that it was against the law of both God and man, and also because it amounted to a usurpation by the court of a fundamental parental right.[13]

What then of racially discriminatory laws such as the Nuremberg laws passed by the Nazis stripping Jews of their citizenship and other rights? Or the apartheid legislation of South Africa in the latter half of the twentieth century? Were these laws 'obviously illegal or immoral'? By today's standards the answer must be Yes. But that conclusion can only be reached by judging the laws in question by the standards of a Higher Law (see Chapter IV). For, what we are really saying when we invalidate a law is that it falls foul of an overriding principle which must prevail over any incompatible piece of legislation. In the case of laws legalising or enforcing racial discrimination, the relevant overriding principle is that of equality, while in the case of, say, a law imposing censorship the principle in question will be that of freedom of expression (see Chapter VII.2).

IV

# Higher Law

### 1. Does European law have higher law status?

**In the event of a clash between European Union law and United Kingdom domestic law European law prevails. Is this doctrine necessarily correct? And, if so, does this allow the courts to declare a United Kingdom statute void if it is in conflict with European law, or at least to suspend its operation until this question is resolved?**

> The EEC Treaty is the supreme law of this country, taking precedence over Acts of Parliament. Our entry into the Community meant that (subject to our undoubted but probably theoretical right to withdraw from the Community altogether) Parliament surrendered its sovereign right to legislate contrary to the provisions of the Treaty on the matters of social and economic policy which it regulated.[1]

This assertion of the supremacy of EU law over UK domestic law has become commonplace. But where did it come from? It is certainly markedly at variance with what the English courts were saying until not long before. Here are a few examples:

> We take no notice of treaties until they are embodied in laws enacted by Parliament, and then only to the extent that Parliament tells us.[2]

> I pause here, however, to make one observation on a constitutional point. Thus far I have assumed that our Parliament, whenever it passes legislation, intends to fulfil its obligations under the Treaty. If the time should come when our Parliament deliberately passes an Act with the intention of repudiating the Treaty or any provision in it or intentionally of acting inconsistently with it and says so in express terms then I should have thought that it would be the duty of our courts to follow the statute of our Parliament … Unless there is such an intentional and express repudiation of the Treaty, it is our duty to give priority to the Treaty.[3]

> The instant appeal does not present an appropriate occasion to consider whether

> … anything short of an express positive statement in an Act of Parliament passed after January 1 1973 that a particular provision is intended to be made in breach of an obligation assumed by the United Kingdom under a community treaty, would justify an English court in construing that provision in a manner inconsistent with a Community treaty obligation of the United Kingdom ….[4]

There is an assumption in all three passages that the UK Parliament could override EU law if it so wished. This was not the view taken by the European Court of Justice, which had long held that European law was superior to the domestic law of any member state and that where there was a clash European law would prevail.

This position emerged as early as 1963 in a case concerned with the raising of import duties within the Common Market, which was held by the European Court of Justice (ECJ) to be contrary to Art 12 of the EEC Treaty (i.e. the Treaty of Rome). The Court also held that EEC law constituted a new legal order of international law for whose benefit the member states had limited their sovereignty. As Article 12 was held to have direct effect it overrode the Dutch law imposing the tariff increase.[5]

In *Costa v ENEL*, decided soon after, the ECJ reasserted the supremacy of European law. Mr Costa challenged the lawfulness of an Italian law nationalising the Italian electricity company on the ground that the law was unconstitutional and contrary to European law. The case came before the *guidice conciliatore* in Milan, the lowest-ranking judge in the Italian judiciary, who, as soon as he heard mention of Europe, bundled all the papers over to Luxembourg. The Italian Government objected that the matter should have gone up through the Italian court hierarchy before being referred to the ECJ, but the ECJ supported the little Milan judge, holding that it was for the domestic court alone - of whatever rank - to decide whether a reference to Luxembourg was necessary. Moreover, it held, where a subsequent domestic law was incompatible with EC law, EC law must prevail.[6]

This position was reaffirmed and further extended in subsequent decisions. In 1978, for example, the ECJ held that in the case of directly applicable EEC provisions, where a provision of national law conflicted with EEC law, the offending national law did not even have to be repealed but could be ignored immediately. Where such an offending national law was repealed, the repeal had retroactive effect. This meant that the decision was taken out of the hands of the member-states and given to the ECJ itself. If a member state failed to repeal an offending piece of legislation this made no difference. The legislation could simply be treated as if it had never existed.[7]

Although this Eurocentric position was reaffirmed time and again by the ECJ it did not make any impression on the British Government or judiciary until *Factortame* 25 years later – by which time the United Kingdom had been a member of the EEC for over 15 years![8]

*Factortame* was an application for an interim injunction suspending part of the UK Merchant Shipping Act 1988 on the ground that it was in conflict with EC law. The 1988 Act restricted registration of ships as British to those all of whose owners were UK nationals, or, in the case of vessels owned by companies, 75% of whose directors and 75% of whose shareholders were British nationals. The case was brought by a British registered company which however was owned by Spanish nationals. Their argument was that by depriving them of the right to register their fishing vessels as British the Act was discriminating against fellow EC citizens, which was in breach of EC law.

The case was initially brought in the English High Court and went up to House of Lords, which agreed with the courts below that the British Constitution did not give the English courts any power to suspend an Act of Parliament even on a temporary basis, as this could only be done by means of an interim (or interlocutory) injunction against the Crown, which the courts had no jurisdiction to grant.

As the case concerned EC law it was referred to the ECJ, and the word from Luxembourg was unequivocal. It is the duty of national courts, it was held, to apply those parts of EC law which have direct effect and to protect rights which Community law conferred on individuals. This duty, said the ECJ, included the obligation to consider giving the individual concerned interim protection in order to avoid irremediable damage. Then came the grand finale, in drab enough language but words which essentially drove the last nail into the coffin of the sovereignty of English law:

> Community law must be interpreted as meaning that a national Court which, in a case before it concerning Community law, considers that the sole obstacle which precludes it from granting interim relief is a rule of national law must set aside that rule.[9]

This was a clear ruling not only allowing but indeed obliging British courts to suspend an Act of Parliament in certain circumstances – something which both the Court of Appeal and the House of Lords had held they could not do in any circumstances as it was contrary to the British Constitution. It was now clear that there was something higher than the British Constitution: the Treaty of Rome.

But that was not the end of the story. The case came back to the House of Lords, whose interpretation of the Luxembourg ruling and application of it to the relevant facts revealed a less than wholehearted endorsement of European supremacy over English law. Having previously held that it had no power to grant an injunction against the Crown, the House of Lords now found that this power had been there all the time - not in the EC Treaty but in section 37 of the Supreme Court Act 1981.

But should this power be exercised in the present case? This, it held, was a matter of discretion. In the words of Lord Goff,

> ... the Court should not restrain a public authority by interim injunction from enforcing an apparently authentic law unless it is satisfied, having regard to all the circumstances, that the challenge to the validity of the law is, prima facie, so firmly based as to justify so exceptional a course being taken.[10]

It was held that the present case *did* indeed qualify under this rather restrictive test, though no damages were available in a case of this kind. And so the Secretary of State was duly restrained by the Court from putting the offending sections into effect. The case then went back to Luxembourg, where the ECJ held that:

> Although it was for the member states of the EEC to determine, in accordance with the general rules of international law, the conditions which had to be fulfilled in order for fishing vessels to be registered in their registers and granted the right to fly their flag, in exercising that power a member state had to comply with the rules of Community law.[11]

The ECJ went on to hold that the relevant part of the Merchant Shipping Act 1988 *was* indeed contrary to EC law, as it offended against the principles of *freedom of establishment* and *non-discrimination* against nationals of other EC member states.

In a further ruling the ECJ declared that in laying down a requirement that no less than 75% of the beneficial owners of UK-registered shipping vessels had to be UK nationals the UK had 'failed to fulfil the obligations incumbent upon it under Articles 7, 52 and 221 of the EEC Treaty'.[12]

Though cataclysmic in its effect on English law, as far as the ECJ was concerned *Factortame* merely represented the culmination of the development of principles developed by the ECJ over the previous 25 years. These principles may now be stated as follows (substituting 'European Union (EU) law' for 'European Community (EC) law':

(1) EU law forms part of UK domestic law, but the supreme part.

(2) EU law therefore takes precedence even over Acts of the UK Parliament.

(3) This means that any UK Act of Parliament which is incompatible with EU law is invalid.

(4) It is within the power of the UK domestic courts to set aside any UK domestic law which is incompatible with EU law.

(5) The UK domestic courts indeed have a duty to do so.

Were Lords Denning and Diplock wrong, then, to suggest that if an Act of Parliament was specifically intended to override European law the courts would be bound to follow the UK statute? The Merchant Shipping Act 1988 was not so worded, and this doctrine has never been put to the test. But there is no doubt that it would never have been acceptable to the ECJ, which routinely gives priority to EU law (and in so doing to its own authority). But why should that have mattered?

Though the ECJ ruling in *Factortame* initially received a less than rapturous welcome from the English courts they quickly came to accept it, as can be seen from the extract from the *B&Q* case quoted at the beginning of this chapter. Nor is that entirely surprising, because the supremacy of EU law effectively gives tremendous power to the UK judiciary, which now has the right - and even the duty - to declare non-conforming Acts of Parliament void, something which the judges never had before and which is contrary to one of the most central tenets of the British Constitution, namely the legislative supremacy of Parliament.

There are two caveats that must be entered here. First, there is the obvious point that the supremacy of EU law extends only as far as EU law itself extends. That is why Hoffmann J in the *B&Q* case cited above referred to the area affected by the supremacy of the Treaty of Rome as 'the matters of social and economic policy which it regulated'.[13] It would now have to be said that it is not only the Treaties that are to be regarded as supreme but EU law as a whole and that the scope of EU law is growing all the time. Nevertheless, there still remain certain areas of English law which are not affected by it.

The second caveat is more fundamental, and that is that as far as the UK is concerned the whole colossal edifice of EU law rests on the very insecure basis of a single UK Act of Parliament. It was the European Communities Act 1972 which took the UK into the the European Communities. If that Act were to be repealed the whole edifice of EU law would come crashing down. Not only would EU law cease to be supreme in the UK: it would cease to have any effect there at all. But could the European Communities Act be repealed? Under the British Constitution as established for at least the past three hundred years no Act of Parliament is entrenched and no Act of Parliament has 'higher law' status of any kind. The fundamental principle of parliamentary legislative supremacy means that any Act of Parliament, no matter how important and regardless of its wording, can be amended or repealed by a simple majority in the House of Commons, a simple majority in the House of Lords and the Queen's assent. The constraints of practical politics however mean that there are some Acts which cannot in fact be repealed. These include all the Acts granting independence to the various former British colonies and possessions, repealing any one of which would be tantamount to a declaration of war against the country concerned. The European Communities Act is not quite in the same category, as its repeal would only signify the UK's withdrawal from the European Union club. Even the Warsaw Pact, a much less voluntary association of states in Eastern Europe under Soviet control, came to an end when one country after another threw off the Soviet yoke. It is highly invidious to the European Union to compare it to such an organisation. But the point is that it is always possible to withdraw from any association or alliance.

Finally, we have to ask whether the ECJ doctrine of the automatic supremacy of EU law is necessarily correct. It is worth noting the somewhat different approach adopted in Germany, that apparently most loyal of EU member states. The most relevant cases here are what are commonly referred to as *Solange I* and *Solange II*.

*Solange I*[14] concerned the validity of certain EEC export licensing regulations. The Frankfurt Administrative Court (*Verwaltungsgericht*) agreed with the applicant, a German exporter, that these EEC regulations constituted a violation of fundamental rights under the German Constitution. But, as the matter concerned the EEC, it referred the case to the ECJ, which adopted its usual Eurocentric approach, holding that:

(a) EC law was always superior to national law.

(b) Respect for fundamental rights formed an integral part of the general principles of law protected by the ECJ. But the question was whether any analogous guarantee inherent in Community law had been disregarded.

(c) The system of export licensing did not violate any right of a fundamental nature.

Instead of simply applying this ruling, as was done by the English courts in *Factortame*, the Frankfurt Administrative court then referred the matter to the German Federal Constitutional Court (*Bundesverfassungsgericht*) for a ruling on the constitutional validity of the EEC regulations in question:[15] The Constitutional Court held as follows:[16]

(a) EEC law was not part of national law nor of international law, but formed an independent system of law flowing from an autonomous source.

(b) So EEC law and German law stood independent of and side by side with one another.

(c) However, the EEC did not yet have a democratically elected Parliament with legislative powers, nor did it have a bill of rights.

(d) So the guarantee of fundamental rights under the German Basic Law (*Grundgesetz*) would prevail in any clash with EEC law.

(e) But the export licensing system itself did not breach any fundamental rights, such as the freedom of trade and choice of occupation under Art 12 of the German Basic Law.

The reason that this case was nicknamed *Solange* ('as long as', 'provided that') is that its essential message was that Germany would recognise the decisions of the ECJ only as long as those decisions did not infringe any rights guaranteed to German citizens under the German Basic Law.

But probably the most significant part of the judgment is the German court's characterisation of the relationship between German law and EEC law:

> [19] This court – in this respect in agreement with the law developed by the European Court of Justice – adheres to its settled view that Community law is neither a component part of the national legal system nor international law, but forms an independent system of law flowing from an autonomous legal source; for the Community is not a State, in particular not a federal state, but 'a *sui generis* community in the process of progressive integration', an 'inter-State institution' within the meaning of Article 24(1) of the Constitution.
> [20] It follows from this that, in principle, the two legal spheres stand independent of and side by side one another in their validity, and that, in particular, the competent Community organs, including the European Court of Justice, have to rule on the binding force, construction and observance of Community law, and the competent national organs on the binding force, construction and observance of the constitutional law of the Federal Republic of Germany. The European Court of Justice cannot with binding effect rule on whether a rule of Community law is compatible with the Constitution, nor can the Bundesverfassungsgericht [the German Federal Constitutional Court] rule on whether, and with what implications, a rule of secondary Community law is compatible with primary Community law. This does not lead to any difficulties *as long as* the two systems of law do not come into conflict with one another [*sic*] in their substance. There therefore grows forth from the special relationship which has arisen between the Community and its members by the establishment of the Community first and foremost the duty for the competent organs, in particular for the two courts charged with reviewing law – the European Court of Justice and the Bundesverfassungsgericht – to concern themselves in their decisions with the concordance of the two systems of law. Only *in so far as* this is unsuccessful can there arise the conflict which demands the drawing of

> conclusions from the relationship of principle between the two legal spheres set out above.[17] (Italics supplied.)

The view that European law does not form part of either domestic or international law is surprising enough. The added remark that this view is 'in agreement with the law developed by the European Court of Justice' is all the more astounding, especially in view of the now settled position of the English judiciary that 'the EEC Treaty is the supreme law of this country, taking precedence over Acts of Parliament'.[18] If this did not come from the ECJ, then where did it come from and why did the English judiciary latch on to this idea, which, as we have seen, is very different from their starting position in the pre-accession period?

Taken as a whole, the quoted extract from *Solange I* presents a stark contrast with the current UK position that European law is an integral part of the domestic law of each member state, and the supreme part. In the judgment of the German Constitutional Court we find a very different image. Not only is European law not accepted as part of German law but it is not even regarded as part of international law either. Moreover, European law is not superior to German law but is in a parallel universe of its own floating free in the stratosphere. It is however admitted that 'as long as' (*solange*) there was no conflict between the two systems of law the precedence of European law over German law would generally be recognised. In the event of a clash of laws, however, the German court reserved the right to rule that a provision of European law was inapplicable in Germany on the ground that it was incompatible with the German Basic Law.

However, by 1987 when *Solange II* came to be decided the EC had become a slightly more democratic institution, thus making the German court less standoffish. In view of the ECJ's increased concern for human rights, the German Constitutional Court was now prepared to forego its previously claimed right to review EC law by the standard of the fundamental rights contained in the German constitution. In addition we now read:

> That partly functional incorporation of the European Court into the jurisdictions of member-States expresses the fact that the legal orders of member-States and that of the Community are not abruptly juxtaposed in a state of mutual insulation but are in numerous ways related to each other, interconnected and open to reciprocal effects.[19]

Since 1987, therefore, the German position has moved closer to that adopted by the UK judiciary. But there is still the conditional *solange* attached to it. Germany will abide by European law as long as – and only as long as – it does not infringe the human rights guaranteed to German citizens under the German Constitution.

Why could Britain not have adopted a more independent stance than it has? English law went from one extreme to the other: from a belief in the potential precedence of English law over Community law to servile acceptance of European law as the supreme part of English law. Could the English judges not have held out for something akin to the German position? The commonest objection to that is that, by contrast with Germany, Britain lacks a written constitution with an entrenched Bill of Rights. That is of course true, but it was in Britain that human rights were pioneered, and they remain embedded in the fabric of the common law.

The cynic might also remark that the UK judges' acceptance of the superiority of European law over UK domestic law has given a huge boost to the power of UK judiciary. The same doctrine which has stripped Parliament, and therefore in practice the Government, of the ability to pass whatever laws it likes, has greatly enhanced the authority of the judges, who now have the power even to declare a UK Act of Parliament void.

## 2. Does human rights law have higher law status?

**The Human Rights Act 1998 has incorporated the European Convention on Human Rights into United Kingdom law. Does this mean that Convention Rights now enjoy higher law status, as some members of the judiciary have claimed?**

In a lecture delivered in October 2000, just after the Human Rights Act 1998 had come into force, Lord Steyn, a law lord, had this to say:

> Now we have a true Bill of Rights, in the shape of the European Convention on Human Rights, incorporated into our law by the carefully and subtly crafted Human Rights Act 1998. It is a Bill of Rights akin to similar measures in many constitutions. In *Reynolds* I said that the Human Rights Act has a *constitutional or higher order legal order foundation*. The Human Rights Act 1998 is now part of what is otherwise an unwritten constitution.
>
> One may then legitimately ask why does it matter whether the Human Rights Act has a constitutional or higher legal order status. It matters greatly. The fact that a right is *entrenched* in a Bill of Rights is compelling testimony that it is to be accorded *a higher normative status than other rights*. This will be particularly important in regard to the interpretation and application of the Convention and the Act. Constitutional adjudication needs to be approached generously in order to afford citizens the full measure of the protections of a Bill of Rights. By contrast, decisions taken day by day by commercial judges in respect of the

> meaning of, say, standard forms of letters of credit may sometimes employ relatively strict methods of construction. The Human Rights Act as a constitutional measure will influence not only the interpretation of statute law but also the development of common law. Decisions under it are not to be regarded as a separate stream of jurisprudence. The common law, statute law and the Human Rights Act coalesce in one unified legal system.[1] (Italics supplied.)

Lord Steyn's argument appears to run as follows:

(a) The fact that the European Human Rights Convention is now incorporated into English law automatically makes the Convention part of the British Constitution.

(b) The fact that the Convention is part of the Constitution automatically gives the Convention higher law status.

(c) The Convention Rights are therefore 'entrenched in a Bill of Rights'.

(d) Which means that the Convention Rights are 'to be accorded a higher normative status than other rights'.

(e) The judicial approach to these rights must be less strict than in ordinary commercial matters.

Upon examination, as we shall see, though the first of these statements is unassailable, assertions (b), (c) and (d) do not follow from it and fly in the face of centuries of British law and also of evidence drawn from other countries; and, if statement (e) is an exhortation for judges to favour those claiming rights against those resisting such claims, this would be unjust.

**Does the European Human Rights Convention now form part of the British Constitution?**

Yes, undoubtedly. But this does not mean much. Any law that has some bearing on constitutional matters may be considered to be part of the Constitution. But, the fact that a particular statute forms part of the British Constitution does not 'entrench' it or set it above any other statute or give it any special 'higher law' status. Such concepts are totally alien to the British Constitution and to English law as a whole.

The British Constitution is commonly said to be 'unwritten'. This is somewhat misleading, as large parts of the Constitution are in fact written down, whether in the form of statutes, case law or other rules and regulations. There are really two respects – one superficial and the other of crucial importance – in which Britain's 'unwritten' Constitution differs from the 'written' constitutions now found in most other countries around the world.

The superficial point is that, unlike a written constitution, which is contained in a single document, Britain's unwritten Constitution is made up of a whole host of disparate sources scattered in a variety of documents, practices and customs. The constitutions of most countries range in length from just a few pages to a fair-sized book. There is none known to the author which cannot be accommodated within the covers of a single volume. By contrast, the British Constitution does not exist in that form at all. There is no single identifiable document or book or series of books, to which one can point and say: 'This is the British Constitution.' That is the superficial difference between a written and an unwritten constitution.

But there is also a much more important and deep-seated difference, and that is in the status enjoyed by a written constitution by contrast with Britain's unwritten one. For, a written constitution is almost invariably invested with the status of a higher form of law than ordinary laws. Such constitutions are commonly referred to as containing the 'fundamental law' or 'basic law' of the state concerned. Another way of putting it is that a written constitution is often accorded the status of a 'higher law' or 'higher form of law'. In order to protect this higher status enjoyed by the constitution, two further features are generally found.

One is that the constitution is deliberately made difficult to amend or repeal. The degree of protection with which a constitution is hedged about can be expressed in terms of 'flexibility' or 'rigidity': the more 'rigid' a constitution is the more difficult it is to change. One can also say that a particular constitution, or a particular article or provision of a constitution, is 'entrenched', by which is meant that it is specially protected against alteration. The whole of the US Constitution, for example, is entrenched, and an elaborate procedure for amendment is laid down in Article V of the Constitution itself requiring any amendment to be proposed by two-thirds of both houses of Congress (or by the legislatures of two-thirds of the states) and ratified by the legislatures of three-quarters of the states (or by constitutional conventions in three-quarters of the states).

The other feature of written constitutions is that if any 'ordinary' law conflicts with the constitution, the constitution prevails. Or, to put it simply, where there is a clash the constitution will 'trump' ordinary law every time. It is this which has given the courts such great power in states with written constitutions, because it falls to them to strike out laws which are 'unconstitutional'. Having arrogated this role to itself two hundred years ago the US Supreme Court now exercises a huge amount of power, which was well demonstrated by the fact that it was the court that decided the presidential election in the year 2000, the first time that anything like that had happened.

There is no parallel in the British Constitution to the entrenchment or the higher law status enjoyed by written constitutions. Many constitutional changes have been made over the years, all by means of ordinary statutes. During the Blair administration alone (since 1997) power was devolved to a Scottish Parliament, a Welsh National Assembly and a Northern Ireland Assembly; the composition of the House of Lords was radically changed; and the European Convention on Human Rights was incorporated into UK law. Though referenda were held on devolution, no special procedure was needed for any of these changes, and – whatever the political constraints may be – legally speaking they could all be repealed tomorrow by the same ordinary procedure as was used to pass them: a majority of one in the House of Commons, a majority of one in the House of Lords, and the Queen's assent.

Even so ancient and sacrosanct a part of the British Constitution as Magna Carta, dating back to 1215, could be repealed at any time by exactly the same procedure as is needed to pass, amend or repeal any statute. Indeed, this is true not only in theory but also in practice. So, for example, the so-called Bill of Rights 1688, which, despite its title, has always been treated as an Act of Parliament, *was* amended by a perfectly ordinary statute called the Defamation Act 1996. And even Magna Carta itself has not really withstood the ravages of time particularly well. One of its chief provisions, at least according to one interpretation, is the guarantee of trial by jury – a right which has been greatly eroded in recent times and which at the time of writing is under threat of yet further erosion. And what procedure has been used to make these constitutional changes? As always, just a simple majority in the House of Commons, a simple majority in the House of Lords and the Queen's assent.

The significance of this becomes even clearer if we compare the position with that obtaining under an entrenched written constitution. So, for example, there can be little doubt that the law governing trial by jury is part of the Constitution in both the UK and the US. The Sixth and Seventh Amendments to the United States Constitution guarantee trial by jury. As the *whole* of the US Constitution is entrenched, these provisions automatically enjoy higher law status. The practical effects of these two features are, first, that the law governing trial by jury can only be changed by the elaborate and deliberately cumbersome procedure laid down in Article V of the US Constitution; and, secondly, that any law conflicting with these constitutional provisions will be deemed unconstitutional and therefore void. But what about the British

Constitution? Here too there is trial by jury. Indeed, that is where the Americans got the idea from! Yet, the circumstances in which trial by jury is available in England and Wales have shrunk drastically over recent decades. How did that happen? The changes were made by parliamentary legislation. Did they require any special majority or procedure? No. Were these changes subjected to any challenges in the courts? No. Why not? For the simple reason that – by contrast with the United States – neither the British Constitution nor any part of it is entrenched and neither the British Constitution nor any part of it enjoys higher law status. This is not something that can be changed by any judge, however elevated, nor even by all the judges in concert.

At the time of writing a threat has been launched by the British Government against the rule of double jeopardy, namely the ancient right not to be tried twice for the same offence. In the United States this right is protected by the Constitution, where it appears in the Fifth Amendment: 'nor shall any person be subject for the same offence to be twice put in jeopardy of life or limb'. The rule against double jeopardy is therefore entrenched together with the rest of the US Constitution, and the only way it can be repealed is by the elaborate process of constitutional amendment as laid down in Article V of the Constitution itself. Does this right form part of the British Constitution as well? Undoubtedly. For centuries the conclusive plea to any attempt to try someone a second time for the same offence has been *autrefois acquit* ('previously acquitted') or *autrefois convict* ('previously convicted'). Yet, as with any other legal provision, whether it is part of the constitution or not, all that is needed to repeal it is an ordinary statute passed in the normal way. What then of the 'new legal landscape' that Lord Steyn claims has been ushered in by the Human Rights Act and which has supposedly given Britain entrenched human rights? Could the validity of an Act of Parliament removing the ancient constitutional right against double jeopardy be challenged in the courts? Any such attempt will almost certainly fail. If it succeeds it will signal the overthrow of the three-century-old British Constitution and the substitution of the supremacy of the judiciary for the sovereignty of Parliament.

Because of the non-entrenchment and non-higher status of the British Constitution it really makes no difference whether a particular statute is part of the constitution or not, or whether part of it is concerned with constitutional issues and the rest is not. Are the laws governing divorce part of the British Constitution or not? Under the Constitution of the Republic of Ireland divorce was strictly forbidden until the Constitution was amended to allow it. As the Irish Constitution is an entrenched written instrument, this change required a popular referendum. In the UK, by contrast, the statutes relating to divorce can be changed with the same ease as any other Acts of Parliament - and have been on several occasions. So, are the UK laws of divorce part of the British Constitution or not? This is not a question that need exercise anyone, because it makes absolutely no difference whether they are so considered or not.

What then about the Human Rights Act? Because of its subject matter it must obviously now be regarded as part of the British Constitution. But that does not give it a status any different from that of any other statute that forms part of the Constitution - which is exactly the same as the status enjoyed by all other statutes, whether they are concerned with constitutional matters or not.

**Does the fact that the European Human Rights Convention is now part of the British Constitution automatically give the Convention higher law status?**

The answer, as we have already seen, is a resounding No. The doctrine of a constitutional law 'trumping' any other inconsistent law has no application in the United Kingdom. There is no hierarchy of 'higher' and 'lower' laws. All laws are equal. If there is a conflict between two statutes, the applicable rule is that of implied repeal: the later one will be preferred to the earlier one. This has nothing to do with the 'status' of the two laws but is concerned only with the *dates* when they were passed.

In the lecture quoted above Lord Steyn cited a letter to *The Times* by a senior barrister claiming that the Human Rights Act had no higher a status than the Dangerous Dogs Act 1991. Lord Steyn rejected this out of hand, adding that the 1991 Act 'has been widely condemned as an appallingly drafted piece of legislation'. This is irrelevant. Indeed, the unnamed barrister no doubt chose an apparently trivial and much-criticised statute deliberately to make the point that under English law all statutes have equal status. Lord Steyn does go on to concede that 'other commentators have also expressed the view that the Human Rights Act is no more than an ordinary statute', but he simply dismisses this view as 'wholly misconceived'. Yet he gives no reason for his assertion other than that 'the European Convention on Human Rights, incorporated into our law by the carefully and subtly crafted Human Rights Act 1998 ... is a Bill of Rights akin to similar measures in many constitutions.' This is true enough of the *contents* of the Convention but it says nothing about its *status*.

It is also a non sequitur to say, as Lord Steyn does elsewhere in the same lecture, that: 'The fact that a right is entrenched in a Bill of Rights is compelling testimony that it is to be accorded a higher normative status than other rights.' *If* a right *were* entrenched it would indeed have 'higher normative status' or 'higher legal order status', but, as shown above, the whole point about the British Constitution is that *nothing* in it is entrenched: the whole concept of entrenchment is alien to the British Constitution.

*Europe*

The fact that a country has a Bill of Rights does *not* automatically invest it with higher law status. In Germany, for example, the European Convention on Human Rights *does* form part of German domestic law but it only enjoys the status of an ordinary statute. It specifically does *not* have any kind of higher law status. Moreover, the decisions of the Strasbourg Court and the Committee of Ministers is merely *persuasive*, not binding. Germany does of course also have its own set of 'Basic Rights' (Grundrechte) which are part of the constitution or 'Basic Law' (Grundgesetz), and which therefore do enjoy higher law status. But the Euopean Convention certainly does not do so. The position of the Convention is similar in Italy and Turkey.[2]

*New Zealand*

New Zealand likewise has a Bill of Rights which specifically does *not* have higher law status. This is laid down in the Bill of Rights Act 1990, section 4 of which provides as follows:

> No court shall, in relation to any enactment (whether passed or made before or after the commencement of this Bill of Rights),
> (a) Hold any provision of the enactment to be impliedly repealed or revoked, or to be in any way invbalid or ineffectuve; or
> (b) Decline to apply any provision of this enactment by reason only that the provision is inconsistent with any provision of this Bill of Rights.

*Human Rights Act 1998*

The UK Human Rights Act was also carefully drafted so as to prevent it from being accorded higher law status. The British Government was anxious not to give the courts the power to set aside Acts of Parliament on the ground of incompatibility with the European Convention, as was frankly explained in the White Paper, *Rights Brought Home: the Human Rights Bill* (Cm 3782), presented to Parliament in October 1997:

> The Government has reached the conclusion that the courts should not have the power to set aside primary legislation past or future, on the ground of incompatibility with the Convention. This conclusion arises from the importance which the Government attaches to parliamentary sovereignty. In this context, parliamentary sovereignty means that Parliament is competent to make any law on any matter of its choosing and no court may question the validity of any Act that it passes. In enacting legislation, Parliament is making decisions about important matters of public policy. The authority to make those decisions derives from a democratic mandate. Members of Parliament in the House of Commons possess such a mandate because they are elected, accountable and representative. To make provision in the Bill for the courts to set aside Acts of Parliament would confer on the judiciary a general power over the decisions of Parliament which under our present constitutional arrangements they do not possess, and would be likely on occasions to draw the judiciary into serious conflict with Parliament.[3]

The White Paper likewise rejected the idea that what was to become the HRA should be 'entrenched' by giving it special protection against subsequent repeal or amendment. The White Paper specifically cited the US Constitution in this connection, which can be amended only by a highly elaborate process involving a two-thirds majority of both houses of Congress and ratification by three-quarters of the state legislatures. 'But', comments the White Paper, 'an arrangement of this kind could not be reconciled with our own constitutional traditions, which allow any Act of Parliament to be amended or repealed by a subsequent Act of Parliament. We do not believe that it is necessary or would be desirable to attempt to devise such a special arrangement for this Bill.' Indeed, whether any UK statute could ever be 'entrenched' is extremely doubtful.

Section 3 of the Human Rights Act provides that the courts must try as far as possible to interpret any legislation, primary and subordinate alike, in a way which is compatible with the Convention rights.

But, if a court is 'satisfied' that a statutory provision is incompatible with a Convention right, it may issue a 'declaration of incompatibility' under section 4(2). What this means is that, far from being able to set aside legislation inconsistent with the Human Rights Convention, all that the courts can do is flag up the inconsistency – and it is then up to the Government to decide whether to remedy the incompatibility or not.

A declaration, we are told in section 4(6), 'does not affect the validity, continuing operation or enforcement of the provision in respect of which it is given'; and it is not even 'binding on the parties to the proceedings in which it is made'. Before actually making a declaration of incompatibility a court has to notify the appropriate Government minister, who is entitled to be joined as a party to the proceedings if he so wishes. But the minister will presumably take this offer up only if he wishes to oppose the issue of a declaration of incompatibility. What, then, if the minister does not wish to oppose it? The declaration will then be duly issued by the court, but it is clear that this is no way invalidates the offending legislation.

It is then for the responsible minister to decide whether the incompatible legislation should be amended in order to bring it into line with the European Convention. If need be this can be done by a special 'fast-track' procedure. Section 10(2) of the HRA provides that:

> If a Minister of the Crown considers that there are compelling reasons for proceeding under this section, he may by order make such amendments to the legislation as he considers necessary to remove the incompatibility.

So the minister essentially has three options. He may either (a) amend the offending legislation by making a 'remedial order' by the fast-track procedure; or (b) put the amendments that he wants through Parliament in the ordinary way; or (c) do nothing. The wording of the section is significant, as it gives the minister the whiphand. It is for the minister to decide whether there are 'compelling reasons' for adopting the fast- track procedure; and it is for the minister to make the amendments; which, significantly, are the ones that he – not the court – 'considers necessary to remove the incompatibility'.

The provision in section 19 of the HRA on 'statements of compatibility' is in similar vein. A 'statement of compatibility' is to be made by the minister steering a Bill through either House of Parliament. The statement must be made before Second Reading of the Bill and must be in writing and be published 'in such manner as the minister making it considers appropriate'. In the statement the minister must say that 'in his view the provisions of the Bill are compatible with the Convention rights': section 19(1)(a). Alternatively, the minister must make a published written statement 'to the effect that although he is unable to make a statement of compatibility the Government nevertheless wishes the House to proceed with the Bill': section 19(1)(b). The Act here goes out of its way specifically to allow legislation incompatible with the Convention to be enacted if the Government so wishes – which could hardly be the case if the Convention enjoyed higher law status!

What then about section 6(1) which states categorically that 'It is unlawful for a public authority to act in any way which is incompatible with a Convention right'? The term 'public authority' is defined in section 6(3) as including courts and tribunals. So, if an Act of Parliament incompatible with the Convention is allowed to remain on the statute book, will it not be 'unlawful' under section 6(1) for the court to continue to recognise and enforce it? No, because there is also section 6(2)(a), which says that section 6(1) does not apply where the court in question has no choice in the matter 'as the result of one or more provisions of primary legislation'. The purpose of this less than pellucid subsection is obviously to preserve the right of Parliament (i.e. in practice of the Government) to allow legislation incompatible with Convention rights to remain valid. It covers new incompatible legislation introduced by the Government after the coming into force of the Human Rights Act as well as pre-existing incompatible legislation.

### *'Parliamentary sovereignty'*

The passage quoted above from the 1997 White Paper, *Rights Brought Home*, will repay close examination. The points made there are essentially as follows:

(a) The Human Rights Act does not allow the courts to set aside Acts of Parliament on the ground of incompatibility with the Human Rights Convention.

(b) The Human Rights Act was deliberately drafted in this way.

(c) If it were not so drafted it would conflict with the important principle of parliamentary sovereignty.

(d) 'In this context, parliamentary sovereignty means that Parliament is competent to make any law on any matter of its choosing and no court may question the validity of any Act that it passes.'

(e) Parliament's power 'derives from a democratic mandate'.

(f) Members of Parliament in the House of Commons possess such a mandate because they are elected, accountable and representative.

(g) If the Human Rights Act were to give the courts the right to set aside Acts of Parliament this 'would confer on the judiciary a general power over the decisions of Parliament which under our present constitutional arrangements they do not possess, and would be likely on occasions to draw the judiciary into serious conflict with Parliament'.[4]

(h) In addition, as mentioned above, the Government also set its face against 'entrenching' the Human Rights Convention.

If the Human Rights Convention had the higher law status that Lord Steyn claims is has, then that would automatically give the courts the right to set aside statutes incompatible with it. Yet it is clear that the Convention does *not* have higher law status and is *not* entrenched. This is clear not only from the fact that the Government deliberately intended not to confer this status on it but also from a reading of the Human Rights Act itself (see above). Any suggestion that the Human Rights Act can be interpreted to mean that the courts have the power to set aside other statutes on the ground that they conflict with the Human Rights Act or the Convention which it incorporates could only be based on a wholesale scrapping and rewriting of the Human Rights Act as it appears on the statute book.

The doctrine of the sovereignty of Parliament, or better, the legislative supremacy of Parliament, has been a fundamental principle of the British Constitution for over three hundred years. It has to some extent become a legal fiction, as control over legislation is in practice under the control not of Parliament, however defined, but of the executive government, namely the Prime Minister and Cabinet. The Government can normally ensure that any law that it wishes Parliament to pass will be passed, and any bill which lacks government backing is practicaly doomed to failure. This is because the British Constitution has been hammered out over the years on the anvil of practical politics. The executive *is* the executive because it commands a majority in the House of Commons.

But, the fact that the driving force behind legislation is the executive rather than the legislature does not make any difference to the issue we are considering here. The executive is made up of Members of Parliament, who have been elected to the House of Commons, together with some members of the House of Lords.

This is what the White Paper meant by 'democratic mandate'. But, it may be objected, ministers are not elected as ministers, and some of them are not elected at all. Because of the close interlocking relationship between executive and legislature, this is a pedantic point. The electorate has the power to turn out an unpopular Government at a general election – and it has exercised this power on numerous occasions. Although voters are ostensibly voting only for a Member of Parliament, in reality they are voting for a party and for a Government, which is why small parties which are not perceived by the electorate as having a genuine chance of forming a Government do poorly in elections. What about ministers who are not in the Commons but in the Lords? Because the outcome of a general election is in reality the people's verdict on the Government, these ministers are effectively accountable to the electorate as well, and if the Government is turned out of office these ministers will be out of a job. A less than persuasive attempt to argue that the democratic credentials of judges are as good as if not better than those of ministers is discussed elsewhere.[5]

**Are the Convention Rights 'to be accorded a higher normative status than other rights', as Lord Steyn claims?**

## *IV. Higher Law*

As the Convention Rights clearly do *not* have higher law status and are *not* entrenched (see above), with one (arguable) exception there is no basis for giving them 'higher normative status' than other rights. The one exception is freedom of expression (see Chapter VII.2), and more particularly freedom of the press, which however gets its special status *not* from the Convention but from section 12 of the Human Rights Act itself.

**Should the interpretation of the Convention Rights be less strict than that applicable to documents in ordinary commercial matters, as Lord Steyn suggests?**

The interpretation of a document as vaguely worded as the European Convention on Human Rights inevitably gives more latitude to the judiciary. There is plenty of room for divergent interpretations. Not surprisingly, the Strasbourg court is rarely unanimous when deciding whether a particular set of circumstances amounts to a breach of a Convention Right or not. But Lord Steyn appears to be going further when he adds: 'Constitutional adjudication needs to be approached generously in order to afford citizens the full measure of the protections of a Bill of Rights.'[6] If this means that judges should interpret Convention Rights in a way that favours those claiming such rights, then it is a less than reassuring example of judicial activism. Every right has a reciprocal duty – something which rights-based lawyers sometimes appear to lose sight of. Moreover, most of the Convention Rights contain limitations and restrictions. Even the right to life (Article 2), for example, is subject to the qualification that 'deprivation of life' is permissible 'when it results from the use of force which is no more than absolutely necessary'. Should judges automatically favour those claiming rights against those resisting their claim? This would be unjust in the extreme.

### *Summary of arguments*

The following is a summary of the arguments contained in this chapter:

(1) The European Human Rights Convention is now part of the British Constitution.

(2) But this most certainly does *not* invest the Convention with higher law status.

(3) The Convention Rights are *not* entrenched.

(4) There is therefore no basis for the Convention Rights (except possibly

freedom of expression) 'to be accorded a higher normative status than other rights'.

(5) It would be unjust for the judiciary to favour litigants claiming rights against those opposing such a claim.

Practical realities, however, may have an impact on these legal points.

*Practical effect*

No Government would like to appear to be flying in the face of human rights, so, even if the courts interpret such rights in ways which are hard to justify in terms either of logic or fairness, it is highly unlikely that either the Government or Parliament would be emboldened to challenge them. As a result human rights law – as interpreted by the judges – may well in practice come to be treated as enjoying higher law status, which is unlikely to serve the interests of ordinary law-abiding citizens as much as it will contribute to the victory of the judiciary in its long-running battle against the executive. The ultimate casualties will be democracy and the rule of law.[7]

*Tariff for mandatory lifers*

A unanimous seven-judge panel of the House of Lords decided that it was incompatible with Art 6 of the European Convention on Human Rights for the Home Secretary to have the right to determine how long a convicted murderer serving a mandatory 'life' sentence should spend in prison for purposes of punishment.[8] This was widely reported in the press as meaning that the Home Secretary had 'lost' this right or been 'stripped' of it by the court. In fact, however, all that the House of Lords had done was to issue a 'declaration of incompatibility' under section 4 of the Human Rights Act, which, as mentioned above, is all that they could do.

The point is that the Home Secretary's sentencing power was granted to him by Act of Parliament, namely section 29 of the Crime (Sentences) Act 1997. The significance of this case is therefore that convicted murderers were mounting a challenge to an Act of Parliament. But not even Lord Steyn suggested that the legislation in question could be set aside on the ground of incompatibility with human rights – nor even, for that matter, on the basis of implied repeal, as the offending Act of course predated the Human Rights Act.

Nevertheless, this decision is a good illustration of the way in which human rights law has given the already staggering power of the judiciary a yet further boost. The House of Lords here reversed the Court of Appeal, where Lord Woolf CJ had held that:

> While the time may well come when the developments in the jurisprudence of the ECtHR require us to come to a different decision, that stage has not been reached. Until it is reached I do not consider we should interfere with the clearly expressed views of the democratically elected Parliament as those views, up to now, are consistent with the approach adopted by the ECtHR.[9]

As Lord Woolf predicted, between the Court of Appeal hearing in *Anderson* and its consideration by the House of Lords the ECtHR had indeed changed its position. In *Stafford v UK* the ECtHR remarked that:[10]

> ... with the wider recognition of the need to develop and apply, in relation to mandatory life prisoners, judicial procedures reflecting standards of independence, fairness and openness, the continuing role of the Secretary of State in fixing the tariff and in deciding on a prisoner's release following its expiry, *has become increasingly difficult* to reconcile with the notion of separation of powers between the executive and the judiciary, a notion which has assumed growing importance in the case-law of the Court. (Italics supplied.)

As the italicised words make clear, this was merely an *obiter dictum*. There was held to have been an infringement of Art 5(4) of the Convention, which says that anyone who is imprisoned 'shall be entitled to take proceedings by which the lawfulness of his detention shall be decided speeedily by a court and his release ordered if the detention is not lawful'. As the Parole Board had recommended that Stafford be released in July 1997 but the Home Secretary kept him in prison until December 1998, Stafford's detention during that period 'was not reviewed by a body with a power to release or with a procedure containing the necessary judicial safeguards, including, for example, the possibility of an oral hearing'.[11] There was no finding, however, of any infringement of Art 6(1), the right to a fair trial, nor indeed had Stafford even made that claim.

But, even if an infringement of Art 6 had been found by the ECtHR in *Stafford*, what status would that decision have had in the English courts? Section 2(1) of the Human Rights Act says that a UK court or tribunal determining a Convention rights question 'must take into account' any Strasbourg decision 'so far as, in the opinion of the court or tribunal, it is relevant to the proceedings in which that question has arisen'. Despite the peremptory 'must', Strasbourg decisions are *not* binding on UK courts and are *not* incorporated into UK law. In short, the UK courts are left to decide whether they wish to follow Strasbourg or not.

What, then, was the basis for the House of Lords decision in *Anderson* that:

> Section 29 of the Crime (Sentences) Act 1997 is incompatible with a Convention right (that is the right under Article 6 of the European Convention on Human Rights to have a sentence imposed by an independent and impartial tribunal) in that the Secretary of State for the Home Department is acting so as to give effect to section 29 when he himself decides on the minimum period which must be served by a mandatory life sentence prisoner before he is considered for release on life licence.[12]

Where does Art 6 of the Convention say that there is a right 'to have a sentence imposed by an independent and impartial tribunal'? The answer is that it does not. In fact, there is no mention of sentencing at all. What it says is that 'everyone is entitled to a fair and public hearing within a reasonable time by an independent and impartial tribunal established by law'. The House of Lords decision depends on including the sentencing process as part of the trial. But what about the provision, then, for a 'public hearing'? If the Home Secretary is to lose his power of fixing the tariff for convicted murderers, then this decision will presumably go to the Parole Board – who do not hold public hearings either.

As the House of Lords decision in *Anderson* is only in the form of a declaration of incompatibility, it does not set aside the offending legislation and does not affect its validity. So, can the Home Secretary not simply ignore it and carry on as before? In theory, yes. But, if he did so Anderson would take his case to Strasbourg, where he would be bound to score a victory against the UK. This too could in theory be ignored by the Government, but it would earn them the opprobrium of flying in the face of human rights law, and in fact no UK Government has ever ignored a Strasbourg ruling.

In practice, therefore, all the Government's carefully contrived wording of the Human Rights Act designed to prevent the Convention from becoming a higher form of law is likely to be thwarted. Should this not be applauded as a victory for human rights? What it really is is a victory for the judiciary over the executive and legislature alike. The immediate beneficiary of this decision is Anthony Anderson, convicted of two brutal murders. In the words of Lord Bingham:[13]

> In September 1986 the appellant [i.e. Anthony Anderson] murdered a 60 year old man in obviously poor health who had allowed the appellant into his house. Once in the house the appellant punched and kicked the victim who suffered cardiac arrest and died. The appellant stole some of the victim's property. In May 1987 the appellant murdered a 35 year old homosexual who had invited the appellant back to his house after a chance meeting. The appellant attacked and kicked his victim, who died from his injuries, and stole his property. The appellant denied both murders but was convicted before Kenneth Jones J and a jury at the Central Criminal Court.

The key word in Art 6(1) of the convention is 'fair'. Fairness must surely apply to both sides, not only to convicted murderers but also to their victims. Current English criminal procedure does not allow the prosecution to ask for a particular sentence or indeed to become involved in the sentencing process in any real sense at all. On the basis that Anderson 'had deliberately picked on vulnerable victims' the trial judge had recommended a minimum term of 15 years for both murders. The Lord Chief Justice made the same recommendation, but the Home Secretary set the term at 20 years.[14]

Was this really too severe? Norman Brennan, Director of the Victims of Crime Trust was quoted in the press as saying: 'Members of the public see sentences handed out by the judiciary as very inadequate.'[15] The argument on the other side is twofold. First, that as a politician the Home Secretary is likely to be susceptible to the pressures of public opinion. Secondly, that it is a breach of the principle of the separation of powers for a member of the executive to perform a judicial function.

Is it so wrong for public opinion to be taken into account in sentencing? The US Supreme Court has recently ruled as unconstitutional an Arizona requirement for 'aggravating circumstances' to be found by a judge before a convicted murderer could be sentenced to death. This was a function that only a jury could perform, it was held, in conformity with the guarantee of jury trial contained in the Sixth Amendment to the US Constitution. Breyer J concurring with the majority went even further, holding that the Eighth Amendment (prohibiting 'cruel and unusual punishments') 'requires that a jury, not a judge, make the decision to sentence a defendant to death'.

Moreover:

> Nor is the fact that some judges are democratically elected likely to change the jury's comparative advantage in this respect. Even in jurisdictions where judges are selected directly by the people, the jury remains uniquely capable of determining whether, given the community's views, capital punishment is appropriate in the particular case at hand.[16]

From the perspective of the UK judiciary this argument may appear topsy-turvy. Juries are Justice Breyer's first preference in determining the death penalty, with democratically elected judges second and appointed judges bringing up the rear. The point Breyer J is making is precisely the desirability and indeed the necessity for public opinion to be taken into account in these life-or-death decisions. Does this argument not apply also where not the life but the liberty of a convicted murderer is at stake?

What about the doctrine of the separation of powers? Lord Diplock famously remarked that 'the British Constitution, though largely unwritten, is firmly based on the separation of powers'.[17] This is plainly wrong. The legislature and executive are so closely intertwined that the Prime Minister and Cabinet owe their position precisely to the fact that they command a majority in the House of Commons, and legislation in practice originates with the executive, which can generally ensure that any Bill which it wishes Parliament to pass will become law and any Bill which it opposes will be defeated. Even the fact that the law lords not only concern themselves with judicial business but can also participate in the legislative business of the House of Lords as a Parliament – more so now than was traditionally the case – flies in the face of the doctrine of the separation of powers.

What then was Lord Diplock thinking of? He went on to explain: 'Parliament makes the laws, the judiciary interpret them.' In this respect Lord Diplock was quite right. This division of power is indeed an important part of the British Constitution. But it rests not so much on the doctrine of the separation of powers as on that of the legislative supremacy of Parliament, dating back to the 'Glorious Revolution' of 1688-89 and beyond. However, it is now honoured more in the breach than in the observance, as judge-made law has made increasing inroads on the fabric of the law.[18] The Home Secretary's power to fix a tariff for convicted murderers was granted to him by Act of Parliament. It could therefore be argued that any interference with it by the courts should be rejected as amounting to a challenge to parliamentary legislative supremacy.

Separation of powers entails a system of checks and balances, as indeed there is in the US Constitution, for example, which enshrines that principle in a very real sense. In the UK, however, though the judiciary can strike down decisions of the executive and in certain circumstances even set aside Acts of Parliament, the judges of the High Court and above are not subject to any real controls by either the executive or the legislature.[19] Election of judges is unknown and impeachment effectively long abolished, though it originated in England and has been successfully used against many judges in the USA (including one Supreme Court Justice, Samuel Chase, who was acquitted).

# V

# Constitutional Principles

## 1. The rule of law

### *England*

The term 'the rule of law' is closely associated with the name of Albert Venn Dicey (1835-1922), whose *Introduction to the Study of the Law of the Constitution*, first published in 1885, is probably the best known and most influential book on the British Constitution ever written. For Dicey 'the supremacy or the rule of law' was one of the two chief features of the British Constitution, the other being what he termed 'the sovereignty of Parliament'. The rule of law is defined by Dicey as comprising 'at least three distinct though kindred conceptions'.[1]

The first of these three concepts is stated by Dicey in the following terms:

> We mean, in the first place, that no man is punishable or can be lawfully made to suffer in body or goods except for a distinct breach of law established in the ordinary legal manner before the ordinary courts of the land. In this sense the rule of law is contrasted with every system of government based on the exercise by persons in authority of wide, arbitrary, or discretionary powers of constraint.[2]

Dicey contrasts the situation in Britain with that, for example, of pre-Revolutionary France, where King Louis XIV's famous boast was 'L'état, c'est moi' ('I am the state'), and where even the effete Louis XVI could say 'It is legal because I wish it'.[3]

The second strand in Dicey's definition of the rule of law is the concept of equality before the law:

> We mean in the second place, when we speak of the 'rule of law' as a characteristic of our country, not only that with us no man is above the law, but (what is a different thing) that here every man, whatever be his rank or condition, is subject to the ordinary law of the realm and amenable to the jurisdiction of the ordinary tribunals.[4]

*V.1. The rule of law*

Dicey's third aspect of the rule of law is the central role played by the common law in the development of the British Constitution:

> There remains yet a third and a different sense in which the 'rule of law' or the predominance of the legal spirit may be described as a special attribute of English institutions. We may say that the Constitution is pervaded by the rule of law on the ground that the general principles of the Constitution (as for example the right to personal liberty, or the right of public meeting) are with us as the result of judicial decisions determining the rights of private persons in particular cases brought before the courts; whereas under many foreign constitutions the security (such as it is) given to the rights of individuals results, or appears to result, from the general principles of the Constitution.[5]

Taken together, the three facets of Dicey's view of the rule of law might lead us to expect to find in him a vocal supporter of a strong judiciary, an adherent of the cause of judicial activism or even perhaps of judicial supremacism. And at first sight this does indeed appear to be the case. For, declares Dicey, 'far from being the result of legislation, in the ordinary sense of that term', what he calls 'the English Constitution' is 'the fruit of contests carried on in the courts on behalf of the rights of individuals.' He concludes roundly: 'Our constitution, in short, is a judge-made constitution, and it bears on its face all the features, good and bad, of judge-made law.'[6]

But what exactly does Dicey mean by the term 'judge-made law'? He devotes a considerable amount of space to this topic in his *Lectures on the Relation between Law and Public Opinion in England during the nineteenth century*, published in 1905. With characteristic clarity, he attributes the existence of judge-made law in England to two ideas:

> The one is that a judge or a Court … when deciding any case must act, not as an arbitrator, but strictly as a judge; or that it is a judge's business to determine not what may be fair as between A and X in a given case, but what, according to some definite principle of law, are the respective rights of A and X.[7]

And:

> The other idea is that a Court or a judge must follow precedents, by which expression is really meant that a Court having once decided a particular case on a given principle (…) must decide all really similar cases in accordance with the same principle, or, to put the same thing in other words, that a Court is bound, as the expression goes, by its own judgments.'[8]

It is clear from this that Dicey's concept of 'judge-made law' is very different indeed from the modern definition of the term. Judges, he stresses, are not allowed to decide a case on the basis of whatever they consider just or fair. They are constrained by 'definite principles of law' and by binding precedent.

This is a perfectly conventional view of the function and powers of the judiciary. Why then did Dicey label it 'judge-made law'? For the functions and powers he attributes to the judiciary bear little resemblance to those of the legislature, i.e. Parliament. By contrast with the judges, Parliament is constrained neither by principle nor by precedent. Parliament may adopt a protectionist stance at one moment and a free trade position the next; it may nationalise the railways by a stroke of the pen and privatise them again by another stroke of the pen; it may create an intermediate tier of local authorities by one enactment and then abolish them by another. These examples are not hypothetical: all of them are drawn from history.

### *Judge-made law*

In a celebrated paper on 'The Judge as Lawmaker' published in 1972, Lord Reid, one of the leading activist judges of the twentieth century, mocked the critics of judge-made law:

> There was a time when it was thought almost indecent to suggest that judges make law – they only declare it. Those with a taste for fairy tales seem to have thought that in some Aladdin's cave there is hidden the Common Law in all its splendour and that on a judge's appointment there descends on him knowledge of the magic words Open Sesame. Bad decisions are given when the judge has muddled the password and the wrong door opens. But we do not believe in fairy tales any more.[9]

'Really?' we may be tempted to retort: 'Are you saying that all the law reports and law books that a judge has supposedly studied and inwardly digested count for nothing?'

> So [Lord Reid continues] we must accept the fact that for better or for worse judges do make law, and tackle the question how do they approach their task and how should they approach it.[10]

His answer is threefold:

> We should, I think, have regard to common sense, legal principle and public policy in that order.[11]

*Why* must we accept that judges do make law? Lord Reid does not tell us. Or was it simply because it happened to suit himself and other activist judges?

## V.1. The rule of law

What is wrong with Lord Herschell's approach, which is to decide cases within the framework of existing principles and precedent and leave changes in the law to be made by the legislature?

But Lord Reid did at least suggest some guidelines for judge-made law. 'Legal principle' is one of the three ingredients here, but only second in order of priority. Pride of place goes to 'common sense', which seems fine until we discover what Lord Reid's view of common sense is:

> Common sense is not static. What passed for common sense three hundred or even one hundred years ago sometimes seems nonsense today. I do not say that modern notions are necessarily better.[12]

What this does is effectively to nullify common sense as a standard. Common sense here is indistinguishable from policy, which is Lord Reid's third ingredient. No examples of this type of changing 'common sense' are given. It would presumably cover such things as changing attitudes towards, say, punishment for crime. A hundred years, and even more so two or three hundred years ago, criminal activity of any kind was considered to deserve harsh punishment. Theft of a loaf of bread might carry the death penalty. With the rise of the social sciences in the twentieth century the emphasis came to be placed more and more on rehabilitation rather than on retribution or even deterrence. This resulted in a much more liberal approach to sentencing. However, by the end of the century there were serious doubts about the success of this policy. In this welter of different opinions how is it possible to identify the commonsense approach? And, even more important, who is to be given the right to make this decision? Should each individual judge have free rein to sentence in accordance with his own view of what conforms to common sense? This would be unlikely to result in fairness or justice - and would therefore amount to a negation of that fundamental aspect of the rule of law, namely equality before the law.

Lord Reid does go on to identify the fundamental conflict here:

> People want two inconsistent things; that the law shall be certain, and that it shall be just and shall move with the times. It is our business to keep both objectives in view. Rigid adherence to precedent will not do. And paying lip service to precedent while admitting fine distinctions gives us the worst of both worlds. On the other hand too much flexibility leads to intolerable uncertainty.[13]

His solution to this dilemma is stated quite simply: 'At any rate if we are to prevent the law from becoming a jungle you must give our young men some unifying principles which they can understand and use.'[14]

Here at last we have a recognition by Lord Reid of the danger of too much individual judicial discretion. Even more significantly, the solution that he offers is in the form of 'unifying principles'. Incidentally, 'our young men' is a reference to law students, as the paper in question was actually delivered at a conference of university law teachers.

Where are these 'unifying principles' to come from? Lord Reid does not say. Yet he is clearly of the view that such principles do exist.

But Lord Reid was not advocating a uniform approach to the law. On the contrary, he identifies three different types of judges, each with a different approach to the law:

> All may be equally good lawyers but they will not always reach the same result. We want a balance of power and I should be sorry to see the day in this country – we have seen it elsewhere – when all are drilled to think alike.[15]

The reference here is presumably to totalitarian states such as Nazi Germany or the Soviet Union. But the parallel is by no means obvious. Banning freedom of thought is one thing; having certain uniform and predictable standards of law is another. A scientist may believe that the earth is flat, but should he be allowed to teach this in a university as the sole truth?

Not surprisingly, Lord Reid prefers to regard law as an art rather than as a science:

> So you will see I have no golden rule for judicial lawmaking. There is much truth in the old saying that law is as much an art as a science. Judges never will nor should they all think alike.[16]

Yet, as he himself had put it just a few pages earlier, 'too much flexibility leads to intolerable uncertainty'[17] and, again, without 'unifying principles' the law would be likely to become a 'jungle'.

Let us return to the task that Lord Reid set himself at the beginning of his paper. 'So we must accept the fact that for better or for worse judges do make law, and tackle the question how do they approach their task and how should they approach it.'[18] This aparently two-pronged question is really two quite separate and very different questions, one objective and the other subjective. What exactly is meant by 'should' in the second question? Is Lord Reid asking how the law requires judges to set about making law, or is he asking how he personally thinks they ought to do it? In fact, as we have already seen, it is only the latter question that he addresses.

But it is the former question that is the really crucial one: what *is* the proper role of judges? The reason Lord Reid did not address this question is no doubt because, as he pointed out, he did not believe in a uniform approach. In other words, Lord Reid did not *like* uniformity. But that is beside the point. What we have to ask is, first, *whether* the law has any view on the role of the judge as lawmaker, and, *if so*, what it is.

Lord Reid, by origin a Scottish advocate, quotes with approval the following passage from Erskine, whom he describes as 'the most conservative of our three most authoritative institutional writers':

> Judgment ought not to be pronounced by examples or precedents. Decisions therefore though they bind the parties litigating the case create no obligation on the judges to follow in the same tract if it shall appear to them contrary to law.[19]

It is easy to see why this old Scots opinion appealed to Lord Reid, as it gives judges great freedom to decide cases without being bound too closely by precedent. But it is worth noting that Erskine does not allow judges a totally free rein. They may depart from precedent – but only if the earlier decision 'shall appear to them contrary to law'.

What law was Erskine referring to? As has been said by a leading Scots lawyer: 'Unlike English law, Scots law has long been a highly systematized body of principles.'[20] It is to this body of principles that Erskine was referring. This puts his quoted remark in a completely different light. What Erskine is talking about is the balance between the two features identified by Dicey, namely principle and precedent. Erskine recognises that there may well be cases where following precedent may actually fly in the face of principle. He is not suggesting that a judge should just make up the law if he does not happen to like the relevant precedents. What he is saying is something very different, namely that where precedent and principle point in opposite directions, the judge should follow principle. It should be pointed out that the 'highly systematized body of principles' comprising Scots law goes back well over three hundred years. First compiled by Viscount Stair in his *Institutions of the Law of Scotland*,[21] published in 1681, the principles themselves go back a good deal further.

The Scottish approach to judicial decision-making is more akin to that of the Roman-based 'civilian' systems (as they are called) of France, Germany and many other mainland European jurisdictions than to the English approach: '... consistently with the civilian tradition, the tendency of Scottish courts and judges is to seek the appropriate general principle and to reason from that to the decision of the case before them, rather than to seek the apt precedent.'[22]

*Parliamentary legislative supremacy*

In fact, when deciding Scottish cases Lord Reid himself adopted this approach. This is well illustrated by the important case of *Burmah Oil v Lord Advocate.*[23]

During World War II oil installations in Burma belonging to Burmah Oil Company Ltd were destroyed by order of the British Government to prevent them from falling into enemy hands. Burmah Oil sought compensation from the Government. This was refused, so Burmah Oil proceeded to sue the British Government. As the proceedings were brought in Scotland the Defendant was named as the Lord Advocate, the senior adviser to the Government on Scots law. More importantly, the case was decided on the basis of Scots law. Having lost in the courts below, Burmah Oil successfully appealed to the House of Lords, which decided in their favour by three votes to two, the leading speech for the majority being delivered by Lord Reid. In accordance with Scots practice, he based his decision on principles drawn from Scottish institutional writings and also from continental civilian authorities of the seventeenth and eighteenth centuries. Despite his extra-judicial justification for judges as lawmakers, on the bench Lord Reid was fully committed to the Diceyan principle of the legislative supremacy of Parliament. Here for example is an extract from his judgment in *Madzimbamuto v Lardner-Burke*[24] at 723:

> It is often said that it would be unconstitutional for the United Kingdom Parliament to do certain things, meaning that the moral, political and other reasons against doing them are so strong that most people would regard it as highly improper if Parliament did these things. But that does not mean that it is beyond the power of Parliament to do such things. If Parliament chose to do any of them the courts would not hold the Act of Parliament invalid.

This is no isolated text. We have a far fuller exposition of the same argument by Lord Reid in another leading case, *British Railways Board v Pickin,*[25] in which there was an application to set aside part of the British Railways Act 1968, a private Act of Parliament, on the ground that its passage had been obtained by fraud. Reversing the decision of a unanimous Court of Appeal under the mischievous leadership of Lord Denning MR, a much more radical judge than Lord Reid ever was, the House of Lords unanimously rejected the whole idea of the right of the courts to look behind the surface of an Act of Parliament. The leading speech was again delivered by Lord Reid (at 782/614c):

> The idea that a court is entitled to disregard a provision in an Act of Parliament on any ground must seem strange and startling to anyone with any knowledge of the history and law of our constitution, but a detailed argument has been submitted to your Lordships and I must deal with it.
>
> I must make it plain that there has been no attempt to question the general supremacy of Parliament. In earlier times many learned lawyers seem to have believed that an Act of Parliament could be disregarded insofar as it was contrary to the law of God or the law of nature or natural justice but since the supremacy of Parliament was finally demonstrated by the revolution of 1688 any such idea has become obsolete.

And:

> The function of the court is to construe and apply the enactments of Parliament. The court has no concern with the manner in which Parliament or its officers carrying out its Standing Orders perform those functions. Any attempt to prove that they were misled by fraud or otherwise would necessarily involve an inquiry into the manner in which they had performed their functions in dealing with the Bill which became the British Railways Act 1968. (at 618f)

### *Can judges set aside Acts of Parliament?*

Lord Reid's 1972 paper discussed above was quoted with approval by Lord Woolf, who served successively as a law lord, Master of the Rolls and Lord Chief Justice. In an article published in 1995 Lord Woolf claimed that the judges had the power and indeed the duty to declare Acts of Parliament invalid if they conflicted with 'the rule of law':

> Our parliamentary democracy is based on the rule of law. One of the twin principles upon which the rule of law depends is the supremacy of Parliament in its legislative capacity. The other principle is that the courts are the final arbiters as to the interpretation and application of the law. As both Parliament and the courts derive their authority from the rule of law so both are subject to it and can not act in manner which involves its repudiation. The respective roles do not give rise to conflict because the courts and Parliament each respects the role of the other.

At first sight this statement does not appear particularly radical. The legislative supremacy of Parliament is acknowledged, though it is said to derive from the rule of law, which contrasts with the conventional Diceyan view according to which the supremacy of Parliament, as a pillar of the British Constitution, is seen as quite distinct from and independent of that other pillar of the Constitution, the rule of law. But Lord Woolf's conclusion is one that no Diceyan could ever have penned. He gives fair warning that if Parliament were ever to pass 'unthinkable' laws the judges would not recognise or enforce them. Lord Woolf offers two examples of 'unthinkable' legislation: first, Nazi-style laws stripping Jews of their citizenship, and the like; and, secondly, any law expressly abolishing judicial review, presumably even in regard to a specific subject or case:

> However, if Parliament did the unthinkable, then I would say that the courts would also be required to act in a manner which would be without precedent. Some judges might chose (*sic*) to do so by saying that it was an unrebuttable presumption that Parliament could never intend such a result. I myself would consider there were advantages in making it clear that ultimately there are even limits on the supremacy of Parliament which it is the courts' inalienable responsibility to identify and uphold. They are limits of the most modest dimensions which I believe any democrat would accept. They are no more than are necessary to enable the rule of law to be preserved.

What exactly is the definition of 'the unthinkable'? None is offered. It is a highly emotive term, for what is unthinkable to one person may be quite acceptable to another. Would an Act of Parliament restoring the death penalty for murder be 'unthinkable' to Lord Woolf and his ilk? If so, would judges be entitled to refuse to recognise it as valid?

In this passage Lord Woolf reveals that his acceptance of the legislative supremacy of Parliament is conditional at best. If Parliament did 'the unthinkable', it would be the judges' 'responsibility' to depart from precedent in order to keep Parliament in check. To whom do the judges owe this duty? There is no answer. But, we are assured, it is in the interests of preserving the rule of law.

It is not easy to understand how an unelected and virtually irremovable judge, answerable to nobody, can be regarded as upholding the rule of law by flinging aside precedent and trampling on the expressed will of a democratically elected legislature. Far from preserving the rule of law, this would surely signal its final demise.

Moreover, how can the right of unelected judges to invalidate laws passed by an elected legislature be squared with Abraham Lincoln's basic concept of democracy, 'government of the people, by the people, for the people'?

Activist British judges of recent times have confronted this problem head-on. Here, for example, is the extra-judicial view of a Court of Appeal judge, Sir John Laws:

> ... a democratic constitution is in the end undemocratic if it gives all power to its elected government.[26]

This is further explained later on in the same article (p. 92):

> Ultimate sovereignty rests, in every civilised constitution, not with those who wield governmental power, but in the conditions under which they are permitted to do so. The Constitution, not the Parliament, is in this sense sovereign. In Britain these conditions should now be recognised as consisting in a framework of fundamental principles which include the imperative of democracy itself and those other rights, prime among them freedom of thought and expression, which cannot be denied save by a plea of guilty to totalitarianism.

This has rather an old-fashioned ring to it. For, even where there is a written constitution, as in the United States, it is clear that the real power rests not with the constitution itself but rather with those who have the right to interpret it, namely the justices of the US Supreme Court. How else can we explain the radical shifts in the meaning of the US Constitution over the years without any change in the relevant words on paper? This will be discussed further below.

The quoted passage is old-fashioned in another sense as well. It represents a paternalistic view of democracy. It rejects 'government *by* the people' in favour of 'government *for* the people'. It appears to suppose that the judges know better than the people themselves what is good for them. Would activist judges refuse to recognise an Act of Parliament restoring the death penalty for murder? Popular support for such a measure would presumably be irrelevant to such judges.

Sir John Laws appears to assume that the only two contenders for sovereignty are the Government and the Constitution. As we have seen, he plumps for the Constitution. But are these the only contenders for sovereignty? There is no mention of the most obvious contender of all, the one that is attributed with sovereignty in most constitutions. It is not for nothing that the opening words of the US Constitution are: 'We the People'.

The same approach is reflected in many more recent constitutions. The Constitution of the Irish Republic contains a typical statement (Article 6):

> All powers of government, legislative, executive and judicial, derive, under God, from the people, whose right it is to designate the rulers of the State and, in final appeal, to decide all questions of national policy, according to the requirements of the common good.

Likewise, Article 3 of the Russian Constitution introduced in 1993:

> (1) The holders of sovereignty and the sole sources of authority in the Russian Federation are its multinational people.
> (2) The people shall exercise their authority directly and also through organs of state power and organs of local self-government.
> (3) The supreme direct expression of the power of the people shall be the referendum and free elections.

Such declarations may of course easily be dismissed as pious but empty professions of faith. However, if the concept of sovereignty being vested in the electorate is unrealistic, the concept of sovereignty being vested in a constitution is even more fictitious, as we shall see below in regard to the US Constitution.

This goes to the heart of the definition of democracy. Abraham Lincoln's well-known definition cited above treats democracy as a means of reaching decisions: it does not say what those decisions should be. It is for the people to decide what is best for themselves. Modern western-style democracy is indirect, for decisions are generally taken not by the people themselves but by their elected representatives. The power of the people is exercised chiefly through the ballot box. What that means is that, though the people do not have an initiating power, they have the ultimate, last resort power, which is crucial. It is in this sense that the statements quoted above from the US, Irish and Russian Constitutions are to be understood.

Like Lincoln's definition of democracy, these are expressions of what may be termed the electoral view, against which may be set the paternalistic view fashionable among activist judges of the present day. This latter view pays homage to certain values regardless of the degree of popular support that those values enjoy.

### *Opposition to 'judicial supremacism'*

Although judicial activism is clearly in the ascendant in Britain at the time of writing, it has not gone wholly unchallenged. One of its most outspoken critics is Lord Irvine of Lairg, Lord Chancellor under Tony Blair's Labour Government, who in an article published in 1996 described the claim that the judges have the right to review the validity of any Act of Parliament as smacking of 'judicial supremacism':

> ... it has to be made plain that those judges who lay claim to a judicial power to negate parliamentary decisions, contrary to the established law and usages of our country, make an exorbitant claim that could only even be advanced were the courts ever to be presented with parliamentary decisions that were inconsistent with the fundamental tenets of a free democracy and therefore

> unworthy of judicial respect. The very basis of the claim, however – the superior political legitimacy of decision-making based on democratic processes – tells against greater activism in judicial review today where no-one would claim that the decisions for review, made under statutory powers, are other than democratically valid. It has therefore to be acknowledged that this claim serves only to underline the theme of my address this evening, that it is the constitutional imperative of judicial self-restraint which must inform judicial decision-making in public law.[27]

This article, written before Lord Irvine became Lord Chancellor, was followed up by some speeches along similar lines delivered while he was in office. Speaking of the growth of judicial review, Lord Irvine had this to say in a 1998 speech:

> ... against this background of what has, at times, appeared to be the inexorable expansion of judicial supervision, the judges have – quite rightly – accepted one constant limit on their power. I refer, of course, to the principle of parliamentary sovereignty. Viewed in its contemporary setting, this constitutional axiom reflects the primacy which is attached to democracy in the United Kingdom. It traces an immovable perimeter of judicial power by absolutely precluding the courts from interfering with that which has received the imprimatur of the elected legislature. Judicial review of legislative, as opposed to administrative, action is therefore unknown.[28]

Lord Irvine is quite right to describe the principle of parliamentary sovereignty (i.e. legislative supremacy) as a 'constitutional axiom'. As he says, the conclusion is therefore inescapable that (with the exception of matters involving European Union law, as he goes on to explain) the English courts do not possess the legal right to declare an Act of Parliament invalid. But, if this is so central a principle of the British constitution, why is it necessary for the Lord Chancellor to spell it out? Precisely because of the claim asserted by some activist judges (see above) of their right to set aside this fundamental principle and to declare invalid any laws which they consider 'unthinkable'.

### *Blackstone*

What we have here therefore is a fundamental disagreement between two of the most senior and powerful figures in the British legal establishment. Lord Woolf, Lord Chief Justice of England, flanked by a number of other judges and a large bevy of law academics, says that in certain circumstances (not restricted to matters of European law) the judges may set aside an Act of Parliament. Lord Irvine, former Lord Chancellor, says that the judges have no such power. There is no doubt about who is right: the weight of authority and convention alike favours Lord Irvine's position.

Where then did Lord Woolf and his supporters get their ideas from? In the 1995 article quoted above, Lord Woolf cites in support of his view Blackstone's comment that 'Acts of Parliament that are impossible to be performed are of no validity; and if there arise out of them collaterally any absurd consequences, manifestly contradictory to common reason, they are, with regard to those collateral consequences void.'[29]

Unfortunately, this extract from Blackstone was quoted at second hand[30] and out of context.

In any case, what is Blackstone saying here? Does this quotation really support the view that judges may invalidate Acts of Parliament that they consider unreasonable or 'unthinkable'? It is important to realise that Blackstone is himself here quoting from an earlier source, Sir Edward Coke's judgment in *Dr Bonham's* case, decided in 1610. But it is a heavily edited version. Coke's original wording goes as follows:

> And it appears in our books that in many cases the common law will control Acts of Parliament and sometimes adjudge them to be utterly void. For when an Act of Parliament is against common right and reason or repugnant or impossible to be performed, the common law will control it and adjudge such an Act to be void.[31]

Which 'books' is Coke referring to here? He relies for this far-reaching proposition specifically on *Tregor's* case, dating from 1335. But, as as has been convincingly shown by Plucknett, Coke completely misinterpreted the case, which does not provide any support for the large principle which he rests upon it. In addition Plucknett shows that none of Coke's other examples can be considered as authority for the doctrine that the courts have any power to 'adjudge an Act to be void'.[32]

Coke here identifies three categories of Acts of Parliament which he says can be declared void by 'the common law', i.e. by judges like himself. The first of these categories, statutes which are 'against common right and reason', is wide enough to allow a judge to strike down practically any law with which he happens to disagree. The second category is even broader: laws which are 'repugnant'. This begs the question: repugnant to what? Presumably, to the relevant judge's notions of justice. These two categories give the judiciary carte blanche to usurp the legislative role of Parliament. By comparison, the last category mentioned by Coke, Acts of Parliament 'impossible to be performed' is very restricted in its scope. What does it mean? It would presumably refer to a law which, for example, ordered everyone to walk on the ceiling. By contrast with the first two categories, this last category is justifiable. For, if a law really demanded something which was a physical impossibility then it would be a dead letter anyway. But such instances would be few and far between.

The differences between Coke and Blackstone are more striking than the similarities. Where Coke lists three characteristics which invalidate an Act of Parliament, namely if it is (1) 'against common right or reason' or (2) 'repugnant' or (3) 'impossible to be performed', Blackstone gives only the last of these. Unreasonableness is no longer a separate category entitling a judge to declare a law void. For Blackstone only 'manifest' unreasonableness, i.e. only where the unreasonableness is so blatant and obvious that it cannot be ignored, does it come into play at all – and even then only if this characteristic is found in a law which is impossible to be performed.

Not only does Blackstone not accept unreasonableness on its own as the basis for invalidating a statute, but he expressly rejects it on the ground that its acceptance would amount to a usurpation of the role of the legislature and be at variance with the fundamental principle of the supremacy of Parliament, which Blackstone proceeds in the same passage to expound and extol:

> I lay down the rule with these restrictions; though I know it is generally laid down more largely, that acts of parliament contrary to reason are void. But if the parliament will positively enact a thing to be done which is unreasonable, I know of no power that can control it: and the examples usually alleged in support of this sense of the rule do none of them prove, that where the main object of a statute is unreasonable the judges are at liberty to reject it; for that were to set the judicial power above that of the legislature, which would be subversive of all government. But where some collateral matter arises out of the general words, and happens to be unreasonable; there the judges are in decency to conclude that this consequence was not foreseen by the parliament, and therefore they are at liberty to expound the statute by equity, and only *quoad hoc* [thus far] disregard it. Thus if an act of parliament gives a man power to try all causes, that arise within his manor of Dale; yet, if a cause should arise in which he himself is a party, the act is construed not to extend to that; because it is unreasonable that any man should determine his own quarrel. But, if we could conceive it possible for the parliament to enact, that he should try as well his own causes as those of other persons, there is no court that has power to defeat the intent of the legislature, when couched in such evident and express words, as leave no doubt whether it was the intent of the legislature or no.[33]

Blackstone here makes it clear that, if Parliament 'positively enacts' even an unreasonable law, the judges must enforce it. And, as if in direct rebuttal of Coke's claims in *Dr Bonham's* case, Blackstone states categorically that if judges were to be free to reject even such 'unreasonable' laws, this would 'set the judicial power above that of the legislature, which would be subversive of all government'.

The only concession that Blackstone makes to judicial power over statute law is in regard to 'equity' in regard to 'collateral matters'. In 1758 Lord Mansfield defined this type of equity as 'synonymous to the meaning of the legislator'.[34]

In other words, applying 'equity' to a statute is a way of discovering the intention of Parliament, not an excuse to invalidate the law. And even this concept disappeared before the end of the eighteenth century and was indeed attacked by leading nineteenth-century judges (e.g. Lord Tenterden in *Brandling v Barrington*; Pollock CB in *Miller v Salamons*[35]).

Once again, as emerges very clearly from Blackstone's concrete example about the manor of Dale, even where a statute should normally be interpreted in a particular way so as to avoid flying in the face of the general principles of the common law, where Parliament has made its intention clear the judges must abide by it. The hypothetical example Blackstone gives is of a statute giving the lord of the manor power to try all cases arising within his manor. If, however, a particular case arises in which the lord is himself a party, applying the statute would amount to flying in the face of the broad principle of natural justice: *nemo debet esse judex in causa sua* – 'No one should be a judge in his own cause'. So, says Blackstone, in these circumstances the court would interpret the statute in the light of the general principle and would therefore refuse to allow the lord to sit in judgment in the case in question. However, if the wording of the relevant statute made it quite plain that Parliament intended the lord to have the power to decide cases in which he was personally involved as well as all other cases, then the courts would be obliged to allow him to sit in judgment in the particular case in question.

Nor was this a purely hypothetical question, as it turned out, because a century after Blackstone had written these words a decision of the High Court expressly denied the right of the courts to question the validity of an enactment allowing a person to be judge in his own cause: *Lee v Bude & Torrington Junction Railway Co.*[36]

In a later passage Blackstone puts the position even more robustly:

> An act of parliament ... is the exercise of the highest authority that this kingdom acknowledges upon earth. It hath power to bind every subject in the land, and the dominions thereunto belonging; nay, even the king himself, if particularly named therein. And it cannot be altered, amended, dispensed with, suspended or repealed, but in the same forms and by the same authority of parliament.[37]

This is a classic statement of parliamentary legislative supremacy. In the last quoted sentence Blackstone makes certain of covering all bases. The wording is so comprehensive as to leave no room for any judicial claim to be able to cancel or change a jot or tittle in any statute: a law passed by Parliament can be repealed or amended only by Parliament itself.

And yet again, putting it in a nutshell:

> So long therefore as the English constitution lasts, we may venture to affirm, that the power of parliament is absolute and without control.[38]

In expressing this view in 1765 Blackstone was merely stating what had become the orthodox position by his day. Statements of the legislative supremacy of Parliament can be found as early as the reign of Queen Elizabeth I (1558-1603), notably in the authoritative and influential *Commonwealth of England* by Sir Thomas Smith (1513-77), first published in 1582 and reprinted many times in succeeding years.

The reigns of James I (1603-25) and Charles I (1625-49) were marked by conflict between Crown and Parliament culminating in a bloody civil war which the king ultimately lost. On 30 January 1649 Charles I was beheaded and the country briefly became a republic. Upon the Restoration of the monarchy the dead king's son, Charles II (1660-85), was content to toe the parliamentary line. Having spent years in exile, he understood only too well the exigencies of politics. 'I will not go on my travels again' was his motto. But his brother James II (1685-88) had learned nothing and forgotten nothing[39] of the bitter struggle with Parliament and was determined to turn the clock back to the days when the Crown had exercised real power. The result was James II's ouster in the so-called 'Glorious Revolution' of 1688. To consolidate their position Parliament this time enshrined its victory in legislation, and it is from this date that the doctrine of the supremacy of Parliament, which had been asserted for well over a century, was finally established as a fundamental principle of the constitution.

### *Coke*

In his *Institutes* even Coke himself, that doughty champion of the rights of the judiciary, espoused the legislative supremacy of Parliament:

> Of the power and jurisdiction of the parliament for the making of laws in proceeding by bill, it is so transcendent and absolute, as it cannot be confined either for causes or persons within any bounds. Of this court it is truly said: *Si antiquitatem spectes, est vetustissima, si dignitatem, est honoratissima, si jurisdictionem, est capacissima* ('If you look at its antiquity, it is the most venerable,

if you consider its dignity, it is the most honourable, if you measure its jurisdiction, it is the most ample').[40]

Interestingly, Coke here describes Parliament as a court, and not just a court but *the* highest court of all, superior in other words to any common law court. This is a reflection of the label applied to the legislature since Tudor times: the High Court of Parliament.

But how can Coke's remarks in *Dr Bonham's* case be squared with this eulogistic description of Parliament? Could the two passages really have been written by the same person? The answer is that Sir Edward Coke (1552-1634) was a man whose views changed in accordance with circumstances. As Attorney-General (1594-1606) he was the fiercest defender of the Crown. His prosecution of Guy Fawkes and the other Gunpowder Plot conspirators in 1605 was little short of savage. Elevated to the bench as Chief Justice of Common Pleas by James I in 1606, Coke soon became the most intractable opponent of royal power. So serious a thorn in the King's flesh did he become that he was eventually dismissed from the bench in 1616. The 1620s saw Coke as a leading member of the parliamentary opposition to the Crown and, after being lodged briefly in the Tower of London for his pains, author of the revolutionary Petition of Right of 1628, a statement of parliamentary rights against the Crown. It is to his last years that the *Institutes* belong.

Not only did *Dr Bonham's* case, heard in 1610, belong to what might be called Coke's judicial supremacist period, there also was a personal reason why Coke adopted the position that he took.

Dr Thomas Bonham was a medical practitioner working in London. He had a Cambridge degree in medicine. The 'censors' of the Royal College of Physicians proceeded to have Dr Bonham arrested and lodged in the Fleet prison for practising medicine without a licence from them. The censors based their action on the private Act of Parliament under which their college had been incorporated, which gave them the right to 'regulate all London physicians and punish infractions with fine and imprisonment'. The objectionable feature of the statute that Coke latched on to was a provision which allowed the censors to keep half of any fine levied under it. This, held Coke, was contrary to the fundamental rule of the common law expressed in the maxim *Aliquis non debet esse judex in propria causa* ['No one ought to be a judge in his own cause']. This enabled Coke to take the next step, which was to declare the statute void, thus securing Dr Bonham's release and enabling him to carry on his practice of medicine without being subject to the regulation of the censors of the Royal College of Physicians.

Like Bonham, Coke was a Cambridge graduate, and a very proud one at that. What he regarded as the pretensions of the Royal College of Physicians irked him. He regarded the College as an upstart institution which was here trying to set itself up against that true seat of learning, Cambridge. Coke's very real anger comes through quite clearly and may well explain his stand on the case as a whole, especially if it is realised that his argument about the right of the common law courts to set aside statute law is only one of five points on which he based his decision:

> No comparison is to be made between that private College [the Royal College of Physicians] and the Universities of Cambridge and Oxford, no more than between the father and his children or between the fountain and the small rivers which descend from it. The University is Alma Mater, from whose breast those of that private College have suck'd all their science and knowledge.

Note too that, though Coke does Oxford the courtesy of bracketing it with Cambridge, it is mentioned second. This is something in itself that Coke felt strongly about. When reminded in Parliament that precedence belonged to Oxford 'by vote of the House', he ignored the rebuke and repeated the offence. When taken to task by Sir Thomas Edmondes, another Member of Parliament, Coke 'aunswered him somewhat short, that Sir Thomas needed not to trouble himself so much about it, for that he belonged to neither universitie'.[41]

But, regardless of the personal motivation for Coke's judgment in Dr Bonham's case, the fact remains that he not only claimed the right to invalidate statutes but did actually set one aside (albeit only a private Act).

That was in 1610, a time when the rights of the executive, the legislature and the judiciary were in competition with one another. The very principles of the constitution were as yet in a state of flux. They were hammered out on the anvil of war and revolution. After 1688 there was no longer any doubt: Parliament was supreme and the judiciary had no right to declare any statute invalid.

Referring to Coke's exorbitant claims for the judiciary in *Dr Bonham's* case, Lord Irvine remarks pointedly: 'Such notions form no part of the modern law.'[42]

Lord Irvine is plainly right. It is no more and no less than the judges themselves had been saying for three centuries – including Lord Reid, as we have seen, who was far from being an upholder of judicial self-restraint, and who flagged up the change that took place in the British constitution in 1688:

> In earlier times many learned lawyers seem to have believed that an Act of Parliament could be disregarded insofar as it was contrary to the law of God or the law of nature or natural justice but since the supremacy of Parliament was

finally demonstrated by the revolution of 1688 any such idea has become obsolete.[43]

### *Rule of law? – United Kingdom*

For Dicey, writing in 1885, the rule of law was one of the two main pillars of the British Constitution, the other being the legislative supremacy of Parliament. Britain's membership of the European Union has given the courts – the domestic courts – a power they never dreamed of: the power to declare an Act of Parliament void if it is incompatible with European Union law. This power is restricted to matters governed by European Union law.

However, it is easy to see how activist judges may have been emboldened by this unlooked-for bounty into resuscitating the exorbitant claim made by Sir Edward Coke in *Dr Bonham's* case four centuries ago.

At the time of writing, such ambitious claims have been confined to extra-judicial remarks. Except in cases involving EU law no judge or court has actually dared in the course of a judgment to pronounce an Act of Parliament void. But there have been some cases where, without purporting to amend a statute or to strike it down, a court has interpreted it in such a way as in effect to amend some of its provisions. A good example of this is *M v Home Office*,[44] where, in the words of an academic commentator, 'an established statute was virtually re-written' by Lord Woolf and his fellow law lords.[45]

The statute in question was the Crown Proceedings Act 1947, which for the first time allowed the Crown to be sued in court. In *M*'s case the House of Lords held that it was even permissible for a court to grant an interlocutory injunction against the Crown, and that, if the Crown failed to obey this court order, the Crown could be held in contempt of court. Though ostensibly in keeping with the Crown Proceedings Act, this opinion reinterpreted the relevant section of the Act so radically that the Scottish Court of Session refused to follow it:

> Section 21 of the [Crown Proceedings] Act of 1947 applies to both England and Scotland. As to the procedure for suing the Crown, I am of opinion that a decision such as *M v Home Office* is not binding in Scotland though it must be considered as having weight ….
>
> So far as the present case is concerned, I am quite satisfied that the granting of interdict or interim interdict is prohibited by virtue of the provisions of section 21 (1) of the [Crown Proceedings] Act of 1947.[46]

As section 21 applied equally to England and Scotland, it would normally have been incumbent upon the Scottish court to apply the ruling of the House of Lords in *M v Home Office*, even though that was an English case. The formal tone of this extract from *McDonald* masks what is actually a serious dissent. It is clear that the Scottish judges were refusing to follow the highest court in the land because they could not accept the House of Lords' interpretation of an Act of Parliament.

The battle lines are drawn. In saying that under the British Constitution judges do not have the right to overturn Acts of Parliament, Lord Irvine was only reiterating a three-hundred-year-old principle. But why was it necessary for him to go to such lengths to restate so fundamental a doctrine?

The reason is that, as we have seen, that principle is now under attack – from elements within the judiciary itself. The appetite of some judges for greater law-making power has been whetted by their new-found role in relation to European law, which in turn has both fed and been fed by the development of judicial review (see Chapter VIII.1). A third factor which has greatly enhanced judicial power is the Human Rights Act 1998, which came into force in the year 2000. Though carefully drafted so as *not* to give judges the power of declaring parliamentary legislation void, at least one senior judge has declared that human rights law has 'higher law' status so that the courts could set aside any 'ordinary' law found by them to be incompatible with the European Human Rights Convention. A fourth source of enhanced judicial lawmaking powers is the completely new Civil Procedure Rules (CPR) introduced in 1999, which breaks with tradition to the point of dispensing with such familiar and time-honoured terms as 'plaintiff' (now 'claimant') and consigning most previously decided cases on procedural issues to the dustbin. This gave judges the power to interpret the procedural rules afresh, thus making law unhampered by precedents.

These developments have enabled the judiciary to assume greater lawmaking power than ever before, at the expense of long-established principles and precedents. Can this development possibly be seen as fostering the rule of law rather than as subverting it? If the rule of law is identified with certainty, uniformity and predictability achieved through adherence to principle and precedent, then are we justified in speaking of twenty-first century Britain as being subject to the rule of law at all?

### *Rule of law? – United States*

'A government not of men but of laws' is how the American founding fathers envisaged their new state. The earliest official document in which the phrase appears, in the form 'a government of laws and not of men', is the

Massachusetts Constitution of 1780 (Part the First, Article XXX), where it is linked with the concept of the separation of powers:

> In the government of this Commonwealth, the legislative department shall never exercise the executive and judicial powers, or either of them: The executive shall never exercise the legislative and judicial powers, or either of them: The judicial shall never exercise the legislative and executive powers, or either of them: to the end it may be a government of laws and not of men.[47]

Here 'a government of laws and not of men' is held up as the goal, with the separation of powers as the means of achieving it. In other words, this much-quoted phrase is elevated to the keystone of the arch of constitutional government. But what exactly does it mean, and in what way can the separation of powers be regarded as contributing towards the attainment of this end?

Though injected here into a solemn constitutional document, the moving force behind the doctrine is politics rather than law. Indeed, 'A government not of men but of laws' is essentially a political slogan advocating a republican form of government against the supposed ills of monarchy. A system of government in which executive, legislature and judiciary are each in separate hands with each essentially limited to its own sphere of activity was regarded by the American founding fathers as the best safeguard of liberty.

How was this system of checks and balances to be implemented? The solution offered by Madison, Jefferson and Jay in *The Federalist Papers* was a written constitution. But a constitution is merely so many words on paper. It has no force in itself and is in any event subject to the vagaries of differing interpretations.

It did not take long for a wag with a cynical eye on the realities of the situation to restate the doctrine: 'A government not of laws but of lawyers.'

This cynical retort has been justified by history: it is not the US Constitution itself but the view of it taken by the US Supreme Court that rules. And this interpretation, which is seldom unanimous in the first place, has changed the import of the Constitution out of all recognition from one generation to the next.

Law always needs to be interpreted, and whoever has the power to interpret it has great power. The American jurist John Chipman Gray (1839-1915), we are told by Justice Felix Frankfurter (1882-1965) of the US Supreme Court, 'was fond of quoting from a sermon by Bishop Hoadley that "Whoever hath an *absolute authority* to interpret any written or spoken laws, it is he who is truly the law-giver to all intents and purposes, and not the person who first wrote or spoke them." '[48]

Gray's conclusion from this was that 'All law is judge-made law'.[49] Felix Frankfurter was not quite so sure: 'By admitting that there is some substance to the good Bishop's statement, one does not subscribe to the notion that they are law-givers in any but a very qualified sense.'

It would certainly be wrong to suggest that anyone vested with the power – or even the 'absolute authority' – to interpret a law is automatically free to place whatever arbitrary meaning on it that he fancies. When it comes to statutory interpretation there are canons of construction, some of which go back centuries. The trouble is that there is not a single uniform standard but several different and sometimes conflicting canons. This is where the judicial activist, or simply the maverick, scores.

Lord Denning (1899-1999), arguably the most influential English judge of the twentieth century, was often rebuked by the former Lord Chancellor Viscount Simonds (1881-1971), a strict constructionist, for adopting an excessively individualistic interpretation of statute law, most famously in *Magor and St Mellons Rural District Council v Newport Corporation,*[50] in which Lord Denning's approach was characterised as 'a naked usurpation of the legislative function under the thin disguise of interpretation'.

In terms of British judicial practice Lord Denning was an innovator. But his creative brand of statutory interpretation had long been known in America, dating back to the days of John Marshall, Chief Justice from 1801 to 1835.

> The history of the Supreme Court [wrote the historian and librarian of Congress Daniel Boorstin], and especially the story of judicial review … is the surprising account of how a few men have used powers of dubious legality to uphold the rule of law in American life. There is no more ironic aspect of our history.[51]

This is a question-begging paradox. For, by transmuting 'judicial review' into 'judicial sovereignty', as Robert McCloskey put it, was Justice Marshall promoting the rule of law or merely the rule of the Supreme Court? Or are they the same thing?[52]

'The prophecies of what the courts will do in fact, and nothing more pretentious,' opined Oliver Wendell Holmes (1841-1935), 'are what I mean by the law.'[53]

Some academic commentators have made heavy weather of this much-quoted definition, elevating it into a separate theory, the 'prediction theory' of law, and then knocking it down for one reason or another, notably that 'it confuses the notion of prediction with the notion of rule'.[54]

But this rather misses Holmes's point, which is quite a simple one. For Holmes the law was a practical matter. The ordinary citizen whose conduct might possibly bring him into conflict with the law – Holmes's 'bad man' –

was not interested in high-flown theories of the law. What he wanted to know was how he was likely to fare in court.

A similar view of the law was held by Holmes's friend and longtime correspondent, Sir Frederick Pollock (1845-1937), who, besides being an enthusiastic advocate of the codification of the law, was also a believer in the scientific nature of the common law:

> The ultimate object of natural science is to predict events – to say with approximate accuracy what will happen under given conditions .... The object of legal science, as we here understand it, is likewise to predict events. The particular kind of events it seeks to predict are the decisions of courts of justice.[55]

For the common law to achieve this 'scientific' objective, Pollock continued, a system of binding precedent was necessary:

'The object is to ensure the same decision being given on the same facts. In English case-law this object is attained by what seem the most obvious and direct means, namely, an understanding that the court shall follow the authority of decisions formerly given on similar facts.'[56]

Pollock sums up his position:

> We have now seen that case-law has a scientific aim, namely, the prediction of events by means of past experience, and that the possibility of such prediction rests, as in other sciences, on a fundamental assumption of uniformity.[57]

After describing and analysing the process used by what he calls 'a sound lawyer' in advising his client, Pollock continues:

> If the case ever comes before a court for decision, it is the business of the court to determine what those consequences [viz. the legal consequences] shall actually be. But this determination has to be not arbitrary, but regulated in such a manner as to keep up the fundamental assumption of uniformity, and to make scientific prediction possible. We have already said that this is ensured by an understanding that the judgment of the court shall be guided by authority.[58]

What must be stressed above all is that Pollock is not talking about the common law as he would have *liked* it to be but as it *was* at the time, in the 1870s and 1880s.

But one of the main problems of American law is the very fact that it has been very difficult to predict, for the simple reason that, in the hands of the US Supreme Court, the law has changed radically from one generation to another.

The oft-quoted remark that 'the Constitution is what the judges say it is' does not originate from some cynical critic of the Supreme Court but from one of the most distinguished members of the Court itself, Charles Evans Hughes (1862-1948). Nominated to the Supreme Court by President Taft, Hughes served six years as an Associate Justice (1910-16) before resigning to contest the 1916 Presidential election for the Republican Party, which he lost to the incumbent Democratic President, Woodrow Wilson. Then, after serving as Secretary of State under Harding and Coolidge and a brief spell as a judge on the International Court of Justice in the Hague, he returned to the Supreme Court as Chief Justice in 1930, presiding over it during its struggle with Franklin Roosevelt.

'The inference that I was picturing constitutional interpretations by the courts as a matter of judicial caprice,' Hughes later testily explained, 'was farthest from my mind.' But it was too late: whether intended by Hughes or not, the inference was commonly drawn.[59]

Such have been the vagaries of constitutional interpretation emanating from the Supreme Court over time that a more radical interpretation of Hughes's remark appeared justified than he may have intended.

Hughes's own tenure as Chief Justice (1930-41) itself affords a good example. On 'Black Monday', 27 May 1935, the Court handed down three unanimous decisions blocking key provisions in Franklin Roosevelt's New Deal programme. In the following year the Court unceremoniously threw out as unconstitutional two of the most important pieces of New Deal legislation, the National Recovery Act and the Agricultural Adjustment Act. In retaliation the President sent to Congress the so-called 'court-packing bill' allowing Roosevelt to enlarge the Supreme Court by naming up to six additional justices. To stop this legislation in its tracks the Supreme Court quickly came round to the President's way of thinking on the New Deal. The first noticeable 'switch in time that saved nine', as the press called it, occurred in *West Coast Hotel Co v Parrish*,[60] in which by 5 votes to 4 the Court approved a minimum wage law from Washington state that was practically identical to the New York statute which had been struck down as unconstitutional only the previous year in *Morehead v New York ex rel Tipaldo*.[61] Though *Parrish* was actually decided before the court-packing bill had been presented to Congress, the President's displeasure at the Court's treatment of his legislative programme was by then pretty obvious. *Parrish* was followed by a succession of pro-Administration opinions. It is not perhaps without significance that the majority opinion in *Parrish* was written by the Chief Justice himself. 'The Constitution', declared Hughes, 'does not speak of freedom of contract' (at 391), thus sounding the death-knell of the doctrine of 'substantive due process' long favoured by the Court, and thereby opening the way to ever greater Federal regulation of private business.

There is no area where the Supreme Court's position has undergone more radical shifts than in regard to race. In 1896 in *Plessy v Ferguson*[62] the provision of 'separate but equal' facilities for Blacks and Whites was held (by 7 to 1) to be in keeping with the US Constitution, yet by a unanimous decision in 1954 in *Brown v Board of Education of Topeka*[63] the very same thing was branded as unconstitutional, thus ushering in a whole new era in the history of American civil rights. Separate facilities, the *Brown* court held, were intrinsically unequal. It is important to realise that the wording of the relevant constitutional provision, namely the Fourteenth Amendment, adopted in 1868, had remained unchanged throughout. How could the same words mean one thing in 1896 and exactly the opposite in 1954? The answer of course is that though the words on the page had remained the same the interpretation of those words by the US Supreme Court had changed.

But *Brown* was not the end of the story. In 1978 the Supreme Court again changed its position: *Regents of the University of California v Bakke*.[64] Bakke was one of 2,664 applicants for a hundred places at the medical school of the University of California, Davis. Eighty-four students were selected on the basis of academic merit, but the remaining 16 places were filled through a special admissions programme designed to favour minority candidates. Bakke, who was white, was rejected twice, although his academic record was superior to most of the minority students admitted under the special programme. The basis of Bakke's legal claim was that the university's admissions policy had denied him the equal protection of the law which was his right under the Fourteenth Amendment and that the Davis program also amounted to a violation of Title VI of the Civil Rights Act 1964, which prohibited racial or ethnic preferences in federally funded programmes. By five votes to four the Supreme Court ruled that racial criteria could indeed be used by a university in selecting students, provided this was not done on the basis of fixed quotas. As it was held that the Davis special program constituted a quota, the university was ordered to admit Bakke. But Bakke's victory was only achieved at the cost of acceptance of the principle of 'affirmative action', whose scope was further expanded and then later contracted again by succeeding Supreme Court decisions.

Whether affirmative action is justified as a form of compensation for past discrimination or whether, on the basis of the 'disparate impact' theory of racial discrimination, it is regarded as a matter of public policy, it certainly represents a marked departure from the traditional colour-blind liberal approach which in principle is (or should be) as much opposed to anti-white as to anti-black discrimination.

So, in regard to racial discrimination, the US Constitution has had three quite distinct and mutually incompatible meanings in the space of a hundred years – without a single word of the relevant Article being changed. Is this an example of the rule of law? Or is it rather the rule of the nine justices who happened to be sitting on the Supreme Court at the time? Truly, it might be said, a case of 'a government not of laws but of lawyers'!

The Supreme Court's attitude to capital punishment has undergone a similar metamorphosis. In *Furman v Georgia* (1972)[65] the Court declared, by a 5:4 majority, that the death penalty amounted to 'cruel and unusual punishment' under the Eighth Amendment to the Constitution and was therefore unconstitutional. Four years later, in *Gregg v Georgia* (1976),[66] an only slightly differently constituted Supreme Court found, by a majority of 7 to 2, that, although a mandatory death penalty still fell foul of the Eighth Amendment, capital punishment as such was not unconstitutional after all!

Again, as in the previous examples, the law had made a U-turn but the constitutional provisions on which it was based had not changed. The U-turn came about partly as a result of a slight change in the composition of the court and partly as a result of a change of mind on the part of two of the justices.

Throughout the American debate on capital punishment it was recognised that public opinion was strongly in favour of the death penalty. Indeed, 'polls taken a few months after *Furman* showed a substantial jump in public approval of the death penalty'.[67]

It may well be that this strong current of public opinion influenced some of the judges in *Gregg*. This would certainly have been in keeping with an important statement made by Justice Oliver Wendell Holmes in *The Common Law* (1881): 'The first requirement of a sound body of law is that it should correspond with the actual feelings and demands of the community, whether right or wrong.'[68]

This brief remark highlights the potential conflict between what may be termed liberal values on the one hand and democracy on the other, or between Abraham Lincoln's populist definition of democracy and a paternalistic approach to it. The death penalty is anathema to liberal thinkers in the broadest sense. But, if it is called for by popular demand, then, according to Holmes, this desire should be respected. Why? For no other reason than that it *is* popular – and, therefore, in terms of the populist definition, democratic. The paternalists would start at the other end. Capital punishment, they would say, is inherently uncivilised and evil: it is by definition contrary to the democratic value of the right to life and cannot therefore possibly be countenanced, regardless of its popularity.

The US Supreme Court has taken constitutional law on a breakneck roller-coaster ride to the point where Robert H. Bork, a leading American jurist, is able to declare that 'the Supreme Court has usurped the powers of the people and their elected representatives .... The effect on law and democracy have been horrendous. It is impossible for a Court that views itself as a political and cultural institution as much as a legal institution to make reasoned decisions whose principles it will adhere to in the future.'[69]

Bork, a distinguished former federal appellate judge, solicitor general and Yale professor, whose nomination to the US Supreme Court by Ronald Reagan was blocked by the senate because of his conservative views in both politics and law, has attacked the court for its 'constitutionalizing of radical individualism'[70] and 'radical egalitarianism'.[71] What Bork finds objectionable are not only the 'politically correct' values protected by recent Supreme Court opinions but also the way in which the court has set about inventing constitutional rights 'not warranted by law'.[72]

We might have been inclined to write Bork's views off as partisan but for the fact that similar criticisms have been levelled at the court from the opposite direction. Judicial activism, now largely identified with broadly left-wing judges, can equally well be engaged in by conservatives. As mentioned above, Franklin Roosevelt's New Deal would probably have been derailed by the conservative Supreme Court had the President not threatened to introduce a 'court-packing' scheme which would have had the effect of giving control of an enlarged court to Roosevelt nominees.

The conservative majority on the Supreme Court of the present day is likewise not above judicial activism where it finds it necessary. The court battle over the presidential election of 2000 is a good recent example: *Bush v Gore*, 12 December 2000.[73] In a strongly worded dissenting opinion, Justice Stevens, joined by Justices Ginsburg and Breyer, held that the Supreme Court should have declined to become involved in the case at all. They also disagreed with the majority view that, in calling for a manual recount, the Florida Supreme Court had been guilty of a constitutional violation. They accused the majority of ordering 'the disenfranchisement of an unknown number of voters' in the interests of finalising the election result as quickly as possible. Justice Stevens concluded with a stinging attack on the majority: 'One thing, however, is certain. Although we may never know with complete certainty the identity of the winner of this year's Presidential election, the identity of the loser is perfectly clear. It is the Nation's confidence in the judge as an impartial guardian of the rule of law.'

## V.1. The rule of law

This is an ironic inversion indeed. For, the charge levelled by Justice Stevens at the conservative majority is the very accusation so often made by conservative jurists against liberal or left-leaning judges. By going off on a frolic of their own in purportedly interpreting the law, runs this type of criticism, the judges concerned have failed to uphold the rule of law.

'Where law ends tyranny begins.' These words are emblazoned over the Justice Department Building in Washington DC. This is just another version of the familiar refrain, 'A government not of men but of laws.' The underlying assumption in both is that law is the very antithesis of arbitrary power. The United States was self-consciously modelled in opposition to the absolute monarchies of eighteenth-century Europe. The tyranny of an autocratic ruler was what particularly exercised the minds of the framers of the American Constitution. But what about the arbitrary power of judges? The possibility was barely considered at all.

Alexander Hamilton, writing in *The Federalist Papers* in 1787, expressed the view that 'the judiciary is beyond comparison the weakest of the three departments of power'.[74] By contrast: 'The legislature not only commands the purse but prescribes the rules by which the duties and rights of every citizen are to be regulated.'

History has shown this to be a somewhat naive analysis. For who has more power to prescribe the rights and duties of every citizen – strictly a legislative function – than the Supreme Court? Yet Hamilton had the foresight to predict the courts' power to declare legislation void. Indeed, he takes it for granted but is arguably too complacent about its likely effect:

> Some perplexity respecting the rights of the courts to pronounce legislation void because contrary to the Constitution has arisen from an imagination that the doctrine would imply a superiority of the judiciary to the legislative power. It is urged that the authority which can declare the acts of another void must necessarily be superior to the one whose acts may be declared void.[75]

But:

> It can be of no weight to say that the courts, on the pretense of a repugnancy, may substitute their own pleasure to the constitutional intentions of the legislature. This might as well happen in the case of two contradictory statutes; or it might as well happen in every adjudication upon any single statute. The courts must declare the sense of the law; and if they should be disposed to exercise WILL instead of JUDGMENT, the consequence would equally be the substitution of their pleasure for that of the legislative body. The observation, if it proved anything, would prove that there ought to be no judges distinct from that body.[76]

Hamilton has here glimpsed the future but just waves it aside. He does at least recognise the dichotomy between what he calls 'will' on the one hand and 'judgment' on the other. He admits the possibility that judges may decide cases arbitrarily ('will') rather than according to law ('judgment'), but he is not prepared to accept this as a serious likelihood. We can hardly blame him for not being able to foresee the effects of judicial activism not only before *Marbury v Madison* (1803)[77] but even before there was a Constitution or a Supreme Court in existence!

To some extent, however, the American judiciary may be kept in check by the other two branches of Government. The most obvious but also the most cumbersome and time-consuming is by means of constitutional amendment. More important in practical terms is the appointment of federal judges by the President subject to confirmation by the Senate.

Then there is impeachment, which though attempted against only two presidents, Andrew Johnson and Bill Clinton - both times unsuccessfully - has been used over the years with telling effect against federal judges. Impeachment is brought by the House of Representatives as prosecutors before the Senate, which sits as a combination of judge and jury. Though, like most legal institutions and procedures, impeachment was imported into America from Britain, in this country the prestige of the institution never recovered from the failed impeachment of Warren Hastings which dragged on from 1787 until his acquittal in 1795. One or two half-hearted attempts were subsequently made to revive impeachment, but it is now plainly well and truly dead, which means that judges of the English High Court and above are now responsible to no one, accountable to no one, answerable to no one and removable only upon an address of both Houses of Parliament, which is a practical impossibility.

The other form of democratic control over the judiciary found in the USA is also lacking in Britain, namely election. The majority of US states have elected judges, something which those English judges who like to lay claim to democratic credentials would be unlikely to welcome.

## Conclusion

Does the rule of law actually exist in Britain today or is it in reality merely the rule of the judges? Although ostensibly a factual question to which it should be possible to provide an objective answer, that answer cannot realistically be an unqualified 'Yes' or 'No'. Whatever answer is given is likely to be clouded by the subjective view of the person giving it. Is judicial activism a good thing, a necessary evil or an avoidable wrong? There are several combinations and permutations of these objective and subjective responses, of which the following three main positions may be identified:

*Position A*: The rule of law depends upon definite principles and binding precedent, which together make for certainty, uniformity and predictability, which in turn provide the foundation of fairness and justice. The role of judges is to understand, interpret and apply the law whether they agree with it or not. Their right to *make* law is strictly limited to marginal clarification and to the application of existing principles to new factual situations. But they do not have the right to invent new principles nor to set aside or ignore established principles. By crossing this line they usurp the role of the elected legislature, thus subverting democracy and thwarting the rule of law.

*Position B*: However desirable it may be for law to be based on principles and precedent, this is a pipe-dream. Existing legal principles are often either too vague or too outdated to be applied. In order to keep law relevant to changing circumstances, judges have to make law themselves. As this is unavoidable in the modern world, it is meaningless to think of it as in any way a denial of the rule of law. On the contrary, it is the only way in which the rule of law can be achieved.

*Position C*: Not only is it inevitable that law should be made by judges; it is desirable that it should be so. The judges are the guardians of democracy and, by definition, the upholders of the rule of law.

*Analysis*

*Position A* may be labelled 'legal conservatism' and its adherents as 'strict constructionists' favouring 'judicial self-restraint'. It is the position which was dominant in the English judiciary from the time of the 'Glorious Revolution' of 1688 until the latter half of the twentieth century.

Leading exponents of this view include Viscount Simonds (now probably best known for his attacks on Lord Denning's judicial activism) and Lord Buckmaster, whose dissenting judgment in the House of Lords in the famous tort case of *Donoghue v Stevenson*[78] encapsulates the opposition of the legal conservatives to the judicial activists.

Lord Buckmaster first launched a broadside against the whole approach of the majority:

> The law applicable is the common law, and, though its principles are of application to meet new conditions not contemplated when the law was laid

> down, yet themselves they cannot be changed nor can additions be made to them because any particular meritorious case seems outside their ambit.[79]

Lord Buckmaster here draws a distinction between, on the one hand, *applying* the principles of the common law to changing circumstances and, on the other, *changing* or adding to the principles themselves. The former exercise is permissible, the latter not. The point Lord Buckmaster is making is that just because Mrs Donoghue's case deserves sympathy does not entitle the judges to change the law in order to accommodate it.

If the law is changed in this way, remarks Lord Buckmaster, where will it end? 'If one step, why not fifty?'[80] In other words, once one well-established and accepted legal principle is arbitrarily cast aside, others are likely to follow, leading to uncertainty. In *Donoghue v Stevenson* itself a wholly new principle was put forward by Lord Atkin as if it had been in existence already. Yet, argues Lord Buckmaster, if this principle were 'well known and accepted, much of the discussion of the earlier cases would have been waste of time'.[81] This reiterates the time-honoured view of the common law as based on definite principles enshrined in binding precedents.

The nearest American equivalent to *Donoghue v Stevenson* in the development of the tort of negligence is *MacPherson v Buick Motor Co*,[82] decided by Judge Benjamin Cardozo, who was also responsible for extending the scope of fraud to cover negligent words, in *Glanzer v Shepard*[83] and *Ultramares v Touche*, the American precursor of *Hedley Byrne v Heller*.[84] Cardozo was also responsible for some major changes in the law of contract (see for example *Jacob & Youngs Inc v Kent*).[85] These decisions all belong to the period of Cardozo's service on the New York Court of Appeals. But once appointed to the US Supreme Court in 1932 he displayed a high degree of judicial self-restraint and enjoined due deference to Acts of Congress, notably in *Steward Machine Co v Davis*[86] and *Helvering v Davis*.[87] Both these cases were concerned with the question of the constitutionality of the Social Security Act of 1935, a piece of legislation which was central to Franklin Roosevelt's New Deal. In both cases Cardozo delivered the majority opinion upholding the statute.

A cynic might suggest that this apparent shift in Cardozo's position may have been motivated by his support for the New Deal rather than by a genuine belief in judicial self-restraint. Yet, at the very time when he was delivering activist decisions from the New York appellate bench, Cardozo wrote a book, *The Nature of the Judicial Process*, in which he argued that judicial law-making was and ought to be very much the exception rather than the rule. It is worthwhile quoting the relevant passage in full:

> No doubt there is a field within which judicial judgment moves untrammeled by fixed principles. Obscurity of statute or of precedent or of customs or of morals, or collision between some or all of them, may leave the law unsettled, and cast a duty upon the courts to declare it retrospectively in the exercise of a power frankly legislative in function .... We must not let these occasional and relatively rare instances blind our eyes to the innumerable instances where there is neither obscurity nor collision nor opportunity for diverse judgment .... In countless litigations, the law is so clear that judges have no discretion. They have the right to legislate within gaps, but often there are no gaps. We shall have a false view of the landscape if we look at the waste spaces only, and refuse to see the acres already sown and fruitful. I think the difficulty has its origin in the failure to distinguish between right and power, between the command embodied in a judgment and the jural principle to which the obedience of the judge is due. Judges have, of course, the power, though not the right, to ignore the mandate of a statute, and render judgment in despite of it. They have the power, though not the right, to travel beyond the walls of the interstices, the bounds set to judicial innovation by precedent and custom. None the less, by that abuse of power, they violate the law.[88]

This passage will repay close study. The contrast that Cardozo draws between 'power' and 'right' is particularly noteworthy. And his concluding sentence is couched in extremely strong terms.

Justice George Sutherland, Cardozo's contemporary on the Supreme Court, likewise pointedly remarked that: 'The judicial function is that of interpretation; it does not include the power of amendment under the guise of interpretation.'[89] But, for all its similarity to Cardozo's remarks quoted above, this observation comes from a dissenting opinion in which Sutherland stood alone against Roosevelt's New Deal, of which Cardozo was an enthusiastic supporter. Sutherland was one of the so-called 'four horsemen [of the Apocalypse]' on the Supreme Court who consistently and vigorously struck down New Deal legislation as unconstitutional. When the Court capitulated before Roosevelt's court-packing threat Sutherland honourably resigned his seat on the bench.

'The Court did not interpret the Constitution – the Court amended it.' This echo of Sutherland was penned by yet another contemporary of Cardozo's, James Byrnes (Associate Justice 1941-42), whose bond with Roosevelt and the New Deal was so close that, as head of the War Mobilization Board between 1942 and 1945, he earned the affectionate nickname of 'assistant president'. Byrnes's sharp attack on the Court (of which he was no longer a member) was made in an article entitled 'The Supreme Court must be curbed' and referred to the unanimous anti-segregation decision in *Brown v Board of Education* (1954).[90]

'Ordinarily,' remarked Justice Byrnes, 'the Court has been controlled by legal precedents. In the segregation opinion it could cite no legal precedent for its decision because all the precedents sustain the doctrine of separate but equal facilities.'

Justice Byrnes sums up his position by declaring that 'the history of liberty is the history of limitations on government'. His message is simple: The Supreme Court has 'usurped' the power of the States and 'must be curbed'.[91]

How can we square Byrnes's strict constructionism, his belief in precedent and his opposition to big government with his active role in the implementation of the New Deal? To the cynic the key may well be seen to lie in the fact that Byrnes, who was governor of South Carolina in the 1950s, was a southern segregationist. Big government was all right when it came to central regulation of the economy but not when it threatened the traditional way of life of the South.

Cardozo, Sutherland and Byrnes all came out at one time or another against judicial activism, but none of them was entirely consistent and while apparently sharing certain views in reality they had very little in common with one another. Cardozo's judicial self-restraint was most in evidence in his deference to the legislature during the New Deal, which Sutherland opposed with a vengeance. For *him*, by contrast, it was deference to the Constitution as originally conceived by its framers that mattered, and this impelled him to reject the New Deal almost in its entirety. Byrnes agreed with Sutherland that the framers' intentions should be respected and followed, but he had no trouble supporting the New Deal; it was only the Supreme Court's later liberal decisions on race and national security that he found infringed the framers' intentions.

Inconsistencies like this enable commentators to conclude either that there is no such thing as 'the will of the law' or else that the distinction drawn since the time of John Marshall (Chief Justice 1801-35) between 'the will of the law' and 'the will of the judges' is 'a distinction without a difference'.[92]

In his dissenting opinion in *TWA v Franklin Mint Corp*[93] Justice Stevens rejected this equation of 'the will of the judges' with 'the will of the law' as unduly cynical but regretted that it was 'given a measure of credibility whenever the Court bases a decision on its own notions of sound policy rather than on what the law commands'. He concluded more in sorrow than in anger: 'It does so today. The task of revising an international treaty is not one that this Court has any authority to perform. I respectfully dissent.'

## 2. No one should be a judge in his own cause

This maxim encapsulates one of the two fundamental principles of natural justice, the other being *audi alteram partem*, literally 'hear the other side', the principle that 'No one shall be condemned unheard'. Its wording varies, but perhaps its best known formulation is that of Coke: *Nemo debet esse judex in propria sua causa* – 'No one should be a judge in his own cause'.[1] In his commentary on Littleton Coke adds an explanation: *aliquis non debet esse judex in propria causa, quia non potest esse judex et pars*: 'No one ought to be a judge in his own cause, because one cannot be both judge and party.'[2]

So sacred is this principle that Lord Chief Justice Hobart is reported as saying in 1615 that 'even an Act of Parliament made against natural equity, as to make a man a judge in his own case, is void in itself; for *jura naturae sunt immutabilia* ("the laws of nature are immutable") and they are *leges legum* ("the laws of laws")'.[3]

The argument adumbrated here by Hobart (Chief Justice of the Court of Common Pleas from 1613 until his death in 1625) may be restated in the form of a syllogism:

(1) Statute law is the highest form of law in England;
(2) *Nemo judex* is a principle of natural law;
(3) Natural law is a form of law even higher than statute;
(4) Therefore a statute making a man a judge in his own case is void.

Hobart here recognises the legislative supremacy of Parliament as a basic principle of the British Constitution. The only exception to it as far as as he is concerned is where a statute clashes with natural justice, or what he calls 'natural equity', which he identifies with natural law. For Hobart natural law is a higher form of law, with which man-made law, including statutes, must conform if they are to be held valid. The principle of *nemo judex* is cited merely as an example of natural law. So that any statute which is incompatible with that principle would be invalid.

What Hobart CJ was doing here was following the lead of his famous predecessor Sir Edward Coke CJ in *Dr Bonham's* case decided five years earlier, in 1610.[4]

As we have seen, by the time Blackstone compiled his *Commentaries on the Laws of England*, which first appeared in 1765, the doctrine of the legislative supremacy of Parliament was firmly established as a fundamental principle of the British Constitution.[5]

What then about the principle *nemo judex*? Does it still override statute law? Or can Parliament ignore it if it so wishes? The answer to this question depends very much on the status of Acts of Parliament. Though in recent years some judges have espoused a different view in extra-judicial remarks,

## V. Constitutional Principles

English law still upholds the untrammelled authority and legislative supremacy of Parliament.

This could hardly be expressed more clearly or robustly than in this statement made by Lord Reid in *Madzimbamuto v Lardner-Burke*:[6]

> It is often said that it would be unconstitutional for the United Kingdom Parliament to do certain things, meaning that the moral, political and other reasons against doing them are so strong that most people would regard it as highly improper if Parliament did these things. But that does not mean that it is beyond the power of Parliament to do such things. If Parliament chose to do any of them the courts would not hold the Act of Parliament invalid.

Does this mean that Parliament could pass a law permitting someone to be the judge in his own cause? The answer must be Yes, as was held by Blackburn J expressing the unanimous opinion of the judges summoned to assist the House of Lords in reaching their decision in *Mersey Docks v Gibbs*:

> It is contrary to the general rule of law, not only in this country, but in every other, to make a person judge in his own cause, and though the Legislature can, and, no doubt, in a proper case, would, depart from that general rule, an intention to do so is not to be inferred except from much clearer enactments than any to be found in these statutes.[7]

In other words, a measure permitting someone to act as judge in his own cause would be so exceptional as to require very clear wording. But there is no doubt that Parliament has the power to pass even such a measure.

Needless to say, no such legislation has ever been enacted. Why then has there been so much discussion over the years of the possibility of a statute allowing someone to be the judge in his own cause? The reason is precisely because of the sanctity of the principle of *nemo judex*. The logic of this is as follows: if Parliament could pass a law in contradiction even of this sacred principle, then there can plainly be no limit to Parliament's legislative power.

We should not be surprised to find, then, that *nemo judex* has been treated with great respect over the centuries. But how is the principle to be interpreted? Its literal meaning is only a starting point. If anyone who is a party to a lawsuit also has the right to decide its outcome, that would be a clear breach of the principle. By extension we come to the category of cases where the person sitting in judgment is not a party but is nevertheless associated in one way or another with one of the parties. What we are dealing with here is partiality or bias, which leads us to our next category, namely cases where, although there may be no actual bias, there may well be an appearance, or at least a suspicion, of partiality.

## *V.2. No one should be a judge in his own cause*

### *Three principles*

In *Webb and Hay v The Queen*,[8] decided by the High Court of Australia in 1994, Deane J suggested a fourfold classification of these cases, based on three related but separate principles. First, there is the principle that no one should be in a position to decide a matter in which he has an interest, whether pecuniary or otherwise. Secondly, there is the principle of avoidance of partiality or bias. What this means is that a judge must not be a respecter of persons, which is related to the principle of equality before the law, which in turn can be seen as forming part of the fundamental principle of the rule of law. Thirdly, we have the principle that justice must not only be done but must also be seen to be done.

### *Pecuniary interest*

One of the most straightforward cases illustrative of the first of these three principles is *Dimes v Grand Junction Canal Co.*[9] The case involved a dispute between a canal company and a landowner. At first instance the Vice-Chancellor found for the company. This decision was affirmed by the Lord Chancellor, Lord Cottenham. The matter then went to the House of Lords, where the issue was the legality of the Lord Chancellor's decrees in favour of the company.

The problem was that Lord Cottenham, who held the office of Lord Chancellor between 1846 and 1850, was a major shareholder in the canal company at the time when he made the decrees, a fact which was unknown to the defendant in the case. When Lord Cottenham's decision was challenged, all the judges were summoned to Westminster Hall to advise the House of Lords on this sensitive issue. This was an ancient procedure which was adopted only in very important cases. Following the judges' unanimous opinion, the House of Lords declared Lord Cottenham's decrees voidable and duly annulled them.

The *nemo judex* principle was simply explained by Lord Campbell (who was himself to become Lord Chancellor a few years later):[10]

> No one can suppose that Lord Cottenham could be, in the remotest degree, influenced by the interest he had in this concern; but, my Lords, it is of the last importance that the maxim that 'no man is to be a judge in his own cause' should be held sacred. And that is not to be confined to a cause in which he is a party, but applies to a cause in which he has an interest .... We have again and again set aside proceedings in inferior tribunals, because an individual, who had an interest in a cause, took a part in the decision. And it will have a most salutary

> effect on these tribunals when it is known that this High Court of last resort, in a case in which the Lord Chancellor of England had an interest, considered that his decree was on that account a decree not according to law, and should be set aside. This will be a lesson to all inferior tribunals to take care, not only that in their decrees they are not influenced by their personal interest, but to avoid the appearance of labouring under such an influence.

Lord Cottenham was spared the indignity of this decision: he had died just a few months before his decrees were struck down.

### *Non-pecuniary interest*

Lord Cottenham's interest in the *Dimes* case was financial, but, as has now been recognised by the English courts, there is no need for the principle to be confined to such instances. For

> there could be cases where the interest of the judge in the subject matter of the proceedings arising from his strong commitment to some cause or belief or his association with a person or body involved in the proceedings could shake public confidence in the public administration of justice as much as a shareholding (which might be small) in a public company involved in the litigation.[11]

This was said by Lord Hutton in the second *Pinochet* case. A law lord was found to have sat on the first *Pinochet* case in the outcome of which he had a non-pecuniary interest. The case in question was an application for the arrest and extradition to Spain of the former Chilean dictator, General (or Senator) Augusto Pinochet, to stand trial for certain crimes against humanity allegedly committed while he was head of state of Chile. The question before the House of Lords was whether a former head of state enjoyed immunity from arrest and extradition.[12] Besides the parties themselves three human rights groups were given leave to participate in the hearing as 'interveners'. One of these bodies was Amnesty International, which had not only put in written submissions but was also represented by a team of four counsel, who addressed the court in favour of extradition. By a majority of three to two the House of Lords decided against General Pinochet, one of the three law lords forming the majority being Lord Hoffmann, whose wife had worked for Amnesty International since 1977 and who himself was an unpaid Director and Chairman of a connected body known as Amnesty International Charity Limited.[13] The information about Lord Hoffmann's personal association with Amnesty International came to light only about a fortnight after the House of Lords' decision to extradite General Pinochet. The General's solicitors received an anonymous telephone call and on the following day it was headline news. However, ignoring the rising tide of criticism of Lord Hoffmann's participation in the decision, the Home Secretary duly signed the authority for the General's extradition to proceed. General Pinochet's lawyers then lodged a petition asking for Lord Hoffmann's opinion to be declared invalid or, alternatively, for the decision of the House of Lords to be set aside. A fresh panel of law lords was summoned to hear this petition.[14] Delivering the leading speech Lord Browne-Wilkinson adopted a low-key approach:

> It is important to stress that Senator Pinochet makes no allegation of *actual bias* against Lord Hoffmann; his claim is based on the requirement that justice should be seen to be done as well as actually being done.[15]

Lord Hope of Craighead struck a more critical note:

> I think that the connections which existed between Lord Hoffmann and Amnesty International were of such a character, in view of their duration and proximity, as to disqualify him on this ground. In view of his links with Amnesty International Charity Ltd he could not be seen to be impartial. There has been no suggestion that he was actually biased. He had no financial or pecuniary interest in the outcome. But his relationship with Amnesty International was such that he was, in effect, acting as a judge in his own cause. I consider that his failure to disclose these connections leads inevitably to the conclusion that the decision to which he was a party must be set aside.[16]

The House of Lords stressed that in this class of case the disqualification of the judge in question was automatic. It is not necessary to show a 'real danger' or even a 'reasonable suspicion' of bias, let alone any actual bias on his part.

But what exactly is the appropriate test? It was stated by the Court of Appeal in these terms in *Locabail v Bayfield Properties*:

> ... if a judge has a personal interest in the outcome of an issue which he is to resolve, he is improperly acting as a judge in his own cause; and ... such a proceeding would, without more, undermine public confidence in the integrity of the administration of justice. In the context of automatic disqualification the question is not whether the judge has some link with a party involved in a cause before the judge but whether the outcome of that cause could, realistically, affect the judge's interest.[17]

How much of a personal interest does a judge have to have in the outcome of a case before he is automatically disqualified? It used to be held that any interest, however small, would disqualify him. But there has been a recent drift away from this. In *Locabail*, for example, it was maintained that there is a '*de minimis* exception':

> This seems to us a proper exception provided the potential effect of any decision on the judge's personal interest is so small as to be incapable of affecting his decision one way or the other.[18]

This remark looks very much like an exercise in back-tracking. For how can the potential effect on a judge's personal interest be measured? Lord Hoffmann presumably thought that his association with Amnesty International was irrelevant to his sitting on the *Pinochet* case. However, the *Locabail* judgment does go on to add: 'But it is important, bearing in mind the rationale of the rule, that any doubt should be resolved in favour of disqualification.' But where the judge is not personally involved disqualification becomes very difficult to obtain:

> In any case where the judge's interest is said to derive from the interest of a spouse, partner or other family member the link must be so close and direct as to render the interest of that other person, for all practical purposes, indistinguishable from an interest of the judge himself.[19]

There are other dicta which muddy the waters further. In the *Pinochet* case Lord Browne-Wilkinson was at pains to stress that that decision did *not* mean automatic disqualification from *any* case involving a charity with which the judge happened to be connected:

> Only in cases in which a judge is taking an active role as trustee or director of a charity which is closely allied to and acting with a party to the litigation should a judge normally be concerned either to recuse himself or disclose the position to the parties.[20]

This is arguably too protective of judges. It is hard to understand why a judge should not routinely be required to disclose any such interest to the parties.

But what if disclosure is made and no party objects to the judge's continuing to hear the case? Can such parties adopt a 'wait and see' approach, challenging the judge's decision only after he has found against them? That was the way the Court of Appeal described the application made by Mrs Emmanuel, the claimant in *Locabail*, against the decision of a solicitor sitting as a deputy High Court judge, who, on the eighth day of the hearing, disclosed that he had just discovered that 'the firm of which I am a partner seems to have had something to do with attempting to get a bankruptcy order against' Mrs Emmanuel's husband.[21] Mrs Emmanuel's lawyers lodged their objection only after an adverse judgment was handed down by the deputy judge over four months later. Her initial application for the deputy judge's decision to be set aside on the ground of his firm's involvement with the case against Mr Emmanuel was heard by the very deputy judge whose decision was being queried, who dismissed the application. The matter then went to the Court of Appeal, which upheld this decision. The Court of Appeal understandably objected that 'Mrs Emmanuel wanted to have the best of both worlds'.[22] But should the deputy judge not have had to recuse himself of his own accord? It was held by the Court of Appeal that this was not a case of automatic disqualification at all. The reason given for this was that, though the deputy judge was head of the litigation department of the firm of solicitors concerned, he did not have any personal knowledge of his firm's involvement in the case against Mrs Emmanuel's husband. But why should the state of the deputy judge's knowledge be the determining factor? Perhaps a more pertinent question is: why did he not know? The Court of Appeal admitted that though he had conducted a 'conflict search' in regard to Mrs Emmanuel he did not do so in regard to her husband. So, perhaps he *ought* to have known of the potential conflict. Moreover, surely the very existence of this potential conflict should have been enough to disqualify him, regardless of his state of knowledge? Or, failing that, how could his judgment possibly be squared with the requirement that justice must not only be done but must also be seen to be done (see below)? Above all, is it really a good idea to allow a judge to hear an application for his own disqualification in a particular case? For, is this not an almost literal example of someone being a judge in his own cause?

### *'A real danger of bias'*

Three other cases were heard by the Court of Appeal together with *Locabail*. Coming as it did so soon after the House of Lords decision to set aside the judgment of a law lord in *Pinochet* and in view of the sensitive nature of the issues involved, the Court of Appeal was made up of its three most senior judges: the Lord Chief Justice (Lord Bingham), the Master of the Rolls (Lord Woolf) and the Vice-Chancellor (Sir Richard Scott). In the interests of certainty and clarity only one judgment was delivered, which was the judgment of the Court as a whole. Only one of the four appeals heard on that occasion was successful. This was *Timmins v Gormley*, a personal injury case, where the application was for setting aside the judgment of a recorder on the ground of bias. Besides having largely a claimant personal injury practice as a barrister – a fact which he had disclosed to the parties – the recorder was a prolific writer on the subject of personal injury litigation, in which he expressed 'pronounced pro-claimant anti-insurer views'. Though there was 'no suggestion of actual bias on the part of the recorder', it was found by the Court of Appeal that there was 'a real danger' that someone holding the views expressed by the recorder might 'unconsciously have leant in favour of the claimant and against the defendant in resolving the factual issues between them'.[23] On this basis, the appeal against the recorder's decision was allowed and a retrial ordered.

At the time of writing, the 'real danger' test applied in *Timmins* was supposedly the correct standard under English law. This was established by the House of Lords in *R v Gough*,[24] in which several competing tests were analysed and evaluated. The fact that this test itself was stated in several different ways in that case alone is not particularly helpful. Lord Goff, concluding his speech, with which his brother law lords all agreed, described the appropriate test as whether 'there was a real danger of bias on the part of the relevant member of the tribunal in question'.[25] In his brief concurring opinion, Lord Woolf endorsed 'the proper test which Lord Goff has identified',[26] yet the wording he used in describing it was not quite the same as Lord Goff's, Lord Woolf's test being 'whether there is a real danger of injustice having occurred as a result of the alleged bias'. This wording places the emphasis not on the alleged bias itself but on its effect on justice. Though presumably intended to be the same test as Lord Goff's it could easily lead to a different conclusion when applied to the facts of a specific case. In addition, Lord Goff himself used a different formulation of his test elsewhere in his speech in *Gough*, asking whether 'there was a real likelihood, in the sense of a real possibility, of bias'.[27] But is 'a real likelihood of bias' the same thing as 'a real possibility of bias'? 'Likelihood' surely means 'probability', whereas 'possibility' represents a considerably lower level of expectation, even with the word 'real' in front of it. In the concluding paragraph of his speech Lord Goff appears to equate 'real danger' with 'real possibility' rather than with 'real likelihood', which he identifies with 'real probability'. It is not easy to tell from this what the requisite level of possibility is. As a result the test is not as clear as it might be. Indeed, it is surprising that the House of Lords should have been content with it after the problems resulting from its lack of clarity in a case involving a juryman just a few years earlier.[28]

### *'Justice must not only be done but must be seen to be done'*

Lord Goff was at pains to reject the test suggested by Lord Hewart CJ in *R v Sussex Justices, ex parte McCarthy*[29] that even a suspicion of bias was sufficient to vitiate the proceedings.[30] The *Sussex Justices* case arose out of a road traffic accident in which McCarthy's car had collided with another vehicle. McCarthy was charged with the criminal offence of drunken driving and the driver of the other car also instituted civil proceedings against him for damages. At his criminal trial the magistrates' clerk was none other than the solicitor acting for the plaintiff motorist in the civil case. When the magistrates retired to consider their verdict this clerk withdrew with them in case they needed to consult him on a point of law. This was customary at the time, although the practice now is for the clerk to join the magistrates only if expressly invited to do so. In fact, the Sussex magistrates did without their clerk's assistance. But Lord Hewart was in no doubt that McCarthy's conviction had to be quashed nevertheless:

> It is said, and, no doubt, truly, that when that gentleman retired in the usual way with the justices, taking with him the notes of the evidence in case the justices might desire to consult him, the justices came to a conclusion without consulting him, and that he scrupulously abstained from referring to the case in any way. But while that is so, a long line of cases shows that it is not merely of some importance but is of fundamental importance that justice should not only be done but should manifestly and undoubtedly be seen to be done. The question therefore is not whether in this case the deputy clerk made any observation or offered any criticism which he might not properly have made or offered; the question is whether he was so related to the case in its civil aspect as to be unfit to act as clerk to the justices in the criminal matter. The answer to that question depends not upon what actually was done but upon what might appear to be done. Nothing is to be done which creates even a suspicion that there has been an improper interference with the course of justice.[31]

This passage has been invoked on many occasions, not least by Lord Denning MR, who restated it in his own characteristically robust manner:

> … in considering whether there was a real likelihood of bias, the court does not look at the mind of the justice himself or at the mind of the chairman of the tribunal, or whoever it may be, who sits in a judicial capacity. It does not look to see if there was a real likelihood that he would, or did, in fact favour one side at the expense of the other. The court looks at the impression which would be given to other people. Even if he was as impartial as could be, nevertheless, if right-minded persons would think that, in the circumstances, there was a real likelihood of bias on his part, then he should not sit. And if he does sit, his decision cannot stand.[32]

Lord Hewart's dictum was criticised in *R v Camborne Justices, ex parte Pearce*:

> While indorsing and fully maintaining the integrity of the principle reasserted by Lord Hewart CJ, this court feels that the continued citation of it in cases to

> which it is not applicable may lead to the erroneous impression that it is more important that justice should appear to be done than that it should in fact be done.[33]

This rather mealy-mouthed comment combines criticism of Lord Hewart's statement with purported support for the principle it embodies. What exactly is that principle? Lord Hewart leaves us in little doubt: it is the principle 'that justice should not only be done but should manifestly and undoubtedly be seen to be done', which he describes as 'of fundamental importance' and which, he stresses, is supported by 'a long line of cases'.

While claiming to uphold this principle the court in the *Camborne Justices* case effectively subverted it. Henry Pearce had been found guilty of selling watered-down milk in a prosecution brought by the Cornwall County Council. The magistrates' clerk at his trial, a certain Donald Thomas, also happened to be an elected member of the county council. This fact came to Pearce's knowledge only after the trial, and he then applied for *certiorari* to quash the conviction. Unlike in the *Sussex Justices* case, the clerk here did not retire with the magistrates but he was sent for to advise the justices on a point of law. The facts of the case were not discussed in his presence, and, after advising the magistrates he returned to court. On the basis of these facts the court held that 'there was no real likelihood of bias', and the application for *certiorari* was dismissed. But perhaps the most illuminating comment came from Lord Goddard CJ in the course of argument, when he conceded that: 'If the court were asked to express an opinion they would say that it were better if Mr Thomas were not to sit when prosecutions were conducted on behalf of the council of which he was a member.'

The 'long line of cases' referred to by Lord Hewart in support of the principle applied in the *Sussex Justices* includes *Eckersley v Mersey Docks*, in which Lord Esher MR, one of the great Victorian judges, stated as the rule applicable to judges 'that not only must they not be biased, yet if the circumstances are such that people – not reasonable people, but many people – would suspect them of being biased, they ought not to sit as judges'.[34]

Some confusion has arisen from the fact that the actual decision in *Eckersley*, which did *not* involve either a judge or a juror, was an exception to this general rule. Lord Esher MR explained extremely clearly why the very strict rule which is applicable to judges of all degrees did not apply to the situation in the case before him. The point is that the test for judges does not depend on actual bias but merely on a suspicion of bias – and not necessarily even reasonable suspicion. Moreover, it cannot be stressed enough that Lord Esher did not invent this doctrine: it was already well established by his day.

### *V.2. No one should be a judge in his own cause*

Has this time-honoured principle now been swept away in England? The House of Lords in *Gough* certainly disapproved of it, without, however, expressly overruling Lord Hewart's judgment in the *Sussex Justices* case, and without so much as mentioning *Eckersley v Mersey Docks* or any of the other cases on which Lord Hewart's judgment was based.

#### *Uniform standard?*

It is not even clear to whom the 'real danger' test applies. In *Gough* Lord Goff thought it 'possible, and desirable, that the same test should be applicable in all cases of apparent bias, whether concerned with justices [viz. justices of the peace, or magistrates] or members of other inferior tribunals, or with jurors, or with arbitrators'.[35] Does this mean that the same standard is to apply across the board from the highest to the lowest level? If so, why is there no mention of High Court judges or the higher echelons of the judiciary? Is this because Lord Goff thought that a different standard was applicable to them? Or because it was unthinkable to him that their judgments would ever have to be set aside for bias? The *Pinochet* episode was of course as yet in the future at the time of *Gough*.

By contrast, in the *Mersey Docks* case both Lord Esher and Lopes LJ expressly stated that the same test – what we might call the 'suspicion of bias' test – was applicable to judges of all degrees (though not necessarily to arbitrators appointed in a contract). Indeed, Lord Esher specifically mentions 'judges of the Superior Court'.

#### *Jurors*

Although Lord Esher did not refer directly to juries, the same test used to be applied to them, most recently by the Court of Appeal (Criminal Division) in *R v Morris.*[36] This decision was expressly disapproved in *Gough* by Lord Goff, who remarked that in *Morris* 'it appears that *R v Spencer* was not cited to the court'.[37] In *R v Spencer*[38] three nurses at a secure mental hospital were charged with ill-treating patients. A member of the jury whose wife happened to work as a cleaner at another psychiatric hospital made no secret during the trial of his belief in the guilt of the defendant nurses. As a result, this juror was discharged by the judge, but he then gave a lift to three other jurors, who disobeyed the judge's instructions not to discuss the case with the discharged juror. The trial judge decided not to accede to the defence request to discharge the rest of the jury. The test he applied was 'that the jury should not be discharged unless it could be shown that there was a very high risk that the apparently biased juror had influenced any of his fellows'. This test was characterised by both the Court of Appeal and the House of Lords as too strict. The Court of Appeal offered instead the following test:

> … in this type of circumstance this court must ask itself whether it thinks there is anything in the events which ex hypothesi should not have occurred which leads it to the conclusion that an injustice may have been done, or that there is a real danger that the appellant may have been prejudiced by what has gone on. In the instant case, we do not think that we should come to that conclusion.[39]

This is a somewhat vague and longwinded version of the 'real danger' test, which was restated rather more pithily by Lord Ackner in the House of Lords: 'The correct test is … whether there was a "real danger" that the appellants' position had been prejudiced in the circumstances ….'[40] However, though the test applied by the House of Lords was essentially the same as that used by the Court of Appeal, the result was exactly the opposite - which hardly inspires confidence in the 'real danger' test.

### *Australia*

The 'real danger' test was expressly rejected by the High Court of Australia in *Webb and Hay v The Queen*.[41] The case involved the trial of two men for the brutal murder of a certain Lance Edward Patrick. During the trial the mother of the murder victim's fiancee was aproached by a member of the jury who handed her a bunch of daffodils with a request that she give them to Mr Patrick's mother. The two defendants immediately objected and asked for a 'mistrial', i.e. for the jury as a whole to be discharged. The trial judge refused this request and also decided not to excuse the juror in question. After conviction and an unsuccessful appeal the defendants were given special leave to appeal to the High Court of Australia on two grounds, one being that, on the basis of the 'flower incident', the trial judge should have discharged the jury.

The trial judge applied a version of the 'real danger of bias' test. But the correct test under Australian law was held to be very different:

> When it is alleged that a judge has been or might be actuated by bias, this Court has held that the proper test is whether fair-minded people might reasonably apprehend or suspect that the judge has prejudged or might prejudge the case.

This is in fact our old friend the doctrine espoused by Lords Denning, Hewart and Esher. It asks not whether it is likely that the judge or juror concerned actually *is* biased but whether his or her conduct is likely to create an *impression* of bias on an outside observer. Mason CJ and McHugh J in *Webb* go on to explain, quoting Lord Hewart:

> The principle behind the reasonable apprehension or suspicion test is that it is of 'fundamental importance that justice should not only be done, but should manifestly and undoubtedly be seen to be done'.

### *USA*

In the US there is a large body of law devoted to the question of the disqualification of judges. American law has remained true to the ancient common law principle requiring not only what has been termed 'the cold neutrality of an impartial judge' but also the appearance of neutrality.[42] It is accepted that whether a judge is disqualified is a question not of fact but of law.[43]

In a number of states of the USA this whole matter is governed by statute. It is generally held that such statutes should be broadly construed so as to afford maximum protection of the public against biased judges. So, for example, it has been held that the grounds for disqualification enumerated in a statute should not be regarded as exhaustive; also, that a judge's disqualifying interest need not be directly involved in the case in question; and moreover, that the term 'party' in a disqualification statute should not be narrowly interpreted but should include all parties 'in interest'.[44]

This last point is particularly instructive in the light of the disqualification of a law lord in England in the *Pinochet* case.

The Federal statute on the subject provides that: 'Any justice, judge, or magistrate of the United States shall disqualify himself in any proceeding in which his impartiality might reasonably be questioned.'[45] This places the onus on the judge himself to stand down wherever his impartiality might 'reasonably' be impugned. Once again, the emphasis is on the impression of bias rather than on the existence of bias. The section then goes on to enumerate a number of specific circumstances in which a judge should recuse himself. These, it should be emphasised, are not by way of explanation of the general provision quoted above but in addition to it:

> (b) He shall also disqualify himself in the following circumstances:
> (1) Where he has a personal bias or prejudice concerning a party, or personal knowledge of disputed evidentiary facts concerning the proceeding;
> ...

(5) He or his spouse, or a person within the third degree of relationship to either of them, or the spouse of such a person:

(i) Is a party to the proceeding, or an officer, director, or trustee of a party;

(ii) Is acting as a lawyer in the proceeding;

(iii) Is known by the judge to have an interest that could be substantially affected by the outcome of the proceeding;

(iv) Is to the judge's knowledge likely to be a material witness in the proceeding.

What if the judge discloses his interest? If the parties do not object, should he be permitted to hear the case anyway? This appears to be taken for granted in England.[46] However, the US Federal statute does not allow this in respect of the specific grounds for disqualification listed in subsection (b) but only in relation to the general grounds identified in subsection (a):

> (e) No justice, judge, or magistrate shall accept from the parties to the proceeding a waiver of any ground for disqualification enumerated in subsection (b). Where the ground for disqualification arises only under subsection (a), waiver may be accepted provided it is preceded by a full disclosure on the record of the basis for disqualification.

In keeping with the original spirit of the English common law, another Federal statute provides that the mere filing of an affidavit by a party alleging bias on the part of the judge is enough in itself to disqualify him.[47] No proof of bias is needed, and there is no determination of the truth or falsehood of the allegation. All that is required is a certificate of counsel of record to say that it is made in good faith.

There is a similar provision in some state statutes. However, it has to be said that in certain other states this kind of provision has been held unconstitutional on the ground that it transfers judicial power from the court to the parties.[48]

### *USA – juries*

By contrast with Britain, in the United States prospective jurors are routinely subjected to examination on the voir dire, which is a crucial part of jury selection.

In England it is not possible to question jurors at all. At the time of writing it is still possible to challenge a juror for cause, but this is extremely rare, as it has to be based on information about him obtained from some source other than the juror himself. In practice such challenges are limited to a situation where a juror recognises the defendant.

*V.2. No one should be a judge in his own cause*

That is why British cases concerned with alleged prejudice on the part of a juror tend to arise only *after* the trial. By contrast, the general practice in the US of jury selection on the basis of voir dire examination leaves little room for any dispute about the fairness of a verdict after it has been returned. Indeed, it is a general rule of US procedural law, whether in a state or federal court and whether in a civil or criminal trial, that once a verdict has been rendered it is too late to apply to disqualify a juror. The rule is not invariable, but the key test is whether the losing party has been prejudiced by the presence of a juror who ought not to have been impanelled in the first place. There is also an understandable reluctance to allow such matters to be decided by an appeal court, which, unlike the trial judge, will not have had the opportunity of seeing and hearing the testimony of the juror concerned and determining his demeanour.[49]

One of the grounds on which a juror may be challenged in the United States is *propter affectum*, i.e. on the basis that the juror was likely to be biased. Where a juror is connected with one of the parties by blood, marriage or commercial ties there is a presumption that he will be biased. So, a juror who is related to one of the parties is automatically disqualified. This ancient rule extends to the ninth degree of relationship! A challenge on this ground is characterised as a challenge 'for principal cause'. Other principal causes include situations where a juror is the employer or employee of either party or their attorney. In such situations the relationship or association between the juror and the party is conclusive, and no court has any discretion to disregard it.[50]

The other form of challenge *propter affectum* is what is termed a 'challenge to the favor'. Does this mean that a juror who shows sympathy for one of the parties can be challenged under this head? It has been held that this in itself will not necessarily disqualify the juror concerned, provided the juror claims that this will not affect his ability to reach a verdict dispassionately.[51]

The key question here is whether the relevant juror has prejudged the case. But how is it possible to tell? Is it enough if the juror has placed a bet on the outcome of the case? However, where a juror made a 1 dollar bet on the penalty in a murder case before the juror knew that he would be called in that case, it was held that there was no prejudice. The fact that the position taken by the juror was contrary to his small financial interest in the outcome no doubt contributed to this result.[52]

In only very rare cases have counsel been allowed to question jurors upon voir dire on their political views or affiliation. A challenge on political grounds was even disallowed in a *quo warranto* case challenging the election of a particular official where the jurors in question were members of a political club which had opposed the defendant in the disputed election.[53]

The reason for the reluctance of US law to allow political prejudice to disqualify a juror is no doubt because of the openness of political party affiliation in American life in a way which is unimaginable in Britain or Europe.

Voir dire examination of jurors on their religious beliefs has, however, been allowed in certain cases. But the most frequent type of bias on which questioning is permitted is racial prejudice. However, even where a juror has admitted holding a prejudice against a particular race or nationality, this has not disqualified him if he can credibly assert that he harbours no prejudice against the party in question or that his prejudice against the race or nationality concerned is not so extreme as to affect the fairness of his verdict.[54]

### *Conclusion*

English law, it turns out, has fallen out of step with the rest of the common law world. In England alone the test is whether there was a real danger of bias. In the USA and Australia, as we have seen, as well as in Canada and New Zealand, some form of the 'reasonable suspicion' test holds sway. This is hardly surprising, as that was the original English test as well. Why then have the English courts seen fit to depart from it?

The justification given for this is essentially that it would be unjust for the mere impression of bias to be enough to set aside a decision. However, this argument can easily be countered:

(a) Bias is insidious. It is impossible to tell whether someone actually is biased or not, so conduct which might give that impression cannot be ignored.

(b) Even if a decision is set aside on this basis, the case can always go to a retrial. But the more alert judges are to the need to avoid doing anything that could give the impression of partiality the fewer decisions there will be that will have to be set aside. Had the time-honoured principle enunciated by Lords Esher, Hewart and Denning not been discredited by the English courts the *Pinochet* debacle would probably never have occurred. For, though it was not realised that Lord Hoffmann was automatically disqualified from sitting on that case, it should nevertheless have been obvious that his doing so would be likely to give an impression of partiality. However, as this did not matter under the already prevailing 'real danger of bias' test, those who knew of Lord Hoffmann's association with Amnesty International presumably considered that there was no obstacle to his sitting.

(c) The abandonment of the traditional doctrine in favour of the 'real danger' test may, ironically, itself be seen as a breach of the principle that no one should be a judge in his own cause. For in changing the rules in this way the English courts have taken it upon themselves not only to act as legislators – which has become increasingly common – but to do so in a matter which affected their own position. The 'real danger' criterion makes a judge's decision much harder to challenge on grounds of bias than it would have been under the old test.

VI

# Legal Rights and Obligations

### 1. 'Where there is a right there is a remedy'

**It is sometimes suggested that the emphasis on rights is a modern development in the law. In fact, the concept of rights has been at the centre of legal discourse for centuries. Every right has a reciprocal obligation, and one person's rights may conflict with another's. Where a right is infringed the law provides a remedy. But not every loss or damage is recognised as amounting to the infringement of a right.**

'Where there is a right there is a remedy' is a translation of the Latin maxim *ubi jus ibi remedium*, which is also sometimes rendered 'Where there is a right there is legal redress' or 'There is no wrong without a remedy', or even 'Equity will not suffer a wrong to be without a remedy'. This last formulation has led to the view that the principle was peculiar to Equity and therefore strictly speaking not part of the common law at all.

#### *Equity*

The best known instance of this specifically equitable jurisdiction was the enforcement of trusts, which were recognised by the Court of Chancery (a court of Equity) but not by the common law courts. So, for example, if Testator T left land to two named individuals, P and Q, to hold it on trust for Beneficiary B, legal title to the land passed to P and Q. Under the old law, if P and Q chose to hold the land for their own benefit B would have had no redress in the common law courts, which looked only to the strict legalities. B had to go to a Court of Equity to obtain redress. This distinction between law and equity ceased to be important with the passing of the Judicature Acts 1873-75, which allowed all courts to apply equitable principles.

Seen as a specifically equitable principle this maxim was limited to filling gaps left by the common law. In fact, however, it was much wider as it was also a common law principle. So much so, indeed, that it is to this maxim that the great growth and flexibility of the common law has been attributed.

*Ashby v White*

This is well illustrated by the old case of *Ashby v White*.[1] Matthias Ashby, a burgess of Aylesbury who was entitled to vote in parliamentary elections, was prevented by the returning officers from casting his vote. Although the candidates for whom Ashby had intended to vote were duly elected Ashby brought an action on the case (i.e. a tort action) against the returning officers and claimed £200 in damages. After obtaining a verdict for £5 at first instance, he lost on appeal, with only the Lord Chief Justice, Sir John Holt, favouring his cause in a judgment which has come to be regarded as one of the leading opinions of all time. The House of Lords endorsed Holt's dissenting judgment by 50 votes to 16, thus giving Ashby a resounding victory and establishing an important principle.

The issue before the court was essentially quite simple. The fact that Ashby had a right to vote and that he had been deprived of that right was not in dispute. The question was: What loss had he suffered? Lord Holt's argument rings down the centuries:

> My brother Powell indeed thinks that an action upon the case is not maintainable, because there is no hurt or damage to the plaintiff; but surely every injury imports a damage, though it does not cost the party one farthing, and it is impossible to prove the contrary; for *a damage is not merely pecuniary, but an injury imports a damage when a man is thereby hindered of his right*. As in an action for slanderous words, though a man does not lose a penny by reason of the speaking them, yet he shall have an action. So if a man gives another a cuff on the ear, though it cost him nothing ... yet he shall have his action, for it is a personal injury. So a man shall have an action against another for riding over his ground, though it do him no damage: for it is an invasion of his property and the other has no right to come there.

It is important to understand the terminology used here. 'Injury', from the Latin *injuria*, means a legal wrong or an infringement of a legal right, whereas 'damage' means 'harm' or 'loss' in a very broad sense.

What Holt CJ is saying, therefore, is that a plaintiff (or claimant) does not need to suffer any actual harm or loss in order to be entitled to legal redress. The infringement of a claimant's legal rights is enough to entitle him to judgment in a court of law. Or, as Holt put it: 'It is a vain thing to imagine a right without a remedy, for want of right and want of remedy are reciprocal.' In finding in favour of Ashby, Sir John Holt characteristically sets out the whole of the relevant law. The examples he gives span three major areas of the common law, namely trespass, personal injury and defamation, all of which he identifies as importing strict liability. Since the rise of negligence as the leading tort following *Donoghue v Stevenson*[2] the concept of strict liability has declined – with certain notable exceptions.

But was Holt CJ suggesting that *any* infringement of a right would automatically give the supposed victim a right of action at law? In *Ashby's* case the defendants had invoked the maxim *De minimis non curat lex* ('The law does not concern itself with trifles') contending that even if Ashby had suffered some damage it was so slight as to be unworthy of notice. This argument was rejected by the House of Lords. But that did not mean that an insignificant and purely nominal infringement of a right would entitle the 'victim' to judgment. The distinction drawn was between an *absolute* right, whose infringement was automatically taken to amount to damage, and a *qualified* right, where actual damage had to be shown in order to establish a cause of action. An example of this was the right of an easement of support, where the withdrawal of lateral support was not enough on its own, in the absence of actual damage, to found an action at law.

### *Rights versus privileges*

In *Ashby v White* the Declaration (i.e. the claimant's statement of case) referred to the plaintiff's entitlement to vote as a *privilege*. Lord Holt however described it as a *right*, which is the way it would now be thought of, and the maxim upon which the decision rested used the Latin word *jus* ('right'), not *privilegium*.

What is the difference between a right and a privilege? A privilege is a special right reserved to an individual person or a limited class of persons, bodies or institutions. Its grant is generally attended by some degree of formality in the form of letters patent or some other document. Rights, by contrast, are likely to be shared more widely, most often by the population as a whole. If we were to represent rights and privileges diagrammatically, privileges would occupy a small circle within a much larger circle of rights. Every privilege is a right but not every right is a privilege. So, the right of free speech belongs to everyone, but Members of Parliament speaking in the House of Commons enjoy a greater degree of freedom of speech than anyone else. The special rights enjoyed by Members of Parliament together form part of 'parliamentary privilege' established by the Glorious Revolution of 1688-89. With certain restrictions (e.g. matters which are *sub judice*) Members of Parliament can say what they like in the chamber, including remarks that would otherwise be defamatory. But this privilege is lost once they step outside the House. That is why an MP attacking a fellow-MP in a speech in the House will often be greeted with a challenge to repeat those remarks outside the House.

Would it have made any difference to Ashby's claim whether his entitlement to vote was classified as a right or as a privilege? No, because, as mentioned above, all privileges are subsumed under the heading of rights. So the infringement or removal of a privilege would be just as actionable as the infringement of a right which was not a privilege.

### *Powers versus duties*

Every right has a reciprocal duty. In *Ashby's* case the returning officers had the *power* to register the vote of every qualified elector, but they also had a *duty* to do so. To put it another way, Matthias Ashby's *right* to vote imposed a *duty* on the returning officers to allow him to exercise this right. From Ashby's point of view the returning officers' refusal to permit him to cast his vote was an infringement of his voting right, but it was also a breach of the returning officers' duty to allow all those entitled to vote to do so. Had the returning officers possessed a *power* without a *duty*, Ashby could not have succeeded in his suit. For, had the returning officers had a power without a duty, this would have meant that they could choose to register or not to register a voter at will.

### *Anns v Merton*

In *Anns v Merton*[3] a block of maisonettes was built on inadequate foundations, as a result of which the structure began to move, leading to the cracking of walls, sloping floors and other defects. The long lessees of the maisonettes sued the local authority for negligence in approving and failing to inspect the foundations. A unanimous House of Lords found the council liable to the lessees and the leading speech, delivered by Lord Wilberforce, came for a time to be regarded as a classic statement of the law of negligence.

The legal position of the local authority was governed by statutes which gave it the *power* to inspect the foundations of buildings in their area and to insist on any necessary corrections, but there was no *duty* or *obligation* upon the local authority to carry out any such inspection in the first place. The council in this instance approved the building plans showing foundations of '3 feet or deeper to the approval of local authority'. In fact, they were built only to a depth of two feet six inches, but the council never inspected the actual foundations.

Lord Wilberforce confronted the distinction between powers and duties head-on, but with a surprising result, claiming as he did that either of these could give rise to a duty of care at common law:

> It is irrelevant to the existence of this duty of care whether what is created by the statute is a duty or a power: the duty of care may exist in either case. The difference between the two lies in this, that, in the case of a power, liability cannot exist unless the act complained of lies outside the ambit of the power.[4]

The local authority, it was held, had a *discretion* whether they should inspect or not. If this discretion was not properly exercised then the council would be in breach of its duty of care to the lessees. On the basis of agreed facts this was found to be the case.

This decision went clean against a previous House of Lords decision, *East Suffolk Rivers Catchment Board v Kent*,[5] which was not overruled but only distinguished although its facts were arguably on all fours with those of *Anns*, as was tacitly admitted by Lord Russell of Killowen in his very brief concurring speech in *Anns*.

The *East Suffolk* case in turn rested on a whole succession of decisions going back a century and more, which enunciated the doctrine that, where there was a power without a duty liability would arise only where the power was exercised negligently but not where the power was not exercised at all. The principle was stated with his usual clarity by that great commercial judge, Scrutton LJ, in a case involving an injury sustained as a result of a fall by an (evidently somewhat intoxicated) pedestrian who had lost his way because a gas-lamp had been extinguished. He sued the local authority in negligence for plunging the area in question into darkness and thereby causing his accident: *Sheppard v Glossop Corporation*.[6] He lost his case on the basis of the principle, as stated by Lord Romer in the *East Suffolk* case, that: 'Where a statutory authority is entrusted with a mere power, it cannot be made liable for any damage sustained by a member of the public by reason of a failure to exercise that power.' Liability would arise only (i) where it was decided to exercise the power, (ii) the power was exercised negligently, and (iii) this negligence was the cause of the claimant's loss or damage.

In *Sheppard's* case the same principle was stated with admirable clarity as follows:

> There is no duty to exercise the power of lighting at all. Nor, if the local authority do light, are they obliged to light the whole of their district or any particular part

> of it .... In this particular case the local authority did not cause the danger; it was already in existence.[7]

These words were spoken by none other than Atkin LJ, who as Lord Atkin was later to become the architect of a greatly broadened view of duty of care in *Donoghue v Stevenson* and who, on the strength of his new vision, took a very different line in the *East Suffolk* case (where his was the sole dissenting speech) from the one that he had adopted in *Sheppard*.

### *Chronology*

It might help to summarise the development of this doctrine thus far in a chronology:

**Before 1977**: The established principle was that a body vested with a discretionary power could not be held liable for choosing not to exercise that power but only for exercising it negligently and thereby causing damage. This doctrine formed the basis of many cases, including:

*Sheppard v Glossop Corporation* (1921), where it was enunciated, among others, by Atkin LJ.

*East Suffolk Rivers Catchment Board v Kent* (1940), where Lord Atkin was the sole dissenting voice, disagreeing not only with his four brother law lords but also with himself in his earlier incarnation as Atkin LJ in *Sheppard's* case. What is more, Lord Romer could not resist quoting Atkin LJ against Lord Atkin in his speech in *East Suffolk*!

**1977**: *Anns v Merton* (1977). The House of Lords decides that the non-exercise of a power may import liability for negligence.
**1990**: *Murphy v Brentwood District Council*.[8] A House of Lords of seven members overrules *Anns v Merton* and all decisions based on it.

### *Murphy v Brentwood*

The facts of *Murphy's* case were on all fours with those of *Anns v Merton*. A house was built over filled ground on a steel reinforced concrete raft foundation which subsided causing major cracks and leaks. The design of the foundation had been approved by the local authority. As in *Anns*, the council did not actually inspect the foundation – or so it appears, as, amazingly, this issue was not even broached in any of the seven speeches delivered in the

House of Lords *Murphy*. As in *Anns*, the council had the *power* to inspect but no *duty* or *obligation* to do so.

Why were there seven law lords instead of the usual five sitting in *Murphy*? Because what they were really deciding was the fate of *Anns v Merton*, the leading case in the field, a House of Lords decision which had stood and been held in the highest esteem for some 13 years. Murphy is one of the comparatively few cases in which the 1966 practice statement was applied allowing the House of Lords to overrule an earlier decision of their own.[9] But that only makes it all the more puzzling that there was no discussion of the fundamental question about *powers* and *duties* upon which the earlier cases had concentrated.

The speeches in *Murphy* were scathing about *Anns*. 'I think it must now be recognised,' opined Lord Keith of Kinkel,[10] that *Anns* 'did not proceed on any basis of principle at all, but constituted a remarkable example of judicial legislation.'

### *'Pure economic loss'*

What, then, is the principle upon which *Murphy* rests? If there is any principle to be found in it at all it must be the doctrine that there is no duty of care arising out of negligent actions (as against negligent misstatements) for pure economic loss, for which damages are therefore irrecoverable. This unfortunately raises more questions than it answers.

*Murphy* is one of a group of decisions which stemmed the rising pro-claimant tide in the law of negligence. So, though the question about powers and duties was not actually considered in *Murphy*, it is highly unlikely that a duty of care would be found to arise on the basis of the failure to exercise a discretionary power.

### *Damnum absque injuria*

The House of Lords' restrictive definition of 'pure economic loss' in *D&F Estates v Church Commissioners*[11] and *Murphy v Brentwood District Council*[12] has led to a fairly common situation where there is no legal redress even though the claimant has suffered a loss clearly caused by the negligence of the defendant. The negligent plasterer in *D&F Estates* is an example of someone who caused a loss to the owners of the flat but was held not to be liable. There was no contract between the flatowner and the plasterer, so the claim could not be brought in contract. And, as the loss suffered by the flatowner was the cost of replastering, which was classified as 'pure economic loss', there was no legal remedy at all. Yet in *Junior Books v Veitchi*,[13] decided by a 4:1 majority by the House of Lords itself only a few years earlier, a claim had succeeded for the replacement of defective flooring. Likewise, the 'purely economic' loss in *Murphy*, as it was characterised by Lord Keith, was hardly distinguishable from that suffered in *Anns*, which had been labelled by Lord Wilberforce as 'material, physical damage'.

What the House of Lords was effectively saying in *D&F Estates* and *Murphy* was that this kind of damage did not infringe the claimant's rights – a highly artificial and arbitrary policy decision. All the more so indeed when it is realised that it is only certain types of 'pure economic loss' that are irrecoverable. 'Pure economic loss' arising out of negligent misstatements falling under *Hedley Byrne v Heller Bros*[14] is still a recoverable head of damage, but if the 'pure economic loss' arises from negligent actions rather than from negligent deeds the claim is doomed.

Such cases must now be taken as examples of *damnum absque injuria*, or 'damage without legal wrong' – a necessary corollary to the doctrine *ubi jus, ibi remedium*. Taken together, what these two maxims say is that there must be legal redress for the infringement of any legal right, but that where no legal right is affected a loss or damage must go unremedied.

More traditional examples of *damnum absque injuria* include such cases as *Gorris v Scott*[15] and *Phillips v Britannia Hygienic Laundry Co.*[16] In *Gorris v Scott* some sheep were being shipped on deck from Hamburg to Newcastle when they were lost as a result of being swept overboard by a freak wave. The owner of the sheep sued the shipowner under legislation, the Animals Order 1871, which required shipowners to transport livestock in pens fitted with battens, or footholds. The claimant's case was that had his sheep been penned in on deck they would not have been washed overboard. Although this was undoubtedly true he lost his case because the legislation on which he was relying was not concerned to prevent sheep from being swept overboard but rather to prevent sheep from infecting one another with a contagious disease.

The decision in *Phillips v Britannia Hygienic Laundry Co* is perhaps less understandable. A laundry company's lorry collided with a van belonging to the claimant. The accident happened when the lorry's axle, which had been negligently repaired just two days before, suddenly broke in two and a wheel came off, hitting and damaging the claimant's van. The case was brought under legislation requiring a motor car to 'be in such a condition as not to cause, or to be likely to cause, danger to any person on the motor car or on the highway'.

Atkin LJ (as he then was) put the position 'on this important and difficult question' as follows:

> I conceive the rule to be that when a statute imposes a duty of commission or omission upon an individual, the question whether a person aggrieved by a breach of the duty has a right of action depends upon the intention of the statute. Was it intended that a duty should be owed to the individual aggrieved as well as to the State, or is it a public duty only? That depends upon the construction of the statute as a whole, and the circumstances in which it was made and to which it relates. One of the matters to be taken into consideration is this: Does the statute on the face of it contain a reference to a remedy for the breach of it? If so, it would prima facie, be the only remedy, but that is not conclusive. One must still look to the intention of the legislature to be derived from the words used, and one may come to the conclusion that, although the statute creates a duty and imposes a penalty for a breach of that duty, it may still intend that the duty should be owed to individuals.[17]

It was held that 'it was not intended to impose a duty enforceable by individuals aggrieved, but only a public duty, the sole remedy for breach of which is the remedy provided by way of a fine.' So, though there was undoubted physical damage to the claimant's van as a result of the collision, the defendant laundry was not liable. The claim in common law negligence against the laundry company also failed, as it had not been negligent. But, after *Donoghue v Stevenson*, which was yet to be decided, there would have been a good claim in negligence against the motor garage which had botched the repair of the axle. Today, therefore, there would be a remedy for the aggrieved claimant.

### 2. 'Nobody shall profit from his own wrongdoing'

This principle, described by Coke as 'maxime of law', is quoted by him in the form 'No man shall take advantage of his owne wrong'.[1] Coke applies it to a particular property law scenario, but it is equally applicable to many other situations.

Its most obvious use is to prevent anyone from benefiting from his own criminal act. A good example of this is to be found in the well-known old New York case of *Riggs v Palmer*. An heir named in his grandfather's will had murdered the old man in order to inherit his estate. It was decided that, though strict construction of the statutes governing inheritance would have permitted the convicted murderer to inherit, there was an overriding general principle which negated this right: 'All laws as well as all contracts may be controlled in their operation and effect by general, fundamental maxims of the common law. No one shall be permitted to profit by his own fraud, or to take advantage of his own wrong, or to found any claim upon his own iniquity, or to acquire property by his own crime.'[2] On this basis, the murderer was debarred from inheriting from his victim.

A more recent English case illustrates a further extension of the principle: *Davitt v Titcumb*.[3] Julie Gilford and Gary Titcumb were lovers. They bought a house together. They were co-owners at law and tenants in common in equity, with Julie entitled to just over half the value. The purchase was made by means of a mortgage secured by an endowment insurance policy on the lives of both of them. If either of them died before the maturity date of the policy, the survivor would be paid the insurance monies. The insurance policy was duly assigned to the mortgage lender, a building society, which therefore took over the benefit of the policy. Just over two years later Julie Gilford was stabbed to death by Gary Titcumb. The insurance premiums had been paid to date and the policy was still on foot. Titcumb was convicted of murder and sentenced to life imprisonment.

There was no question of the murdered woman's share of the proceeds going to her murderer. The issue confronting the court was what to do about the murderer's share. The trial judge admitted that the facts presented him with 'a very real dilemma'. On the one hand, it could be argued that Titcumb's entitlement to his share was not affected by his murder of his partner. On the other hand, there was what the judge called 'the inescapable fact' that if the murderer was allowed to claim his share of the money, he would be 'claiming a fund that would not have come into existence but for his criminal act'.

It was this latter argument that carried the day, and it was decided that the murderer was not entitled to any part of the proceeds of the sale of the house as he would otherwise be benefiting from his criminal act.

Not only is the perpetrator of a crime himself debarred from enjoying any such benefit but also anyone whose claim depends on his. This was established in a surprising spin-off from the story of Dr Crippen, the notorious wife-killer: *Re Crippen (decd)*.[4] The murdered woman died without making a will. According to the rules of intestacy under English law, Dr Crippen would in the normal course of things have stood to inherit the whole of his wife's estate. But what was to become of it once he had been executed for her murder? Shortly before being hanged the doctor had made a will appointing his mistress, Ethel le Neve, as executrix and universal legatee of his estate, and she had the audacity to claim Mrs Crippen's estate as well. Her claim was given short shrift by the High Court: 'It is clear that the law is that no person can obtain or enforce any rights resulting to him from his own crime; neither can his personal representative claiming under him obtain or enforce any such rights .... The human mind revolts at the very idea that any other doctrine could be possible in our system of jurisprudence.'

Although the judge was applying the principle that nobody should profit from his own wrong, he actually based his decision on a specific statute, the Court of Probate Act 1857, which expressly gave the court discretion to override the normal law of intestacy in regard to the appointment of administrators in 'special circumstances'.

Likewise *Cleaver v Mutual Reserve Fund*,[5] in which a man murdered by his wife had taken out an insurance policy with his wife as beneficiary. It was held by the Court of Appeal that the wife could not benefit but that the money was payable to the deceased's executors who, instead of holding it on trust for the wife, would hold it on a resulting trust for the deceased's estate and for the beneficiaries of the estate, excluding the wife.

The principle has even been applied where there was no actual proof of crime: *Re Pollock*.[6] The dead bodies of a husband and wife were found at their home. It appeared that the husband had shot his wife and then turned his revolver on himself. The wife had made a will leaving her residuary estate to her husband, but his will had left his estate to other members of his family. The question before the court was whether the wife's property was to pass to the husband's estate and then go to whoever was named in the husband's will, or whether the wife should be treated as having died intestate. Even though there was no positive proof that the husband had murdered his wife, the fact that the wife was shot in the face and the husband in the mouth led to the conclusion that he had indeed killed her.

But what if the husband had been insane at the time? Clearly, then, he would have had to be found not guilty by reason of insanity. It was held, however, that, as there was no evidence of the husband's state of mind, the court had to proceed on the assumption that he had been guilty of murder. It was therefore decided that the wife's will should be disregarded and that her estate should pass as on an intestacy.

### *Exceptions*

However, not even the important principle against allowing anybody to profit from his own wrong has been consistently applied, and it has sometimes not been applied at all.

### *Mary Bell*

In 1998 something of a stir was caused in England by the publication of a book entitled *Cries Unheard* by Gitta Sereny. This dealt with the life of a certain Mary Bell, the original name of a woman who had served twelve years in detention after being convicted of manslaughter for killing two boys, one aged three and the other four, at a time when she herself was eleven years old in 1968. The reason the appearance of this book aroused such great interest was the report that Mary Bell had 'received a sum of more than £50,000 from the proceeds of publication of the book'.[7]

Although the amount involved was disputed, was this not a clear case of a convicted criminal benefiting from her crime? As it happens, there was a comparatively recent Act of Parliament dealing with this very question. The Proceeds of Crime Act 1995, an unnecessarily complicated piece of statutory draftsmanship, specifically gave the court the right to order the confiscation of the proceeds of crime. However, this right was expressly restricted to the period of six years after the relevant conviction: 'No application shall be entertained by the court under this section if it is made after the end of six years beginning with the date of conviction': Criminal Justice Act 1988, section 74A(10), as amended by section 5 of the Proceeds of Crime Act 1995.

On this basis it was decided that no action could be taken to stop Mary Bell from benefiting from her crime. The Home Secretary at the time, Jack Straw, was quoted as expressing impotent rage: 'Now Mary Bell was convicted many, many years ago, but I think that the population as a whole are deeply offended by the idea she should be making this kind of money out of those terrible murders, and so am I.'[8] Even the Prime Minister of the day, Tony Blair, was quoted as sympathising with the 'great distress and great anguish' of the victims' families.

An Act of Parliament therefore actually got in the way of the implementation of the principle that no one should profit from their own wrong. But what if there had been no statute at all? The position would probably not have been any better, as no one would then have had the right to apply for a confiscation order – in any circumstances.

What the Mary Bell episode shows is just how insubstantial a principle can be if it is allowed to float free. For this particular principle to have real practical effect in the future it would need to be enshrined in a less restrictive statute which would give practical backing to the principle by putting procedures in place to enable the principle to be applied.

It has to be said, however, that this is not the sort of problem that occurs with most other principles. But it does illustrate the paramountcy of statute law in the British Constitution – which is itself a fundamental principle.

But what if the author of that book had broken her contractual undertaking to pay Mary Bell her promised share and Mary Bell had then sued her for breach of contract? Here the ordinary procedure of a contractual action would have given the court the opportunity of adjudicating on the lawfulness or enforceability of the contract between Mary Bell and the author. Would the contract have been struck down as illegal? It is hard to say, as the criterion for such a decision is essentially a matter of public policy. Could a contract to pay a convicted criminal for collaborating on a book about their life be construed as a contract *contra bonos mores*, i.e. contrary to good morals? Such contracts have been held void. The only contracts actually struck down under this head have been to do with sexual immorality, such as contracts for prostitution. However, there is no reason why 'good morals' should be so narrowly construed.

### *Drug trafficking*

In the wake of the public outcry in 1998 over Mary Bell's profiting from the proceeds of *Cries Unheard*, the Home Secretary promised that the Government would 'look at the Proceeds of Crime Act', presumably with a view to broadening its scope. However, instead of this a judicial decision two years later actually made it more difficult for confiscation orders to be made.

This was in *McIntosh v HM's Advocate*,[9] decided by a 2:1 majority vote in the Appeal Court of the Scottish High Court of Justiciary on 13 October 2000. Robert McIntosh had been convicted under section 4(3) of the Misuse of Drugs Act 1971 of an offence involving Diamorphine, a Class A drug. He was sentenced to four years' imprisonment. His offence was clearly a 'drug trafficking offence' for the purposes of the Proceeds of Crime (Scotland) Act 1995 section 49(5)(a)(ii), which triggered the operation of section 1(1) allowing the court to make a confiscation order 'requiring the accused to pay such sums as the court thinks fit'.

After McIntosh's conviction the prosecutor applied for such an order against him, which McIntosh challenged on fundamental grounds. The problem in regard to confiscation orders is: How much should the offender be required to pay? For it is rarely possible to ascertain exactly how much a criminal has made out of his criminal activities. For this reason section 3(2) of the 1995 Act permits the court to *assume* that 'any property appearing to the court' to have been received by him 'as a payment or reward in connection with the drug trafficking carried on by him' could be confiscated. This section shifted the burden of proof on to the shoulders of the accused.

McIntosh challenged the legality of this provision on the ground that it conflicted with Article 6(2) of the European Convention of Human Rights providing that 'Everyone charged with a criminal offence shall be presumed innocent until proved guilty according to law'. Lords Prosser and Allanbridge agreed with this contention and found in McIntosh's favour. Allowing the court to make assumptions about the provenance of money in a person's possession was, they held, a clear violation of the fundamental right of the presumption of innocence. The fact that, though these assumptions could be rebutted, it was for the accused to rebut them, was a further argument in McIntosh's favour.

In his dissenting opinion, Lord Kirkwood, however, made the simple but trenchant point that an application by the prosecution for a confiscation order does not amount to a further criminal 'charge' against the accused. Such an application can be made only after the accused has already been convicted. In other words, the hearing on the confiscation order is not part of the trial but only of the sentencing process. The question of guilt or innocence does not arise at this stage: it has already been decided. And so, held Lord Kirkwood, the provisions for a confiscation order in the 1995 Act are not repugnant to the presumption of innocence.

The McIntosh case illustrates the problem arising when two principles are in conflict with each other – or appear to be so. On the basis of Lord Kirkwood's simple but compelling logic, there is no reason why confiscation orders need be seen as interfering in any way with the right to a fair trial. If, however, the majority view prevails, such orders will be doomed, to the detriment of the public interest in deterring crime.

### 3. The presumption of regularity

One of the most important principles in the law of evidence is the presumption of the lawfulness of any document or action: *Omnia praesumuntur rite et solemniter esse acta* – 'Everything is presumed to have been done rightly and properly' or 'Everything is presumed to have been properly and duly performed.'[1] Its most frequent use is in regard to documents, where it has been applied to deeds, wills and contracts alike. But it can be applied to actions as well.

The principle amounts to a rebuttable presumption of law, as is clear from the fuller formula also found in Coke's *Institutes*: *Omnia praesumuntur rite et solemniter esse acta donec probetur in contraria* – 'Everything is presumed to have been properly and duly performed until the contrary is proved.'[2]

The nineteenth-century case of *Gibson v Doeg*[3] is a good example. The residential lease of a house contained a standard covenant against use of the premises for business purposes. The tenant converted the whole place into a public house and grocery shop. The landlord knew about this but turned a blind eye to it, being happy to accept the rent for over twenty years. When the landlord sold the property the new owner sought to eject the tenant for breach of covenant. But it was held that the fact that the breach had gone on for as long as it had with the knowledge of the previous landlord was evidence from which a jury might presume that the alteration had his consent.

Where a document contained an attestation clause stating that it had been duly signed, sealed and delivered as a deed it was presumed that the document was indeed a properly sealed and valid deed even though it had not in fact been sealed.[4] But in a similar case the presumption was rebutted and the burden of proof shifted to the party claiming that the deed was genuine.[5]

Similarly, the date appearing on the face of a document is presumed to be its true date.[6] The maxim can also be used to select the most likely possibility in situations where there are two or more alternatives, as was explained by Sir Frederick Pollock CB:[7] 'Where the maxim *omnia rite acta praesumuntur* applies, there indeed, if the event ought properly to have taken place on *Tuesday*, evidence that it did take place either on *Tuesday* or *Wednesday* is strong evidence that it took place on the *Tuesday*.'[8]

### *Wills*

In *Smith & Smith v Smith*[9] the question was whether a will was validly executed. There were two witnesses to the fact that the testatrix had written something, but they did not see what it was and did not even know that it was a will. In the words of the judge, Sir J.P. Wilde: 'They were present, and saw something written, although they do not know what it was. There is a full attestation clause in the handwriting of the testatrix, containing her signature. The question is whether it was signed in the presence of the two witnesses. Is not that sufficient evidence that it was?'

The judge explained the significance of the principle:

> The presumption *omnia rite esse acta* is strong in a case like the present, and the Court ought to be very careful not to defeat the intention of the testatrix by setting aside the will, unless the evidence clearly rebuts the presumption .... If the Court were to hold that [the attestation was insufficient] ... it would invalidate a great many wills ....[10]

In *Harris v Knight*[11] the purpose behind the maxim was explained by Lopes LJ:

> The maxim, '*Omnia praesumuntur rite esse acta*', is an expression in a short form, of a reasonable probability, and of the propriety in point of law of acting on such probability. The maxim expresses an inference which may reasonably be drawn

> when an intention to do some formal act is established; when the evidence is consistent with that intention having been carried into effect in a proper way; but when the actual observance of all due formalities can only be inferred as a matter of probability. The maxim is not wanted where such observance is proved, nor has it any place where such observance is disproved. The maxim only comes into operation where there is no proof one way or the other; but where it is more probable that what was intended to be done was done as it ought to have been done to render it valid; rather than that it was done in some other manner which would defeat the intention proved to exist, and would render what is proved to have been done of no effect.[12]

Its purpose is precisely to protect genuine and honest people against an unduly technical and literalistic interpretation of the law. It has not always been uniformly applied, however. The test as stated by Phillimore J in *In the Estate of Bercovitz* is as follows:

> The vital question in my judgment is whether when they attest they intend to attest the operative signature of the testator, having seen or had the opportunity to see that signature either made or acknowledged.[13]

Applied to *Bercovitz's* case, the principle was held not to operate. The whole will was on a single sheet of paper, with the testator's signature at both top and bottom. There was an attestation clause at the top with the witnesses' signatures immediately below. Which of the testator's signatures were the witnesses attesting, the one at the top or the one at the bottom? As the witnesses' own signatures appeared just below the top signature the inference was that it was that signature which was attested. The Wills Act 1837 section 9 however at that time required a will to be 'signed at the foot or end thereof by the testator', and it was that signature which had to be witnessed. As the witnesses had probably not witnessed the testator's signature appearing at the bottom of the paper the will was held invalid.

This seems unduly harsh. The unusual lay-out of the will was clearly motivated by the testator's desire for secrecy, as one of the witnesses recalled that the whole page below the space for the signatures at the top was covered by blotting paper. The reason the law requires the testator's signature to appear at the end is precisely to prevent forgery. Otherwise a testator might be prevailed upon to sign at the top of a blank piece of paper, allowing anything to be added beneath. But the same might occur with a signature at the foot of a blank sheet of paper! And in this case, although the will itself was typed, a handwriting expert could presumably have compared the testator's two signatures, which seem to have been done within a short time of each other.

Though the will in *Bercovitz* was held invalid, the principle of *omnia praesumuntur* was accorded due respect. This was not the case in the much more recent first instance decision in *Wood v Smith*.[14] Two days before he died the testator had written out a document by hand headed 'My Will by Percy Winterbone'. He did not sign it at the foot of the document but it was signed at the foot by two attesting witnesses. One of these pointed out to him that he had not signed, but he said: 'Yes I have. I've signed it at the top', referring to the heading, adding that he could sign it anywhere.

The first question before the court was whether the heading constituted a signature. The plaintiff executors did not seek to dispute this, but they argued that the position of the words 'Percy Winterbone' invalidated them as a signature, and the judge agreed with this contention. The Wills Act 1837 section 9 had originally required that a will be signed 'at its foot', but this requirement was abolished by section 17 of the Administration of Justice Act 1982. On what basis, therefore, was the signature held to be invalid? The argument was that at the time the testator put his name to the paper in question there was no disposition of property on it, so *at that moment of time* the piece of paper was not a will. The argument is a clever-clever schoolboy's debating point, which ought to have been laughed out of court in the circumstances of the case. For there was never any doubt:

(a) that the *whole* instrument was in Percy Winterbone's handwriting,
(b) that it *did* contain dispositions of property,
(c) that the dispositions were penned immediately after the heading containing the signature,
(d) that the signature was attested by two subscribing witnesses who signed at the foot of the holograph will and only after the dispositions of property had been made, and
(e) that the phrase 'My Will by Percy Winterbone' is itself evidence of a clear intention on Mr Winterbone's part that the document he was executing *should* constitute a will.

Despite all these points, the first instance judge held that the will had not been duly executed and could not be admitted to probate. The Court of Appeal reversed this part of the decision, holding that the will had been duly executed, though it was still not admitted to probate on the ground of insufficient testamentary capacity.[15]

But why did it take a trip to the Court of Appeal in order to obtain the right decision on the validity of the will in these circumstances? The first instance decision may be said to offend against no fewer than three fundamental principles of the common law:

(i) *Omnia praesumuntur rite et solemniter esse acta.* In *Re Sandilands*[16] there was an attestation clause to a purported deed stating that the deed had been signed, sealed and delivered. The presumption that the deed had been properly sealed was held to operate even though there was no trace of any seal on the face of the document. This is not a million miles away from the case of *Wood v Smith* itself, yet the presumption was apparently never cited in that case either to or by the court, nor indeed on appeal.

(ii) *Benigne faciendae sunt interpretationes ... ut res magis valeat quam pereat;*[17] *et verba intentioni, non e contra, debent inservire.*[18] – 'A document should be construed in a liberal spirit, so that it is held valid rather than that it should be destroyed; and the words of a document ought to serve the intention of the parties and not the contrary.' These two closely related maxims of the common law are fundamental to the interpretation of any kind of document, enjoining a broad purposive approach. The first maxim requires a court to treat a purported contract as a contract, a purported will as a will, a purported deed as a deed – subject to negative evidence rebutting this presumption. Despite its obvious relevance to *Wood v Smith* this maxim was also not cited in that case. Applying it to Percy Winterbone's will would obviously have resulted in holding it valid, and an application of the second maxim would have resulted in an interpretation of the will in the way intended by the testator.

But these two maxims are doubly relevant. They are relevant not only to the will but also to the statute governing the execution of wills, the Wills Act 1837. The relevant section is section 9, which now reads as follows (as amended by section 17 of the Administration of Justice Act 1982):

> No will shall be valid unless – (a) it is in writing and signed by the testator, or by some other person in his presence and by his direction; and (b) it appears that the testator intended by his signature to give effect to the will; and (c) the signature is made or acknowledged by the testator in the presence of two or more witnesses present at the same time; and (d) each witness either – (i) attests and signs the will; or (ii) acknowledges his signature, in the presence of the testator (but not necessarily in the presence of any other witness), but no form of attestation shall be necessary.

The first instance judge interpreted section 9(b) as meaning that the testator 'must have made his will before signing it'. It is hard to see how this extremely restrictive interpretation could be derived from the wording, and this interpretation was rejected on appeal. But not only does this narrow interpretation serve no practical purpose; it also happens to fly in the face of a fundamental principle of construction of the law.

(iii) Precedent: precedent is of course the very life-blood of the common law, and there is no shortage of authority on the validity of wills. *Smith and Smith v Smith,*[19] discussed above, was a similar but far weaker case than *Wood v Smith*, yet the disputed will was upheld in the earlier case, which was not cited to or by the court in *Wood v Smith*.

### *Official acts*

The principle *omnia praesumuntur rite et solemniter esse acta* is particularly useful in authenticating official acts. It is presumed that a person purporting to act in an official capacity was properly appointed and is duly authorised so to act: *Ross v Helm.*[20] It is likewise presumed that the decisions of a court of competent jurisdiction are regular and valid.

### *Acts of Parliament*

The same principle is also applicable to the authenticity of Acts of Parliament. As long as a statute appears on its face to be valid, it must be taken to be so. The requisite formula is that it was passed by Crown, Lords and Commons. As long as a purported Act of Parliament claims to have received this threefold assent it must be taken to be valid, as was pointed out by Sir Edward Coke CJ in *The Prince's Case:*[21]

> If an Act of Parliament be penned by assent of the King and of the Lords Spiritual and Temporal and of the Commons, it is enacted by authority of Parliament, it is a good Act; but the most usual way is that it is enacted by the King by the assent of the Lords Spiritual and Temporal and of the Commons ... but if an Act be penned that the King, with the assent of the Lords, or with the assent of the Commons, it is no Act of Parliament, for three ought to assent to it, *scil* the King, the Lords and the Commons or otherwise it is not an Act of Parliament.

Four centuries later the same doctrine applies. Here is how Lord Reid put it in *Pickin v British Railways Board:*[22]

> The function of the court is to construe and apply the enactments of Parliament.

## VI.3. *The presumption of regularity*

> The court has no concern with the manner in which Parliament or its officers carrying out its Standing Orders perform those functions. Any attempt to prove that they were misled by fraud or otherwise would necessarily involve an inquiry into the manner in which they had performed their functions in dealing with the Bill which became the British Railways Act 1968 …

The presumption of the validity of Acts of Parliament on the basis of what they say on their face owes more, however, to the principle of parliamentary legislative supremacy than to the maxim under consideration.

Lord Diplock himself, that great advocate of increased judicial power in public law, conceded that even an administrative decision which was void ab initio 'should be given all the effects in law of a valid decision' if not challenged within the applicable time limit: *O'Reilly v Mackman*.[23]

### *The principle whittled down*

In recent years, in keeping with the general drift away from principle, the force of this maxim has been eroded by the courts.

In *Dillon v The Queen*,[24] a Privy Council case on appeal from Jamaica, a police officer was charged with negligently permitting two prisoners lawfully in his custody to escape. His defence was that it was for the Crown to prove that the prisoners were in lawful custody and that it had failed to do so. The Court of Appeal of Jamaica rejected this contention, holding that there was a presumption that the prisoners were in lawful custody. However, the appeal succeeded before the Privy Council, which held 'that it was essential for the Crown to establish that the arrest and detention were lawful and that the omission to do so was fatal to the conviction of the appellant .... The lawfulness of the detention was a necessary precondition for the offence of permitting escape, and it is well established that the courts will not presume the existence of facts which are central to an offence.'

The doctrine that a presumption cannot be used to establish facts central to the case in hand is supported by *Scott v Baker*.[25] A motorist who was found to be over the permissible alcohol limit in two breath tests and a blood test challenged his conviction on the ground that it had not been proved that the 'Alcotest' device used to test his breath had been approved by the Home Secretary. In fact, a circular had been sent by the Home Office to the police, magistrates and courts all round the country. But Lord Parker CJ in the Divisional Court described the idea that this circular could be taken as evidence of the Home Secretary's approval as 'naive', and found in favour of the motorist. He dismissed the contention that this should be governed by the maxim *omnia praesumuntur* on the ground that a fact as 'central' to the case as the Home Secretary's approval could not be proved 'by way of a rebuttable presumption' which had been challenged.

This seems remarkable, both because of the threefold evidence of the motorist's guilt and the circular sent out in the Home Secretary's name. Moreover, although the presumption was rebuttable it had not been rebutted, merely challenged, which is a very different thing indeed.

What is even more remarkable is that this case departed from the precedent of *Boyd-Gibbins v Skinner*,[26] where a motorist was convicted of exceeding the speed limit. The conviction was based on a law making it an offence to drive over 30 miles an hour 'on a road in a built up area'. There were no lamp-posts on the road in question, but it was held by Lord Goddard CJ that on the basis of section 1(7) of the Road Traffic Act 1934 there was a prima facie case that the stretch of road in question was in a 'built up area'. Lord Goddard made a trenchant point about this kind of challenge:

> It would indeed be a serious thing if the police, every time they prosecuted a person for driving over thirty miles an hour on a stretch of road which was deemed to be in a built up area, had to produce a witness from the local authority to give formal proof of the order containing the direction that the road was to be so deemed .... If, therefore, there is a sign of the type prescribed by the Minister under section 1(8) erected at the beginning of a length of road indicating a speed limit of thirty miles an hour, that in my opinion is prima facie evidence that all necessary steps have been taken to prescribe that that road should be regarded as being in a built up area.

VII

# Human Rights

## 1. Individual liberty

**It is sometimes assumed that the legal basis of individual liberty is the European Human Rights Convention incorporated as it is into the Human Rights Act 1998. In fact, liberty, or freedom of the individual, has since time immemorial formed the bedrock of the common law, and still does. Ironically, however, the interpretation now favoured by the courts makes the law less protective of the liberties of ordinary citizens than it used to be.**

### *European Convention on Human Rights*

'Liberty and security of person' are guaranteed by Article 5 of the European Human Rights Convention, which was incorporated into English law by the Human Rights Act 1998. Most of the cases under Article 5 have been brought to object to detention or imprisonment, and this is the way the article is generally understood. But does the wording not admit of a broader construction? 'Everyone has the right to liberty and security of person.' 'Liberty' is open to several interpretations, one of which is the right to do whatever you like as long as it does not interfere with anyone else's rights. 'Security' comes from a Latin root meaning 'lack of worry', or 'lack of anxiety'. What it means is the right to stay at home and go about your business without let or hindrance – without having to look over your shoulder all the time.

### *Common law*

Whether this broader interpretation can be read into Article 5 or not, it is part of the English common law – and always has been since time immemorial. Eighteenth-century Britain was renowned for its high degree of liberty coupled with a high degree of inequality. As we shall see, this combination is not a paradox at all. It was the French Revolution which lumped 'liberty' and 'equality' together – adding 'fraternity' for good measure. In a very real sense, however, far from being complementary, liberty and equality are at loggerheads with each other. This is discussed below in Excursus B to this chapter.

### *'An Englishman's home is his castle'*

This well-known adage actually comes from Sir Edward Coke's report of *Semayne's* case heard in 1605:[1]

> That the house of every one is to him as his castle and fortress, as well for his defence against injury and violence as for his repose; and altho' the life of a man is a thing precious and favoured in law; so that altho' a man kills another in his defence, or kills one *per infortun'*, without any intent, yet it is felony, and in such case he shall forfeit his goods and chattels, for the great regard which the law has to a man's life; but if thieves come to a man's house to rob him, or murder, and the owner or his servants kill any of the thieves in defence of himself and his house, it is not felony, and he shall lose nothing, and therewith agree [there follow citations of some old cases]. So it is held in 21 Henry VII c. 39 every one may assemble his friends and neighbours to defend his house against violence: but he cannot assemble them to go with him to the market, or elsewhere for his safeguard against violence: and the reason of all this is, because *domus sua cuique est tutissimum refugium* ('Everyone's home is to him the safest refuge').

Coke is here in expansive mode, explaining that although killing a man in self-defence or even accidentally is normally a felony, this is not the case when a householder or his servants kill 'in defence of himself and his house' a thief who has come to rob or murder him. Backing this up with authority he then goes on to cite a statute dating from the reign of Henry VII (1485-1509), a century earlier, which specifically allows a householder to assemble his friends and neighbours 'to defend his house against violence'.[2] The statute draws a sharp distinction between gathering supporters together at the house – which is allowed – and taking them on a vigilante expedition around the streets.

There are two key concepts here: those of home and self-defence. First, Coke is at pains to distinguish the legal position if you kill someone threatening your home from that if you kill someone anywhere else. Secondly, he stresses the importance of self-defence. But what exactly is meant by that term? The Henry VII statute is instructive here, as it permits a householder to 'assemble his friends and neighbours to defend his house against violence'. This can only mean that you are allowed under the law to prepare a welcoming party for the intending thieves or burglars and that you are exculpated if you kill them in the process.

This law does not appear ever to have been repealed. Unfortunately, however, it was not prayed in aid in the recent much-publicised Tony Martin case in which a householder shot at two intruders to his remote home, aptly named Bleak House, killing one and wounding the other. Tony Martin based his case on self-defence, but by a majority of 9 to 2 he was convicted of murder and wounding with intent and was sentenced to life imprisonment.

On appeal his conviction was downgraded from murder to manslaughter and his sentence reduced from life to five years' imprisonment.[3] The basis of this decision was a finding of diminished responsibility in reliance upon psychiatric evidence which had not been adduced at trial. The judgment of the Court of Appeal was delivered by Lord Woolf CJ, who remarked that:

> At the time the offences were committed, Mr Martin was being burgled by the two people whom he shot. Because he was being burgled at the time there was considerable public sympathy for Mr Martin and media interest in his case. There were also suggestions that the law was in need of change.

To say that Tony Martin had attracted 'considerable public sympathy' was an understatement. The reaction to his conviction for murder was little short of a public outcry. As for the state of the law, the main authority cited by the Court of Appeal was *Beckford v R*,[4] a Privy Council advice on an appeal from Jamaica. Solomon Beckford was a police officer who had shot and killed a suspect in the belief that the man was armed and posed a threat to the police officer's life. Like Tony Martin, therefore, Solomon Beckford pleaded self-defence but was found guilty of murder. However, his conviction was quashed by the Privy Council on the ground that the trial judge had misdirected the jury on the test for self-defence.

The correct test for self-defence was enunciated by the Court of Appeal in *Martin* as follows:

> When this defence is raised, the prosecution has the burden of satisfying the jury so that they are sure that the defendant was not acting in self-defence. A defendant is entitled to use reasonable force to protect himself, others for whom he is responsible and his property. In judging whether the defendant had only used reasonable force, the jury has to take into account all the circumstances, including the situation as the defendant honestly believes it to be at the time, when he was defending himself. It does not matter if the defendant was mistaken in his belief as long as his belief was genuine. Accordingly, the jury could only convict Mr Martin if either they did not believe his evidence that he was acting in self-defence or they thought that Mr Martin had used an unreasonable amount of force.

In short, the test for self-defence enunciated here is twofold.

First, the defendant has to have a 'genuine belief' that he was acting in self defence. This is subjective. He may be mistaken or his belief may be unreasonable. That makes no difference. As long as he really believes that he was acting in self-defence this limb of the test is satisfied. But then comes the objective limb: Did the defendant use a reasonable amount of force in the circumstances? In Lord Woolf's words: 'It is only if the jury are sure that the amount of force which was used was unreasonable that they are entitled to find a defendant guilty if he was acting in self-defence.'

Overarching these two limbs is the crucial matter of the burden and standard of proof. It is for the prosecution to prove either that the defendant did *not* have a genuine belief that he was acting in self-defence, or that the amount of force he used was *not* reasonable in the circumstances. Proving a negative is difficult at the best of times. Proving that a person did not have a certain belief, is virtually impossible, especially as the reasonableness or rationality of that belief is immaterial. Deciding whether the amount of force used was excessive is a little easier. But even this has to be proved to the criminal standard of proof beyond reasonable doubt if a plea of self-defence is to be rejected.

Despite the heavy evidential burden involved in disproving a plea of self-defence, the Court of Appeal made no attempt to disturb what they took to be the jury's rejection of this defence on the part of Tony Martin. Moreover, no distinction was drawn between self-defence in a home situation and self-defence in any other situation. The *Beckford* case mentioned above was the only authority on self-defence cited by the Court of Appeal. Yet the circumstances of that case were very different from those of *Martin*. In particular, Solomon Beckford was not in his own home at the time of the shooting. Yet, even in that case it was specifically stated by the Privy Council that: '… a man about to be attacked does not have to wait for his assailant to strike the first blow or fire the first shot: circumstances may justify a pre-emptive strike.'[5]

Was it not relevant that the man shot dead by Tony Martin was an intruder in the process of burgling his home? To the law of self-defence in homicide as stated by the Court of Appeal this fact would appear to be of no consequence. It is true that the relevant statute law, section 3 of the Criminal Law Act 1967, makes no specific mention of protection of the home either:

> (1) A person may use such force as is reasonable in the circumstances in the prevention of crime, or in effecting or assisting in the lawful arrest of offenders or suspected offenders or of persons unlawfully at large.
>
> (2) Subsection (1) above shall replace the rules of the common law on the

> question when force used for a purpose mentioned in the subsection is justified by that purpose.

The key words here are 'in the circumstances'. What this means is that the amount of force that is to be regarded as reasonable will vary according to circumstances. Is this not where protection of one's home against burglars comes in? Is this not therefore a relevant circumstance justifying greater force than might otherwise be the case? But does the provision in subsection 3(2) that subsection 3(1) replaces the rules of the common law not abrogate the old principle that a man's home is his castle? No, because 3(1) has built into it a variable in the words 'in the circumstances'. This is tailor-made to accommodate the old common law rule. And what about the Henry VII statute? If, as appears to be the case, it was never repealed, the applicable principle would be *leges posteriores priores contrarias abrogant* – 'later statutes repeal earlier incompatible ones'. This is the doctrine of implied repeal, according to which an earlier statute will be deemed to have been repealed if incompatible with a later one. However, it is not a principle which is lightly invoked, and is only to be used subject to another ancient principle: *generalia specialibus non derogant* – 'general words do not detract from specific ones'. In short, if the statute cited by Coke was not expressly repealed then it must still be deemed to be in force, as the provisions of the 1967 act cited above do not contradict it, and even if they did the 1967 Act, couched as it is in general terms, cannot overule the very specific provisions of the earlier statute.

## *USA*

A comparison with the situation in the United States is instructive. The relevant law is as follows:[6]

> The right of a person to defend his home from attack is a substantive right governed by rules analogous to those applicable to defense of the person, with the major exception that a person faced with danger of attack in his own home is under no duty to retreat. The modern rule as to homicide in defense of the habitation is that if an assault on a dwelling and an attempted forcible entry are made under such circumstances as to create a reasonable apprehension that it is the design of the assailant to commit a felony or to inflict on the inmates a personal injury which may result in the loss of life or great bodily harm, and the danger that the design will be carried into execution is imminent and present, the lawful occupant of the dwelling may lawfully prevent the entry, even by the taking of the life of the intruder. In such case, the occupant may meet the assailant at the threshold and prevent him from breaking in by any means

> rendered necessary by exigency, and upon the same ground and reason that one may defend himself from peril of life or great bodily harm by means fatal to the assailant, if rendered necessary by the exigency of the assault. This permits the taking of life in case the assailant purposes the commission of any felony, or other crime of violence to the purpose. In some jurisdictions statutes have been enacted expressly justifying homicides committed in defense of the habitation. Generally, however, a householder is deemed to have no right to take life to prevent a mere unlawful entry into his house, if the entry is not under such circumstances as to afford reasonable grounds for apprehension that the intruder's purpose is to take life, or to inflict serious bodily harm on the inmates, or to commit a felony.

Under US common law, therefore, Tony Martin would have been entitled to kill the intruder as he did. This becomes all the clearer if we take each test individually:

*Q. Was there a forced entry to Mr Martin's property?*

A. Yes.

*Q. Were there 'reasonable grounds for apprehension that the intruder's purpose' was 'to commit a felony'?*

A. Yes. Not only was there an 'apprehension' on Tony Martin's part, but 'both men were wearing gloves and carrying a torch and holdall bags'. It was accepted by the court that 'the circumstances gave rise to at least a very strong inference that they were intent on burglary'. (The term 'felony' is no longer used in English law, but burglary and robbery would both fall into this category.)

*Q. Was there a danger that this purpose was likely to be carried out imminently?*

A. At the time of the shooting Tony Martin was certainly under the impression that a break-in was imminent.

### *The Bulger murder*

In marked contrast to the way Tony Martin was treated by the English legal system was the treatment received by the young murderers of the two-year-old toddler, Jamie Bulger. Both were high-profile cases arousing very strong public feeling. In the case of Tony Martin public sympathy was plainly largely on his side; in the Bulger case the public were equally plainly revolted by the brutal and senseless murder of an innocent child. Yet in both cases the legal system was on the opposite side from that of public opinion.

Both cases were concerned with individual liberty, in Tony Martin's case in a twofold sense: first, his right to an undisturbed home life and secondly whether he had the right to defend himself against intrusions in the way that he did. In the case of the Bulger murderers the legal issue quickly shifted from the murder itself to the right of the convicted murderers to be released early coupled with their right to privacy and anonymity.

Tony Martin was partially successful in his appeal, as his conviction for murder was quashed and his sentence reduced from life to five years. But he was still branded a criminal, guilty of manslaughter, and left with a considerable amount of time to spend behind bars – in a situation where in the US he would not have been convicted of any crime. A further indignity was subsequently visited upon Tony Martin by the grant of public funding (what used to be known as legal aid) for the surviving burglar, a man with a string of convictions, to sue Tony Martin in a civil action for trespass to the person. By contrast, Tony Martin's own appeal against his murder conviction was privately funded, and it was only once his appeal had been (partially) allowed that his counsel was able successfully to request costs out of central (public) funds.

The two killers of Jamie Bulger were only 10 years old at the time, yet it was a brutal murder described by the trial judge as an act of 'unparalleled evil and barbarity' and by Lord Woolf MR (in 1997) as 'exceptionally horrific'. The murderers lured the child away from his mother at a shopping centre, abducted him, dragged him over two miles and subjected him to torture, including beating him over the head with a 28lb iron bar and subjecting him to sexual abuse before battering him to death and then laying his body on a railway line to make the murder look like an accident. They later even returned to the scene to join the many people laying flowers near where Jamie's body had been found.

After being convicted of murder, these two boys, Robert Thompson and Jon Venables, were sentenced to 'detention during Her Majesty's pleasure' under section 53(1) of the Children and Young Persons Act 1933, a mandatory indeterminate sentence with a tariff to be fixed by the Home Secretary for retribution (or punishment) and deterrence. The trial judge expressed the view that the murderers would remain in custody for 'many, many years' until the Home Secretary was satisfied that they no longer posed a danger to the public. He suggested eight years as the minimum tariff period, Lord Chief Justice Taylor recommended ten years and the Home Secretary finally set it at 15 years, but it was expected that the murderers would actually spend longer than this in custody.

The two young killers challenged this by means of judicial review – and won. The case went all the way to the House of Lords, where by three votes to two it was decided that the Home Secretary had acted 'unlawfully' by applying a tariff. By four votes to one it was decided that in fixing the tariff the Home Secretary was exercising a judicial power and, like a sentencing judge, should therefore have remained detached from the pressure of public opinion.[7]

The one law lord who was in the minority throughout was Lord Lloyd, who stressed that the question before the court was not whether they agreed with the Home Secretary's decision but only whether that decision was lawful or not. Lord Goff joined him in holding that there was nothing unlawful in the Home Secretary's policy to employ a tariff nor in the setting of the tariff period at 15 years. As for the *way* in which the Home Secretary had chosen to exercise the power entrusted to him by Parliament, Lord Lloyd made the trenchant remark that:

> If the courts are going to tell the Home Secretary how to perform a function which has been entrusted to him, and to him alone, by Parliament, then there would appear to be no limit to the bounds of judicial review. Of course, the court will interfere if the Home Secretary acts unlawfully or abuses his powers, or behaves unfairly, or on any of the other well established grounds of judicial review. But there was nothing remotely unfair in the Secretary of State assessing the tariff on the information which he already had, without calling for further reports.[8]

Lord Lloyd's was a voice of fairness, logic and common sense crying in the wilderness. But the majority in the House of Lords did nevertheless admit that a sentence of 'detention during Her Majesty's pleasure' was meant to have a punitive element and was not purely intended to rehabilitate youthful offenders. The Home Secretary's power to set a tariff was also accepted, provided it was sufficiently flexible to enable him to vary it in the light of the development of the young offender in question. However, the 15-year tariff imposed on the two Bulger killers was quashed.

The case went to Strasbourg, where the very right of the Home Secretary to be involved in the sentencing of Venables and Thompson was challenged - again successfully. The Strasbourg court pointed out that the fixing of the tariff amounted to 'a sentencing exercise', to which Article 6(1) of the Convention was therefore applicable. Article 6(1) guarantees a fair trial 'by an independent and impartial tribunal established by law'. 'Independent', said the Strasbourg court, meant 'independent of the parties to the case and also of the Executive. The Home Secretary, who set the applicant's tariff, was clearly not independent of the Executive, and it follows that there has been a violation of Art 6(1).' In addition, as the young murderers had been 'deprived' since their conviction 'of the opportunity to have the lawfulness of [their] detention reviewed by a judicial body in accordance with Art 5(4)', there was a violation of that article as well.[9]

The decisions protecting the privacy of Venables and Thompson are yet a further illustration of the way the courts have gone out of their way to favour them, as discussed in the next section of this chapter.[10]

## 2. Freedom of expression

**(1) Both common law and ECHR Article 10 protect the right to freedom of expression in the very broadest sense.**

**(2) Protection is accorded to individuals as well as to the press, but in practice the press and other media tend to enjoy special treatment.**

**(3) Where freedom of expression conflicts with other rights, freedom of expression generally prevails.**

**(4) Despite the claim that English libel law has a 'chilling effect' on the press, the law is now more favourable to the press than ever.**

It is often said that the rights recognised by the common law are negative, by contrast in particular with the rights accorded by the Human Rights Convention. Under the common law everything is lawful unless it is specifically prohibited. There is no law to stop you from picking your nose, so it is lawful. Is that the same as saying that there is a right to pick your nose? No. But it may well be that too much is made of the distinction.

Nowhere does the common law specifically guarantee a right of freedom of expression. It is a right which exists in the interstices between the laws governing defamation, obscenity, treason, confidence and the like.

### *The law before the Human Rights Act 1998*

In *Cassell v Broome*[1] Lord Kilbrandon remarked obiter that 'at least since the European Convention was ratified' there had been in the United Kingdom 'a constitutional right to free speech'.[2] The case was a *cause célèbre* primarily concerned with the award of exemplary or punitive damages in libel. There were no fewer than seven law lords sitting on it, of whom Lord Kilbrandon was the most junior, and none of the others made the point quoted above. Were it not for the mention of the European Convention Lord Kilbrandon's remark would hardly merit notice thirty years after it was made.

By 'the European Convention' Lord Kilbrandon presumably meant the European Convention on Human Rights, which at the time of his remark, in 1972, had not yet been incorporated into English law. That was only to come with the Human Rights Act 1998, which came into force in October 2000. Was Lord Kilbrandon suggesting that freedom of speech became a constitutional right through the ratification of the Human Rights Convention (in 1953)? The words 'at least' indicate that he was not quite sure. But the idea that the constitution could have been changed by the Convention reveals a rather strange notion of the way in which the British Constitution is made and develops. The Constitution is made up of three main elements: statute law, common law and convention, with the possible addition of authoritative old texts.

It is contrary to all principles of English law to suggest that the British Constitution could have been automatically amended by a Convention which had not been incorporated into United Kingdom statute law and which could be used only against the state (although so-called 'horizontal effect' has in fact crept in in practice), and then only by means of a lengthy and cumbersome process, first before a commission, and eventually a court in Strasbourg, whose decisions were unenforceable.

The truth of the matter is that freedom of speech had been accepted as a principle of the common law of England for centuries before the ratification of the European Human Rights Convention. The famous case of *Entick v Carrington*,[3] decided as long ago as 1765, was concerned with the attempts of the government to silence its critics by the use of general warrants. Lord Chief Justice Pratt declared general warrants illegal both in *Entick* and also in the saga involving that colourful rebel, John Wilkes (1727-97). In *Wilkes v Wood*[4] heard in 1763, Pratt CJ went so far as to pronounce general warrants 'illegal and contrary to the fundamental principles of the constitution'. But these cases were just as concerned about freedom of expression as about unlawful searches.

But the real protection of free speech came from the existence of juries. For juries were in the habit of acquitting those charged with sedition or with the writing of seditious libels. So, for example, in *John Tutchin's* case[5] in 1704, Chief Justice Holt, a judge noted for his fairness, concluded his summing up to the jury in these words: 'Gentlemen, I must leave it to you; if you are satisfied that he is guilty of composing and publishing these papers at London, you are to find him guilty.' But the jury used a legal loophole, finding Tutchin guilty of composing and publishing but not of writing the offending documents. As a result Tutchin was eventually acquitted. In *Entick v Carrington* Lord Pratt warned against this kind of jury nullification. Making it clear that he was no 'advocate for libels' and adding that 'calumny' deserved severe punishment, he made a plea to juries 'always to convict when the proof is clear'. He went on to reveal his understanding of the practical political realities of liberty:

> They [viz. juries] will do well to consider, that unjust acquittals bring an odium upon the press itself, the consequences whereof may be fatal to liberty; for if kings and great men cannot obtain justice at their hands by the ordinary course of law, they may at last be provoked to restrain that press, which the juries of their country refuse to regulate. When licentiousness is tolerated, liberty is in the utmost danger; because tyranny, bad as it is, is better than anarchy, and the worst of governments is more tolerable than no government at all.[6]

### *ECHR Article 10*

In *Attorney General v Guardian Newspapers Ltd* (No 2)[7] Lord Goff expressed the view that there was 'no inconsistency' between the right of freedom of expression under Article 10 of the Convention and the English law of confidence:

> This is scarcely surprising, since we may pride ourselves on the fact that freedom of speech has existed in this country perhaps as long as, if not longer than, it has existed in any other country in the world.[8]

'In the field of freedom of speech' there is 'no difference in principle between English law on the subject and Art 10 of the convention': Lord Keith of Kinkel in *Derbyshire County Council v Times Newspapers*.[9]

Could freedom of speech or expression be regarded as a constitutional right prior to the Human Rights Act 1998? As mentioned above, as early as 1763 Lord Chief Justice Pratt had declared general warrants to be 'illegal and contrary to the fundamental principles of the constitution'. The phrase 'the fundamental principles of the constitution' has a very modern ring to it. In using this strong language did Pratt LCJ intend to suggest that the principle to which he was referring was 'entrenched' or belonged to a 'higher legal order' which could not be repealed by ordinary legislation? Not at all. Indeed, he made the point in *Entick v Carrington* that if Parliament wished to legalise these general warrants that he had just excoriated as unconstitutional, all they had to do was revive the so-called Licensing Act, which had permitted general warrants but which had expired in 1693. In short, this eminently sensible judge recognised full well the principle of Parliamentary legislative supremacy, which indeed had been the basis of the 'Glorious Revolution' of 1688-89.

What about Lord Kilbrandon's 1972 remark (quoted above) about freedom of speech as a constitutional right? By 'constitutional right' did he mean to imply that it was 'entrenched' or that it belonged to some 'higher legal order'? If so, it is hard to see where he could have got that idea from. For it is a central principle of the British Constitution that no part of it is or can be 'entrenched' and that it does *not* constitute or form part of any 'higher legal order'.

Has the position changed in the thirty years since Lord Kilbrandon uttered his remark? The answer must be Yes and No. Yes, because very soon after, on 1 January 1973, the United Kingdom became a member of what is now the European Union, whose law was subsequently accepted as having automatically become part – and the supreme part – of United Kingdom law. The result is that where there is a conflict between United Kingdom law and European Union law, the latter prevails. European Union law is therefore in a sense a 'higher legal order' in the United Kingdom. (This is fully discussed in Chapter III.2.)

But what about the Human Rights Act 1998? Do the Convention rights incorporated into that Act constitute or belong to a 'higher legal order'? The wording of the Act goes out of its way to prevent any such effect, but it would not be surprising if the Convention came to enjoy higher law status as a result of judicial activism or indeed judicial supremacism.

Yet there are certain members of the judiciary who have a different view. Here for example is what Lord Steyn had to say on the matter after the Human Rights Act had been passed but before it had come into force, in *Reynolds v Times Newspapers*:[10]

> The starting point is now the right of freedom of expression, a right based on a constitutional or higher legal order foundation. Exceptions to freedom of expression must be justified as being necessary in a democracy. In other words, freedom of expression is the rule and regulation of speech is the exception requiring justification. The existence and width of any exception can only be justified if it is underpinned by a pressing social need. These are fundamental principles governing the balance to be struck between freedom of expression and defamation.[11]

There is no justification for this view, as is fully argued elsewhere in this book.[12]

### *Freedom and equality*

But how much freedom of speech is there in reality? Paradoxically enough, true freedom requires equality, which is a practical impossibility. For example, everybody has the right to mount a soapbox at Hyde Park Corner and sound off on whatever subject he fancies, but his voice will soon be drowned out by the person armed with a bullhorn or a megaphone, who in turn will find his freedom of speech eclipsed by someone who can reach millions through the printed word or who can command the airwaves of radio or television.

The effect of this disparity is particularly noticeable where an individual who has been unjustifiably maligned by the media wants to set the record straight. He can sue the publishers and journalists concerned for defamation, but, unless he is himself a millionaire, this is not usually very practical. There have been several private members' bills introduced into Parliament in recent years to give individuals in this situation a 'right of reply' in the newspaper or publication which wrongly attacked them in the first place. Not one of these bills has ever reached the statute book – further evidence of the power of the media.

### *Internet*

What about the internet, or the 'world wide web'? The internet allows anyone to communicate with potentially vast audiences at little or no expense. For once, as a result of a fluke of technology, the playing field appears just a little more level than before. But, inevitably, this was perceived as a threat by some, and the perfectly genuine concerns of the public about paedophilia, pornography, violence and national security have been used to curb the burgeoning of free expression on the internet.

Defamation law has also been used in this connection. So, for example, in a recent English case two website operators were ordered by the court to disclose the identity of 'Z Dust', the anonymous author of allegedly defamatory postings on their websites.[13]

The judge remarked that the postings were 'plainly defamatory' and that: 'The claimants are not seeking to discover whether a tort has been committed; that is plain from the evidence ....' And again: 'I have come to the conclusion that it was perfectly plain from the outset that the postings on both websites were highly defamatory and that, accordingly, the claimants were the victims of a sustained campaign amounting to an actionable tort.'

For a finding of liability for defamation it would not have been enough to examine the postings; it would surely also have been necessary to give the author the opportunity of putting forward a defence! Having branded 'Z Dust' a tortfeasor, the judge made a *Norwich Pharmacal* order for disclosure of 'Z Dust's' identity. This is a special type of discovery order which may be granted where a defendant 'has got mixed up in the tortious acts of others so as to facilitate their wrongdoing'.[14] This is all very well where it is known for sure that a tort has been committed. In the original *Norwich Pharmacal* case itself, for example, the application was brought by a pharmaceutical company which knew that its patents were being infringed but did not know by whom – a very different situation from that of 'Z Dust', where the allegation of defamation was just that, merely an allegation.

If this case is anything to go by it bodes ill for freedom of expression on the internet, as authors' identities will no longer be able to be protected, and website operators may even try to control what appears on their sites.[15]

### *Freedom of expression v freedom of the press*

It is a serious mistake to equate freedom of expression with freedom of the press – though this is often done, especially by newspapermen. In practice the rights of the press are favoured under Article 10 and even more so in the United Kingdom by HRA section 12. What has this to do with the common law? Everything, because it is for the courts to interpret these enactments, and their decisions then enter the corpus of the common law.

There is no specific protection in the Convention for freedom of the press, which indeed is not even mentioned there. On the face of it, therefore, the Convention treats individuals with the same respect as the press barons and media moguls. In practice this is not actually the case.

This comes through occasionally in judgments of the European Court of Human Rights in Strasbourg. See for example the unanimous judgment in *Informationsverein Lentia v Austria*:[16]

> The Court has frequently stressed the fundamental role of freedom of expression in a democratic society, in particular where, through the press, it serves to impart information and ideas of general interest, which the public is moreover entitled to receive.

The idea that there are different 'echelons' or levels of speech which are entitled to differing degrees of protection is the product of Strasbourg jurisprudence rather than anything in the Convention itself. According to this doctrine the press is entitled to enjoy the highest degree of protection, which must mean that where there are competing interests those of the press will be favoured – a thought which is likely to be as unsettling to some as it is reassuring to others.

### *Human Rights Act section 12*

As far as UK law is concerned, the rights of the press in Article 10 of the Convention are supplemented by section 12 of the Human Rights Act itself, which 'applies if a court is considering whether to grant any relief which, if granted, might affect the exercise of the Convention right to freedom of expression'.

Section 12(2) makes it very difficult to obtain an ex parte injunction against the press without notice. It provides that:

> If the person against whom the application for relief is made ('the respondent') is neither present nor represented, no such relief is to be granted unless the court is satisfied –
>
> (a) that the applicant has taken all practicable steps to notify the respondent; or
>
> (b) that there are compelling reasons why the respondent should not be notified.

This goes well beyond the ordinary rule generally applicable in these circumstances, as contained in Civil Procedure Rules 25.3:

> (1) The court may grant an interim remedy in an application made without notice if it appears to the court that there are good reasons for not giving notice.

In general, therefore, it is possible to obtain an injunction without alerting the other side to what you are doing as long as there are 'good reasons' for not letting them know. But when freedom of expression is involved there have to be 'compelling reasons' for not notifying the other side in advance, which makes it much more difficult for the applicant. What would such 'compelling reasons' be? During the committee stage of the Human Rights Bill through the House of Commons the then Home Secretary, Jack Straw, helpfully suggested that there might be 'compelling reasons' 'in a case raising issues of national security where the mere knowledge that an injunction was being sought might cause the respondent to publish the material immediately. We do not anticipate that that limb would be used often.'[17] This last throw-away sentence is the key to the purpose behind the phrase 'compelling reasons'. It is clearly intended to make it so difficult for applicants to go ex parte as to be virtually impossible.

What about the hybrid type of application traditionally known as 'ex parte on notice'? This means that only the applicant is officially represented but the other side can come along and raise points of law, but it is not an 'inter partes' hearing properly so called. This has the advantage from the respondents' point of view that they are not kept in the dark, but it is frustrating for them as well as they are not permitted to make proper submissions. Would this hybrid solution pass muster under section 12 of the HRA? Probably not.

But even if the applicant were able to persuade the court that there were compelling reasons why the respondent should not be notified, that would be unlikely to help the applicant very much, as sub-section 12(3) provides:

> No such relief is to be granted as to restrain publication before trial unless the court is satisfied that the applicant is *likely* to establish that publication should not be allowed. (Italics supplied.)

This restriction on what is termed 'prior restraint' is clearly intended to assist the press. The scenario it is concerned with is where a person gets wind of the fact that a newspaper is about to publish a damaging article about him and he then applies to the court for an injunction to stop publication. This sub-section makes it very difficult to obtain such an injunction.

Why is the word 'likely' used here instead of 'probable', which is the normal *American Cyanamid*[18] test for interlocutory injunctions? In *Imutran Ltd v Uncaged Campaigns Ltd*[19] the defendants argued that 'likely' represented a higher standard of probability than 'probable', and this was not disputed by the applicants, though the judge felt that 'the difference between the two is so small that I cannot believe that there will be many (if any) cases which would have succeeded under the *American Cyanamid* test but will now fail because of the terms of s 12(3)'.

Sub-section 12(4) goes much further in favour of the press:

> The court must have particular regard to the importance of the Convention right to freedom of expression and, where the proceedings relate to material which the respondent claims, or which appears to the court, to be journalistic, literary or artistic material (or to conduct connected with such material), to –
> (a) the extent to which –
> (i) the material has, or is about to, become available to the public; or
> (ii) it is, or would be, in the public interest for the material to be published;
> (b) any privacy code.

This effectively elevates the right to freedom of expression above all other Convention rights (except for freedom of thought, conscience and religion, which is given similar but much vaguer protection by HRA section 13). In reality it is not freedom of expression that is protected here but freedom of the press. This is clear from the phrase 'journalistic, literary or artistic material' as well as from the practical application of the section to litigation.

What is the relevance of the question whether the 'journalistic, literary or artistic material' in question 'has, or is about to, become available to the public'? This is a reference to the 'public domain' defence. If the newspaper or publisher concerned can say that the material complained of is already in the public domain there would clearly be little point in suppressing its publication. This was a problem encountered in the *Spycatcher* saga (see below). Amazingly, however, section 12 extends the same protection even to material which is 'about to become available to the public', presumably from another source, though that is by no means clear from the wording.

Then comes the 'public interest' defence. If the publisher can show that it is or would be in the public interest for the material to be published it must not be suppressed. Unfortunately, the press – and particularly those parts of the press least entitled to adopt such a stance – frequently don the mask of the guardians of morality when their true motive is probably profit derived from public prurience. There is no satisfactory definition of 'public interest', which plays into the hands of an already overmighty press. The *Naomi Campbell*[20] case is but one recent example of this, where at first instance it was accepted that there was no overriding public interest in finding out about the private life of a leading model but on appeal it was decided that there was such a public interest – with the resulting tail-wags-dog situation where costs greatly outweigh the value of the claim (see further below).

The only apparent concession that the section makes to the rights of applicants is the reference in section 12(4)(b) to 'any relevant privacy code'. But this too is designed to protect the press, not their victims. It is noteworthy that the reference is not to 'the right to respect for private and family life' contained in Article 8 of the Convention but only to 'privacy codes'. These are the codes applicable to the press and broadcasting media compiled by their own self-regulating complaints commissions. During the passage of the Human Rights Bill through Parliament Jack Straw revealed that the Government's intention in inserting this provision was to bolster press and broadcasting self-regulation. 'The fact that a newspaper has complied with the terms of the code operated by the Press Complaints Commission – or conversely, that it has breached the code – is one of the factors that we believe the courts should take into account in considering whether to grant relief.'[21] The Press Complaints Commission has been notoriously slow to find a newspaper in breach of the privacy code. So, if the courts act in accordance with the Government's intention and treat these codes with the same scant respect that is evinced in decisions of the Press Complaints Commission then this provision will prove cold comfort to applicants.

It is clear therefore that HRA section 12 offers the press additional protection over and above that already provided by the Convention. The British Government has freely admitted that that was their purpose in adding section 12. During the passage of the Human Rights Bill through Parliament the then Home Secretary, Jack Straw, casually remarked: 'We have taken the opportunity to enhance press freedom in a wider way than would arise simply from the incorporation of the Convention into our domestic law.'[22] Why was it felt necessary to take this 'opportunity'? And what about the rights of others that would inevitably suffer as a result of this enhancement of press freedom? There is no mention of this.

### *Freedom of expression versus other rights*

Taken together with HRA section 12, Article 10 gives freedom of expression precedence over all other rights. However, there are a few notable exceptions, but they are not always easy to predict or justify. Here is how the position was put in an oft-quoted Court of Appeal judgment:

> It cannot be too strongly emphasised that outside the established exceptions (or any new ones which Parliament may enact in accordance with its obligations under the Convention) there is no question of balancing freedom of speech against other interests. It is a trump card which always wins.[23]

The last sentence is often quoted out of context. Nevertheless, the dismissive tone in which the exceptions are referred to is significant. And in practice they are not accorded as much respect as might have been expected even from the wording of Article 10 itself.

A case where confidentiality prevailed over press freedom was *X Ltd v Morgan-Grampian Ltd.*[24] A draft business plan stolen from a company (Tetra Ltd, whose identity was protected in the English proceedings, where it was referred to as X Ltd) was communicated to a journalist on a magazine published by Morgan-Grampian. The journalist telephoned the company to check certain facts. The company sought an injunction to stop publication and an injunction under section 10 of the Contempt of Court Act 1981 for an order disclosing the identity of the journalist's source. It was held that the damage to the company's business outweighed the public interest in publication, so not only was publication prohibited but it was also held that the disclosure of the journalist's source was in the interests of justice, especially as the information had been imparted in breach of confidence. Disclosure was accordingly ordered as it 'overrode the policy underlying the statutory protection of sources'. In fact the journalist never disclosed his source and was fined £5,000 for contempt of court.

This victory of confidentiality over freedom of expression was short-lived. The journalist in *Morgan-Grampian* took the case to Strasbourg on the ground that the order to disclose his source infringed Article 10. By 11 votes to 6 the

Human Rights Commission upheld his complaint, and this was confirmed by the ECtHR by a majority of 11 to 7. The Court accepted that the aim of the disclosure order was 'legitimate', but held that the company's interests in knowing the identity of the source was outweighed by the journalist's right to protect his source:

> In sum, there was not, in the Court's view, a reasonable relationship of proportionality between the legitimate aim pursued by the disclosure order and the means deployed to achieve that aim. The restriction which the disclosure order entailed on the journalist's exercise of his freedom of expression cannot therefore be regarded as having been necessary in a democratic society, within the meaning of Art 10(2), for the protection of Tetra's rights under English law, notwithstanding the margin of appreciation available to the national authorities.

However, seven of the eighteen judges dissented on the ground that the domestic court was in a better position to evaluate the strength of the conflicting interests and that the House of Lords decision was within the margin of appreciation allowed to national authorities: *Goodwin v UK*.[25]

This decision plainly subordinated any conflicting rights to freedom of expression, and, in particular freedom of the press, which was bolstered still further by HRA section 12 (see below).

*Interbrew v Financial Times & others*

However, in a more recent case involving the leaking to the press of sensitive confidential (and in this case allegedly partially forged) company documents the Court of Appeal followed the House of Lords in *X Ltd v Morgan Grampian* rather than the Strasbourg court in *Goodwin v UK*. The newspapers concerned were ordered to reveal the source of the leak: *Interbrew v Financial Times & others*.[26]

Does this mean that the UK courts are free to ignore a Strasbourg judgment in favour of a House of Lords decision? Supposedly not, as section 2 of the HRA requires 'A court or tribunal determining a question which has arisen in connection with a Convention right' to 'take into account' any judgments, decisions, declarations and advisory opinions made by the European Court of Human Rights, the Human Rights Commission and even the Committee of Ministers of the Council of Europe. The operative phrase here is 'take into account', which is so vague as to beg the whole question of the status that Strasbourg jurisprudence should enjoy in the UK courts.

The key issue in these cases was whether the curbs placed on freedom of expression were 'necessary in a democratic society' within Article 10(2). There has been some unintentionally amusing judicial discussion of the relationship between *X Ltd* and *Goodwin* in this regard. There are essentially two questions here:

(i) Are the principles applied by the Strasbourg court in *Goodwin* and by the House of Lords in *X Ltd* the same or different?

(ii) If different, which set of principles should the English courts follow?

Some have maintained that the Strasbourg court in *Goodwin* established 'a stricter standard of necessity' than the House of Lords in *X Ltd* while others insisted that the principles in both cases were the same. But, if so, why did the two courts reach diametrically opposed conclusions? Schiemann LJ explained this difference quite simply in yet another case involving the leaking to the press of confidential company information: *Camelot Group v Centaur Ltd*:[27]

> In my judgment the tests which the Court of Human Rights and the House of Lords applied were substantially the same. I am conscious that they reached different conclusions on the same facts but this is a no more surprising legal phenomenon than this court concluding that a particular course of conduct amounted to negligence when the court of first instance concluded that the very same course of conduct did *not* amount to negligence. This phenomenon of judges coming to different conclusions although applying the same principles to the same facts is illustrated in *Goodwin's* case.

Not only, therefore, was there a difference of opinion about whether the principles informing *Goodwin* were the same as those set out in *X Ltd*. In addition, if there was a difference there was the question of which set of principles should be followed. It is less than reassuring that there should be such uncertainty on such important questions.

But even more remarkable is the view expressed in the passage from *Camelot* quoted above that appears to see nothing untoward in different courts' reaching different conclusions on the same principles even when applied to the same facts. What is the value of principles if this sort of thing is regarded as normal – or at least as not abnormal? And what does it do to the certainty of the law? Or to the whole concept of justice? For the more uncertain the law is, the more unpredictable it inevitably becomes; and the more unpredictable the law is, the less justice there is. If equality before the law means anything at all, it must include the principle that the law is the same for all; and this must surely mean that the appropriate principles must be readily identifiable and must be applied in the same way to all relevant cases. What hope is there for this if different results are reached even when the same principles are applied to the same facts? But, if principles count for little and the outcome of litigation is unpredictable, what determines the outcome of a case? By a process of elimination what we are left with is the power of the judiciary to make law. But is the rule of lawyers - or, more particularly, the rule of judges - the same thing as the rule of law (see Chapter V.1)? And, for that matter, what does this say about the level or indeed the existence of democracy?

But, even if these really big issues can be satisfactorily addressed, this still leaves unanswered the question: How did it happen that two courts reached opposite conclusions on the basis of the same principles applied to the same facts? And, more important, what can be done about it? The inescapable answer to the first question is that the principles of human rights law (to mention but one affected area of the law) are not sufficiently clear. This points to an equally obvious solution, namely to clarify those principles. That is something to which this book is intended to attempt at least to make a modest contribution. However, as long as the courts, both domestic and European, continue to take the law into their own hands by making it up as they go along and as long as there is either no power or not enough determination on the part of any other institution or group in society to challenge the judiciary, the situation is inevitably going to go from bad to worse, at the expense of the rule of law and democracy alike.

### *Naomi Campbell v Mirror Group Newspapers*

Even where there is a claim for damages without any attempt to stop publication in advance, the rights of the press are still likely to prevail over confidentiality. Naomi Campbell, a well- known fashion model, launched an action against Mirror Group Newspapers, who had published articles indicating that the model was a drug addict including photographs showing her attending meetings of Narcotics Anonymous. Naomi Campbell argued that her connection with this organisation and her attendance at their meetings was confidential and that there was 'no overriding public interest justifying publication'. She won at first instance but was awarded only £2,500 in compensatory damages plus a further £1,000 in aggravated damages.[28]

This was overturned on appeal[29] on the basis of 'public interest' following the guidelines laid down by the Court of Appeal in *A v B & Another, sub nomine Garry Flitcroft v Mirror Group Newspapers Ltd.*[30] A newspaper had been approached by two women who claimed to have had sexual affairs with a married professional footballer. The footballer sought injunctions to restrain publication of these accounts on the ground that this was a breach of confidentiality and would infringe the footballer's privacy. The Court's ruling on this was:

> Where an individual is a public figure he is entitled to have his privacy respected in the appropriate circumstances. A public figure is entitled to a private life. The individual, however, should recognise that because of his public position he must expect and accept that his actions will be more closely scrutinised by the media. Even trivial acts relating to a public figure can be of great *interest* to readers and other observers of the media. Conduct which in the case of a private individual would not be the appropriate subject of comment can be the proper subject of comment in the case of a public figure. The public figure may hold a position where higher standards of conduct can be rightly expected by the public. The public figure may be a role model whose conduct could well be emulated by others. He may set the fashion. The higher the profile of the individual concerned the more likely that this will be the position. Whether you have courted publicity or not you may be a legitimate subject of public attention .... The courts must not ignore the fact that if newspapers do not publish information which the public are *interested* in, there will be fewer newspapers published, which will not be in the public *interest*. (Italics supplied.)

There appears to be a blurring here of two meanings of the word 'interest'. They both have the same Latin etymological origin but they have come to be quite distinct. The difference is best illustrated by an example: 'There can be little doubt that the public – or a large part of it at any rate – have an *interest* in pornography, but does it follow that publication of pornography is in the public *interest*?' Few would maintain that it does. Yet that appears to be the argument in the *Flitcroft* case: namely, that as the public is *interested* in the peccadilloes of so-called celebrities there is a public *interest* in not suppressing publication of such material. This is a non-sequitur. As for the point about public figures as role models, that too seems somewhat strained. Does the fact that someone is a well-known football player turn him into a role model of morality? That footballers are role models to the young is undoubted – in areas such as fashion, hairstyles and drinking habits, but morality? Hardly. Does anybody really expect a footballer to lead an exemplary home life just because he is a 'celebrity'? And the point about the number of newspapers is equally strange. It is doubtless true that if a newspaper does not pander to the tastes of the public it may have to fold. But, first of all, would this be such a bad thing? And, moreover, is this an argument for a court? Why should the courts be concerned to protect the proliferation of newspapers on the basis of cheap intrusive sensationalist reporting?

Yet the approach to the 'public interest' set out in *Flitcroft* was applied to Naomi Campbell's case, with the result that the first instance judgment in her favour was reversed. The fact that the model had initially denied involvement with drugs before it emerged that she was attending meetings of Narcotics Anonymous certainly did not do her any good. Against the background of Article 10 of the Convention coupled with HRA section 12 the decision of the Court of Appeal ought not to have come as a great surprise. But why then was the first instance decision different? This only underlines the alarming uncertainty pervading the whole of human rights law.

### *Prior restraint*

With some surprising exceptions, HRA section 12 makes it very difficult to obtain a court order to stop publication of a particular book or article, or 'prior restraint', as it is called. As we have seen, one case where an order for prior restraint succeeded was *X Ltd v Morgan Grampian,*[31] but this decision by a unanimous House of Lords was later disapproved by a majority of the ECtHR in *Goodwin v UK.*[32] As mentioned above, section 12 of the HRA now makes it far more difficult than ever before to obtain prior restraint:

> (1) This section applies if a court is considering whether to grant any relief which, if granted, might affect the exercise of the Convention right to freedom of expression.
>
> ...
>
> (3) No such relief is to be granted so as to restrain publication before trial unless the court is satisfied that the applicant is likely to establish that publication should not be allowed.

If section 12(3) provides tacit protection of the press, section 12(4) (already quoted above) is, as we have seen, quite open about it:

> The court must have particular regard to the importance of the Convention right to freedom of expression and, where the proceedings relate to material which the respondent claims, or which appears to the court to be journalistic, literary or artistic material (or to conduct connected with such material) to –
> (a) the extent to which –
> (i) the material has, or is about to, become available to the public; or
> (ii) it is, or would be, in the public interest for the material to be published;
> (b) any relevant privacy code.

In other words, books and newspaper or magazine articles should not be prevented from appearing not only where their subject-matter is already in the public domain but also where it is 'about to' become public; and, in addition, there is that favourite journalistic argument, that publication is 'in the public interest' – a notoriously difficult and inevitably subjective test. As mentioned above, the reference to privacy codes may appear to work against the press, but in fact the opposite is true. The privacy codes in question are those incorporated into the Code of Conduct of the Press Complaints Commission and other similar bodies, which, with some notable exceptions, have provided little succour to individuals whose privacy has been invaded by the media.

The wording of this legislation clearly owes a good deal to the long and inglorious *Spycatcher* saga. In *Attorney-General v Guardian Newspapers,*[33] the House of Lords by three votes to two decided to keep in place interlocutory injunctions restraining newspapers from serialising extracts from *Spycatcher*, a book written by Peter Wright, a former British Secret Service agent. The two dissentients, Lords Bridge and Oliver, were not noted as radicals, yet they were, in Lord Bridge's words, 'in profound disagreement' with the majority. Lord Bridge adopted a characteristically commonsense approach. He fully accepted that *Spycatcher* contained material publication of which amounted to a breach of confidence on the part of its author. But, as the book had already been published in the USA, Lord Bridge rejected the remedy of what he called 'a futile injunction' and instead suggested an action for an account of profits. Moreover:

> The maintenance of the ban, as more and more copies of the book *Spycatcher* enter this country and circulate here, will seem more and more ridiculous. If the government are determined to fight to maintain the ban to the end, they will face inevitable condemnation and humiliation by the European Court of Human Rights in Strasbourg. Long before that they will have been condemned at the bar of public opinion in the free world.

Lord Bridge's comment on the likely outcome at Strasbourg was prophetic. In *The Observer & The Guardian v UK*[34] the ECtHR held that the injunctions were initially justifiable but that their continuation by the House of Lords after Spycatcher's publication in America amounted to a violation of Article 10 of the ECHR.

### *Douglas v Hello!*

When film stars Michael Douglas and Catherine Zeta-Jones got wind of the fact that *Hello!* magazine was about to publish unauthorised photographs of their wedding they immediately that very evening obtained an injunction from an English High Court judge over the telephone prohibiting publication of the offending pictures. On the following day there was a hearing before another High Court judge, who continued the injunction. *Hello!* immediately appealed against this decision. The case then went to a two-judge Divisional Court, who were unable to agree. So it was then heard by a three-judge Court of Appeal, which unanimously discharged the injunction. Of the seven judges who had considered the matter, therefore, three were in favour of granting the injunction and four were against. In view of the *Goodwin* decision in Strasbourg and, even more so, section 12 HRA, it is surprising that any judge would have entertained the idea of an injunction in these circumstances, especially as the order would have killed the relevant issue of *Hello!* completely, which the Court of Appeal was not prepared to do. As a sop to the film stars the judges indicated that in their opinion the Douglases had 'a powerfully arguable case to advance at trial' – though they must have known that without an injunction the case was most unlikely ever to go to trial. The real interest of this case is in regard to privacy.[35]

It also represents an attempt to give the Convention 'horizontal effect'. None of the parties involved was a public authority, though the Convention is meant to be restricted to actions against such bodies. Yet the case was not simply dismissed on this ground.

### *Venables & Thompson v News Group Newspapers*

A case with a very different outcome was *Venables & Thompson v News Group Newspapers*.[36] The application was made by Robert Thompson and Jon Venables, the two Bulger murderers, by then aged 18, shortly before the two were released on licence with new identities and possibly even some plastic surgery to disguise their appearance. They were successful in obtaining perpetual injunctions *contra mundum* (i.e. against the world at large) protecting: (a) their physical appearance; (b) their new identities; (c) their whereabouts; and (d) information about the seven years that they had spent in detention.

So ironclad is the protection afforded Venables and Thompson that when the *Manchester Evening News* published an artist's impression of what they might look like at the age of 18 it was found guilty of contempt of court and fined £30,000 plus costs of £120,000.[37] The scope of these orders is so wide that it is hard to think of any new information about the two murderers that *could* lawfully be published, and it must also be remembered that these restrictions are enforceable not only against the defendants in the case itself but against anyone at all who dares to contravene them. What if the two murderers were to kill again or commit some other crime? Could that be reported? If at all, presumably only under their new assumed names and without any indication of their true identities. Which would mean that the success or failure of treating them in this privileged fashion could never be tested!

On the face of it this seems an astounding result. Why should the perpetrators of the brutal and horrific murder of a two-year-old infant be accorded such exceptional, not to say unique, protection – and at public expense to boot? It was admitted by the court that 'until now the courts have not granted injunctions in the circumstances which arise in this case'. So what made this case different? Simply the likelihood that, if their identities and whereabouts were known, the two murderers would be pursued. 'Among the pursuers may well be those intent on revenge.'[38] But the real question is *why* these particular murderers should be at such great risk. The gruesome nature of their crime and the youthful innocence of their victim is not enough to explain it. The problem is the widespread public perception that they have not been adequately punished for what they did. Had they emerged from a proper adult prison after fifteen years behind bars – the tariff proposed by the Home Secretary – the chances of a revenge attack on them would have been minimal, and there would have been no need for any special measures to protect them. What message does the special treatment that these murderers have enjoyed send to other violent youngsters? Or to the parents of vulnerable young children? Or for that matter, to the public at large? Taken together with some other recent cases it is not difficult to see how this decision may strengthen the cynical observation that convicted murderers belong to a specially favoured class of litigants.

Public perceptions aside, what is the legal basis for this remarkable decision? 'In my judgment,' concluded Butler-Sloss P, 'the case stands or falls on the application to it of the law of confidence.' The law of confidence or confidentiality has come to be used to fill the gap in English law occupied in other systems by a law of privacy. But why should information about convicted murderers be confidential?

Butler-Sloss P freely admitted that section 12 HRA and ECHR Article 10 'together give an enhanced importance to freedom of expression and consequently the right to publish'. However, her judgment goes on to attempt to justify the remarkable restrictions on freedom of expression contained in the injunctions granted to the two Bulger killers. Turning first to Article 10 itself, Butler-Sloss P remarked: 'The right to confidence is, however, a recognised exception within Art 10(2) ....'[39] In fact, however, the scope of this exception is far narrower than that of the law of confidence as developed by the English courts. '... in the vast majority of cases,' said Lord Goff in a leading case on confidentiality, 'the duty of confidence will arise from a transaction or relationship between the parties ... but it is well settled that a duty of confidence may arise in equity independently of such cases': *Attorney General v Guardian Newspapers (No 2).*[40] In what circumstances could a duty of confidence arise in the absence of any transaction or relationship between the parties? It is in this area that the law of confidence has expanded to fill the void in English law as a result of the absence of a law of privacy.

But Article 10 does not appear to include this extension. Article 10(2) refers specifically to 'preventing the disclosure of information received in confidence'. It is hard to see how this could possibly apply to information obtained by a newspaper about convicted murderers. In normal circumstances, anyone offering such information to the press would be most unlikely to ask for it to be treated as confidential. On the contrary, provided his financial reward was adequate an informant would probably be only too happy to see it in print. But what if this information had originally been imparted to this informant in confidence? Would the informant's broken duty of confidence automatically pass to the newspaper, so that it could be said that the information was 'received in confidence' by the paper? It is hard to see how it could.

Butler-Sloss P even prayed in aid of her protective injunctions ECHR Articles 2, 3 and 8. These articles oblige contracting states to uphold everyone's right to life (Article 2), to prevent anyone from being 'subjected to torture or to inhuman or degrading treatment or punishment' (Article 3), and to maintain everyone's 'right to respect for his private and family life, his home and correspondence' (Article 8). Butler-Sloss P's argument appears to run along the following lines: As the courts are 'public authorities', it is their duty to see to it that the rights of the vulnerable young murderers are not interfered with by vigilantes out for revenge.

There is only one thing wrong with this argument and that is: Why should the courts be more concerned with the rights of two brutal killers than with those of anyone else? In particular, what about the rights of Jamie Bulger? It is ironical indeed that these three rights should have been singled out, for these are the very rights of which that innocent little child was deprived. He was tortured, killed and torn from the bosom of his family.

In a radio interview Lord Woolf CJ specifically expressed his support for the anonymity granted to the young killers: 'It would not bring baby Bulger back to life if one or other of those young men had in turn been killed.'[41] As a statement of biological fact this is incontrovertible, but what does it say about the attitude of the courts to criminals and their victims? If murderers were given the punishment that the public believed they deserved, that might or might not act as a deterrent. But would it not at least indicate a more positive attitude towards the rights of the law-abiding population as a whole?

## VII. Human Rights

### *Shouting 'Fire!'*

Do you have the right to shout 'Fire!' in a crowded theatre when there is no fire? This has never actually been tested in a court of law, but it is generally assumed that such a right would not exist because your cry may cause a stampede resulting in injury or even death. But are we asking the right question? The proper question to ask should surely be not whether you have the right to shout 'Fire!' but rather whether you could be held legally responsible for any damage resulting from your cry. To establish legal liability it would have to be shown that it was 'reasonably foreseeable' that your cry would result in a dangerous stampede and that your cry actually caused the stampede and the ensuing injuries. Though ignorant of the legal niceties required for legal liability most people would nevertheless recognise the danger of shouting 'Fire!' in a crowded theatre.

In *Wilkinson v Downton*[42] a practical joker went round to his friend's house and announced to his wife: 'Your husband has been smashed up in an accident and is lying at the Elms pub with both legs broken.' In fact the whole story was a fabrication, but the wife went into shock. The practical joker was found liable in tort and had to pay the wife £100 in general damages.

Does this mean that there is no right to make remarks to people to which they may react badly? No, it does not mean that at all, but it is as well to consider their likely reaction before embarking on a career as a practical joker. This is common sense, which cannot however curtail the legal right of freedom of speech.

Similarly, though there is no doubt a right to shout 'Fire!' in a crowded theatre, reflection upon the likely consequences may well inhibit the prospective shouter from actually doing so. In this way, he will be limiting his own rights by reference to the rights of his fellow theatregoers - notably the right to live their lives without interference by others.

The panic and stampede following a false alarm might easily result in injury or even death. So, one person's right to shout 'Fire!' for his own personal amusement must be balanced against the right of the theatregoers in general not to have their lives placed in danger. This problem has often been discussed, among others, by the US Supreme Court Justice Oliver Wendell Holmes Jr (1841-1935). Two socialists were convicted in 1917 of attempting to cause insubordination amongst soldiers drafted to fight in World War I. Although the pamphlet published for this purpose did not call upon the draftees to use unlawful or violent means to oppose the draft, in the circumstances, held Holmes, it created 'a clear and present danger', so their conviction was justified: *Schenk v United States*.[43]

## *VII.2. Freedom of expression*

> The most stringent protection of free speech would not protect a man in falsely shouting fire in a theater, and causing a panic. It does not even protect a man from an injunction against uttering words that may have all the effect of force.

This is particularly noteworthy in view of Holmes's reputation as a champion of human rights. Alan Dershowitz, a modern American liberal jurist, has gone so far as to suggest that falsely shouting 'Fire!' in a crowded theatre is not speech at all. Characterising Holmes's view as a 'flawed analogy' and a 'silly argument', he urges:

> So let us hear no more nonsensical analogies to shouting fire in a crowded theater. Those who seek to censor speech will just have to come up with a somewhat more cogent illustration – one that bears at least some relationship to real speech.[44]

But, if shouting 'Fire!' is *not* speech, what is it? Dershowitz recognises that falsely shouting 'Fire!' in a crowded theatre does not deserve legal protection but he does not want it to be used as the basis for what he calls 'censorship'. With the shouting of 'Fire' out of the way as irrelevant to the question of freedom of speech, any form of 'real speech' will qualify for legal protection.

This is all the more surprising in view of the wide definition of 'speech' that the US Supreme Court is prepared to accept. Even flag-burning is now classified as speech – and speech which *does* qualify for First Amendment protection! See for example two cases both decided by a 5:4 majority: *Texas v Johnson;*[45] *Eichman v United States.*[46]

Falsely shouting 'Fire!' in a crowded theatre clearly is speech, but speech which does not enjoy legal protection. Other examples of speech – including what the US Supreme Court calls 'symbolic speech' or 'nonverbal expression' – will qualify for protection according to its nature and the circumstances in which it is used.

Shouting fire is not just a theoretical conundrum but an important practical problem for any democracy: In what circumstances can the right of free expression be curbed, or, to put it another way, to what other right or rights could freedom of expression yield precedence? Perhaps the most important practical manifestation of this problem is in regard to revolutionary or anti-social views.

### *National security*

Can a government invoke national security to starve certain groups or organisations of what Margaret Thatcher called 'the oxygen of publicity'? An attempt by her Government to do so backfired because of inept wording. In 1988 the Government issued notices to the BBC and the Independent Broadcasting Authority requiring them 'to refrain at all times from sending any broadcast matter ... where the person speaking the words represents or purports to represent' one of the named organisations. The broadcasting media easily got round this over-precise wording by having the offending words dubbed by a 'voice-over'. This resulted in the comical spectacle of spokesmen for the named organisations being seen on television but appearing to speak in a beautifully clear actor's voice instead of in their own sometimes less than perfectly modulated tones. As a result, far from starving them of the oxygen of publicity this exercise gave them greater publicity than ever plus entertaining novelty value.

One may wonder, then, why a legal challenge was launched against the Government's directives. In fact, the case, brought by a number of broadcast journalists, went all the way up to the House of Lords: *Brind v Secretary of State for the Home Department*.[47] The Government sought to justify its directives on the ground that they were necessary in the public interest to combat terrorism. In the judicial review hearings in the English domestic courts it was held that this reasoning could hardly be regarded as '*Wednesbury* unreasonable'. As the ECHR had not yet been incorporated into English law, an application was then lodged with the European Commission of Human Rights under Article 10 of the Convention: *Brind v UK*.[48] But the applicants were rebuffed again. The Commission recognised 'the need to protect the State and the public against armed conspiracies seeking to overthrow the democratic order which guarantees this freedom and other human rights'. As the UK Government's measures were not 'disproportionate to the aim sought to be pursued' and 'bearing in mind the margin of appreciation permitted to States', the Commission found the application inadmissible.

Would these decisions have been any different if the words of the spokespeople of the named organisations had been suppressed altogether instead of the ludicrous situation which actually obtained where their words were only too clearly heard, as they were spoken by actors? It is hard to say, though the Commission certainly was aware of the true situation.

### *Spycatcher*

The *Spycatcher* saga is also in point here. When the interlocutory injunctions mentioned above were put in place against *The Guardian* and *The Observer*, three other newspapers began publishing extracts from the disputed book.

Did this amount to a contempt of court? On the one hand, it seems strange that someone who is not a party to the original action can be held in contempt for doing something which on the face of things he is perfectly entitled to do. On the other hand, however, for one newspaper to contravene a publishing ban placed by a court on another newspaper makes a nonsense of the court ban. In *Attorney-General v Times Newspapers*[49] it was held by the House of Lords that where C knowingly impedes or interferes with the administration of justice in an action between A and B, C is in contempt of court. By publishing extracts of the book, it was held, the three other newspapers had put into the public domain material which the Government sought to keep confidential, and for this reason was guilty of a contempt of court.

Though never challenged in the ECtHR, this facet of *Spycatcher* seems also to be under threat, as appears from *Attorney-General v Punch.*[50] In 1997 the Attorney-General had obtained an injunction restraining David Shayler, a former member of the Security Service, from disclosing information obtained by him relating to security or intelligence matters. Some three years later, however, an article by David Shayler on the Bishopsgate bombing appeared in *Punch* magazine. A majority of the Court of Appeal, reversing the judge at first instance, held that this did not amount to a contempt of court as the Attorney-General 'had not established that [Mr Shayler] knew that the publication [of the *Punch* article] would interfere with the course of justice by defeating the purpose underlying the injunctions and had therefore failed to prove the necessary element of mens rea'.

It was also held that an attempt to extend the injunction to cover the *Punch* article was contrary to section 12(3) of the HRA (see above) and, moreover, was 'disproportionate to any public interest' and therefore a violation of Article 10 of the ECHR.

This decision shows how difficult it is likely to be for the UK Government to bring proceedings for contempt against anyone who is not directly bound by an injunction. This may seem strange in view of the fact that the derogations from freedom of expression contained in Article 10(2) expressly include 'preventing the disclosure of information received in confidence'.

It should be mentioned on the other side, however, that the Government *was* successful in prosecuting David Shayler for disclosing information and documents contrary to the Official Secrets Act 1989, the hearings before the Court of Appeal and House of Lords coming in the immediate aftermath of the terrorist attack on the World Trade Center in New York on 11 September 2001.[51] The House of Lords, affirming the decisions below, rejected the defence that disclosure had been 'necessary in the public interest'. That defence, it was held, was not available under the relevant sections of the

Official Secrets Act, which however did not mean that those sections were not compatible with Article 10 of the ECHR, because the Official Secrets Act provided a built-in machinery for security agents to obtain authorisation for disclosure; and a refusal of such authorisation could always be challenged by way of judicial review. Moreover, 'public interest' cut both ways, as there must also surely be a public interest in national security. Applying the principle of proportionality, a favourite European import of comparatively recent vintage, Lord Hope concluded that the restrictions on freedom of expression in the Official Secrets Act were not disproportionate to the protection of national security.

### *Defamation versus freedom of expression*

On the face of it the English law of defamation looks as though it favours claimants. This is well illustrated by the tongue-in-cheek summary provided by Tony Weir in his *Casebook on Tort*.[52] Describing defamation as 'the oddest' of torts, he goes on to explain that the claimant 'can get damages (swingeing damages!) for a statement made to others without showing that the statement was untrue, without showing that the statement did him the slightest harm, and without showing that the defendant was in any way wrong to make it (much less that the defendant owed him any duty of any kind)'.

This is all perfectly true. What it does not mention, however, is that there is no legal aid for defamation and that bringing a claim can be ruinously expensive. As a result, it is generally only 'celebrities' and the super-rich who can contemplate using this blunt legal instrument. The outcome is frequently unpredictable, making it even less appealing to the ordinary person who has been mauled by the press. And, perhaps most important of all, being a claimant in a defamation case is not dissimilar from being a defendant in a criminal prosecution. By bringing such a claim you are effectively putting yourself in the dock. As in a criminal prosecution, the burden of proof is on the other side, but as a defamation claimant you are practically inviting them to repeat the bad things they said about you - and any report of the court proceedings is privileged.

Yet the press are convinced that *they* are disadvantaged by the law of libel. A recent academic book on *Libel and the Media* is sub-titled *The Chilling Effect*[53] to reflect the supposedly negative effect that the law of libel has on the media. One recommendation for reform is that the burden of proof should be on the claimant and not the defendants, as it has always been up to now. Under the present law, there is a presumption that the offending statement is false. If the defendants can prove that it is true they will succeed on the defence of what is termed justification. One can just imagine what would happen if the burden were to shift to the claimant. This would mean that the victim of a scurrilous press campaign alleging, for example, unspeakable sexual excesses on his part would have to prove a negative, which is difficult enough at the best of times. But in this case his whole life would come under scrutiny, putting him on the defensive even more than a defendant in a criminal prosecution. This would be quite intolerable. But the arguments for such a reform are, first, that the presumption of falsity is incompatible with freedom of speech and, secondly, that: 'After all, the plaintiff will always know the truth about his or her conduct.'[54]

This may appear plausible, but it represents a serious threat to the rights of the individual. The following points are worth bearing in mind:

(a) For the media to equate freedom of the press with freedom of expression generally is seriously misleading. In theory individuals have the same rights as the press barons but their rights are meaningless unless backed by financial muscle and political clout. If what an individual – or even a group of people – wishes to say does not have the right backing it will never be heard and may effectively be suppressed. In such circumstances press freedom and individual freedom of speech may actually be opposed to each other. The press is highly protective of their own rights but much less so of the rights of others, especially those who disagree with them.

(b) If the victims of press attacks had a genuine right of reply then perhaps the presumption of falsity of any statement which formed the subject of a libel action might be less excusable.

(c) In addition, there are other rights, such as the right not to have one's name and reputation ruined by inaccurate or misleading reporting – and of course the right of privacy.

(d) Why is there not some other remedy available to curb press excesses? The self-regulation which is meant to be provided by the Press Complaints Commission simply does not work, which is hardly surprising when it is realised that this body is made up largely of editors of newspapers. A light slap on the wrist is occasionally administered to a newspaper which has overstepped the mark, but it is difficult for a complainant to achieve even this degree of success. The press is one of the last bastions of self-regulation. The situation cries out for a proper independent regulatory regime which strikes a genuine balance between press freedom and the rights of individuals, but the power of the press moguls is far too great to allow any such system ever to be established.

(e) To oblige a claimant to prove his own innocence would be the ultimate indignity and would place individuals at the mercy of the press even more than is already the case now.

(f) Even the authors of *Libel and the Media* recognise that 'some tabloids will carry stories with known libel risks owing to the fear that otherwise their rivals will have exclusive coverage or because the stories are just too good to ignore; it is a nice question whether this on occasion amounts to reckless behaviour'.[55]

If English libel law does indeed have a 'chilling effect' on freedom of expression it inhibits those parts of the media which least deserve to be affected, and in particular the serious broadsheets and publishers of books. One particularly irksome aspect of the law is the need to check for accidental defamation.

In an amusing leading case a Sunday newspaper ran a light-hearted article in which a certain Artemus Jones, described as a churchwarden at Peckham, was said to have been seen at the Dieppe motor races 'with a woman who is not his wife, who must be you know – the other thing!' The author of the piece had assumed that the name Artemus Jones was fictitious, but there was a real Artemus Jones, a barrister, who sued the paper for defamation on the basis that anyone who knew him would have thought it was about him, even though he was not a churchwarden, did not come from Peckham and had not been to Dieppe. He was awarded damages of £1,750, – a lot of money in 1910 – a jury award which was upheld by both the Court of Appeal and the House of Lords: *Hulton & Co Ltd v Jones*.[56] It may seem unfair to penalise the press for an innocent mistake like this – and to force every author and publisher to check every intended fictitious name against records. Yet this is the least that the victim of such a libel would expect. This aspect of libel law is rare and has no effect whatsoever on the most irresponsible branch of the press, namely the tabloids.

### *Damages*

What the public associates most with libel is the astronomical awards of damages made in some high-profile cases – sometimes for apparently trivial insults. Until recently you were likely to be awarded more for injured pride than for broken bones or paralysis. This was commonly blamed on the libel juries, but it was not really their fault. Ironically, it was at least partly the fault of the very tabloid press against which such awards were most likely to be made. Their sensational style of reporting gave the public the impression that six-figure awards were the norm for libel. As a result, when members of the public found themselves on a libel jury these awards became their model. This was because, unlike judges, juries were not allowed to be given any figures during the trial by either judge or counsel.

This curious rule was established (or, to be more precise, re-established) by the Court of Appeal *Ward v James*,[57] where it was enunciated with enthusiasm by none other than Lord Denning MR himself. Why is it, he asked, that when a case is heard by a judge sitting alone he may be referred by counsel to conventional awards of damages but that no figures could ever be mentioned to a jury?

'Why should the jury not receive the same guidance as a judge? This sounds well in theory, but in practice it is open to strong objection.' As counsel on both sides would mention different figures, the poor jury would become confused. Yet, is this not what happened anyway? For, though not permitted to cite specific figures to a jury, counsel could and did attempt to guide them by making cryptic remarks such as: 'If you do find for the plaintiff, think of fridges rather than of Rolls Royces.' Such coded messages were doubly confusing, because not only was the jury caught in a welter of conflicting values but they also had to place a monetary figure on them.

In *John v MGN Ltd*[58] a jury award of £350,000 (£75,000 compensatory damages plus £275,000 exemplary damages) to the musician, Elton John, for a false allegation that he was on a 'diet of death', was reduced by the Court of Appeal to a total of £75,000 (£25,000 compensatory damages plus £50,000 exemplary damages). The power of the Court of Appeal to intervene in this way dates back only to the Courts and Legal Services Act 1990.

In addition, the Court of Appeal held, there was no reason why in future the judge or counsel could not give the jury an indication of what they considered an appropriate level of damages. The resulting reduction in the level of libel damages must be welcomed in terms of proportionality, though it does also of course favour the press at the expense of libel claimants.

### *Local authorities*

Other recent developments have tended in the same direction. So, in *Derbyshire County Council v Times Newspapers Ltd*[59] the House of Lords decided that a local authority – or indeed any other organ of government – did not have the right to bring a defamation action, as this would be contrary to public policy:

> It is of the highest importance that a democratically elected governmental body, or indeed any governmental body, should be open to uninhibited public

> criticism. The threat of civil action for defamation must inevitably have an inhibiting effect on freedom of speech.

This was based on *City of Chicago v Tribune Co*,[60] decided by the Illinois Supreme Court and approved by the US Supreme Court in *New York Times Co v Sullivan*.[61] The Chicago decision rested on a broad principle:

> The fundamental right of freedom of speech is involved in this litigation and not merely the right of liberty of the press. If this action can be maintained against a newspaper it can be maintained against every private citizen who ventures to criticise the ministers who are temporarily conducting the affairs of his government.

While recognising the important distinction discussed above between freedom of the press and freedom of speech generally, this passage neatly asserts the convergence of interests of the press and the general public in criticising government institutions. This identity is perhaps more apparent than real. For, how would a private citizen set about criticising public institutions without a media platform? Also, if a government body is unable to sue for libel, this gives carte blanche to the press, which can be as irresponsible as it likes knowing that it is immune from suit. If individual councillors or government officials were attacked as well, they would of course be entitled to bring a libel claim in their own names. But, unless they were extremely rich they would be unlikely to do so.

### *The Human Rights Act 1998*

The most important recent development in English defamation law is the passing of the Human Rights Act 1998, which, besides incorporating the European Human Rights Convention, including of course the right to freedom of expression, into English law, affords special protection to freedom of expression (in section 12), and especially to 'journalistic, artistic or literary material'. This has a broad relevance going well beyond defamation. (See above.)

### *'Political information'*

As far as defamation itself is concerned, the effect of the Human Rights Act was felt even before it came into force, notably in *Reynolds v Times Newspapers Ltd*.[62] The former Irish Taoiseach (Prime Minister), Albert Reynolds, sued the *Sunday Times* newspaper for publishing an article accusing him of making certain dishonest statements. At first instance the jury found in favour of Mr Reynolds but awarded him no damages. The judge substituted an award of one penny, the smallest coin of the realm. The matter went on appeal chiefly on the question of whether 'political information' was protected by what is called qualified privilege. Qualified privilege is an important defence in the law of defamation. What it means is that where, for example, a statement is made in the performance of a legal, moral or social duty, the occasion on which it is made is deemed to be privileged in the sense that, even if the statement is untrue it is not an actionable defamation unless the claimant can show that it was made 'maliciously', i.e. deliberately. So, where an invigilator at an examination announced to the assembled candidates that 'This fellow Bridgman has cribbed and will get no marks in consequence', it was held that the occasion was privileged, as the invigilator was acting out of a sense of duty. Though the accusation was false, there was no evidence of malice on the invigilator's part, so the action must fail.

But, to return to *Reynolds*, should 'political information' be accepted as a new category of qualified privilege similar to that of the 'public figure' defence enunciated by the United States Supreme Court in *New York Times Co v Sullivan*? By 3 votes to 2 the House of Lords said No. In his speech Lord Hobhouse identified the power that such an extension of the qualified privilege defence would put in the hands of the media: 'Such an approach would of course be attractive to the media but it would be handing to what are essentially commercial entities a power which would deprive the subjects of such publications of the protection against damaging misinformation.'

The two dissenters wanted the question of qualified privilege to be remitted to the judge at the retrial of the issue, which had been ordered, which would have thrown the whole law in this area into confusion.

One of them, Lord Steyn, went so far as to suggest that with the coming into force of the Human Rights Act 1998 freedom of expression was now 'a right based on a constitutional or higher legal order foundation'[63] (for full quotation see above, p. 168).

The problem, as Lord Hobhouse clearly recognised, is that, far from striking a balance, this approach favours the rights of the press barons over ordinary people. As we have seen, freedom of the press is not the same thing as freedom of expression generally. Those attacked by the press cannot retaliate unless they too have access to the mass media. Their only legal recourse is to the extremely costly blunt instrument of the law of defamation, which is not an option for any other than the super-rich.

## *VII. Human Rights*

### *Tolstoy Miloslavsky v United Kingdom*

Another English defamation case which has had a human rights dimension is one in which Count Nikolai Tolstoy Miloslavsky, a historian, wrote a pamphlet alleging the commission of war crimes at the end of World War II on the part of Lord Aldington, Warden of Winchester College. Aldington sued Tolstoy for defamation and won, being awarded damages of £1.5 million plus costs together with an injunction against further publication of the defamatory statements. Tolstoy took the matter to Strasbourg claiming that the judgment constituted a violation of his right to freedom of expression. The Commission unanimously upheld this allegation. But the Human Rights Court equally unanimously held that the judgment against Tolstoy was 'prescribed by law' and as such did not violate Article 10, but that the level of damages was disproportionate.[64]

This was an unusual case, not least because the pamphlet in question was privately printed and circulated. This may explain why Tolstoy did not receive the same degree of protection that the corporate press normally enjoys. In that respect the case resembles *Janowski v Poland.*[65] A journalist had insulted municipal guards for ordering street vendors to leave a public square and was given a suspended sentence of eight months' imprisonment for his pains. Here again the journalist was acting in a private capacity. Once again, too, the Strasbourg Commission took a more sympathetic view than the Court, the Commission finding by 8 votes to 7 that the journalist's rights under Article 10 had been infringed, while the Court held by 12 to 5 that there had been no violation of his right of freedom of expression.

By contrast, journalists writing in their professional capacity can normally count on support in Strasbourg, though when it comes to a battle between journalists and the judiciary this is rather less likely. Three cases involving the same Austrian journalist but with different results are a good illustration of this: *Oberschlick v Austria; Oberschlick (No 2) v Austria;* and *Prager & Oberschlick v Austria.*[66]

However, in *De Haes & Gijsels v Belgium,*[67] a magazine launched a virulent attack on Belgian Court of Appeal judges for awarding custody of children to their father, who had been accused of incest and child abuse but who had been acquitted. The judges sued the magazine for defamation and won. But in Strasbourg both the Commission (by 6 votes to 3) and the Court (by 7 to 2) found that this constituted a violation of the magazine's freedom of expression.

## Excursus B

## Liberty and equality

**Does the well-known belief that there are 'two concepts of liberty' have any validity, or any relevance to law? Instead of the dichotomy between 'positive' and 'negative' liberty, would it not be more useful to compare liberalism and libertarianism? Even more valuable is recognition of the inherent contradiction between liberty and equality.**

In his celebrated Oxford inaugural lecture delivered in 1958 Sir Isaiah Berlin identified two concepts of liberty: positive and negative. Negative freedom he defined as 'not being interfered with by others. The wider the area of non-interference the wider my freedom.' He cited Thomas Hobbes: 'A free man is he that … is not hindered to do what he hath the will to do.'[1]

However, Hobbes also recognised that a total absence of restraint on what anyone may do will ultimately result in chaos. This is what he termed the 'state of nature' in which, as he famously put it, there is a war of every man against every man and human life is 'solitary, poore, nasty, brutish and short'.[2] Berlin does not discuss this aspect of negative freedom.

Positive freedom, according to Isaiah Berlin, 'derives from the wish on the part of the individual to be his own master'.[3] But how different is this from 'negative freedom'? Berlin comments:

> The freedom which consists in being one's own master, and the freedom which consists in not being prevented from choosing as I do by other men, may, on the face of it, seem concepts at no great logical distance from each other – no more than negative and positive ways of saying much the same thing. Yet the 'positive' and 'negative' notions of freedom historically developed in divergent directions not always by logically reputable steps, until, in the end, they came into direct conflict with each other.[4]

What is Berlin thinking of? He identifies the French Revolution in its Jacobin form as 'an eruption of the desire for "positive" freedom of collective self-direction on the part of a large body of Frenchmen who felt liberated as a nation, even though the result was, for a good many of them, a severe restriction of individual freedoms.'[5]

Jean-Jacques Rousseau probably got closest to this contradiction in his distinction (not mentioned by Berlin) between *la volonté de tous* ('the will of all') and *la volonté générale* ('the general will'). 'The general will is rarely that of all' is how Rousseau put it in the first draft of *Du Contrat Social*. This was revised to read:

> There is often a marked difference between the general will and the will of all: the former looks only to the common interest; the other looks to the private interest and is nothing other than the sum of individual wills. But, remove from these same individual wills the more or less mutually destructive interests and what remains as a sum of the differences is the general will.[6]

The 'will of all' is the expression of the desires of all the individuals concerned and is selfish in its motivation. The 'general will', by contrast, is unselfish and aims at the general good. But how is it reached? Rousseau goes on to explain:

> If the people made decisions only after being sufficiently informed, the citizens would not have discussions amongst themselves, so that from the large number of minor differences the general will would always emerge, and the decisions would always be good.

However, the passage continues, if parties and factions are allowed to arise, the general will is likely to be sacrificed to the particular will of the dominant group. Despite this, for Rousseau, the irrepressible optimist and idealist, the general will 'is always constant, unalterable and pure', and indeed 'indestructible'.[7]

It has to be remembered that Rousseau came from Geneva, a city-state, and his model states were the Swiss cantons, where the individual citizens enjoyed a far greater say than was possible even then in a large nation-state such as Britain or France. In practice, especially in large states with diverse populations, different parties or factions tend to have different views of what the 'general will' is, and the cynic may even doubt whether there necessarily is such a thing as a common good for any given society.

Had Roussseau's writings been consigned to the oblivion which normally swallows up quirky curiosities of utopian idealism, none of this would matter. But as his ideas were taken up by political activists in the French Revolution and later, the relationship between the 'general will' and the 'will of all' became a live issue. What happened was that the concept of the general will became a tool in the hands of totalitarian parties and leaders of both the left and the right. Nothing could have been further from Rousseau's mind. Nevertheless, it is easy to see how his essentially mystical concept of an eternal, indestructible and pure 'general will' could be transmogrified into the twentieth-century doctrines of Fascism or Communism, where the will of the individual was subordinated to that of a single party and its leader.

For Rousseau, as we have seen, the general will is essentially a purified form of the individual wills of all the people. All the petty differences in the 'will of all' cancel one another out and what emerges is the pure and eternal 'general will'. Both concepts are expressions of the will of the individuals making up the society concerned, and both are therefore manifestations of liberty.

Yet the twentieth-century totalitarian reinterpretation of the general will is of course a complete denial of the concept of freedom or liberty. How did this reversal come about?

The two leading masters of this intellectual sleight of hand were Hegel (1770-1831) and Marx (1818-83). Hegel agreed with Rousseau in treating the will to freedom as fundamental, but for Hegel the general will was not the product of a counting of heads after the cancelling out of petty selfish individual differences. Hegel objected that Rousseau's general will was not different enough from his will of all. By means of 'dialectic' (i.e. a process of reasoning by combining two opposites, namely 'thesis' and 'antithesis', to produce a 'synthesis') Hegel reconciled the concepts of individual liberty and obedience to the state. He rejected the conventional wisdom which saw individual freedom as based on a whittling down of state power. For Hegel the rights of individuals were not threatened by the state but embodied in the state. From this concept it is not a huge leap to the Nazi credo: 'Ein Volk, ein Staat, ein Führer' ('One Nation, one State, one Leader').

Marx said he found Hegel standing on his head and turned him right way up. Like Hegel, Marx used dialectical reasoning, but to a very different end. While Hegel's dialectic led to state power, Marx's led inexorably to the concept of 'the dictatorship of the proletariat' theoretically culminating in the 'withering away of the state' coupled with total equality throughout society. This utopian vision was employed by some hard-headed and ruthless political leaders to establish the power of a Communist Party in Russia and elsewhere. What the self-styled disciples of Hegel and Marx had in common was the creation of a totalitarian system of government and society.

We have come a long way from any idea of individual liberty. All forms of totalitarianism, whether of the fascist or communist variety, amount to a negation of individual liberty. We can see how both brands of totalitarianism used ideas which can be traced back to Rousseau's 'general will'. And we can also see how this idea itself may be seen as a form of what Isaiah Berlin has labelled 'positive liberty'.

What does this tell us about Berlin's 'two concepts of liberty'? Only that so-called positive liberty has in practice turned out to be a sham. But does it even exist as an idea? Or, in other words, are there really two concepts of liberty in Berlin's sense?

## *VII. Human Rights*

### *Liberals and libertarians*

Whatever we may think of Isaiah Berlin's dichotomy between 'positive' and 'negative' liberty, there *are* undoubtedly at least two concepts of liberty based on a very different classification. These are probably best characterised by the labels attached to them in current American usage, namely liberalism and libertarianism. There is a certain overlap between them on particular issues, but they derive from fundamentally different philosophical wellsprings and are temperamentally opposed to each other. So, for example, both are likely to resist the introduction of compulsory identity cards, which both would see as an invasion of privacy. Likewise, both oppose censorship, though some modern liberals may favour a ban on pornography and possibly also on violence in films. For libertarians the less government control there is the better. For them the doctrine 'laissez faire, laissez passer' applies not only to the economy but to pretty well every other sphere of activity as well. What has been termed the 'nightwatchman state' is their ideal, according to which the true function of the state is purely negative, merely to defend its citizens against crime and foreign invasion. Liberalism, on the other hand - of which there are many shades - may actually welcome active government involvement in certain respects: anti-discrimination laws, for example, or social welfare programmes designed to assist the poor and funded by progressive taxation.

Upon analysis modern liberals (in the American sense) place greater emphasis on equality than on liberty. In order to enforce non-discrimination, for example, employers, educational establishments and individuals generally have to be coerced into behaving in ways which they would not otherwise do. The employer who, under the threat of anti-discriminatory laws, hires a black female applicant when his own personal preference would have been to offer the job to someone else is effectively being coerced into curtailing his own free will. That is why libertarians oppose such egalitarian laws.

It can be seen from this that, far from being complementary, liberty and equality are essentially at loggerheads with each other. This is so in a more general sense as well. No society in the history of the world has enjoyed less liberty - and greater equality - than Maoist China. During the so-called 'cultural revolution' doctors were ordered out into the fields to become peasants and peasants were uprooted from the land to become 'barefoot doctors'. Everybody was forced to wear regulation 'Mao suits' and to read Mao Tse-tung's 'little red book'. Chinese society was in turmoil. This was deliberate policy on the part of Mao. It was intended to obliterate class distinctions and to blend individuals from all different backgrounds into a homogenised social and economic soup. This aggressive policy robbed individual Chinese citizens of their liberty but it did produce a high degree of equality, with one important exception – Mao himself, the chef standing by the cauldron and stirring the soup continuously with a big wooden ladle.

The overzealous enforcement of anti-discrimination laws can easily lead to reverse discrimination or 'affirmative action' – which is just another form of discrimination. Once this stage is reached liberty and equality are joint casualties.[8]

### *Equality of opportunity*

Equality of opportunity is another concept which gives rise to misunderstanding. What is the relationship between equality and equality of opportunity? Equality of opportunity is commonly seen as a moderate concept whereas equality itself is generally identified as a radical belief.

The definition of socialism as adopted by the Soviet Union was: 'From each according to his ability, to each according to his work.' According to Soviet propaganda the Soviet Union had reached the stage of socialism in its development. The ultimate goal according to Marxist theory is of course communism: 'From each according to his ability, to each according to his needs.' It is interesting to compare these two concepts. Neither of them is totally egalitarian. Under socialism, according to this, a person's earnings will vary in proportion to the quality and quantity of the work he does. But even under communism the amount that individuals contribute to society will vary with their ability and – more surprising perhaps – what they take out of society will vary according to their 'needs'. We are *not* told who is to assess the level of these 'needs', nor how they are to be assessed.

Equality is a highly artificial goal which is practically impossible to achieve. The closest to it that any real society has ever got is probably, as discussed above, Mao Tse-tung's China. But this could only be achieved by having one larger than life figure who was – to use the language of George Orwell's *Animal Farm* – very much 'more equal' than everyone else.

By contrast with equality itself, equality of opportunity appears a fairly modest and attainable goal. The Education Act 1944 – or the 'Butler Act', as it was popularly known – was designed to produce equality of opportunity by setting a uniform 'eleven-plus' public examination for children of all classes and degrees (with the exception of those whose parents could afford to send them to independent schools). Those who passed this examination went on to a grammar school and from there to university, while those who failed were consigned to secondary modern schools and to more menial occupations. The theory was that as all children sitting the eleven-plus would stand an equal chance of passing, this was an eminently fair way of sifting the wheat from the chaff. In this way, its supporters assumed, merit and not birth or wealth would reign supreme: it would be a 'meritocracy'.

It was Lord Melbourne, Queen Victoria's first Prime Minister, who remarked: 'I like the Garter: there's no damned merit in it.' The old cynic was pouring scorn on the then new-fangled fashion for awards for 'merit' – which he suspected was simply a hypocritical and pretentious label. That was a century before the vogue for 'meritocracy' came into its own in the mid-twentieth century.

The real problem with meritocracy is that, by whatever standards, it has never delivered the promised result. So, after a generation of schoolchildren had grown up under the Butler Act the position was that the universities were still almost as middle-class as they had been before. What 'Rab' Butler and his ilk had not realised was that by the age of eleven a child's social and cultural identity was already largely formed. Middle-class parents were much more likely to encourage their children to read and to do well at school than their working-class counterparts. Moreover, the physical environment of a middle-class home was likely to be much more conducive to learning and education than that of the average working-class home.

What this meant was that equality of opportunity had not worked. The system was simply not able to offer all eleven-year-olds an equal opportunity. What then is the solution? It is clear that the age of eleven is eleven years too late. Unless children start from a level playing field there can be no equality of opportunity. And that means at birth. Hence the concept of comprehensive education, which was intended as a conscious corrective to the failure of the Butler Act. The theory of comprehensive education is that by lumping all children together from the beginning they will have true equality of opportunity. But this too has failed to deliver the expected result. Middle-class children still do better than their working-class classmates. This is largely because the whole environment of a typical middle-class home is more supportive of education than that of the average working-class home. This difference is present from birth. Ironically, therefore, the only way to achieve true equality of opportunity is by ensuring that all children are equal in every way from birth. But, as we have seen, equality is an impossibility.

The whole concept of equality of opportunity needs further investigation in any event. The term tends to be used glibly. But what exactly does it mean? Opportunity for what? It can surely mean only one thing: equality of opportunity to become *unequal*. Hence the description of modern western life as a 'ratrace' and the constant talk of a 'level playing field'. Every game has a winner and a loser. These sporting analogies make it plain therefore that the purpose of the initial equality is to produce an ultimately unequal result - but one which is achieved fairly.

As merit is so subjective and as there are so many other intervening or indeed supervening factors - such as birth, connections, wealth, appearance and guile - the system has not led to any real increase in the genuine recognition of merit. Discrimination in one direction has sometimes been replaced by discrimination in the opposite direction - but any form of discrimination is inevitably inimical to true meritocracy.

Like beauty, merit is in the eye of the beholder. As a cynic has put it: 'Mediocrity is excellence to the mediocre.'[9] In other words, if the judge of merit is himself of limited ability he may well identify his own modest level of competence with excellence so that when it comes to selecting someone for a position or an honour he will be likely to prefer the mediocre candidate to the one who really deserves it. The classic example of this is the case of Mozart, who in his own day was generally regarded as inferior to the court composer Antonio Salieri, who is now remembered only for his association with Mozart.

By labelling people as 'winners' or 'losers' the modern ratrace society has produced widespread psychological stress, anxiety and depression. Unlike more traditional societies, where success or failure was recognised as being the product of chance, luck, fate or divine predestination, it has come to be seen in modern western society as a reflection of the merit, or in other words, the worth, of the individual concerned, so that failures are branded - in their own eyes as well as in those of others - as somehow less worthy, less valuable members of society.

VIII

# The Administration of Justice

## 1. Judicial review

**In the famous *Wednesbury* case it was said that judicial review was governed by 'perfectly well understood principles'. These time-honoured doctrines have recently been under concerted attack. What then are the principles, if any, governing this important and rapidly expanding branch of the law today?**

Judicial review is available only from the High Court, or, to be more precise, from what is now known as the Administrative Court. It can be used to challenge the legality of a decision taken by a public authority such as a government minister or department, a local authority, a lower court or a statutory body such as the Monopolies and Mergers Commission or the Human Fertilisation and Embryology Authority. Judicial review also happens to be the most important and commonest way of bringing a human rights claim. Claims specifically based on an alleged violation of a right under the European Convention of Human Rights (ECHR) can only be brought by the 'victim' of the decision in question.[1]

Judicial review is different from an appeal. In order to have the right to appeal against a decision there has to be a statute, i.e. an Act of Parliament, specifically providing for it. Appeals are mostly made against court judgments, though there also are certain administrative bodies from whose decisions it is possible to appeal. There is a hierarchy of courts, with the possibility of appeal lying from one level to the next and culminating in the House of Lords. Permission is generally required in order to lodge an appeal. The court hearing the appeal will normally have the right to decide the whole case again and, if it wishes, to substitute its own decision for that of the court below.

This is precisely where a judicial review differs from an appeal. The court conducting a review is concerned to determine the lawfulness, but not the merits, of the decision under review. The natural corollary to this is that though the court could quash the impugned decision, i.e. set it aside, it could not substitute its own decision for that of the original decision-maker. However, a recent procedural change now allows the court to do just that, with the result that the substantive law has been changed by the back door.[2]

Does the distinction between a review and an appeal have any practical meaning any more or is it merely a distinction without a difference? If properly respected the distinction is an important one with very real practical effects. But, the recent 'procedural' change is only the latest of a series of nails which have been driven into the coffin of judicial self-restraint.

Nevertheless, the very clear way that Lord Brightman put the position in 1982 is still supposedly the law today:

> Judicial review is concerned, not with the decision, but with the decision-making process. Unless that restriction on the power of the court is observed, the court will in my view, under the guise of preventing the abuse of power, be itself guilty of usurping power.[3]

### *Wednesbury*

In the most famous judicial review case of all, commonly known as *Wednesbury*, decided in 1947, the issue was the lawfulness of a decision taken by a local authority. The Sunday Entertainments Act 1932 gave local authorities the power to grant a licence to cinemas to show films on Sundays 'subject to such conditions as the authority think fit to impose'. A cinema in the Wednesbury area applied to the local council for such a licence. The council agreed to grant them a licence but attached to it the condition that no children were to be admitted to the Sunday shows even if accompanied by an adult. This condition made the licence practically useless to the cinema. What was the point of Sunday cinema if children could not attend? It has to be remembered that this all happened in the days when English family life still existed.

The cinema proprietors challenged the lawfulness of this restrictive condition. In his judgment Lord Greene was at pains to stress that the question was not whether he or his fellow judges would have allowed children in but the very different and much narrower question whether the local authority had been acting lawfully in taking the decision that they took. In short, the court engaged in a judicial review is not allowed to 'second guess' the original decision. In a review the power of the court is much less than in an appeal.

In the words of Lord Greene MR:

> The power of the court to interfere in each case is not as an appellate authority to override a decision of the local authority, but as a judicial authority which is concerned, and concerned only, to see whether the local authority have contravened the law by acting in excess of the powers which Parliament has confided in them.[4]

This last phrase is fundamental: the right to make the decision under review was given by Act of Parliament not to the courts but to the local authority. For a court to substitute its own decision for that of the local authority would amount to a usurpation of the right of the local authority and could even be seen as an attempt to subvert the intention of Parliament.

*Wednesbury* is now over half a century old and has been subjected to a tremendous onslaught from judicial activists or judicial supremacists who want to expand the power of the judiciary. One senior judge has gone so far as to predict that

> the day will come when it will be more widely recognised that the *Wednesbury* case was an unfortunately retrogressive decision in English administrative law, in so far as it suggested that there are degrees of unreasonableness and that only a very extreme degree can bring an administrative decision within the legitimate scope of judicial invalidation.[5]

This remark appears to miss the point that Lord Greene was at such pains to make. In cases of this kind, said Lord Greene, 'The law recognises certain principles .... What, then, are those principles? They are perfectly well understood.' Lord Greene then goes on to set out these principles. They really are quite simple.

(a) *Illegality*: is the decision under review lawful? In *Wednesbury* itself, as we have seen, Parliament had allowed the local authority to grant Sunday licences 'subject to such conditions as the authority think fit to impose'. This is a very wide discretion indeed. Was the local authority acting within what Lord Greene called 'the four corners' of this discretion? If they had stepped outside these four corners they would have been acting 'ultra vires' (beyond their powers), and their decision could have been quashed by the court. But so wide was the discretion granted them by Parliament that this was not the case here at all. Their decision to include the restriction against children under fifteen was therefore lawful and could not be set aside by the court even if the judges had disagreed with it.

(b) *Unreasonableness*: once it is found that the decision under review was not unlawful, that would normally be the end of the matter – unless the decision was perverse or unreasonable in the extreme. Lord Greene's formulation of what is still termed '*Wednesbury* unreasonableness' echoes down the years. For a decision to be set aside as 'unreasonable', said Lord Greene, it has to be 'so unreasonable that no reasonable authority could ever have come to it'. The word 'ever' emphasises just how extreme the degree of unreasonableness has to be before the court can act. This is deliberate. If the threshold of unreasonableness were lowered judges would be allowed to set aside administrative decisions simply because they did not happen to agree with them. This would amount to a usurpation of the power of the original decision-maker by the judge concerned.

Lord Greene explained this important point as carefully as he could:

> Some courts might think that no children ought to be admitted on Sundays at all, some courts might think the reverse. All over the country, I have no doubt, on a thing of that sort honest and sincere people hold different views. The effect of the legislation is not to set up the court as an arbiter of the correctness of one view over another. It is the local authority who are put in that position and, provided they act, as they have acted here, within the four corners of their jurisdiction, the court, in my opinion, cannot interfere.

(c) *Procedural impropriety*: this third ground of judicial review is concerned not with the actual decision itself but with the way the decision was taken. In short, it is about natural justice. As this was not in issue in *Wednesbury* it is not mentioned there but it is a very ancient and important ground. More will be said about it later.

**Q. Is *Wednesbury* still good law? And does it really make any difference whether it is or not?**

**A. *Wednesbury* is still supposedly good law, though now under frontal attack from activist judges and their academic supporters. And yes, it makes a great deal of difference whether it is in force or not.**

In a lecture given in 1995, Lord Irvine of Lairg, the future Lord Chancellor, delivered a powerful blast against 'judicial supremacism' and in favour of the traditional *Wednesbury* approach advocating 'judicial self-restraint in public law matters ... which the vast majority of lawyers would still acknowledge to be the guiding principle of our system of judicial review'.[6]

Lord Irvine took issue with the idea expressed by a High Court judge that 'the greater the intrusion proposed by a body possessing public powers over the citizen into an area where his fundamental rights are at stake, the greater must be the justification which the public must demonstrate'.[7]

The main target of attack of those opposed to *Wednesbury* is the high threshold of '*Wednesbury* unreasonableness'. Such critics favour what Lord Irvine described as 'a lower standard of *Wednesbury* unreasonableness in fundamental rights cases' and a more 'interventionist role' for the courts. 'On this approach, the court would be invited to exercise a much tighter control over the merits of a decision where it perceives a threat to fundamental rights.' Lord Irvine warned that this approach led the judges 'into dangerous territory':

> The political and legal choices which import consideration of fundamental rights protection are among the most difficult and the most subjective, and offer immmense scope for political and philosophical disagreement. It cannot be right that such questions should be regarded as more rather than less suitable to judicial determination. The approach adopted in *Brind*,[8] which states conclusively that the *Wednesbury* threshold of unreasonableness is not lowered in fundamental rights cases, must prevail.[9]

Those words were written before the passing of the Human Rights Act 1998 (HRA). With the Act in place the anti-*Wednesbury* forces have been able to draw sustenance from the European Convention on Human Rights, which is partly incorporated into English law by the Act.

**Q. Do the courts now have greater powers in judicial review cases involving human rights? If so, what practical effect does this have?**

**A. The courts have tended to arrogate greater powers to themselves where 'fundamental rights' are concerned. But the law on judicial review is in disarray, with several approaches competing with one another.**

In a leading case four homosexual members of the armed forces challenged their discharge from the service as irrational. At first instance the approach adopted was described as follows:

> I approach the case ... on the conventional *Wednesbury* basis adapted to a human rights context and ask: can the minister show an important competing public interest which he could reasonably judge sufficient to justify the restriction? The primary judgment is for him. Only if his purported justification outrageously defies logic or accepted moral standards can the court, exercising its secondary judgment, properly strike it down.[10]

Except for the requirement that 'the most anxious scrutiny is accorded when fundamental rights are in issue' the standard of irrationality applied here is, if anything, stricter than the well-known definition of *Wednesbury* unreasonableness.

The Court of Appeal adopted the position that where fundamental human rights were involved a 'heightened scrutiny' test was applicable: 'The more substantial the interference with human rights, the more the court will require by way of justification before it is satisfied that the decision is reasonable' in the sense that it is within 'the range of responses open to a reasonable decision-maker'.[11]

Nevertheless, the Court of Appeal upheld the first instance decision against the four service personnel, who then took their case to Strasbourg, where a unanimous court found a 'grave violation' of their rights under Art 8.[12]

Subject to the doctrine of 'the margin of appreciation' (i.e. the varying degree of latitude given to the domestic authorities) the Strasbourg court had no hesitation in judging the merits of the Ministry's decision:

> The court recognises that it is for the national authorities to make the initial assessment of necessity, though the final evaluation as to whether the reasons cited for the interference [with the applicants' private lives] are relevant and sufficient is one for this court. A margin of appreciation is left open to contracting states in the context of this assessment, which varies according to the nature of the activities restricted and of the aims pursued by the restrictions.[13]

The Strasbourg court took the opportunity of aiming a broadside at what they saw as the undue restrictions placed on the domestic courts by the conventional approach to judicial review:

> The threshold at which the High Court and the Court of Appeal could find the Ministry of Defence policy irrational was placed so high that it effectively excluded any consideration by the domestic courts of the question of whether the interference with the applicants' rights answered a pressing social need or was proportionate to the national security and public order aims pursued, principles which lie at the heart of the Court's analysis of complaints under Article 8 of the Convention.[14]

Now that the HRA and the Convention can be applied directly by the domestic courts, can they too go for the jugular as the Strasbourg court did here?

### *'Proportionality approach'*

The last-quoted passage was cited with approval in *Daly*, a case involving the rights of convicted prisoners. Lord Steyn there identified two alternative approaches to judicial review: the traditional *Wednesbury* approach and the 'proportionality approach', which he admitted may 'sometimes yield different results'. What exactly is the difference? 'The intensity of review,' according to Lord Steyn, 'is somewhat greater under the proportionality approach.' And: 'Even the heightened scrutiny test developed [by the Court of Appeal in the case on homosexual service personnel] is not necessarily appropriate to the protection of human rights.' Does this mean that in human rights cases the courts should exercise even greater powers than envisaged there to set aside administrative decisions?

Apparently recognising that this 'proportionality approach' looked very much like an attempt on the part of the court to judge the merits of the decision under review – which was totally forbidden under the traditional approach as a usurpation of the position of the original decision-maker – Lord Steyn found it necessary to state quite starkly: 'This does not mean that there has been a shift to merits review.'[15]

### *'Merits review'?*

Yet is that not exactly what *Daly* was, a 'merits review'? George Daly, a long-term prisoner, objected to the new policy requiring a prisoner's privileged legal correspondence to be searched in the prisoner's absence. Daly lost in the Court of Appeal, which held 'that the policy represented the minimum intrusion into the rights of prisoners consistent with the need to maintain security, order and discipline in prisons'.[16]

But this decision was reversed by a unanimous House of Lords. The relevant legislation, section 47(1) of the Prisons Act 1952, provides that: 'The Secretary of State shall make rules for the regulation and management of prisons ... and for the classification, treatment, discipline and control of persons required to be detained therein.' This is a very widely drawn power indeed. Moreover, there was no challenge to the right of prison officers to search a prisoner's cells including his privileged documents. In other words, there was a tacit recognition by the applicants themselves that convicted prisoners were not entitled to the same rights of 'respect for their private and family life' as everyone else. The only objection was to the requirement that the prisoner step outside his cell while the search was being conducted. In these circumstances it is hard to see the House of Lords judgments in *Daly* as anything other than an attempt to substitute their own decision for that of the Home Secretary.

### *'Context is everything'*

Lord Steyn adopted the view that 'the intensity of review in a public law case will depend on the subject matter in hand', adding: 'That is so even in cases involving convention rights. In law context is everything.'[17]

Context is everything? What does this mean? If this means that principles are subordinate to facts and that the courts should decide matters 'on a case by case basis' (to use a phrase much beloved of some members of today's judiciary) then it is less than reassuring, as it threatens to increase subjectivity and uncertainty at the expense of objectivity, certainty, predictability and therefore of justice.

Context is everything? If this means that the subject-matter of the case is all-important then it becomes even more disquieting. For what this implies is that a case will be treated differently according to the identity of the applicant. And this is borne out by an examination of court decisions. Is it entirely fanciful to suggest that the courts appear unduly concerned to protect the rights of convicted killers and other criminals, prisoners in general and asylum seekers? The recent cases of Venables and Thompson (the murderers of Jamie Bulger), the child-killer Mary Bell, the murderer Anthony Anderson and the Afghan hijackers differ in many respects, but all have one thing in common: victory for convicted criminals.[18]

*'Policy decisions' versus 'determination of rights'*

Yet another fashionable approach to judicial review was suggested by Lord Hoffmann, who drew a distinction between 'policy decisions' and 'a determination of rights'. In the interests of democracy, policy decisions, or decisions as to what the public interest (or general interest) requires should be made 'by democratically elected bodies or persons accountable to them'. Examples of such decisions are questions of taxation, town and country planning, and road construction. 'In that way,' said Lord Hoffmann, 'democratic principle is preserved.'[19]

When it comes to individual rights, however, Lord Hoffmann recommends a different approach:

> There is no conflict between human rights and the democratic principle. Respect for human rights requires that certain basic rights of individuals should not be capable in any circumstances of being overridden by the majority, even if they think that the public interest so requires. Other rights should be overridden only in very restricted circumstances. These are rights which belong to individuals simply by virtue of their humanity, independently of any utilitarian calculation. The protection of these basic rights from majority decision requires that independent and impartial tribunals should have the power to decide whether legislation infringes them and either (as in the United States) to declare such legislation invalid or (as in the United Kingdom) to declare that it is incompatible with the governing human rights instrument. But outside these basic rights, there are many decisions which have to be made every day (for

example, about the allocation of resources) in which the only fair method of decision is by some person or body accountable to the electorate.[20]

Unfortunately, however, the distinction between 'policy decisions' and 'determinations of rights' is not as clearcut as Lord Hoffmann's classification might lead us to believe. Immigration policy is a good example. Is it a matter of public interest or of individual rights? If treated as a matter of public policy the appropriate approach by the courts should be judicial self-restraint, with a reluctance on the part of the judges to interfere with decisions taken by the elected legislature and democratically accountable executive. In fact, however, this is one of the prime areas of particularly marked judicial activism or even judicial supremacism, presumably on the assumption that it concerns fundamental individual rights.

Lord Hoffmann's assertion that 'there is no conflict between human rights and the democratic principle' is really an expression of an elitist theory of democracy, which is at loggerheads with the normal 'electoral' theory of democracy. The electoral view sees democracy as a system of government designed to give voice to the wishes of the majority. By contrast the elitist view sees democracy as a system of government embodying certain 'liberal' or even 'politically correct' social and political values whether they are held by the majority or not. The problem with the elitist theory of democracy is that it is an attempt to impose certain values on society regardless of the views of the majority. In the normal sense, therefore, this elitist approach can be seen as fundamentally undemocratic or even anti-democratic.

To return to our example, is it wrong for Parliament and the Government to seek to control the influx of asylum seekers? Seen as a policy decision with wide popular support, such measures should surely be subjected to minimal interference from the courts. Instead we find that it is an area where the courts are more inclined than in almost any other to strike down Government policy. The justification for this is that, when looked at from the point of view of individual asylum seekers, which is how the courts tend to view it, it is an area of fundamental human rights entitling the courts to maximum interference.

Which view is correct? It cannot be stressed enough that a right enjoyed by one person necessarily entails a reciprocal obligation owed to him by another. So, if asylum seekers are accorded the right to be supported at public expense, this right imposes an obligation on council taxpayers to support them. Likewise, one person's rights will be likely to compete with those of others. So, for example, if asylum seekers are given the right to free housing, this cannot but detract from others' rights to free housing, not to mention the burden that it places on taxpayers without their consent.

Upon examination, therefore, the assertion that there are some human rights which are so fundamental that they have to be upheld by the courts in the face of opposition by the majority turns out in reality to be a doctrine giving judges the power to impose their own social and political values on society.[21]

### *Conclusion*

What then are the principles now governing judicial review? Amidst the welter of competing theories the formulation adopted by Lord Diplock in the so-called GCHQ case still commands considerable respect:[22]

> Judicial review has I think developed to a stage today when, without reiterating any analysis of the steps by which the development has come about, one can conveniently classify under three heads the grounds on which administrative action is subject to control by judicial review. The first ground I would call 'illegality', the second 'irrationality' and the third 'procedural impropriety'.

There is a certain amount of ambiguity in Lord Diplock's definition of illegality, the exact terms of which are as follows:

> By 'illegality' as a ground for judicial review I mean that the decision-maker must understand correctly the law that regulates his decision-making power and must give effect to it. Whether he has or not is par excellence a justiciable question to be decided, in the event of dispute, by those persons, the judges, by whom the judicial power of the state is exercisable.[23]

It will be noticed that this test is twofold, as the decision-maker (a) 'must understand' the relevant law 'correctly' and (b) 'must give effect to it'. It appears from the wording that the decision-maker must comply with *both* these conditions. Failure under either head will presumably be enough to entitle the court to quash the decision. And, of course, as Lord Diplock makes quite plain, it is for the court to decide whether the decision-maker has indeed complied with these conditions. Does this mean that unless the decision-maker makes the 'right' decision the court can strike it down as illegal?

This ties in with the whole discussion relating to error of law in relation to ouster clauses and centring on *Anisminic Ltd v Foreign Compensation Commission*.[24] The question is essentially whether an authority entrusted with a decision-making power has the right to decide the case 'wrongly' or whether *any* error of law automatically takes the decision outside the authority's jurisdiction.[25]

This question is also relevant to an understanding of the scope and indeed the validity of the much-attacked ultra vires principle, which was long held to form the very cornerstone of the whole edifice of judicial review.

Another related head is that of abuse of power, which likewise raises a jurisdictional problem: is it possible for a public authority to abuse its power without stepping outside its jurisdiction? Or does any abuse of power automatically amount to an ultra vires act? In other words, are there degrees of abuse of power ranging from the comparatively minor to the very serious? And how relevant is this question if any abuse of power is enough to entitle the decision in question to be quashed?

What this boils down to is a question of the power of the judiciary over the executive. If any abuse of power, however trivial, amounts to an ultra vires act, this boosts the power of the courts even beyond its previous level. For, the question of whether there has been an abuse of power in the first place - by, say, the Home Secretary or some other Government minister - is one which is reserved to the judges. And the question of whether any abuse of power is automatically ultra vires is another question which the judiciary has arrogated to itself. Once a decision is classified as ultra vires, it can be quashed - a further judicial power. And, with the recent judicial attack on the ultra vires principle, once a decision is branded as an 'abuse of power' the judges have the right to set it aside.

But perhaps the most important problem of all in Lord Diplock's formulation has to do with his attitude to principle. After enunciating his three grounds for judicial review in *GCHQ*, he continued:

> That is not to say that further development on a case by case basis may not in course of time add further grounds. I have in mind particularly the possible adoption in the future of the principle of 'proportionality' which is recognised in the administrative law of several of our fellow members of the European Economic Community; but to dispose of the instant case the three already well-established heads that I have mentioned will suffice.[26]

Is Lord Diplock claiming the right to add new grounds to the three which he has already identified? It is worth noting that the one candidate that he singles out for mention in this connection, namely proportionality, he specifically designates as a 'principle'. Lord Diplock does not say what level of court he thinks should have the right to make a change of such magnitude to the law. Would it have to come from the House of Lords as the highest court in the land, or could any judge just decide to add a ground here or there whenever he felt like it? One thing is certain: Lord Diplock does not see this as a function which should belong to Parliament. This is clear from his language, and in particular from the telltale phrase 'on a case by case basis'. Yet, is not adding grounds for judicial review a legislative function, and one that *should* therefore belong to Parliament?

As a staunch upholder of the doctrine of the separation of powers, Lord Diplock might have been expected to stop short of claiming for the courts the right to invent new grounds of judicial review.[27] The concept of the separation of powers holds that there should be as little overlap as possible in the membership of the three branches of Government, namely the executive, the legislature and the judiciary, and that these three institutions should check and balance each other so as to prevent the concentration of power in the hands of any one of them.

The grounds for judicial review are a matter of *principle*, as indeed Lord Diplock clearly recognised. It is the function of the courts to *apply* principles to a whole host of differing factual situations. It is for the courts to decide which principle is applicable to any given set of factual circumstances, in the course of which it is inevitable that principles will be expanded, contracted, modified or even reinterpreted to greater or lesser extent. This process - the process of *applying* principles to facts - cannot but be done on a 'case by case basis'.

But is it permissible for *new principles* to be added on a case by case basis? It smacks of an arbitrary approach to law. Moreover, it amounts to a usurpation of the legislative function of Parliament and is also likely to lead to a denial of justice. For what it means is presumably that when the 'right' case comes along the court will say: 'None of the existing grounds is applicable here, but, as we think this is a deserving case, let us just create a new ground to cover it.' Would this be an exercise of the rule of law - or of its very antithesis?

However, it has to be said that the three grounds which Lord Diplock actually enunciates in *GCHQ* are in no sense novel or revolutionary, but in fact conform closely to the principles accepted for centuries. What then about proportionality, upon which Lord Diplock certainly appears to have looked with favour? It is not perhaps irrelevant that it was already a principle not only of the domestic law of a number of European states but also of the European Union itself. For, where European Union law impinges on UK domestic law, the principles of EU law come into play. In addition, proportionality is closely related to irrationality as a ground for judicial review, so that in a sense it is already present as a subset under that head. So, if, for example, a penalty is out of proportion to the offence, does this not make it unreasonable as well?

The objection is therefore not primarily to proportionality itself but to the concept - which Lord Diplock appears to have taken for granted - that the courts can introduce new principles as and when they choose.

Under the influence of the European Court of Human Rights in Strasbourg the UK domestic courts have embraced with gusto the concept of the separation of powers. For the Home Secretary, a member of the executive, to set a 'tariff' for a convicted murderer has been excoriated as a breach of Article 6 of the ECHR. The fact that this power was given to the Home Secretary by Act of Parliament has not saved it. And, under the same pressures, at the time of writing the ancient post of Lord Chancellor is about to be abolished, largely because its functions traditionally straddled the now-sacred divide between executive, legislature and judiciary.

The irony is that this same concern for separation of powers is not in evidence in regard to encroachments by the judiciary into the preserves of the other two branches of government. For judges to create or introduce new principles of law actually amounts to just such an encroachment. Yet it goes on unabated. Judicial review is beset by such a welter of principles and supposed principles as to make it a highly unpredictable and therefore unclear and potentially unjust area of law.

But amid all the clamour there can even now be heard the still small voice of Lord Greene and *Wednesbury*. This was well demonstrated by an immigration case decided in 1996.[28] Jayaram Khadka, the 20-year-old heir to Richard Morley, a millionaire, was ordered to be deported after living in the United Kingdom since 1990, when he was informally adopted by Mr Morley in accordance with a promise made to Mr Khadka's natural father, who had saved Mr Morley's life in a Himalayan climbing accident. In the first court decision backing the Home Secretary in many months, Laws J held as follows:

> I am unable to conclude that the Secretary of State's decision in this case was beyond the range of responses open to a reasonable decision-maker. His decision was taken as the people's democratic representative. If I were to overturn it I would usurp that role - which it is no business of mine to do - and it goes without saying that my personal view of the case's merits has no relevance whatever.

In brief compass this is as classic a statement of the conventional principles of judicial review as any. The 'range of responses' language does not actually constitute a different standard from *Wednesbury* unreasonableness itself.

There is also express recognition of the danger of usurping the role of the Home Secretary by introducing the judge's own personal view of the merits of the case. In addition, if the report is accurate, there is a somewhat gratuitous salute to the Home Secretary as 'the people's representative'. In fact, the Home Secretary's power to make immigration decisions is based not on his elective status – not directly, at any rate – but rather on the fact that he has been entrusted with this power by an Act of Parliament.

The most remarkable thing about this case is that this exemplary model of judicial self-restraint resulted in the rejection of a claim whose merits were patent – an application against deportation by a law-abiding young man of impeccable character who was not and was never likely to become a burden on the state and who had spent his formative years in the United Kingdom. In recognition of these factors, shortly after coming to power in 1997 the new Home Secretary, Jack Straw, gave Jayaram Khadka indefinite leave to remain in the United Kingdom.[29]

This only underlines just how viable the *Wednesbury* principles are. Laws J was undoubtedly quite right to decide the case as he did. As he himself pointed out in graphic terms, he would have been usurping the Home Secretary's role had he done anything else.

This scrupulously correct decision by Laws J came hard on the heels of a case in which that same judge had been reversed by a unanimous Court of Appeal, in which Sir Stephen Brown P found it necessary to summarise the legal basis of the jurisdiction.[30]

> After the most critical, anxious consideration, I feel bound to say that I am unable to say that the health authority in this case acted in a way that exceeded its powers or which was unreasonable in the legal sense. The powers of this court are not such as to enable it to substitute its own decision in a matter of this kind for that of the authority which is legally charged with making the decision.

What have we here if not our old friends the ultra vires principle and *Wednesbury* unreasonableness coupled with the prohibition on treating a review as if it were an appeal? This case is in itself an eloquent warning of the dangers of sweeping away the conventional principles and replacing them with vague concepts of 'fundamental human rights'.

If judges ignore the established principles they will be in danger of usurping the constitutional position of both legislature and executive. Moreover, though by no means always easy to apply, these old principles have proved remarkably resilient and adaptable over the years, and to replace them with woolly concepts that are far more problematical will not be serving the interests of justice or the rule of law, two of the most important criteria of which are the related qualities of certainty and predictability.

## 2. Ouster clauses

**Can the jurisdiction of the courts be excluded by an ouster clause? Contrary to common belief, ouster clauses are not invariably invalid.**

An ouster clause is generally a provision in an Act of Parliament saying that the decision of some executive or administrative authority, tribunal or other body shall be final, or words to that effect. The purpose of such a clause is to ensure a quick and final determination in certain types of cases without the involvement of the courts. From a Government point of view any attempt by the courts to override such an exclusion is likely to be seen as judicial interference. On the other hand, the judiciary tend to regard ouster clauses as a threatened curtailment of their authority, a gross infringement of the principle of the separation of powers and an attempt to subvert the rule of law. Not surprisingly, therefore, ouster clauses have figured prominently as a key battleground in the struggle for power between the judiciary and the executive.

Some ouster clauses however reserve final decision-making power to a court, either a county court or the High Court. Where the power is reserved to the High Court, the approach of the judiciary is very different. Far from being hostile to the ouster clause, they are suddenly supportive of it, as that kind of ouster clause of course poses no threat to their authority at all, but if anything bolsters it.

But what is the status of ouster clauses? Are they in keeping with the principles of the British Constituition or do they fly in the face of the fundamental principles of justice and the rule of law? Their validity clearly rests on that most fundamental principle of the British Constitution, the sovereignty of Parliament, or rather parliamentary legislative supremacy, which is discussed in Chapter I.

### *Anisminic*

The leading authority on the status and effectiveness of ouster clauses is still *Anisminic Ltd v Foreign Compensation Commission.*[1] After the 1956 Suez crisis, mining property belonging to Anisminic worth £4 million was sequestrated by the Egyptian Government and sold on to an Egyptian organisation known as TEDO. In 1957 TEDO paid Anisminic £500,000 for their whole Egyptian undertaking under an agreement reserving Anisminic's rights to pursue their claim for full compensation against any government authority other than that of Egypt. In 1959, under a treaty between the UK and Egypt, the British Government received £27.5 million 'in full and final settlement' for a number of sequestrated businesses, including that belonging to Anisminic. How that sum was to be distributed among the individual companies was left to the British Government. There was already an administrative tribunal set up in Britain to hear such claims for compensation: the Foreign Compensation Commission. Anisminic applied to this body, whose powers were limited to compensating British nationals only. The relevant statutory instrument required that the original owner of the property and 'any person who became successor in title' to him had to be British nationals. As TEDO, which was deemed to be Anisminic's 'successor in title', was not and never had been a British national, Anisminic's application was dismissed.

The tribunal's decision was patently unjust. The fact was that Anisminic's property was specifically listed among those for which the Egyptian Government had paid the British Government £27.5 million. Why then should Anisminic be denied their rightful share of this money merely because their business had after sequestration been sold to TEDO, an Egyptian organisation? It would make little sense to interpret the term 'successor in title' as applying to TEDO in these circumstances. As Lord Reid put it: '... "successor in title" must refer to some person who somehow succeeded to the original owner as the person now having the original owner's hope or expectation of receiving compensation. The obvious case would be where the original owner had died.'[2]

Essentially what Lord Reid was saying was that the whole question of 'successors in title' was a red herring. It would only have been germane where it was a successor in title who was the claimant. But where, as here, it was the original owner who was the claimant, the whole to-do about successors in title was irrelevant. On this basis, held Lord Reid, 'the commission made an enquiry which the order did not empower them to make, and they based their decision on a matter which they had no right to take into account. If one uses the word "jurisdiction" in its wider sense, they went beyond their jurisdiction in considering this matter.'[3]

By a writ action Anisminic sought a declaration of the court that the tribunal's determination had been made without, or in excess of, jurisdiction, and was a nullity. But there was a serious obstacle to court intervention. For the legislation constituting the tribunal, the Foreign Compensation Act 1950, contained an ouster clause reading as follows:

> The determination by the Tribunal of any application made to them under this Act shall not be called in question in any Court of Law.

Despite this apparently conclusive bar on court involvement, it was held by the House of Lords that the tribunal's decision was a nullity and that the court did not therefore lose its right of jurisdiction over the matter. In this way the perfectly clear and peremptory language of the ouster clause in the statute was effectively negated.

The House of Lords' decision in *Anisminic* was by a 3:2 majority. Of the nine judges involved in the case (one at first instance, three in the Court of Appeal and five in the House of Lords) there was actually a majority *against* the final decision (all three judges in the Court of Appeal plus two in the House of Lords). The case also revealed a diversity of approaches and indeed of principles among the judges.

Three different approaches to the question of ouster clauses and the broader issues surrounding them may be identified:

(1) The tribunal whose determination was being challenged had committed an error of law in reaching its determination which had taken it beyond its jurisdiction (ultra vires), so that its determination was only a purported determination and therefore a nullity. As there was no actual determination, the ouster clause did not apply. (*This was the view taken by the majority in the House of Lords, restoring the original decision of the trial judge.*)

(2) The tribunal had been guilty of an error of law, but it was quite entitled to make such an error. Its determination was a genuine determination, albeit mistaken. So the ouster clause must be honoured and the court had no jurisdiction to intervene. (*The view taken by Lord Morris of Borth-y-Gest in the House of Lords and all three judges in the Court of Appeal, including Diplock LJ.*)

(3) The tribunal had not been guilty of an error of law at all. (*Lord Pearson in the House of Lords.*)

Even the majority in the House of Lords drew a distinction between errors of law that are serious enough to take the tribunal outside its jurisdiction on the one hand and, on the other, errors of law that are made within the tribunal's jurisdiction. This is a distinction that Lord Denning had made in his early days in the Court of Appeal, and a dictum of his was quoted with approval by Lord Wilberforce in the *Anisminic* case:

> No one has ever doubted that the Court of King's Bench can intervene to prevent a statutory tribunal from exceeding the jurisdiction which Parliament has

> conferred on it, but it is quite another thing to say that the King's Bench can intervene when a tribunal makes a mistake of law. A tribunal may often decide a point of law wrongly while keeping well within its jurisdiction.[4]

In fact, not a single member of the House of Lords in *Anisminic* suggested that there was no difference between errors of law going to jurisdiction and non-jurisdictional errors of law. Yet, despite this, a tradition has grown up that *Anisminic* obliterated the distinction between errors of law going to jurisdiction and non-jurisdictional errors of law.

Even Lord Diplock appears to have believed something approximating to this. In *O'Reilly v Mackman* he said that the House of Lords decision in *Anisminic*, 'and particularly the leading speech of Lord Reid', had 'liberated English public law from the fetters that the courts had theretofore imposed on themselves so far as determinations of inferior courts and statutory tribunals were concerned, by drawing esoteric distinctions between errors of law committed by such tribunals that went to their jurisdiction, and errors of law committed by them within their jurisdiction'.[5]

Is Lord Diplock saying that since *Anisminic* there has been no such thing as a non-jurisdictional errors of law? Not quite. But, in maintaining that the 'esoteric distinction' between errors of law going to jurisdiction and non-jurisdictional errors of law is a distinction without a difference, he is effectively saying that *any* error of law in a decision will now be enough to make that decision a nullity. (Surprisingly, perhaps, this radical position is expressly qualified by restricting it to 'inferior courts and statutory tribunals', thus presumably excluding executive decisions – though in *Re Racal Communications Ltd* he referred to *Anisminic* as applying to 'an administrative tribunal or other administrative authority'.[6]

In fact, however, as we have seen in regard to Lord Wilberforce, *Anisminic* did not obliterate the distinction between jurisdictional and non-jurisdictional errors of law at all. Lord Reid, whose speech in that case was specifically cited by Lord Diplock in that connection (see above) was equally at pains to draw a distinction between the two types of error:

> It has sometimes been said that it is only where a tribunal acts without jurisdiction that its decision is a nullity. But in such cases the word 'jurisdiction' has been used in a very wide sense, and I have come to the conclusion that it is better not to use the term except in the narrow and original sense of the tribunal being entitled to enter on the enquiry in question. But there are many cases where, although the tribunal had jurisdiction to enter on the enquiry, it has done or failed to do something in the course of the enquiry which is of such a nature that its decision is a nullity. It may have given its decision in bad faith. It may have made a decision which it had no power to make. It may have failed in the

course of the enquiry to comply with the requirements of natural justice. It may in perfect good faith have misconstrued the provisions giving it power to act so that it failed to deal with the question remitted to it and decided some question which was not remitted to it. It may have refused to take into account something which it was required to take into account. Or it may have based its decision on some matter which, under the provisions setting it up, it had no right to take into account. I do not intend this list to be exhaustive. But if it decides a question remitted to it for decision without committing any of these errors it is as much entitled to decide that question wrongly as it is to decide it rightly. I understand that some confusion has been caused by my having said in *Armah v Government of Ghana* (6) that, if a tribunal has jurisdiction to go right, it has jurisdiction to go wrong. So it has if one uses 'jurisdiction' in the narrow original sense. If it is entitled to enter on the enquiry and does not do any of those things which I have mentioned in the course of the proceedings, then its decision is equally valid whether it is right or wrong subject only to the power of the court in certain circumstances to correct an error of law.[7]

And the third member of the majority, Lord Pearce, expressed a similar view.[8]

Where then did the myth come from that *Anisminic* had decided that *any* error of law was enough to destroy an ouster clause? It is probably not unconnected with some of the more robust dicta on this point falling from Lord Denning after he had repented of his conventional reasoned view (quoted above) expressed in *Shaw*.[9]

Completely departing from this position, in *Pearlman v Keepers & Governors of Harrow School*,[10] Lord Denning adopted a much more radical stance. In *Pearlman*, as in *Anisminic*, there was an ouster clause. The relevant statutory provision, Schedule 8 to the Housing Act 1974, provided that the decision of the matter in question was to be that of the county court 'and any such determination shall be final and conclusive'. This is the relevant part of Lord Denning's judgment in that case:[11]

... the distinction between an error which entails absence of jurisdiction and an error made within the jurisdiction is very fine. So fine indeed that it is rapidly being eroded .... So fine is the distinction that in truth the High Court has a choice before it whether to interfere with an inferior court on a point of law. If it chooses to interfere, it can formulate its decision in the words: 'The court below had no jurisdiction to decide this point wrongly as it did.' If it does not choose to interfere, it can say: 'The court had jurisdiction to decide it wrongly, and did so.' Softly be it stated, but that is the reason for the difference between the decision of the Court of Appeal in *Anisminic* and the House of Lords.

I would suggest that this distinction should now be discarded. The High Court

> has, and should have, jurisdiction to control the proceedings of inferior courts and tribunals by way of judicial review. When they go wrong in law, the High Court should have power to put them right .... The way to get things right is to hold thus: no court or tribunal has any jurisdiction to make an error of law on which the decision of the case depends. If it makes such an error, it goes outside its jurisdiction and certiorari will lie to correct it.

It has been suggested by certain commentators that this view was approved by the House of Lords in *Re Racal Communications Ltd*[12] and 'has been accepted as the orthodox position in English administrative law'.[13] But far from being endorsed by the House of Lords in *Racal*, Lord Denning's position in *Pearlman* was expressly disapproved by Lord Edmund-Davies in that case, who cited with approval instead the dissenting judgment of Geoffrey Lane LJ (as he then was) in *Pearlman*, who held that:

> The judge is considering the words ... which he ought to consider. He is not embarking on some unauthorised or extraneous or irrelevant exercise. All he has done is to come to what appears to this court to be a wrong conclusion on a difficult question. It seems to me that, if this judge is acting outside his jurisdiction, so then is every judge who comes to a wrong decision on a point of law. Accordingly, I take the view that no form of certiorari is available to the tenant.[14]

*Racal* involved the interpretation of section 441(3) of the Companies Act 1948, concerning orders for the inspection of a company's books. The section provided that: 'The decision of a judge of the High Court or of any of the Lords Commissioners of Justiciary on an application under this section shall not be appealable.' Why did it require a trip to the House of Lords to interpret so straightforward a piece of legislation? And a unanimous House of Lords did indeed find it straightforward. As Lord Diplock put it, there could be no appeal from the judge's decision under the section 'on the sole and simple ground that the statute says that the judge's decision shall not be appealable'.[15] Why then all the fuss? Lord Scarman revealed the true problem:

> My Lords, were it not for the decision in the Court of Appeal allowing the appeal, I would have thought this case too plain for argument. Parliament has enacted that the decision of a judge of the High Court on an application under s 441 of the Companies Act 1948 'shall not be appealable': see s 441(3). The Court of Appeal has allowed this appeal. How can their decision be justified in the face of the unambiguous prohibition imposed by Parliament?[16]

In short, there was no appeal from the decision of a High Court judge (or the

Scottish equivalent) under the section because Parliament said that there could be no appeal. But, how did this differ from *Anisminic*? Was there not an equally clearly worded and peremptory ouster clause involved there? Like the *Racal* ouster clause, it too was a statutory ouster clause, this time in section 4 of the Foreign Compensation Act 1950, and, as discussed above, providing that: 'The determination by the Tribunal of any application made to them under this Act shall not be called in question in any Court of Law.'

What was the difference between this ouster clause, which was struck down in *Anisminic*, and the one in *Racal*, which was upheld? In fact, the only real difference was that the *Anisminic* ouster clause gave the final say to a tribunal, whereas the *Racal* clause gave it to a High Court judge. So, was this really just a case of the judges of the House of Lords looking after their own – their brother High Court judges? It is certainly hard to see how *Racal* can stand with *Anisminic*. When Parliament says 'a High Court judge's decision is final' then that is taken at face value, but when Parliament says 'the tribunal's decision is final', that is overturned. Can High Court judges not make errors of law? In fact, every time that a judge decides a case wrongly, that is an error of law. Lord Diplock recognised this but had a ready answer:

> Mistakes of law made by judges of the High Court acting in their judicial capacity as such can be corrected only by means of appeal to an appellate court; and if, as in the instant case, the statute provides that the judge's decision shall not be appealable, they cannot be corrected at all.[17]

'They cannot be corrected at all' – an amazing statement in the light of *Anisminic*!

The anomaly had not been lost on Lord Denning sitting on the *Racal* case in the Court of Appeal, but he had his own characteristic solution. He recognised, as the House of Lords did not, that reason and consistency demanded that the ouster clause in *Racal* be treated in the same way as that in *Anisminic*:

> The first question which arises is: can the Director of Public Prosecutions appeal to this court? Section 441(3) provides: 'The decision of a judge of the High Court … on an application under this section shall not be appealable.' In my opinion, that subsection is not a bar to the appeal to this court. There are many cases now which show that if a judge misconstrues a statute by giving himself jurisdiction when he has none or by refusing jurisdiction when he has it, then he makes an error which goes to the jurisdiction: and there is an appeal to this court, no matter how wide the words which seem to exclude it. For authority in this

> regard I need only refer to *Anisminic Ltd v Foreign Compensation Commission*, and especially to what was said by Lord Reid, by Lord Pearce and by Lord Wilberforce, to which I would add a few words of my own in the later case of *Pearlman v Keepers and Governors of Harrow School*: ... no court ... has any jurisdiction to make an error of law on which the decision of the case depends.' It seems to me that in this case, if the judge made an error of law in construing the words of the section, if he construed the words 'an offence' etc too narrowly, then he made an error of law which made him refuse jurisdiction when he ought to have entertained it. So the appeal can be entertained here in this court.[18]

The principles to be extracted from the decision of the majority of the House of Lords in *Anisminic* may be summarised as follows:

(1) Parliament is entitled to give exclusive or final jurisdiction over certain types of disputes to whoever it likes.

(2) A decision by a judicial body containing an error of law going to jurisdiction is not really a decision at all: it is a nullity.

(3) Therefore, such a decision is not exclusive or final but may be challenged in the courts.

In *Anisminic* the body given the final say by Parliament happened to be a tribunal, whereas in *Racal* it was a High Court judge. Lord Denning recognised that this made no difference to the principles. However, in the light of the House of Lords decision in Racal, these principles presumably have to be modified so as to read as follows:

(1) Parliament is entitled to give exclusive or final jurisdiction over certain types of disputes to whoever it likes.

(2) A decision by an administrative tribunal or other administrative authority containing an error of law going to jurisdiction is not really a decision at all: it is a nullity.

(3) Therefore, such an erroneous decision by such a body is not exclusive or final but may be challenged in the courts. However, this does not apply where the body invested by Parliament with exclusive or final jurisdiction is itself a court of law, in which case the ouster clause must be taken literally.

Put like this, which presumably must be taken to be the law today, it makes very little sense. Lord Denning's disarmingly candid explanation in *Pearlman* (quoted above) of the real basis on which the courts decide these matters certainly has the ring of truth about it: namely that the decision of the High

Court depends in reality not on legal niceties but on whether it 'chooses to interfere' or not. If it does, it will say, 'The court below had no jurisdiction to decide this point wrongly as it did'; and 'if it does not choose to interfere, it can say: "The court had jurisdiction to decide it wrongly, and did so."' Then comes a pure Denning gem: 'Softly be it stated, but that is the reason for the difference between the decision of the Court of Appeal in *Anisminic* and the House of Lords.'[19]

What exactly is Lord Denning suggesting here? Presumably that the Court of Appeal (surprisingly, he was not himself sitting) had decided in advance not to interfere, but the House of Lords had other ideas.

It would be hard to find a better example of this kind of judicial politics than *Racal*, where it was clear that the House of Lords were determined at all costs to uphold the right of a High Court judge not to have his decision interfered with. Ironically, as we have seen, the chief obstacle to this was their own decision in *Anisminic*. So they simply declared that the supposedly sacred principles of *Anisminic* did not apply to courts of law - a textbook example of Lord Denning's somewhat cynical description of the way in which judges play games with the law.

Another such case is *Page v Hull University Visitor*,[20] where the House of Lords by a majority held that the decision of a university 'visitor', i.e. the person with supervisory functions over an academic, ecclesiastical or charitable foundation, was to be regarded as final and was not subject to judicial review. This remarkably conservative view appears to fly squarely in the face of the trend towards ever greater access to judicial review, even in regard to non-statutory quasi-public authorities.[21]

In *Thomas v University of Bradford*[22] a unanimous House of Lords struck out a claim brought by a university lecturer for wrongful dismissal. The lecturer had chosen to take her case to court in preference to petitioning the visitor. It was held that the visitor had exclusive jurisdiction - rejecting the view expressed by Lord Hailsham LC in his capacity as visitor of another university in *Casson v University of Aston in Birmingham*,[23] in which he refused jurisdiction on the ground that 'a visitor can have no jurisdiction in any matter governed by the common law, e.g. contract'.[24]

In *Thomas* the possibility of a subsequent judicial review of a vistor's decision was left open. Lord Ackner's conclusion was that the lecturer's 'claim falls within the exclusive jurisdiction of the visitor, *subject always to judicial review* [italics supplied]'.[25] Lord Griffiths likewise expressed the view that the visitor's decision would be subject to judicial review for mandamus or prohibition, and, on the basis of an abuse of his powers, for certiorari as well.[26]

The question whether a university visitor's decision was susceptible to judicial review arose expressly in *Page*, another case involving the dismissal of a university lecturer, who, had petitioned the visitor – and been rebuffed. To the question, 'Does certiorari go beyond quashing for abuse of power and allow judicial review for errors of law within jurisdiction?'[27] Lord Slynn, supported by Lord Mustill, replied as follows:[28]

> With deference to the contrary view of the majority of your Lordships, in my opinion if certiorari can go to a particular tribunal it is available on all the grounds which have been judicially recognised. I can see no reasons in principle for limiting the availability of certiorari to a patent excess of power (as where a visitor has decided something which was not within his remit) and excluding review on other grounds recognised by the law. If it is accepted, as I believe it should be accepted, that certiorari goes not only for such an excess or abuse of power but also for a breach of the rules of natural justice there is even less reason in principle for excluding other established grounds. If therefore certiorari is generally available for error of law not involving abuse of power (as on the basis of Lord Diplock's speeches I consider that it is available) then it should be available also in respect of a decision of a visitor.
>
> I am not persuaded that the jurisdiction of the visitor involves such exceptional considerations that this principle should be departed from and that some grounds be accepted and others held not to be available for the purposes of judicial review.

This position was rejected by the majority of the House, Lords Browne-Wilkinson, Keith and Griffiths, bolstered by an array of old authorities going back to the seventeenth and eighteenth centuries. Lord Griffiths paid homage to this long line of authority:

> For three centuries the common law courts have recognised the value of the visitor acting as the judge of the internal laws of the foundation and have refused to trespass upon his territory. I do not believe that it would be right to reverse this long line of authority and declare that certiorari should now lie to reverse the decision on a question of law.[29]

What then if the visitor was guilty of an error of law? 'Although,' admitted Lord Browne-Wilkinson, 'the general rule is that decisions affected by errors of law made by tribunals or inferior courts can be quashed, in my judgment there are two reasons why that rule does not apply in the case of visitors.'[30] The two reasons were:

(a) First, that 'the constitutional basis of the courts' power to quash is that the decision of the inferior tribunal is unlawful on the grounds that it is ultra vires' (108c), but this concept was inapplicable to a visitor because ultra vires referred to 'the general law of the land' whereas a visitor was concerned only with the 'domestic law' of the institution in question. This, it has to be said, is a strained argument indeed. The plain fact is that the concept of ultra vires is *not* necessarily to do with the general law. One of the chief applications of the ultra vires principle was in Company Law, where the question was whether a company had acted within or beyond its Memorandum of Association – which could well be described as the company's constitution or, indeed, its domestic law! Far from being inapplicable to a vistor's jurisdiction, it could be argued that the concept of ultra vires is eminently suited to it. In deciding the matter before him, has the visitor strayed beyond his powers under the 'domestic law' of the university in question? That is what a reviewing court would be concerned to discover – a perfectly straightforward application of the ultra vires principle.

(b) Secondly, that there was a distinction between an error of law going outside the jurisdiction of the relevant decision-maker and an error of law within his jurisdiction. This Lord Browne-Wilkinson based on the passage cited above from the dissenting judgment of Geoffrey Lane LJ (the later Lord Chief Justice) in *Pearlman*, as approved by the Privy Council in *South East Asia Fire Bricks v Non-Metallic Mineral Products Manufacturing Employees Union*[31] and by the House of Lords in *Racal* (see above). Lord Browne-Wilkinson interpreted the phrase 'within his jurisdiction' in the narrow sense of whether the visitor 'had inquired into and decided a matter which he had no right to consider'.[32] There was no question but that the visitor had the right to inquire into the matter which he had decided. 'Accordingly, unless this House is prepared to sweep away long-established law, there is no jurisdiction in the court to review a visitor's decision for error of law committed within his jurisdiction.'[33]

This second reason is impressive indeed – or would be if it were not confined exclusively to university visitors! For, just two pages further back in that same speech of Lord Browne-Wilkinson's we read that, the decision in *Anisminic* 'rendered obsolete the distinction between errors of law on the face of the record and other errors of law by extending the doctrine of ultra vires. Thenceforward it was to be taken that Parliament had only conferred the decision making power on the basis that it was to be exercised on the correct legal basis: a misdirection in law in making the decision therefore rendered the decision ultra vires.'[34]

There are two problems with this passage:

(a) What exactly is meant by it? There can be no doubt that an error of law does not have to appear on the face of the record for it to form the basis of a judicial review. But is Lord Browne-Wilkinson suggesting that *Anisminic* obliterated *all* distinctions between errors of law, so that *any* error of law in the making of a decision would be enough to make the decision a nullity? There is no mention here of any distinction between errors of law going to jurisdiction and non-jurisdictional errors of law. However, as we have already seen, despite a self-perpetuating myth to the contrary *Anisminic* certainly did *not* obliterate *that* distinction.

(b) If Lord Browne-Wilkinson *is* suggesting that *Anisminic* is to be interpreted as meaning that any error of law in a decision automatically vitiates that decision, then why does that not apply equally to the decisions of university visitors? For, as we have seen, when it comes to visitors' decisions, Lord Browne-Wilkinson invokes Geofrey Lane LJ's distinction between the two categories of error.

The respect shown in *Page* for precedent is touching. But we can only wonder why it is that this respect is so selective. The traditional privileged position of university visitors is sacred – but, as has been well demonstrated by the *GCHQ* case[35] and *M v Home Office*,[36] when it came to the position of the Crown the judges had no difficulty in sweeping aside the mountain of authority that stood in their way.

*Page* leaves us with the nagging question: Why this special treatment for university visitors? We may possibly gain a clue from some remarks in the judgments. Here, for example, is Lord Griffiths in *Thomas v University of Bradford*:[37]

> It is true that the decision of the visitor is final and the parties are thus deprived of challenging a decision in the Court of Appeal and perhaps the House of Lords. But is this a disadvantage or an advantage? I rather think it is an advantage. Today the visitors of universities either are or include independent persons of *the highest judicial eminence*. Would not most people consider it better to accept the decision of such a person rather than face the risk of the matter dragging on through the years until the appellate process has finally ground to a halt. There is also the advantage of cheapness, lack of formality and flexibility in the visitatorial appeal procedure which is not bound by the intimidating and formalised procedures of the courts of law.

There is no doubt a good deal of truth in this. But, when it comes to speed, expense and convenience, could the same argument not be used in favour of administrative tribunals – like the one in *Anisminic*? It would be a cold day in hell before an English judge would be caught advancing such arguments in favour of tribunals. Why? The answer may possibly be lurking in the italicised words in the passage quoted above: for university visitors are often themselves drawn from the ranks of the judiciary.

Likewise, in *Page*, Lord Griffiths remarked that:[38]

> The visitor either is a person holding a high judicial office or is advised on questions of law by such a person, in whose decision on matters of law, it is reasonable to repose a high degree of confidence. I say this not because any holder of judicial office should ever regard it as an affront to be overruled by an appellate court but merely to emphasise that as a practical matter the chances are that the visitor probably will get it right.
>
> If it is thought that the exclusive jurisdiction of the visitor has outlived its usefulness, which I beg to doubt, then I think that it should be swept away by Parliament and not undermined by judicial review.

Is it purely coincidental that the two protected species who have been given special consideration by the courts are High Court judges – in *Racal*, see above – and university visitors, who are often High Court judges themselves?

Lord Griffiths's regard for parliamentary supremacy is again noteworthy, coupled as it is with his pillorying of judicial review in this connection as amounting to 'undermining'. This is all the more remarkable as the privileges of university visitors do not derive from statute but from the common law. It would therefore have been all the easier for the courts to bring university visitors into line with the other changes in the law – if they had wanted to.

The principle espoused by the majority in *Anisminic* was not in itself revolutionary or even novel. Lord Pearce in particular cited a number of old authorities showing that 'no certiorari' or general ouster clauses in Acts of Parliament could be bypassed by the courts where the decision-making authority in question had exceeded its jurisdiction, by, for example, in effect 'directing itself to an enquiry other than that which was laid on it by Parliament' or asking itself 'the wrong question in deciding whether to make an order'.[39] Among other dicta relied upon, Lord Pearce quoted Cockburn CJ in *Ex parte Bradlaugh*, who, referring to an ouster clause, said:[40]

> … I am clearly of opinion that the section does not apply when the application for the certiorari is on the ground that the inferior tribunal has exceeded the limits of its jurisdiction.

But, if all that *Anisminic* did was to confirm this old line of authority, why is it regarded as marking such an important departure? The answer lies not so much in what *Anisminic* actually decided as on the way it has been interpreted. As we have seen, it is now commonly suggested that *Anisminic* obliterated all distinctions between errors of law so that *any* mistake of law in a decision is now enough to make that decision a nullity, thereby effectively deleting any ouster clause.

If this is really what *Anisminic* decided it would mark a radical departure. For, *any* mistake in a decision will almost invariably be a mistake of law. So, in order to bypass any ouster clause all the court will have to do is to disagree with the decision in question. The logic will then be:

(a) This decision is wrong.
(b) Therefore there is a mistake of law here.
(c) Therefore the decision is a nullity.
(d) Therefore the ouster clause is inapplicable.

But is this really what *Anisminic* decided? Despite the self-perpetuating myth to this effect, the answer is No. Not a single member of the House of Lords or Court of Appeal was of opinion that *any* error of law in a decision would make that decision a nullity.

Lord Pearson accepted that *if* the tribunal had acted in excess of jurisdiction the court would be entitled to intervene by way of judicial review. However, on the facts, he held that the tribunal 'did not ask any wrong question or exceed their jurisdiction in any way .... The decision ... was plainly within their jurisdiction, and therefore by virtue of s 4(4) of the Foreign Compensation Act 1950, it cannot be called in question in any court.'[41] This appears to mean that Lord Pearson regarded the tribunal as having made no error of law at all, and certainly no error taking them outside their jurisdiction.

Lord Morris in the House of Lords, in common with a unanimous Court of Appeal made up of Sellers, Diplock & Russell LJJ, also accepted that where a tribunal acts in excess of jurisdiction the court is entitled to intervene by way of judicial review. However, if the tribunal made 'a mistake of law within the jurisdiction' in reaching its decision, that would not vitiate the decision. Lord Morris gave some illuminating practical examples of the distinction, including adopting a passage from *Halsbury's Laws*[42] which had been approved by Greer LJ in *R v Minister of Health, ex parte Committee of Visitors of Glamorgan County Mental Hospital*:[43]

> There the proceedings are regular upon their face and the magistrates had jurisdiction, the superior court will not grant the writ of certiorari on the ground that the court below has misconceived a point of law. When the court below has jurisdiction to decide a matter, it cannot be deemed to exceed or abuse its jurisdiction merely because it incidentally misconstrues a statute, or admits illegal evidence, or rejects legal evidence, or misdirects itself as to the weight of the evidence, or convicts without evidence ....

Lord Morris also quoted Slesser LJ's view in the same case that if the decision-maker had done no more than 'arrive at an erroneous decision', that did not render the decision ultra vires.[44] Applying these principles to the facts of *Anisminic*, Lord Morris concluded: 'In agreement with Sellers, Diplock and Russell LJJ,[45] I consider that the commission acted entirely within their designated area of jurisdiction. I do not think that their decision or determination is to be jettisoned as being a nullity.'[46]

Lords Reid, Pearce and Wilberforce, forming the majority in the House of Lords, held that the tribunal *had* gone beyond their jurisdiction in reaching their purported decision, thus nullifying it and entitling the court to intervene. But did these judges leave any room for an error of law that did *not* go to jurisdiction? Despite the current belief to the contrary, the answer is that they all did.

Lord Reid explained the difference between the two sorts of error in the passage quoted above. Likewise, Lord Wilberforce quoted with approval the passage cited above from Denning LJ's judgment in *R v Northumberland Compensation Appeal Tribunal, ex parte Shaw*, the concluding sentence of which puts the position in a nutshell: 'A tribunal may often decide a point of law wrongly while keeping well within its jurisdiction.'[47]

Similarly, in addition to the passage of his speech cited above, Lord Pearce held that:

> If the tribunal is intended, on a true construction of the Act, to enquire into and finally decide questions within a certain area, the courts' supervisory duty is to see that it makes the authorised enquiry according to natural justice and arrives at a decision *whether right or wrong*. They will intervene if the tribunal asks itself the wrong questions (i.e. questions other than those which Parliament directed it to ask itself). But if it directs itself to the right enquiry, asking the right questions, they will not intervene merely because it has or may have come to the wrong answer, provided that this is an answer that lies within its jurisdiction.[48]

### *Anisminic: conclusion*

Despite the self-perpetuating myth referred to above, there can therefore be no doubt that *Anisminic* is *not* authority for the proposition that *any* error of law is enough to turn a decision into a non-decision.

The distinction between errors of law going to jurisdiction and non-jurisdictional errors of law remains. But is it a genuine distinction or a distinction without a difference? It is certainly true that the definition of 'jurisdiction' espoused by the House of Lords majority is considerably wider than that adopted by the minority.

Nevertheless, on the facts of *Anisminic* itself it is not difficult to agree with the majority that the tribunal had indeed exceeded their jurisdiction. The point is that, in basing their rejection of Anisminic Ltd's claim on the question of the nationality of the company's 'successors in title', the tribunal were considering something which was not only irrelevant but which, in Lord Reid's words, 'they had no right to take into account'. He continued as follows:

> If one uses the word 'jurisdiction' in its wider sense, they went beyond their jurisdiction in considering this matter. It was argued that the whole matter of construing the order was something remitted to the commission for their decision. I cannot accept that argument. I find nothing in the order to support it. The order requires the commission to consider whether they are satisfied with regard to the prescribed matters. That is all they have to do. *It cannot be for the commission to determine the limits of their powers.*[49] (Italics supplied.)

The last sentence is crucial. No statutory body can possibly have the right to decide on the scope of its own powers. By definition, its powers are limited by the instrument under which it is constituted. This is far from being a new principle, as is clear from the passages by Lord Alverstone CJ and Farwell LJ cited by Lord Pearce in *Anisminic*.[50]

If this is what Lord Reid means by using the word 'jurisdiction' in its 'wider sense', then it clearly still allows room for non-jurisdictional errors of law. But that leaves the formidable practical problem of deciding where the dividing line comes. The disagreements in *Anisminic* itself, both on the definition of jurisdictional errors and on whether such an error has or has not been made in a particular case, are enough to show the difficulties involved. However, it is worth taking heed of the warning sounded by Lord Reid himself in *Ridge v Baldwin* against the 'perennial fallacy that because something cannot be cut and dried therefore it does not exist'.[51] So, just because the distinction between jurisdictional and non-jurisdictional errors of law is not an easy distinction to draw should not be taken to mean that there is no such distinction – nor, as Lord Denning urged in *Pearlman*, that because the distinctions are 'fine' they should be 'discarded'. That way lies the substitution of arbitrary judicial discretion for rules and principles.

### *Post-Anisminic ouster clauses*

In an article published in 1995 Lord Woolf remarked: 'In that case [viz *Anisminic*] even the statement in an Act of Parliament that the Commission's decision "shall not be called in question in any court of law" did not succeed in excluding the jurisdiction of the court. Since that case Parliament has not again mounted such a challenge to the reviewing power of the High Court.'[52]

This last remark is not borne out by the evidence. On the contrary, the Foreign Compensation Act 1969, which was passed in the immediate aftermath of the *Anisminic* decision, introduced a new attempt to restrict judicial intervention. Section 3 of the Act provides that, with the exception of certain specific rights of appeal, 'anything which purports to be a determination' of the Commission shall not be called in question in any court of law. This new stronger formula – specifically intended to get over the problem encountered in *Anisminic* by its predecessor in the 1950 Act on the same subject – has succeeded, at least insofar as it has never been the subject of litigation.

Similarly, the Interception of Communications Act 1985 section 7(8) and the Security Service Act 1989 section 5(4) both contain ouster clauses preventing the judicial review of decisions 'as to jurisdiction'. These provisions have also not been tested in the courts.

What exactly is meant by the phrase 'as to jurisdiction'? The intention is presumably to prevent a decision from being challenged by way of judicial review on the ground that it is ultra vires. This does however leave open the possibility of challenging the decision on other grounds. But, any other ground would actually be a lesser ground and so, a fortiori, should not be permitted either. The contention would have to be: 'While conceding that the decision-maker here has not exceeded his jurisdiction, we contend that he has made a mistake of law and ask for it to be quashed on that ground.' This argument would carry no weight – unless the mythical interpretation of *Anisminic* exploded above is taken to be correct.

### *Time-limited ouster clauses*

The commonest type of statutory restriction on access to the courts is now to be found in provisions which give potential applicants only a short time in which to take the matter to court. If they miss the deadline, they have no further legal redress.

An example of this type of clause is to be found in section 242(1) of the Town and Country Planning Act 1971, which provides that:

> Except as provided by the following provisions of this Part of this Act, the validity of ... any such order as is mentioned in subsection (2) of this section ... shall not be questioned in any legal proceedings whatsoever.

This is then picked up in section 245(1), which provides that:

> If any person – (a) is aggrieved by any order to which this section applies and desires to question the validity of that order, *on the grounds that the order is not within the powers of this Act, or that any of the relevant requirements have not been complied with in relation to that order*; or (b) is aggrieved by any action on the part of the Secretary of State to which this section applies and desires to question the validity of that action, *on the grounds that the action is not within the powers of this Act, or that any of the relevant requirements have not been complied with in relation to that action*, he may, within six weeks from the date on which the order is confirmed or the action is taken, as the case may be, make an application to the High Court under this section. (Italics supplied.)

These provisions came before the court in *Griffiths v Secretary of State for the Environment*,[53] where, surprisingly perhaps, the only question considered by the court was how the six-week deadline was to be calculated, in particular whether the six-week period ran from the date when the Secretary of State's letter was dated and posted or from the date when it was received by the addressee.

It was held by the House of Lords (by 4:1) upholding the decisions below, that the Government's more restrictive interpretation was correct. As a result, Mr and Mrs Griffiths were out of time – albeit by only three days – in lodging their application to the High Court against the Minister's decision, it was time-barred and had been properly struck out. Even Lord Scarman, voicing the only dissent in the House of Lords, did so on the narrow basis that the wording of the section allowed the interpretation contended for by the Griffithses. There was no attempt at all to bypass the restriction on access to the court on more fundamental grounds. So, this type of ouster class – if such it can be called – appears to be effective.

Once again, however, there remains at least a theoretical possibility of seeking judicial review out of time on grounds other than those specifically mentioned in the Act. For the Act places a time restriction only on judicial review 'on the grounds that the action is not within the powers of this Act, or that any of the relevant requirements have not been complied with in relation to that action'. The first of these grounds is a straightforward ultra vires ground and the second one could be interpreted as applying only to errors of omission. So it could be contended that any non-jurisdictional error of law which is an error of commission rather than of omission is not covered by the time-limit. But, as mentioned above, this would succeed only if the mythical interpretation of *Anisminic* were held to apply.

In a lecture delivered in Hong Kong in 1998, Lord Irvine LC expressed the view that it was 'undeniable that, in this case [viz *Anisminic*], the House of Lords came close to the perimeter of judicial power which is set by the bedrock principles of the constitution ... constitutional logic dictates that some form of words must exist which would be sufficiently clear to insulate a given discretionary power from judicial review. If this was not the case, Parliament would not be truly sovereign. Thus, if at some point in the future the courts are presented with a sufficiently clear ouster clause, it will be their constitutional duty to give effect to it.[54]

This trial of strength between the Government and the judges is yet to come. If previous clashes are anything to go by, the judges will not be the first to blink.

## Excursus C

### Pollock on the common law

**The judiciary have always regarded themselves as the guardians of the common law. Modern judicial activists go further and tend to see it as their role to shape and mould the common law so as to keep pace with modern life. Judicial activism, however, shades into what has been termed 'judicial supremacism', with elements of the judiciary vying for power with the executive and the legislature. The judicial protagonists in this war are at pains to enlist in their support the big guns of the past, including the highly respected name of Sir Frederick Pollock. However, this particular attempt rather backfires.**

A present-day Lord Justice of Appeal, Sir Stephen Sedley, compares statute law unfavourably with the common law: 'Apart from the historic texts – Magna Carta, the Bill of Rights – statutes were until this century regarded, by lawyers if not by parliamentarians, as dangerous reefs in the great ocean of the common law, to be observed chiefly in order to circumnavigate them.'[1] In support of this view Sedley quotes a remark of Sir Frederick Pollock's as cited by Lord Steyn in a 1996 Bentham Club lecture: 'Parliament generally changes the law for the worse, and ... the business of the judges is to keep the mischief of its interference within the narrowest possible bounds.'[2]

Though an undistinguished lecturer, Sir Frederick Pollock (1845-1937) was a highly prolific, respected and influential academic jurist and a friend of Oliver Wendell Holmes Jr 1841-1935), the famous US Supreme Court justice, with whom he conducted a long correspondence.

The words quoted from Pollock by Lord Steyn and Sedley LJ are wrenched from their context, and the view which they purport to express was not one which Pollock was putting forward but in fact rejecting. In a word, so far from holding up the common law as a superior alternative to legislation, Pollock is actually attacking it. The Pollock essay in question, titled 'Some Defects of our Commercial Law', published in 1882, was not concerned to compare statute law with the common law. Pollock's purpose was, first, to show how uncertain English commercial law was, and, secondly, how it could be improved. His critique of the existing law is largely an attack on the common law, not a defence of it:

> Nature loves variety, and the growth of English law, left as it has been to the natural course of litigation, is full of varied surprises. So far as the ways of nature are thus manifested, she is by no means prodigal in finding distinct answers for questions of practical importance. But her courses are no less precipitate in some directions than they are dilatory in others. There are points not intricate in themselves, and demanding rather to be settled one way or another than to be settled in the best conceivable way, which are still the subject of lengthened and indecisive discussion. There are others of the most delicate kind, and requiring the most careful balancing of different interests, which have been decided not only without adequate discussion, but without any rational discussion at all.[3]

Citing the vexed topic of contracts by correspondence as an example, Pollock remarks:

> This is a singularly good example of the kind of difficulty before which case-law, and advisers with nothing but case-law to guide them, may stand helpless for years together.[4]

Pollock then launches into a critique of the law of property, which at the time was still largely judge-made:

> Results of the same kind have been produced in various departments of the law of property by the excessive subtilties and refinements forced upon it, *sometimes in the teeth of positive legislation*, by the Court of Chancery.[5] (Italics supplied.)

Pollock's attitude to the common law is therefore far from flattering. But does he not criticise statute law as well? Yes, but not on the basis suggested by Sedley. What Pollock objected to was the piecemeal nature of British legislation and what he refers to as 'the singular entanglement of statute-law and case-law'.[6]

He gives a graphic description of the way this comes about. Parliament finds some rule of common law ('often some modern judicial development')[7] 'inadequate or inconvenient'. Parliament thereupon amends the law, but this does not restate the whole law on the subject but assumes a knowledge of the pre-existing common law. As a result, 'in most cases and for most persons' the amended Act of Parliament 'is not intelligible without a great deal of trouble'.[8] The next step is for this Act to be interpreted by the courts:

> The Statute-book would be a real book if the fiction that every one knows the law were a fact. In that case every new statute would be in itself a real and complete piece of information addressed to all persons concerned. But since the fiction is not a fact, statutes are composed on the plan above mentioned are a kind of hieroglyphics to the ordinary Englishman. Nor is their reading always an obvious matter even to experts. There is a whole science of interpretation better known to judges and parliamentary draftsmen than to most members of the legislature itself. Some of its rules cannot well be accounted for except on the theory that *Parliament generally changes the law for the worse, and that the business of the judges is to keep the mischief of its interference within the narrowest possible bounds*. Our modern law of real property is simply founded on judicial evasion of Acts of Parliament, which, however, was of such a flagrant kind as could not take place now-a-days.[9] (Italics supplied.)

The italicised words are the ones quoted by Lord Steyn and Sedley LJ, but they now appear in context and it can be seen how the omission of the first 14 words of the sentence reverses its meaning.

Pollock then concludes his tracing of the 'entanglement of statute-law and case-law':

> The law as amended and interpreted is discovered to need re-amendment; and upon the fresh amendment the work of judicial interpretation begins again. And so it goes on till we have a series of statutes which to an uninitiated observer might seem to deal with their whole subject, but are really mere islands scattered in an ocean of case-law.[10]

Is Pollock here suggesting that there was too much statute-law? Just the opposite, in fact. His point is that British statute law is not comprehensive enough. He attacks the British approach to legislation, what he calls 'desultory legislation' or 'partial legislation', and sings the praises of the much more thoroughgoing type of legislation favoured on the continent and also in India, namely codification:

> The remedy lies straight before us, and has already been applied with success by the majority of civilized nations. It is the statement of the law by the supreme authority of the legislature, and in an orderly and lucid form; in one word, codification. If Parliament is afraid of undertaking this, it is afraid of

> undertaking that which the Italian Parliament, the German Reichstag, and the Swiss Federal Assembly have been doing without fear and without failure for several years past.[11]

Nothing, therefore, could be further from the truth than the suggestion that Pollock saw legislation 'as dangerous reefs in the great ocean of the common law to be observed chiefly in order to circumnavigate them'.[12]

### *Pollock on 'the science of case-law'*

Although, as we have seen, Sir Frederick Pollock was an enthusiastic advocate of the codification of the law, he was also a believer in the scientific nature of the common law of his day, by which he meant predictability:

> The object is to ensure the same decision being given on the same facts. In English case-law this object is attained by what seem the most obvious and direct means, namely, an understanding that the court shall follow the authority of decisions formerly given on similar facts.[13]

IX

# Contract

## 1. Contract as agreement

**(1) Is a contract essentially an agreement? Or is its formation to be seen rather in terms of offer and acceptance? Or promise for promise? These three models all overlap but it is far less difficult in practice to identify a valid contract than is sometimes suggested.**

**(2)(a) The 'innocent' party to a breach of contract is always entitled to judgment.**

**(2)(b) If he has suffered a loss he will also be entitled to (compensatory) damages, the level of damages being calculated so as to compensate him for his loss.**

**(2)(c) But the actual damages awarded will be subject to mitigation, whether the person himself has actually mitigated his loss or not.**

What is a contract? How can a legally binding promise be distinguished from one which has no legal force? What is the distinction between contractual obligations and those imposed by the law of tort? Is a contract primarily an agreement? Is a contract an exchange of promises? Or is it to be viewed in terms of offer and acceptance?

In practice these problems are far less intractable than some academic commentators have tried to maintain. But the position now is that there is a good deal of confusion surrounding even the question of what a contract is.

Three overlapping models lie at the heart of the classical doctrine of contract law: (i) contract as agreement; (ii) contract as offer and acceptance; and (iii) contract as an exchange of promises.

The concept of contracts as agreements is the most fundamental of the three and also the easiest to understand, which is perhaps why academics have long preferred to concentrate on contract as offer and acceptance and contract as an exchange of promises, because there are some obvious problems with these two models.

For example, whenever anyone buys a newspaper, goes to the cinema or boards a bus there is a contractual relationship. How are such simple transactions to be squared with the classical promise-for-promise model? Is it realistic to suggest that the purchase of a newspaper can be classified in terms of mutual promises? And if so, what exactly do the parties promise each other? The newspaper is generally thrust into the hand of the purchaser either at the same time as payment is made or else very shortly before or after. It is not easy to see this as in any sense an exchange of promises. Even the concept of offer and acceptance is difficult to apply here. Does the offer come from the newspaper vendor or from the buyer? And in what sense can we really speak of offer and acceptance at all?

Whether such everyday activities can be squeezed into a promise-for-promise mould or an offer-and-acceptance framework, what is plainly present in all of them is an *agreement*. The concept that contracts are agreements *is* widely taught, but what is not always made clear is the relationship that this simple model has with the promise-for-promise model and with the concept of offer and acceptance.

Some contracts conform to all three models at once. A contract of employment is a good example. There is clearly an offer and acceptance situation here, with the offer generally coming from the employer and the acceptance from the employee. An employment contract is also not hard to classify as an exchange of promises, with the employee promising to perform certain duties and the employer promising to pay him a certain agreed wage or salary in return.

Other contracts, like, for example, a simple cash purchase from a shop, conform to the offer-and-acceptance model as well as to the agreement model but are hard to characterise in terms of promises. Yet others, while clearly qualifying as agreements, cannot easily be squared with either of the other two models.

Ironically, perhaps, it is the biggest and most complex transactions that tend to be the easiest to fit into all three of the conventional models. Contracts for the sale of land, for example, are undoubtedly agreements and there is a very clear process of offer and acceptance involved. In addition, such contracts really do conform to the promise-for-promise model, as they are normally executed at a time before the property is transferred or the whole purchase price is paid. In other words, at the time the contract is entered into the performance by both parties is still in the future. So the contract is a true exchange of promises of land for cash.

The purchase of stocks and shares is another example of this. It is usually done over the telephone, with the contract being made at a time before payment and also before delivery of the share certificate. It is a clear example of a promise for a promise as well as of offer and acceptance - and there can be no doubt that there is an agreement there as well.

The conventional contractual models have been the butt of attack by certain academic commentators. Here for example is P.S. Atiyah:

> The truth is, I would suggest, that there is no such thing as a typical contract at all .... Consider such simple transactions as the boarding of a bus, or a purchase of goods in a supermarket, or a loan of money. Is it really sensible to characterize these transactions as agreements or exchanges of promises? Is it meaningful or useful to claim that a person who boards a bus is promising to pay his fare? If so, would it not be just as meaningful to say that when he descends from the bus and crosses the road he promises to cross with all due care for the safety of other road users?[1]

The technique here is to raise a cloud of dust over the whole subject, blurring the conventional distinctions and allowing the academic commentator in question to suggest that the traditional concepts are meaningless or incorrect.

In fact, two of the three examples singled out by this academic commentator do actually fit quite naturally into the conventional models. It is hard to understand how Atiyah can deny, as he does, that the loan of money is an agreement. If it is in the form of a mortgage or any other type of large loan, its character as an agreement is underlined by being enshrined in a more or less elaborate document which has to be signed by both parties signifying their agreement. Such loans are also quite easy to see as mutual promises, as they are normally agreed well before any money actually changes hands. What such an agreement is saying is essentially: 'We promise to advance you a loan of £x in return for monthly payments of interest at such-and-such a rate and repayment of the principal by the year YYYY.' It is also not difficult to see a loan of money as an example of offer and acceptance, the offer almost invariably coming from the lender.

In the case of simpler loans, say the borrowing of £100 from a friend, the money would usually be handed over straight away. There would then be only one promise, namely that of the borrower, to repay the money, at some specific or indefinite time in the future. But there is certainly no problem about classifying even this kind of loan as an agreement, and it also conforms to the offer-and-acceptance model. It may not always be easy to determine whether the offer came from the lender or from the borrower, but this really makes no difference, as is well illustrated by the purchase of goods in a supermarket.

Surprisingly, Atiyah doubts the classification of a supermarket purchase not only as an exchange of promises but even as an agreement at all! Yet supermarket shopping provides one of the best examples imaginable of free and voluntary agreement between two parties. It may well be that by placing slabs of chocolate at eye-level just by the check-out the supermarket proprietor is trying to influence the shopper and make her buy something that she does not need and would probably not otherwise have bought, but she is certainly not compelled to buy it. In terms of psychology there may be an element of influence involved here, but in terms of law and commerce this is a free and voluntary agreement on both sides.

The legal nature of a supermarket purchase was analysed by the English Court of Appeal in *Pharmaceutical Society v Boots*, in which it was held that the contract was made at the check-out, with the offer coming from the customer and acceptance from the cashier on behalf of the shop.[2] The reason the case was brought had nothing to do with contract law. The Pharmaceutical Society was concerned that chemist shops operating a self-service system might be contravening the law requiring certain medicines to be sold under the supervision of a qualified pharmacist. When the customer took a bottle of aspirin off the shelf and put it in her basket, did that constitute a purchase? If so, that would be unlawful, as the open shelves were not under the control of a pharmacist. Boots argued successfully that that was not when the purchase, i.e. the contract, was concluded. The contract was made only when the customer paid for her final selection of goods at the check-out. This made good sense. For, if a contract was concluded every time a shopper selected an item from the open shelves and put it in her basket or trolley, it would be impossible for her to change her mind. If, for example, she first selected a standard size tube of toothpaste only to find that a 'family size' tube offered better value, she would be locked into the 'contract' that she had already concluded to buy the standard tube. In practice, of course, shoppers are free to change their minds as many times as they like until they reach the check-out. It is only then, once an item has been rung up and paid for, that the contract is concluded.

Like the purchase of a newspaper and other simple transactions, a supermarket purchase cannot easily be analysed in terms of an exchange of promises. But, as we have seen, there can be no doubt that it is an agreement made by offer and acceptance.

Contrary to what Atiyah says, it is remarkable just how well the classical models fit modern types of transactions – and, not least, that of promise-for-promise. The buying and selling of shares over the telephone has already been alluded to. This type of contract not only constitutes an agreement but is also an example of offer and acceptance and is also an exchange of promises: 'I will pay you £20,000 in return for the transfer of 150 shares in Mousetraps plc into my name', with a reciprocal promise by the broker. Because there is a contract in existence by the time the telephone conversation has ended, neither buyer nor seller can cancel it. So, if the purchaser finds even a minute later that the shares that he has just bought at 102 pence have now dropped to 97 pence each, he cannot go back on his original agreement.

The principle here was upheld in *White & Carter v McGregor*,[3] a Scottish case which ended up in the House of Lords and therefore applies equally to English law. A garage entered into a contract with an advertising agency to place plates advertising the garage on litter bins all round town for three years. The first instalment had to be paid seven days after the first advertisements were put up. If any instalment remained unpaid the whole contract price for the full three-year period became payable in full immediately. On the same day as they placed the order the garage wrote to the advertising agency asking them to cancel it. The advertising agency had not yet done any work on the order. But they refused to cancel, on the basis that a binding contract had been concluded and that the garage's purported cancellation amounted to a repudiatory breach which the advertising agency refused to accept. The advertising agency then went ahead and performed their side of the agreement, placing the advertisements with the garage's name on them on litter bins. When the garage refused to pay the first instalment the advertising agency demanded the full contract price. When this was not forthcoming either, the advertising agency sued the garage for the money. The sheriff court and the Court of Session found for the garage, but by a majority of three to two the House of Lords allowed the appeal of the advertising agency and awarded them the full three-year contract price.

It is worth noting that there was no disagreement in the House of Lords about the fact that there was a breach of contract here. Indeed, not even the garage proprietor disputed that he was in breach of contract. The essential issue before the court was a very different one, namely quantum. The garage proprietor contended that he could surely not be expected to pay for a three-year advertising contract as no work had yet been done on the order when he asked for it to be cancelled. In other words, the dispute was on the question of mitigation, and it was on this point that the two dissenting speeches focused.

The reason this case is important to us here is that it provides us with a good high-level example of a contract as an exchange of promises. The moment the garage's order had been accepted by the advertising agency, both parties were locked into a binding contract. The fact that no work had been done and no money had changed hands when the garage wanted to pull out made no difference. A contract had been concluded and failure by either party to perform their side of the bargain would amount to a breach.

Without mentioning *White & Carter v McGregor*, Atiyah characterises this type of 'wholly executory' contract as a 'conundrum':

> A, let us say, orders goods from B, to be specially made to his requirements. The next day, A discovers that he can buy what he wants ready-made elsewhere and cancels the order. B, let it be supposed, has so far done nothing whatever under the contract. There is no doubt in law that B can hold A liable and sue him for damages without having to lift a finger to perform his part of the contract. A receives no benefit, B suffers no detriment, no reliance, and yet he is entitled to damages. How can this be so, and how is it that common lawyers have continued to define the doctrine of consideration in terms of benefit and detriment when this definition does not fit the paradigm case of classical contract theory?[4]

This hypothetical case is so close to *White & Carter* that we may wonder why it is necessary to use it in preference to the actual case. But there is one important difference between *White & Carter* and Atiyah's hypothetical example, and that is that in the decided case not only was there an exchange of promises but there was actual performance by the advertising agency, whereas in the hypothetical case we are not told whether or not B went ahead and made the ordered goods after A had purportedly cancelled the order. Yet that is the crucial point in *White & Carter*. As was agreed on all hands, had the advertising agency not gone ahead and performed their part of the contract in spite of the purported cancellation, they would not have been entitled to claim the full contract price, which they were awarded by the House of Lords.

Without performing their part of the contract, would they have been awarded anything at all? They would most likely have been awarded nominal damages only, which at that time were pegged at 40 shillings (or £2). More importantly, where the winner of a case is awarded nominal damages only, he may well fail to be awarded costs, as this is a matter which is within the discretion of the court.[5]

It is misleading to suggest that in the hypothetical case cited above where 'A receives no benefit' and 'B suffers no detriment', B is nevertheless entitled to damages – unless this is understood as including nominal damages. Significantly, while claiming that this is the normal situation, Atiyah fails to cite a single decided case as an example of this. The reason is simple: it is by no means the normal situation but is a rare exception.

One example that Atiyah *could* have cited in support of his contention is *Thompson Ltd v Robinson,*[6] a first instance decision involving a contract for the purchase of a car. After entering into the contract the buyer refused to take delivery. The sellers, who were a motor dealership, sued for their loss of profit on the aborted sale – and won. In *Charter v Sullivan*,[7] by contrast, on very similar facts, only nominal damages were awarded.

The difference between these two cases is that in the earlier case the car involved was a Standard Vanguard, of which supply exceeded demand, whereas *Charter v Sullivan* was concerned with a Hillman Minx, where the opposite was the case. The significance of this was that, when the buyer rejected the car in *Thompson*, the seller could not sell it to anyone else, as there was a glut of this model of car on the market. So the dealer did actually suffer a loss of profit. In *Charter*, on the other hand, there was a ready market for the rejected car, so no loss was sustained.

Both these cases were fought in terms of an 'available market' within section 50(3) of the Sale of Goods Act 1893, but that is essentially just a statutory application to sale of goods contracts of a principle of the general law of contract.

In fact, these cases provide a good example of the practical application of several of the most fundamental principles of contract law:

(1) *Contractual liability*: the principle here is that contractual liability is strict (see the discussion in part 2 of this chapter). What this means is that the moment there has been a breach of contract the 'innocent' party is entitled to judgment against the party in breach. However, this does *not* necessarily entitle the 'innocent' party to damages. What, then, it may be asked, is the point of going to court and obtaining judgment? The answer is that there are other remedies available besides damages, including injunctions and of course specific performance.

(2) *Compensatory damages*: following on from this is the principle that the function of damages is to compensate the 'innocent' party for his loss. What we are talking about here is the ordinary type of damages, or compensatory damages, as distinct from nominal damages on the one hand and, on the other, exemplary or punitive damages. The Latin phrase associated with compensatory damages is *restitutio in integrum*, meaning 'restoration to a whole'. In the case of contract, the function of compensatory damages is to place the 'victim' of a breach in the position he would have been in if the party in breach had performed his part of the contract as promised. The level of damages awarded to the 'innocent' party is calculated so as to compensate him for his loss: no more and no less. If he has suffered no loss, he *is* entitled to judgment under the principle of strict liability but he will only be awarded nominal damages.

(3) *Mitigation*: by equally relentless logic we come to the third fundamental principle of contract law, which is that the 'victim' of a breach of contract cannot just wallow in his misfortune and demand that the party in breach compensate him fully for his loss. He has the duty to mitigate that loss to the best of his ability. In other words, if, let us say, an employee is held by the court to have been wrongfully dismissed, his employer is in breach of contract. The employee will obtain judgment, but how will his loss be calculated? If he was earning £50,000 a year and he has not bothered to look for another job, can he simply expect the court to award him £50,000 a year until he reaches the age of retirement? Certainly not. If he does not actively seek a new position, the court will take into account the state of the labour market for his particular kind of work, his chances of getting another job and the likely level of remuneration that he would have been able to achieve. So, if the court finds that he could quite easily and quickly have found a position paying £30,000 a year, instead of being awarded damages on the basis of an annual loss of £50,000 his loss will be calculated as only £20,000 a year. But, it may be objected, is this not contradictory to the basic principle (2 above) of compensatory damages, according to which the innocent party will be awarded the amount of his loss? In fact, it is quite in conformity with that principle. For, to go back to our employment example, what is the actual loss of the sacked employee? It is not £50,000 but only £20,000, the difference between the job he has lost and his new position. But, what if he has not bothered to look for a new job? Will not his loss then be the full £50,000? No, because the law says that it is his duty to mitigate his loss, and, if he has not done so the court will nevertheless presume that he has.

These three principles can be restated more simply as follows:

**(a) The 'innocent' party to a breach of contract is always entitled to judgment.**

**(b) If he has suffered a loss he will also be entitled to (compensatory) damages, the level of damages being calculated so as to compensate him for his loss.**

**(c) But the actual damages awarded will be subject to mitigation, whether the person himself has actually mitigated his loss or not.**

These principles are not only logical but also practical. How would they apply to Atiyah's hypothetical example mentioned above, in which A orders goods to be produced by B but cancels before paying and also before B has done any work on the order? Can B obtain damages from A still without doing any work on the order? Under principle (a), B is entitled to judgment. But, contrary to what Atiyah says, B will not be entitled to anything more than nominal damages unless he has suffered a real loss, which, on the hypothetical facts as given by Atiyah, does not appear to be the case. In what sense then is this a 'puzzle' or 'conundrum', as Atiyah claims?

On the contrary, the common law, both in theory and in practice, awards real (i.e. compensatory) damages only where there has been a real loss. The only anomaly is *White & Carter v McGregor* (not mentioned by Atiyah in this connection at all), but it has to be remembered that in that case the contracted work was actually performed. As discussed above, the customer did not want the work to be done and had purportedly cancelled his order, but as the law recognised a concluded contract this 'cancellation' amounted to a breach of contract entitling the 'innocent' party either to repudiate the contract or else to treat the contract as still on foot and perform their part of the agreement. This is what they did, advertising the defendant garage's name on litter bins all around town in accordance with the contract. Had that not occurred, the advertising agency would not have succeeded in their claim. That was agreed by all members of the House of Lords.

What would have happened if, instead of being a contract for advertising the garage on litter bins, it had been a contract for painting the garage premises? Let us assume that, as in the actual case, the garage proprietor then changed his mind and decided to 'cancel' the order. Let us also assume that, as also happened in the decided case, the other party refused to cancel but insisted that there was a binding contract which they were going to honour. What could they have done? Could they have come round to the garage the next day and demanded to be admitted in order to paint the building? Clearly, having 'cancelled' the order, the garage proprietor would not have let them in and they would not have been able to perform their part of the contract. Could they in those rather different circumstances, not having done the work, still demand the contract price? Certainly not. But, is it not unfair to make the success or failure of their claim depend on the purely accidental feature of whether or not they needed the co-operation of the garage in order to do the work? That was what the minority in the House of Lords thought, and it is easy to see why.

On the other hand, if we go back to our three basic principles, the actual decision in *White & Carter* becomes more understandable. That there was a breach of contract is undeniable. That gave the 'innocent' party a choice (or an 'election', to use the proper old term) of whether to treat the contract as dead or alive. In treating it as alive and performing their obligations under it, they were perfectly within their rights. And, once they had done the work, they must surely have had the right to be paid for it. That is the underlying logic of the majority decision in *White & Carter*.

This also effectively answers the question why they were awarded the full contract price – for a three-year contract that the customer did not want – and not some lesser figure. In most contract cases the award is for damages for loss of profits. That is not what happened here. It *would* have been the appropriate measure if the advertising agency had *not* done the work but not in a situation where they fully performed their obligations under the contract.

There is also another, more technical, explanation for the fact that they were awarded the full three-year contract price, and that is that the claim was not for damages but for the price, a hangover from the ancient form of action known as 'debt', as distinct from damages.

### *Executory contracts*

Another of Atiyah's broadsides aimed at the promise-for-promise model of contracts is introduced by his remark 'that wholly executory contracts are rarer, more ephemeral in practice, and somewhat less binding than the classical model of contract would suggest'.[8] A wholly executory contract is one based on an exchange of promises made before either party has performed its side of the bargain. In fact, the number of such contracts has clearly increased, not declined, in recent times. This is largely the result of the rise of telephone, fax, email and other forms of instantaneous or near-instantaneous communication. One of the commonest modern contracts is the ordering by telephone of the delivery of a pizza, a curry or some other form of fast food. In the majority of cases no payment is made over the telephone. Instead, all there is is an exchange of promises: a promise to deliver certain specified dishes in return for a promise to pay.

Contracts for the buying and selling of shares are generally made in almost precisely the same way, as is discussed above. The purchase and sale of a house is yet another good example of a promise-for-promise contract. Here it is usual for the buyer to put down a deposit of 5% or 10% on the purchase at the time contracts are 'exchanged', but possession of the property comes only at the stage of 'completion', which may be weeks or even months later, and it is only at this stage that the bulk of the purchase price is actually paid. Purchases on credit represent yet another huge category of promise-for-promise contracts.

However, our academic commentator has not yet exhausted his armoury. He next purports to show 'how easy it is to interpret transactions or arrangements as binding or not binding in their inception, according to the predilections of the interpreter'.[9]

The case which Atiyah fastens on as a prime example of this is *Luxor v Cooper*.[10] The owners of a cinema orally agreed to pay an estate agent a commission on completion of the sale of the cinema to a purchaser introduced by the agent. The agent duly announced that he had found a prospective buyer, but the cinema proprietors then changed their mind and disposed of their interest in the cinema by way of a sale of shares (to a different purchaser, found by themselves) rather than by a sale of the property itself. Even though the property sale did not go through, the agent claimed his commission. When this was refused, he sued the cinema proprietors.

The trial judge had little difficulty in rejecting the claim. This decision was reversed by a unanimous Court of Appeal, which read into the agency contract an implied term that, once the agent had found a willing purchaser, the vendors would not have the right to pull out 'without just cause' or 'without reasonable cause'. This was based on *Trollope v Martyn Bros*,[11] another estate agent case, in which the full terms of a contract of sale had been agreed and the purchaser had actually signed when the vendor decided not to proceed with the sale. But even on these rather different facts, Scrutton LJ, arguably the leading commercial lawyer of the day, had dissented.

The Court of Appeal's decision in *Luxor* was reversed by a unanimous House of Lords restoring the trial judge's decision – a classic back-and-forth outcome or what might be termed a yo-yo case. Lord Russell of Killowen put the matter succinctly:

> The only right of the plaintiff [estate agent] was to receive his commission out of the purchase moneys, if and when received. *His right was a purely contingent right.* He stood to earn a very large sum at comparatively small pains, taking the risk of either side withdrawing from the negotiations before any binding contract of sale and purchase was concluded, or the risk of the contract (if any) for any reason not being carried to completion. My Lords, upon this view of the oral contract which is the foundation of the plaintiff's claim, the action must fail.[12] (Italics supplied.)

The key phrase here is 'contingent right': the estate agent's right to receive commission was contingent, i.e. conditional upon completion of a sale of the property to the prospective buyer that he had found. This is what makes an agent's commission contract different from an ordinary straightforward contract for services. It is a contract which is contingent upon another contract. In other words, it may be seen as a form of collateral contract.

But the contract in the *Luxor* case was conditional in another respect as well. It depended upon the agent's finding a suitable prospective purchaser who was ready, able and willing to buy the property on terms agreeable to the sellers.

The agent's contract was oral, but there was no doubt about its essential terms. What it was essentially saying was that if the agent found a purchaser who was acceptable to the vendor and if the vendor sold the property to this prospective purchaser, £10,000 commission would go to the agent once the sale contract was completed. As usual in the case of collateral contracts, therefore, consideration for the agent's finding a suitable purchaser would be entry by the vendor into the main contract, i.e. the contract of sale with the purchaser introduced by the agent, which in turn would trigger the payment of commission to the agent.

There was no obligation on the agent to do anything at all. He was *not* obliged to go out and find a purchaser any more than the cinema proprietors were obliged to accept any prospective purchaser found by him or indeed to sell the property at all. This is what differentiates this type of contract from most contracts. In the average contract both parties are bound to perform. Typically, one party is obliged to provide goods or services and the other is obliged to pay for them. Both parties are bound the moment the contract is made. But the contract in *Luxor* was a conditional contract. Neither party was bound to do anything unless a certain condition was fulfilled. This is typical of commercial arrangements made with commission agents.

There has been no shortage of litigation over such contracts. As the wording differs from one contract to another, so court decisions have varied. But the commercial realities are essentially the same in all these cases. From a businessman's point of view it makes little commercial sense to bind yourself to pay an agent's commission in circumstances where you are not benefiting from any work on the agent's part. Conversely, agents are likely to be anxious to be able to claim commission in as wide a range of circumstances as possible – and it is the agent who normally determines the wording of the contract. Lord Denning put the position in characteristic fashion:

> We have had many cases on commission claimed by estate agents. The common understanding of mankind is that commission is only payable by the vendor when the property is sold. It is payable out of the purchase money; but some agents have sought, by their printed forms, to get commission even though the property has not been sold or the purchase money received. At first, it was 'when a binding contract is signed'. Next, it was if they introduced a person

> 'ready, able and willing to purchase'. Then they missed out 'able' and wanted commission if they only got a 'prospective' purchaser or a 'willing' purchaser who was unable to purchase. Now we have got to the widest clause that I have yet seen: 'Should you be instrumental in introducing a person willing to sign a document capable of becoming a contract to purchase ....'
>
> Can an estate agent insert such a clause and get away with it? I think not. I regard this clause as wholly unreasonable and totally uncertain. Suppose a man signed a piece of paper which had just got on it the address of the premises and the price. That could be said to be 'a document capable of becoming a contract', even though there was not an offer contained in it. So, also, if a man signed a document which was expressly 'subject to contract'; or even signed a blank form with all the blanks to be filled in. It might be said to be 'a document capable of becoming a contract'. Even if the man were quite unable to complete, he might still be a person 'willing' to sign.[13]

Seen in the light of common commercial sense, therefore, the general rule governing estate agents' commission contracts is really quite simple. *If* the agent (A) introduces a suitable prospective purchaser (P) to the seller (S), and *if* this results in a contract of sale between S and P, then and only then does A become entitled to his commission.

Does this mean that an estate agent's commission contract is a 'unilateral' contract? Atiyah maintains that the House of Lords in *Luxor* 'decided that it was a unilateral promise in which the agent himself undertook to do nothing'.[14] This is not in fact what the House of Lords said. Not only does the word 'unilateral' *not* appear anywhere in any of the speeches, but the situation was very different from that found where there is a 'unilateral' promise. The typical unilateral promise occurs in reward cases. The owner of a lost dog, for example, will put up posters offering a reward for the return of the dog. Unless this offer is revoked (also by means of posters) before the dog is returned, the owner will be obliged to pay the reward to anyone who finds the missing dog and restores it to him in response to the advertisement. The point about a contract with a commission agent is not only that the agent is not obliged to do anything but also that, even if the agent does actually find a prospective purchaser, the vendor is still not under any obligation to sell the property to him – or indeed to anyone. So labelling *Luxor* and commission agent contracts in general as 'unilateral' is not only unhelpful but also incorrect. The correct label, as discussed above, is 'conditional'. Payment of the commission depends on the fulfilment of a double condition: it is conditional not only upon the agent's introducing a suitable prospective purchaser but also on the vendor's proceeding to sell the property to that person.

## 2. Strict contractual liability

**(1) Contractual liability is strict: no negligence or fault need be proved in order for the 'innocent' party to obtain judgment.**

**(2) The main exception to this is the doctrine of frustration.**

**(3) The influence of tort law coupled with judicial activism has led to the partial eclipse of the doctrine of strict contractual liability, which however remains a fundamental principle of law.**

One of the most basic – and one of the most neglected – principles of contract law is that a breach of contract imports strict or absolute liability. What this means is that the 'innocent' party is automatically entitled to judgment, though not necessarily to damages. The reason the word 'innocent' is printed in quotation marks is that this very doctrine of strict liability means that a breach of contract is not in any sense immoral and does not imply any fault on the part of the party in question. So, for example, if you buy a can of baked beans from a supermarket and the beans turn out to be rotten, the supermarket is in breach of contract – even though the fault probably lies elsewhere, most likely with the canning company.

Is it not unfair, then, to hold the supermarket liable? Not at all. In commercial dealings there is normally a contractual chain. In the case of baked beans this chain would stretch from the farmer at the one end to the consumer at the other. Each link in the chain would be connected to the one before and the one after it (if any) by means of a contract. So, if a supermarket had to refund its customers for a bad batch of baked beans, the supermarket could go back to *its* suppliers and ask them for a refund. The buck would stop at the point where the fault arose, because that is where the original breach occurred. It is important to realise, however, that 'fault' in this context does not mean negligence but merely indicates the point where something went wrong with the baked beans.

As if to emphasise the morally neutral nature of contractual liability, some judges have taken to speaking of primary and secondary duties under the contract:

> A basic principle of the common law of contract … is that parties to a contract are free to determine for themselves what primary obligations they will accept …
>
> Every failure to perform a primary obligation is a breach of contract. The secondary obligation on the part of the contract breaker to which it gives rise by implication of the common law is to pay monetary compensation to the other party for the loss sustained by him in consequence of the breach.[1]

In other words, the obligations set out in the contract itself are regarded as 'primary obligations', with payment of damages for breach seen merely as a 'secondary obligation'. This classification of contractual obligations underlines the fact that the duty of the party in breach to make reparation for his breach is in no sense to be regarded as a punishment but merely as substituted performance. This probably goes too far, because it makes it appear as though the parties to a contract have a choice either to perform their contractual duties or to pay damages instead. If this were the case it should not be necessary to go to court in order to obtain an award of damages. It is of course possible to settle a breach of contract case without going to court, but this will usually result in a compromise of some sort and not with full compensation for the loss suffered by the injured party.

### *Beswick v Beswick*

What if there is a breach of contract but the innocent party has not actually suffered any loss? This is what happened in the famous leading case of *Beswick v Beswick*.[2] Peter Beswick was a coal merchant who retired, handing his business over to his nephew in return for a promise that the nephew would pay him £6.50 per week as a consultant for the rest of his life and then £5 per week to his widow. The nephew paid the uncle during his lifetime but after his death made only one payment to his aunt, Mrs Beswick. This created a dilemma. Mrs Beswick had suffered a loss but could not sue on her own behalf as she was not a party to the contract. On the other hand, her late husband (or his estate, which in law is the same thing) *was* a party to the contract but had suffered no loss. Mrs Beswick was in a cleft stick - or would have been had it not been for some fancy legal footwork on her lawyers' part and that of Lord Denning's Court of Appeal. As administratrix of her husband's estate she was entitled to step into his shoes and sue her nephew. The estate was clearly entitled to judgment - but judgment for what? As the estate had suffered no loss, only nominal damages would be likely to be awarded. So she sued instead for specific performance of the agreement to pay her the annuity. Having lost at first instance she won in the Court of Appeal and in the House of Lords. This was the first time that a court allowed specfic performance for a money payment - a logical extension to the principle of strict contractual liability.

### *Paradine v Jane*

The old case of *Paradine v Jane*[3] is still an authority in this area of the law. A landlord sued his tenant for three years' arrears of rent. The default occurred during the English Civil War, and the tenant's defence was that he had not been in occupation of the land during the period in question as he had been expelled by an 'alien enemy', Prince Rupert. In actual fact, Prince Rupert was a German cousin of King Charles I's who had come over to help the king against the parliamentarians. But this was beside the point. The tenant's plea that he had been dispossessed by an alien enemy was not challenged, but the court nevertheless held that 'although the whole army had been alien enemies, yet the defendant ought to pay the rent'.

Were there no circumstances that would excuse a party from performing his duties under the law? The court made it clear that there were: 'where the law creates a duty or charge, and the party is disabled from performing it without any default in him, and has no remedy over, there the law will excuse him. As in the case of waste, if a house be destroyed by tempest or by enemies, the lessee is excused.'

However, the brief judgment continues in a different vein:

'But, when the party by his own contract creates a duty or charge upon himself he is bound to make it good, if he may, notwithstanding any accident by inevitable necessity because he might have provided against it by his contract. Therefore, if the lessee covenants to repair a house, although it is burnt by lightning or thrown down by enemies yet he ought to repair it.' The distinction drawn here is between a duty imposed by the general law - breach of which would be a tort - and a contractual duty. An act of God or inevitable accident may excuse a person from performing a duty laid down by law, but this does not apply to contractual duties, for, as a contract is a voluntary agreement it is open to the parties to provide for any contingency that might arise.

### *Frustration*

This rather harsh doctrine is still the law, though it has been mitigated to some extent by the development of the doctrine of frustration, which has been defined as follows:

> ... something must be the subject-matter of every contract. If that something has disappeared, the contract disappears with that on which it was founded ....
>
> ... if the foundation of the contract goes, either by the destruction of the subject-matter or by reason of such long interruption or delay that the performance is really in effect that of a different contract, parties can if they wish (and no doubt they often do) provide for what in that event is to happen, but, if they do not, then the performance of the contract is regarded as frustrated.[4]

Probably the best-known case of frustration in English law is still *Taylor v Caldwell*.[5] Taylor hired a music hall for a series of concerts, but before the first date booked, and through no fault of either party, the hall burnt down. As a result the concerts had to be cancelled. The contract made no provision for any such eventuality. The hirers of the hall had not paid any part of the hire charge but had incurred advertising and printing costs. It was to recover these expenses that the hirers brought the case, but they failed on the ground that the contract had been frustrated. Blackburn J, one of the great Victorian commercial judges, began by setting out the ordinary legal position:

> There seems no doubt that, where there is a positive contract to do a thing not in itself unlawful, the contractor must perform it or pay damages for not doing it, although, in consequence of unforeseen accident, the performance of his contract has become unexpectedly burdensome, or even impossible.

Then, remarkably, Lord Blackburn (as he was later to become) prays in aid a principle drawn from the civil law, namely Justinian's *Digest*: 'If Stichus has been promised to be delivered on a certain day but he dies before that date, the promisor is not bound.'[6] Stichus is the name of a slave. What this means is that if there is a contract for the sale and purchase of a slave but the slave dies before the date set for delivery, the seller is not liable. Lord Blackburn then cites the celebrated *Treatise on Obligations* by the eighteenth-century French jurist Pothier:

> The principle which we have established, that the debtor of a thing certain is discharged from his obligation when the thing has perished without his act or fault, and before he has been put in arrear, receives an exception in the case in which the debtor makes himself by a particular clause of the contract liable for the risk of accidents.[7]

But, it may well be asked, what authority do civilian sources enjoy in English common law? Blackburn J's answer is twofold:

> Though the civil law is not of itself an authority in an English court, it affords great assistance in investigating the principles on which the law is grounded, and it seems to us that the common law authorities establish that, in such a contract, the same condition of the continued existence of the thing is implied by English law.

This is an important statement. Lord Blackburn here frankly admits the importance of Roman law as a source of legal principles, though he adds that this particular principle was already recognised by the common law:

> The principle seems to us to be that in contracts in which the performance depends on the continued existence of a particular person or thing, a condition is implied that the impossibility of performance arising from the perishing of the person or thing shall excuse the performance.[8]

The word 'frustration' does not appear anywhere in Lord Blackburn's judgment, yet *Taylor v Caldwell* has come to be regarded as the classic frustration case. It is also a good example of a marriage of convenience between Roman and English legal principles. Lord Blackburn conveniently found the relevant principle lurking in the backwaters of the English common law: namely, the implication of a term in the contract that the essential subject-matter of the contract – in this case the concert hall – would be in existence at the time stipulated in the contract. But was that really the operative principle here or was it the one drawn from Justinian?

By the time the music hall burnt down neither party had performed (no pun intended): no concerts had taken place and the hirers had not paid any part of the hire charge. But what if they had?

The cancellation of the coronation of Edward VII in 1902 produced a veritable feast of relevant cases, even though the coronation was not actually cancelled but only postponed to the following year. The king suffered a burst appendix shortly before he was due to be crowned and his great girth made the operation more dangerous than it would otherwise have been. But the fact that the king had had an appendectomy made the operation extremely popular.

In *Krell v Henry*[9] Henry hired some rooms in Pall Mall overlooking the coronation procession route for £75, of which £25 was paid in advance, the balance to be paid on the very day, as it happened, that the postponement of the coronation was announced. Henry never paid the balance, and a strong Court of Appeal found in his favour, upholding the first instance judge, who had actually gone even further in Henry's favour by awarding him in addition a refund of the £25 that he had paid (a claim which he dropped in the Court of Appeal).

But the opposite result was reached in the very similar case of *Chandler v Webster*.[10] Here the hire charge was £141 15s, with £100 paid on account, which the hirer sought to recover when the coronation was postponed. Surprisingly, the Court of Appeal not only decided against him but even ordered him to pay the outstanding £41 15s, on the ground that in this case the full hire charge was due and payable immediately on the booking, well before the king fell ill.

Though the outcome of these two cases was different, there was a common principle underlying them both, which was expressed in yet another of the coronation cases:

> All that can be said is that, when the procession was abandoned, the contract was off, not that anything done under the contract was void. The loss must remain where it was at the time of the abandonment.[11]

The distinction drawn here is between the situation where the contract is 'wiped out altogether' or 'rescinded *ab initio*' and the coronation cases, where the parties were 'merely released from further performance'. What is the justification for this distinction? Probably a deep-seated reluctance on the part of the judges to set aside a contract altogether.

This principle, that 'the loss lies where it falls', was finally disapproved by the House of Lords in *Fibrosa Spolka Akcyjna v Fairbairn*,[12] in which a Polish company ordered machinery from a British company for delivery to Gdynia in Poland. A deposit of £1,000 was paid with the order, but Gdynia was then occupied by German forces and delivery was frustrated. The Polish company sued for the return of the £1,000 and won in the House of Lords, which specifically overruled *Chandler v Webster*. The new principle, which is still the law today, was explained by Lord Atkin by means of a simple example:

> A sells a horse to B for £50, delivery to be made in a month, the price to be paid forthwith, but the property not to pass till delivery, and B to pay A an agreed sum for keep of the horse during the month. The horse dies in a fortnight. A is excused from delivery and B from taking delivery; B is bound to pay the sum due for the fortnight during which the horse was kept; but what is the position as to the £50, the price paid in advance? … The answer which I venture to think would occur to most people, whether laymen or lawyers, would be that the buyer ought to get his money back, having had nothing for it; and the lawyer would support the claim by saying that it is money had and received to the use of the buyer, being money paid on a consideration which has wholly failed.[13]

Lord Atkin summed up his position in terms of what he termed 'an old-established principle of the common law':

> What is being now decided is that the application of an old-established principle of the common law does enable a man who has paid money and received nothing for it to recover the money so expended. At any rate, it can be said it leaves the man who has received the money and given nothing for it in no worse position than if he had received none.[14]

Lord Macmillan, a Scottish judge, likewise held that the distinction drawn in *Chandler v Webster* was wrong, labelling it 'a complete misapprehension'.

## IX.2. *Strict contractual liability*

### *Overlap between contract and tort*

There is an apparent exception to the doctrine of strict contractual liability where contract and tort overlap, as in professional negligence, employment and certain types of personal injury cases. Like frustration, this too can be explained on the basis of implied terms. But, unlike frustration, which is a genuine exception to strict contractual liability, these overlapping situations only give the appearance of being exceptions to strict contractual liability.

Contractual liability arises out of breach, which in turn depends on the terms of the contract. This much is obvious. But the contract will very often include implied terms, and it is not always easy to tell exactly what these implied terms are.

In *Readhead v Midland Rail Co*[15] a railway passenger who had bought his own ticket was badly injured when the carriage in which he was travelling broke away from the rest of the train and overturned. The cause of the accident, it emerged later, was a defect in one of the tyres. The injured passenger sued the railway company not in tort, as one might have expected, but in contract. The injured passenger lost at first instance (before two judges) and again on appeal (heard by six judges). The problem was that the defect in the tyre was not detectable by either eye or ear, and the railway company had carried out all the usual checks on the wheels. Not only was no negligence found on the part of the railway company but even the manufacturers were exonerated from all blame. It was no doubt in anticipation of these findings that the injured man's counsel chose to sue in contract rather than in tort. But this did not help either. What then about the doctrine of strict contractual liability it might be asked? For, even if there was no negligence found on the part of the railway company, were they not in breach of contract?

This is where the implied terms came in. Did the contract include an implied warranty that the railway company would carry its passengers safely to their destination or that the rolling stock was 'free from all defects likely to cause peril although those defects were such that no skill, care or foresight could have detected their existence'? It was held that the contract contained no such term, the only obligation on the railway company being

> to take due care, including in that term the use of skill and foresight, to carry the passenger safely. It, of course, follows, that the absence of such care, in other words negligence, would alone be a breach of this contract; and as the facts of this case do not disclose such a breach, and, on the contrary, negative any want of skill, care, or foresight, we think the plaintiff has failed to sustain his action, and that the judgment of the court below in favour of the defendants ought to be affirmed.[16]

The principle ruling at the time was shortly stated in an 1825 case in the following terms: 'A carrier of goods is liable at all events, a carrier of passengers is only liable for negligence.'[17]

A carrier of *goods* was strictly liable for loss or damage of any kind arising out of any cause other than 'acts of God' or 'the king's enemies', but liability for injury to *passengers* depended on proof of negligence. From a modern perspective this seems perverse. Should it not be the other way round, one might be tempted to ask?

The classic statement of the obligations of carriers of goods still remains the magnificent judgment of Holt CJ in *Coggs v Bernard*,[18] in which that great jurist identified six types of bailments, i.e. situations where goods are left by their owner with someone else. Not all bailments are contractual, as the term includes gratuitous bailments as well as bailments for reward.

The facts of *Coggs v Bernard* are straightforward enough. Bernard undertook to move some hogsheads (i.e. large barrels) of brandy belonging to Coggs from one cellar to another, but so negligently was this done that one of the barrels was cracked open and a large quantity of brandy was spilled. To this day it is not known whether this was a bailment for reward or whether Bernard had merely agreed to move the barrels as a favour to Coggs. Nevertheless, Coggs succeeded in his action for damages.

Holt CJ's sixfold classification of bailments is as follows:

(a) 'A bare naked bailment of goods' (*depositum*), where goods are left without reward in the custody of another. Here liability will attach only in the event of 'gross negligence'.

(b) A loan to a friend free of charge (*commodatum*). Here liability is stricter: 'if the bailee be guilty of the least neglect he will be answerable'.

(c) Lending for hire (*locatio et conductio*). Here too the test is one of negligence.

(d) Pawn (*vadium*). Here the test is one of 'ordinary care' or 'true diligence'.

(e) Bailment without reward (*mandatum*). Here the test for liability is also one of ordinary negligence.

(f) Carriage of goods for reward. Holt CJ divides this into two subcategories: carriage by a 'common carrier' on the one hand, and, on the other, carriage by a 'private person'. The term 'common carrier' included ship's captains and others exercising a 'public employment' as carriers. Here alone liability is strict: 'The law charges this person thus entrusted to carry goods against all events but acts of God and of the enemies of the King. For though the force be never so great, as if an irresistible multitude of people should rob him, nevertheless he is chargeable.' In the case of a private person carrying goods for reward without being a professional 'common carrier', liability will attach only where there is negligence.

This places the rule in *Readhead v Midland Rail Co* in context. In all but one of Sir John Holt's categories of bailment, liability depends on a finding of negligence. The sole exception is a contract for the carriage of goods by a common carrier, which alone is governed by strict liability. Holt CJ explains this as an ancient policy decision in order to protect the public from dishonesty. If you entrusted goods to a carrier and your goods were stolen in transit, what was to stop the carrier from stealing them himself or, in Holt CJ's words, from 'combining with thieves etc and yet doing it in such a clandestine manner as would not be possible to be discovered'? The only way to prevent this was by making the carrier strictly liable, even in the event of theft.

It is important to note that none of Holt's six categories relates to the carriage of passengers, which is not regarded as a bailment at all. It is equally important to note that carriage of goods by a common carrier is a bailment but a contractual bailment, the terms of the contract being laid down by 'the custom of the realm'. But could a common carrier not then introduce an exemption clause into the contract so as to limit his liability? Of course he could, and this is precisely what happened. Carriers soon began to substitute the onerous terms of the customary contract with a 'special contract' relieving themselves of strict liability.[19]

However, the concept of 'common carrier' has not disappeared altogether. Interestingly enough, in theory it extends even to carriers of goods - and passengers - by air.[20] But the introduction of blanket exclusion clauses into contracts of carriage effectively put paid to the distinction between common carriers and other types of carriers.

### *Concurrent liability*

Would *Readhead v Midland Rail Co* be decided the same way today as it was in 1868? Probably not - but not because of any change in the law of contract. So narrow was the scope of the tort of negligence that plaintiff's counsel in *Readhead* did not even bother to attempt it, putting all their hopes in a contractual cause of action, which, as we have seen, failed.

Thanks to a celebrated semi-decomposed snail, the normal cause of action for personal injury claims today is the tort of negligence. Indeed, the only reason for the existence of *Donoghue v Stevenson*[21] was precisely the fact that, as the ginger beer float in that case was bought not by Mrs Donoghue but by a friend as a 'treat' for her, Mrs Donoghue was not in a contractual relationship with anyone.

But what if Mrs Donoghue *had* bought the contaminated drink herself? This would have given her a contractual cause of action against Minchella, the cafe proprietor. *Lockett v Charles*, discussed in a different connection in Chapter II, was just such a case.[22] As we saw there, a husband and wife had lunch together at a hotel. Both ordered whitebait, but after taking a single mouthful the wife felt sick and refused to eat any more of it. Though the husband finished his whitebait, the wife alone got food poisoning, and it was accepted by the judge that her illness had been caused by the whitebait. The husband paid for the meal, but neither spouse was found to have been 'in charge of the proceedings', and so, conveniently enough, each of them was held to have had a contractual relationship with the restaurant. The action, brought jointly by husband and wife, was originally framed in both contract and tort (in the alternative), but during the trial the tort claim was abandoned and plaintiffs' counsel relied solely on a claim of breach of an implied warranty that the food was fit for human consumption. Contractual liability was duly found and the restaurant proprietor was ordered to pay damages totalling £200.

This was a first instance decision and the case never went on appeal. But it is interesting to compare it with its far better known near contemporary, *Donoghue v Stevenson*. Would *Lockett* have succeeded in tort? The plaintiffs' leading counsel evidently felt less than confident on this head. One problem concerned the claim that Mrs Lockett had got her food poisoning from the meal consumed in the restaurant. In view of her husband's robust good health throughout, this was far from self-evident. For, not only had he ordered the whitebait as well but he had consumed his whole portion. These doubts may possibly have been relevant to tort. But were they not equally relevant to a contractual cause of action, it may be asked? The judge, Tucker J, explained the difference:

> With regard to the female plaintiff's position in respect of breach of warranty, every proprietor is under a duty to take reasonable care to see that the food which he supplies to his guests is fit for human consumption. If he does not take such reasonable steps, and if he is negligent, a person who buys the food which he supplies can recover damages from him based on his negligence. As, however, there is no allegation of such negligence in this case, it must be assumed that the proprietor of the hotel and his servants could not be at fault in any way, and either plaintiff can recover only if he or she establishes that there was a contract between him or her and the proprietor of the hotel.

This brings home the practical force of the principle of strict contractual liability. No negligence need be proved: indeed, it can be assumed that there was none. Yet there was clearly something wrong with the whitebait. Who was to blame for this? The point is that that is completely irrelevant to a contractual cause of action.

In a 1921 New York case, *Jacob & Youngs Inc v Kent*[23] a builder was engaged to construct a house conforming to certain precise specifications. In particular, the contract called for all wrought-iron pipes to be 'well galvanized, lap welded pipe of the grade known as "standard pipe" of Reading manufacture'. It turned out, however, that only about two-fifths of the pipe was of this type. But by the time the houseowner was alerted to this most of the pipework was encased within the walls. In order to replace it with the correct type a good deal of the structure would have had to be demolished. The owner's architect nevertheless directed the builder to replace the pipework with the stipulated brand. When he refused the architect refused to give the builder a certificate for final payment and the builder sued for the unpaid balance of the contract price and won in the New York Court of Appeals.

The majority opinion, delivered by Cardozo J, the future US Supreme Court justice, accepted the builder's contention 'that the brands installed, though made by other manufacturers, were the same in quality, in appearance, in market value and in cost as the brand stated in the contract'. The builder's evidence to this effect had been excluded at the original trial. Cardozo J's argument then proceeds as follows:

> We think the evidence [i.e. that there was no real difference between Reading pipe and the brands used instead], if admitted, would have supplied some basis for the inference that the defect was insignificant in its relation to the project. The courts never say that one who makes a contract fills the measure of his duty by less than full performance. They do say, however, that an omission, both trivial and innocent, will sometimes be atoned for by allowance of the resulting damage, and will not always be the breach of a condition to be followed by a forfeiture ...
>
> In the circumstances of this case, we think the measure of the allowances is not the cost of replacement, which would be great, but the difference in value, which would be either nominal or nothing.

Cardozo J's argument on behalf of the majority may be set out as follows:

(a) The use of the wrong brand of pipe was of no significance.
(b) It could not therefore be the basis for terminating the contract.
(c) The houseowner's only remedy lay in an 'allowance' of the difference

in value between the brand of pipe stipulated and that of the pipe actually used.

(d) But this difference in value was 'either nominal or nothing'.

(e) Therefore judgment absolute should be directed in favour of the builder.

So strongly did Cardozo J feel about this case that, not content to award the builder the full contract price, he also gave him 'costs in all courts', a highly unusual order for any American case.

Yet there is clearly something very wrong with Cardozo's reasoning. What is missing from it is the most important point of all, namely a recognition of the concept of strict contractual liability. The use of the wrong brand of pipe was a breach of contract – something that Cardozo was at pains to avoid saying. He uses the non-legal terms 'defect' and 'omission' instead. And, having shied away from admitting that the builder was in breach of contract, Cardozo also carefully avoids using the word 'damages' for the remedy to which the houseowner is entitled, referring instead to an 'allowance' (a term drawn from the doctrine of substantial performance, which, as McLaughlin J argued in his dissenting opinion (see below), had no bearing on this case).

However, whatever label is stuck on it, the builder's non-compliance with the stipulation plainly did amount to a breach of contract, which in turn should have triggered an automatic judgment in favour of the houseowner. Up to this point the law of contract is clear and unambiguous. The normal remedy for a breach of contract is damages, which are of course intended to compensate the injured party for his loss. It was only at this point that the case should have presented any problem at all, namely: how serious was the breach? And had the defendant houseowner suffered any actual loss? Even if, as Cardozo J maintained, the defendant had not suffered any loss, he should still at least have been entitled to nominal damages.

Instead, not only did the houseowner get nothing, but, as we have seen, he also had to pay the builder's legal costs in all courts. Had judgment been entered for the houseowner, as it should have been, no such costs order could have been made. (In addition, it is worth mentioning that 'a substantial minority of [United States] courts have allowed an award of nominal damages to sustain an award of punitive damages',[24] though there was no suggestion of that in *Jacob & Youngs* itself.)

In a refreshingly robust dissenting opinion McLaughlin J took issue with Cardozo J:

> The plaintiff did not perform its contract. Its failure to do so was either intentional or due to gross neglect which, under the uncontradicted facts, amounted to the same thing, nor did it make any proof of the cost of compliance, where compliance was possible …
>
> If the plaintiff had intended to, and had, complied with the terms of the contract except as to minor omissions, due to inadvertence, then he might be allowed to recover the contract price, less the amount necessary to fully compensate the defendant for damage caused by such omissions. But that is not this case …
>
> The defendant had a right to contract for what he wanted. He had a right before making payment to get what the contract called for. It is no answer to this suggestion to say that the pipe put in was just as good as that made by the Reading Manufacturing Company, or that the difference in value between such pipe and the pipe made by the Reading Manufacturing Company would be either 'nominal or nothing'. Defendant contracted for pipe made by the Reading Manufacturing Company. What his reason was for requiring this kind of pipe is of no importance. He wanted that and was entitled to it. It may have been a mere whim on his part, but even so, he had a right to this kind of pipe, regardless of whether some other kind, according to the opinion of the contractor or experts, would have been 'just as good, better, or done just as well'.

In sum McLaughlin J's argument runs like this:

(a) The use of the wrong pipe constituted a breach of contract on the part of the builder.

(b) As with any breach of contract, this entitled the houseowner to judgment.

(c) The appropriate remedy for a breach of contract is damages (with or without more).

(e) The correct measure of damages is the sum of money which would compensate the innocent party for his loss.

(f) The calculation of this figure would depend on whether it was possible to award damages in a contract case for disappointment, mental anguish and emotional distress or whether it was to be calculated in purely commercial terms. If the latter, and if it was found that there really was no difference in value between the pipe stipulated in the contract and the pipe actually used, then a nominal award of damages would be appropriate.

In terms of law and logic alike, the dissenting opinion of this unknown judge is demonstrably far superior to that of his famous colleague. For, it was agreed on all hands that the builder had not complied with the specification in the contract. In law this amounts to a breach of contract. That too is incontrovertible. And a breach of contract entitles the injured party to judgment. That, as we have seen, is a fundamental principle of the law of contract.

But how serious a breach of contract was the builder's non- compliance? Here too McLaughlin J was plainly right and Cardozo J demonstrably wrong. For, the contract in *Jacob & Youngs* actually contained an express term which gave the houseowner the right to treat the breach in question as a very serious breach indeed:

> Any work furnished by the Contractor, the material or workmanship of which is defective or which is not fully in accordance with the drawings and specifications, in every respect, will be rejected and is to be immediately torn down, removed and remade or replaced in accordance with the drawings and specifications, whenever discovered.

It is hard to imagine a more explicit clause justifying the houseowner's position. Yet, amazingly, it is not even mentioned in Cardozo J's judgment!

There can be few practitioners who have never come across a client who, having signed a contract, has subsequently tried to wriggle out of his obligations. One obvious way of doing this is by using some trivial breach as a pretext. Is this what the houseowner in *Jacob & Youngs* was doing? Cardozo J seems to have thought so. To latch on to some insignificant breach in order to bring down the whole contract would be unconscionable:

> It is in society's interest to accord each party to a contract reasonable security for the protection of his justified expectations. But it is not in society's interests to permit a party to abuse this protection by using an insignificant breach as a pretext for avoiding his contractual obligations.[25]

This passage, from a leading American textbook, goes on to draw a distinction between a total and a partial breach. If the houseowner in *Jacob & Youngs* was thought to be trying to portray what was actually a very partial breach as a total breach, then he would only have been entitled to damages to compensate him for his loss; and if there was no loss, then only nominal damages.

But, however trivial or insignificant the breach, the houseowner was certainly entitled to judgment – unless of course Cardozo J's judgment in this case can be taken as changing the law of New York so as to abolish strict contractual liability. That is plainly not the case. Cardozo J did not even address the point, and American law texts continue to state the principle as before. Thus Williston:

> As a contract consists of a binding promise or set of promises, a breach of contract is a failure, without legal excuse, to perform any promise which forms

> the whole or part of a contract. It is immaterial for this purpose whether the failure in performance is great or small, or whether any damage of a substantial nature has been caused. Any breach of contract gives rise to a right of action.[26]

The footnote to this last sentence reads: 'This is universally recognized as myriad cases illustrate this proposition.'

Cardozo's judgment is an example of a new type of judicial activism, as is clear from following passage:

> Those who think more of symmetry and logic in the development of legal rules than of practical adaptation to the attainment of a just result will be troubled by a classification where the lines of division are so wavering and blurred. Something, doubtless, may be said on the score of consistency and certainty in favor of a stricter standard. The courts have balanced such considerations against those of equity and fairness, and found the latter to be the weightier. The decisions in this state commit us to the liberal view, which is making its way, nowadays, in jurisdictions slow to welcome it. Where the line is to be drawn between the important and the trivial cannot be settled by a formula .... The same omission may take on one aspect or another according to its setting .... This is not to say that the parties are not free by apt and certain words to effectuate a purpose that performance of every term shall be a condition of recovery. That question is not here.

If you penetrate this thickly obscure language you eventually come up against a less than frank argument for judicial arbitrariness. Not one of the points made here will stand up to scrutiny in the cold light of day.

(a) There is much bandying about of terms such as 'just result', 'equity' and 'fairness'. Yet it is hard to see why it was fairer to allow an incompetent builder judgment with costs than finding in favour (with or without compensatory damages) of the houseowner.

(b) Cardozo is at pains to stress just how difficult it was to decide whether the builder's 'omission' was important or trivial. This is true, but what Cardozo fails to recognise throughout is that this 'omission' was a breach of contract entitling the injured houseowner to judgment.

(c) In the last sentence of the quoted passage Cardozo purports to respect the right of the parties to a contract to stipulate 'that performance of every term shall be a condition of recovery'. As we have seen, there was just such a clause in the contract in *Jacob & Youngs*, yet Cardozo simply denies it with a categorical: 'That question is not here.'

A recent English case, *Ruxley Electronics v Forsyth*,[27] was concerned with a similar situation. Here a houseowner engaged builders to construct a swimming pool with a depth of 7+ ft at the deep end, but the pool turned out to have a maximum diving depth of only 6 ft. By contrast with *Jacob & Youngs*, it was never doubted that this non-compliance constituted a breach of contract, the only question being to what damages, if any, the houseowner was entitled, and on this rather thorny point the case went all the way up to the House of Lords.

# X

# New Principles?

## 1. Legitimate expectation

**Where a person is the victim of an unfavourable decision taken by a public authority, this may amount to an infringement of that person's legitimate expectations where, for example, the decision contradicts an earlier promise or course of conduct on the part of the public authority concerned.**

### *Meaning*

As with so many principles, this one is probably easier to understand from a concrete example than from a bald abstract statement. In *R v Brent Council ex parte Gunning,*[1] parents objected to the closure and amalgamation of schools by a local authority. It was held that though the parents had no statutory rights in the matter they did have a legitimate expectation to be consulted. But in *Re Westminster City Council*[2] the House of Lords held that the concept of legitimate expectations could not be extended to a general duty to consult.

Straight away, then, there is a distinction drawn between rights and expectations, which will be discussed in more detail below. But is legitimate expectation a principle at all? And, if so, where did it come from?

### *Origins: EC law*

Like several other new principles of English law, the concept of legitimate expectations can be traced back to European Community law. So, for example, when Mr Mavridis was refused a post in the EC civil service on the ground that he was too old he objected that there had been no mention of an age limit in the official advertisement. This, he argued, amounted to a breach of his 'legitimate expectation' that the information in the advertisement was complete. The Advocate General agreed with him, but the European Court of Justice rather fudged the issue by holding that, though the furnishing of incomplete information *might* in certain circumstances amount to a breach of legitimate expectations, the appropriate remedy in such cases was damages, which Mr Mavridis had not asked for. So his application was dismissed.[3]

### *Lord Denning*

Surprisingly, the phrase 'legitimate expectation' was first used in an English court by Lord Denning MR in 1968, though he did not find it applicable to the case in hand. The claimants were foreign students who had been admitted to the United Kingdom to study at a College of Scientology: *Schmidt v Secretary of State for Home Affairs*.[4] The Home Secretary rejected their application for an extension of their stay on the grounds, in Lord Denning's words:

> that the Minister does not regard scientology as a religion or as a church, as it claims to be. It is a pseudo-religion and a pseudo-church which he regards as socially harmful.[5]

The students contended that the Home Secretary was in breach of natural justice by turning their application down without a hearing. Lord Denning commented:

> … an administrative body may, in a proper case, be bound to give a person who is affected by their decision an opportunity of making representations. It all depends on whether he has some right or interest, or, I would add, some legitimate expectation, of which it would not be fair to deprive him without hearing what he has to say.[6]

His conclusion, however, was that aliens had no such 'legitimate expectation'.

### *McInnes v Onslow Fane*

A useful classification was provided by Sir Robert Megarry V-C in *McInnes v Onslow Fane*.[7] McInnes was a boxing trainer who had had his licence revoked by the British Boxing Board of Control because of his conduct as master of ceremonies at a boxing tournament in Bournemouth. He applied five times for a boxing manager's licence and was turned down each time. He asked for an oral hearing but the board refused. He then sought a declaration that the board had acted in breach of natural justice or unfairly in failing to comply with his request to be informed of the case against him or to grant him an oral hearing. It was held by Megarry V-C that the board's duty to act fairly was no more than a duty to decide the application honestly and without bias or caprice. They were not under a duty to give their reasons for refusing. As

McInnes had not shown that the board had acted unfairly his claim was dismissed.

The importance of the case lies not in the disposition of this particular application itself but in the way Sir Robert Megarry set out the ruling principles of law. He distinguished three types of cases: (a) forfeiture cases; (b) expectation cases; and (c) application cases. A forfeiture case is one where the claimant has been deprived of some existing right, benefit or vested interest, such as, for example, a current valid driving licence. Anyone subjected to a decision of this kind would be entitled to the highest level of natural justice. Cases where there is a legitimate or reasonable expectation include renewals, as where someone whose passport has expired applies unsuccessfully for a renewal. A person affected by this kind of decision must clearly have some recourse but the level of natural justice to which he is entitled will not be as high as in a forfeiture or deprivation situation, as for example if he had been deprived of a passport while it was still current. In *R v Secretary of State for Foreign and Commonwealth Affairs, ex parte Everett*[8] it was said by Taylor LJ that a passport was a 'normal expectation of every citizen', but it was held that by giving the claimant the reason for refusing his renewal application the Foreign Secretary had done all that the law required. Application cases have the lowest claim to natural justice. These are situations, like the *McInnes* case itself, where someone has applied 'cold' for, say, a licence or a passport and has been turned down.

This is a neat classification, but the precise level of natural justice applicable to each category is far from clear-cut.

### *Catch-phrase or principle?*

However, it is only comparatively recently that legitimate expectation has been accepted as a principle of English law at all. The House of Lords in *Lloyd v McMahon*[9] did not think so. There had been a finding by the district auditor of 'wilful misconduct' on the part of some Liverpool city councillors. The councillors had submitted detailed written representations but had neither asked the district auditor for an oral hearing nor been offered one by him. The councillors contended in court that they had a legitimate expectation of an oral hearing and the auditor's failure to invite them to one amounted to a breach of natural justice.

Lord Templeman gave this argument short shrift, disparaging the concept of 'legitimate expectations' as a catch-phrase rather than a principle:

> In the voluminous evidence and in the addresses of counsel I have been unable to discern any grounds for the assertion that the oral representations of a councillor could have supplied a defence which was lacking from the written representations of the appellants or could have validated or reinforced possible defences foreshadowed in those written representations. The facts disclosed by the documents were incontrovertible and damning. The auditor had no choice but to find the appellants guilty of wilful misconduct.
>
> Counsel for the appellants urged that although the appellants did not request an oral hearing, they were deprived of a 'legitimate expectation' of being invited to an oral hearing. Counsel for the appellants does not allege that the appellants in fact expected to be invited to an oral hearing and does not speculate whether they would have accepted an invitation. He submits that a legitimate expectation of being invited to an oral hearing is an objective fundamental right which, if not afforded, results in a breach of law or breach of natural justice which invalidates any decision based on written material. This extravagant language does not tempt me to elevate a catch-phrase into a principle. The true principle is that the auditor, like any other decision-maker, must act fairly. It was not unfair for the auditor to reach a decision on the basis of the written material served on and submitted by the appellants. In *Council of Civil Service Unions v Minister for the Civil Service* [1984] 3 All ER 935, [1985] AC 374 it was unfair for the government to decide to deprive a civil servant of his right to belong to a trade union without first consulting the civil servant or his union; this House would have quashed the decision but for the overriding interests of national security which justified the government's decision. Lord Roskill pointed out that 'legitimate expectation' is a manifestation of the duty to act fairly (see [1984] 3 All ER 935 at 954, [1985] AC 374 at 415). A decision may be unfair if the decision-maker deprives himself of the views of persons who will be affected by the decision. In the present case the appellants were afforded ample opportunity to express their views, and the auditor was enabled to reach a decision in the light of every defence which it was possible for the appellants to urge.[10]

In his speech Lord Bridge was hardly less scathing:

> My Lords, the so-called rules of natural justice are not engraved on tablets of stone. To use the phrase which better expresses the underlying concept, what the requirements of fairness demand when any body, domestic, administrative or judicial, has to make a decision which will affect the rights of individuals depends on the character of the decision-making body, the kind of decision it has to make and the statutory or other framework in which it operates. In particular, it is well established that when a statute has conferred on any body the power to make decisions affecting individuals, the courts will not only require the procedure prescribed by the statute to be followed, but will readily imply so much and no more to be introduced by way of additional procedural safeguards as will ensure the attainment of fairness.[11]

Even if there *had* been some defect in procedure, it was held, the auditor's certificate would not have been quashed. The point made by the law lords was that the technical breach of a procedural rule should not automatically be allowed to get in the way of justice. In certain circumstances there would clearly be an expectation of an oral hearing, but not always. To label this an invariable 'legitimate expectation' and to elevate this 'catch-phrase', as Lord Templeman characterised it, into an inviolable principle was not in the interests of justice.

### *Four categories of legitimate expectation*

However, this restrictive approach has not survived. Instead, the concept of 'legitimate expectations' has taken on a life of its own. In *R v Devon County Council, ex parte Baker*[12] Simon Brown LJ found himself able to identify no fewer than four different types of legitimate expectations:

(a) **'A substantive right: an entitlement that the claimant asserts cannot be denied him.'** Examples cited include *R v Home Secretary ex parte Ruddock,*[13] a case concerning telephone tapping, which would now have to be decided in terms of the right of privacy as established under human rights law (see Chapter IV). Another example cited by Simon Brown LJ is *R v Secretary of State for the Home Department, ex parte Khan.*[14] A Home Office circular set out the criteria required if a foreign child was to be allowed to enter the United Kingdom for the purposes of adoption. The claimant objected that these published guidelines created a legitimate expectation that they would be observed. Watkins LJ emphasised the fact that this was an area governed by the discretion of the Home Secretary, who in the judge's opinion had not exercised it 'in the least unfairly'. But the majority of the Court of Appeal disagreed with this and quashed the Home Secretary's decision not to allow the child in question into the country for adoption.

However, it is not even certain that there is such an animal as substantive legitimate expectation. In *R v Secretary of State for the Home Department, ex parte Pierson,*[15] to counsel's submission that the doctrine of legitimate expectation 'has no substantive effect: it merely gives protection against procedural unfairness', even so radical a judge as Lord Steyn merely remarked: 'This is a controversial question. Counsel is not necessarily right.'[16]

(b) **'Perhaps more conventionally the concept of legitimate expectation is used to refer to the claimant's interest in some ultimate benefit which he hopes to retain (or, some would argue, attain). Here, therefore, it is the interest itself rather than the benefit that is the substance of the expectation.'** This less than pellucid definition is illustrated by what Simon Brown LJ described as three 'clear examples': *Schmidt v Secretary of State for*

*Home Affairs*, *O'Reilly v Mackman* and *R v Rochdale Metropolitan BC, ex parte Schemet*.[17] In *O'Reilly* several convicted criminals serving prison sentences sought to set aside a decision refusing them the usual remission of one-third of their sentences. It was held that this remission gave them a legitimate expectation of being allowed an opportunity to challenge the ruling. (In fact they lost the case because this legitimate expectation, it was held, existed only in public law by way of judicial review, but, as the claimants were out of time to apply for judicial review they had simply brought the case by way of writ, i.e. as a private law claim.)

(c) **'Frequently, however, the concept of legitimate expectation is used to refer to the fair procedure itself. In other words it is contended that the claimant has a legitimate expectation that the public body will act fairly towards him.'** But Simon Brown LJ himself recognised that this definition was less than helpful, as 'it confuses the interest which is the basis of the requirement of procedural fairness with the requirement itself'. More simply, as there is already always a requirement of procedural fairness it is superfluous to say that procedural fairness is a legitimate expectation.

(d) **'The final category of legitimate expectation encompasses those cases in which it is held that a particular procedure, not otherwise required by law in the protection of an interest, must be followed consequent upon some specific promise or practice.'** So, for example, in both *Re Liverpool Taxi Owners' Association*[18] and *Attorney General of Hong Kong v NG Yuen Shiu*,[19] the public authority concerned acted contrary to an express undertaking to offer those affected by their decision the opportunity of a hearing.

### *Rights versus expectations*

In 1983 Margaret Thatcher prohibited employees at Government Communications Headquarters (GCHQ) from belonging to a trade union. This was done without the usual consultation with the trade unions concerned, who then took the Government to court: *Council of Civil Service Unions v Minister for the Civil Service*.[20] It was held that the civil servants and trade unions affected had a legitimate expectation that they would be consulted over this. Had national security not been involved (GCHQ being the headquarters for British intelligence communications), the Government would have lost the case and Mrs Thatcher's order would probably have been quashed – even though she had not infringed anyone's legal rights.

But if a legitimate expectation is not quite a right, how could it have such a potentially devastating effect? Moreover, had Mrs Thatcher's order been set aside, would that not have infringed *her* right to issue the order in the first place?

The trend is clearly for the scope of this new principle to broaden. As long ago as 1993 Neill LJ, not noted as a judicial activist, remarked: 'I am very doubtful whether, save perhaps in exceptional circumstances, the principle of legitimate expectation can be invoked to invalidate either primary or secondary legislation which is put before Parliament': *R v Secretary of State for the Environment, ex parte National & Local Government Officers' Association*.[21] Save in exceptional circumstances? What circumstances would those be? One can only wonder. How *could* an expectation which does not even amount to a right *ever* invalidate an Act of Parliament? And what gives the courts the right to set aside statutes in such circumstances?

### *Damages*

Nothing underlines the growing importance of the doctrine of legitimate expectation more than the tendency of the courts to award damages for infringement. The function of such an award was explained by Sedley LJ in *R v Commissioners of Customs and Excise, ex parte F & I Services Ltd*:[22]

> … the unfairness which a change of policy may work on those who have relied on the earlier policy can often be adequately mitigated by … compensating them in money. The point, however, is that such a payment of money is not an anticipatory payment of damages: it is a practical means of eliminating unfairness.

### *Legitimate expectations versus estoppel*

What is the relationship between legitimate expectation and estoppel? The two doctrines are clearly related and appear to overlap. One important difference, as was pointed out by Lord Diplock in *O'Reilly v Mackman*,[23] is that legitimate expectation is confined to public law while estoppel is to be found in public and private law alike. A legitimate expectation will arise where a public authority makes a promise and then reneges on it or where there has been some established practice entitling the claimant to expect that practice to be followed and it is not followed. It has been held, however, that for an actionable legitimate expectation to arise it is *not* necessary for the claimant actually to have relied on the promise or practice to his detriment: *R v Department for Education and Employment, ex parte Begbie*.[24] This is another difference from estoppel, where detrimental reliance is generally required.

Perhaps the best general definition of estoppel is still that set out by Lord Wright in 1946:

> Estoppel is a complex legal notion, involving a combination of several essential elements - statement to be acted upon, action on the faith of it, resulting detriment to the actor.[25]

A simple example of what is sometimes labelled proprietary estoppel is an old case where a father gave his son the impression that the son could have a particular piece of land, although no formal conveyance was executed. On the strength of this the son spent £14,000 in building himself a house on the land in question with his father's full knowledge and approval. The House of Lords held that the father (or his estate) was 'estopped', i.e. stopped or prevented, from claiming a right of ownership over this piece of land, and ordered the land to be formally conveyed to the son without payment.[26]

Though extended by Lord Denning in the *High Trees*[27] case, as was seen in Chapter II, estoppel is an old and long-established principle. The same cannot be said for the doctrine of legitimate expectation.

*Comment*

Like most of the other new principles of English law, legitimate expectation is a product of judicial law-making and shows all the usual signs of its provenance. It is vague, unclear, fuzzy and open to a variety of interpretations. But, like so many other new principles, it is going from strength to strength, serving as it does as yet another weapon in the armoury of the judiciary in its undeclared war against the executive and even against the legislature.

## 2. 'Fair, just and reasonable'

*Is 'fair, just and reasonable' a valid legal test?*

Nobody would suggest that deciding a legal dispute is an easy task. A number of different issues have to be determined. The facts of the case will generally be in dispute between the parties. So, a judge must establish what he considers to be the true material facts. What is equally important is for the appropriate principles and rules of law to be identified. These principles and rules have to be applied to the facts. A conclusion must then be reached, and finally a finding (either wholly or partly) in favour of one party or the other together with a remedy.

There is enough room for disagreement without having a question mark hanging over what the applicable rules and principles are and doubts about what they mean. Yet that is what has happened in ever-increasing areas of the law in recent years. It is a move away from principle and towards arbitrary judicial decision- making.

One of the worst examples of this is the so-called 'fair, just and reasonable' test. This cumbersome label is a warning signal in itself. After all, should not *every* legal decision be fair, just and reasonable? And has that not always been the requirement? The trouble is that 'fair, just and reasonable' is really a slogan rather than a test. It is simply too vague to use as a test, with the unfortunate results that are only too obvious.

This test is of recent origin. In *Caparo v Dickman* the test for a duty of care in the law of tort was stated by Lord Bridge in these terms:[1]

> What emerges is that, in addition to the foreseeability of damage, necessary ingredients in any situation giving rise to a duty of care are that there should exist between the party owing the duty and the party to whom it is owed a relationship characterised by the law as one of 'proximity' or 'neighbourhood' and that the situation should be one in which the court considers it fair, just and reasonable that the law should impose a duty of a given scope upon the one party for the benefit of the other. But it is implicit in the passages referred to that the concepts of proximity and fairness embodied in these additional ingredients are not susceptible of any such precise definition as would be necessary to give them utility as practical tests, but amount in effect to little more than convenient labels to attach to the features of different specific situations which, on a detailed examination of all the circumstances, the law recognises pragmatically as giving rise to a duty of care of a given scope.

This passage was cited by Lord Woolf MR in *Mohammed Khalif Farah v British Airways*[2] 'not only because it sets out the three requirements necessary to establish the duty of care, but also because it emphasises the imprecision of the test and that what one is considering can be regarded as no more, or little more, than convenient labels'.

Where the requisite test is a mere 'convenient label', how is it to be applied? 'Pragmatically', says Lord Woolf, which presumably means on a case by case basis. The trouble with this is not only that principles have been discarded in favour of 'labels' but also that the meaning and applicability of these labels has to be considered afresh in each case. The result is uncertainty.

### 'The Nicholas H'

In '*The Nicholas H*'[3] a ship developed a crack in its hull while carrying a cargo of lead. It was inspected by a surveyor employed by the vessel's classification society, Nippon Kaiji Kyokai (NKK), who, after first recommending permanent repairs then changed his mind and pronounced the ship fit to proceed on her voyage after some temporary repairs had been done. It sailed the same day, but, with the temporary welding repairs cracking, sank a week later. The cargo-owners sued the classification society, NKK, in negligence. The case came before the House of Lords on the assumption (a) that the loss of the ship and its cargo was the fault of the NKK surveyor, (b) that the damage to the cargo was physical damage, and (c) that this damage was foreseeable as the likely consequence of the surveyor's negligence.

At first instance the cargo owners had won, but this had been reversed by a unanimous Court of Appeal, a decision that was upheld by the House of Lords by 4 votes to 1.

Speaking for the majority, Lord Steyn held that:[4]

> … since the decision in *Home Office v Dorset Yacht Co Ltd*[5] it has been settled law that the elements of foreseeability and proximity as well as considerations of fairness, justice and reasonableness are relevant to all cases whatever the nature of the harm sustained by the plaintiff.

Lord Steyn went on to quote with approval the explanation of this test given by Saville LJ in the Court of Appeal:

> … whatever the nature of the harm sustained by the plaintiff, it is necessary to consider the matter not only by inquiring about foreseeability but also by considering the nature of the relationship between the parties; and to be satisfied that in all the circumstances it is fair, just and reasonable to impose a duty of care.[6]

Lord Steyn endorsed Saville LJ's explanation as 'a correct summary of the law as it now stands'. He therefore rejected the claimants' contention that 'since the claim involved foreseeable physical damage to the cargo owners' property, the additional requirements of proximity and that it is fair, just and reasonable to impose a duty of care are inapplicable'. While assuming that there was a sufficient degree of proximity here, Lord Steyn found against the cargo owners on the basis that 'recognition of a duty' would be 'unfair, unjust and unreasonable' towards classification societies, primarily for policy reasons.

In a powerful dissenting speech based foursquare on fundamental principles, Lord Lloyd of Berwick found in favour of the cargo owners. Besides the foreseeability of physical damage, which in the instant case was assumed, what was required to establish a duty of care was a sufficient degree of proximity between the parties. And, said Lord Lloyd, 'the degree of proximity in this case was very close indeed'. Was it 'fair, just and reasonable' to impose a duty of care on the surveyor? Lord Lloyd agreed with the first instance judge, who 'did not consider that there were any considerations of public policy which militated against such a duty'.

Lord Lloyd therefore viewed the 'fair, just and reasonable' test as a matter of policy, as he explained further on:[7]

> The concept of proximity, and the requirement that it should be fair, just and reasonable to impose a duty of care on the defendant in the particular circumstances of the case, have been developed as a means of containing liability for pure economic loss under the principles stated in *Donoghue v Stevenson*.

However, '*The Nicholas H*' was not a case of economic loss:

> We are not here asked to extend the law of negligence into a new field. We are not even asked to make an incremental advance. All that is required is a straightforward application of *Donoghue v Stevenson*.

His conclusion is a ringing attack on the approach adopted by the majority of his brother lords:

> Where the facts cry out for the imposition of a duty of care between the parties, as they do here, it would require an exceptional case to refuse to impose a duty on the ground that it would not be fair, just and reasonable. Otherwise there is a risk that the law of negligence will disintegrate into a series of isolated decisions without any coherent principles at all, and the retreat from *Anns* will turn into a rout. Having given Mr Aikens' arguments my best consideration, I can see no good reason why, on the facts of this case, ordinary well-established principles of the law of negligence should not be allowed to take effect.[8]

### *Paternity*

The 'fair, just and reasonable' test is not confined to the law of negligence but is to be found rearing its ill-defined head in other branches of the law as well. So, for example, in *Child Support Agency v Rust*[9] a magistrates' court decided that a putative father was not in fact the father of the child in question and issued a declaration to that effect. When this was challenged by the Child Support Agency the court ordered the putative father to have a blood test. He refused, and the court then decided that his reasons for doing so were 'fair, just and reasonable', a conclusion the magistrates reached by considering 'what the reasonable man would have done when placed in the same set of circumstances to that in which we found the respondent to be'. On this basis the court found that the Child Support Agency had not discharged its burden of proof and again declared the putative father not to be the father. On appeal by way of case stated to the Queen's Bench Divisional Court the question was whether the magistrates had adopted the right test for paternity. The High Court not only found that the magistrates had used the wrong test but held that, so far from being 'fair, just and reasonable', the putative father's refusal to provide a blood sample could be taken as proof that he was the father, and a declaration was made to that effect.

If 'fair, just and reasonable' is open to two such diametrically opposed interpretations, of what value can it possibly be? Nor was *Rust's* case unique. Two years earlier, in *Child Support Agency v G (Refusal of Paternity Test),*[10] a magistrates' court had found a putative father's refusal to take a DNA test 'fair, just and reasonable' even though the magistrates had also found that his refusal amounted to an 'almost inescapable inference' that he was the father. Once again the magistrates' determination was overturned.

Where there is evidence militating against the putative father's paternity, whether this is evidence of the appearance of the child, the conduct of the mother or the the date of conception, his refusal to take the test may possibly be characterised as 'fair, just and reasonable'. But, in the absence of such evidence, for his refusal to be held to amount to an 'almost inescapable inference' of paternity is to go from one extreme to the other. For the plain biological fact is that a man may simply not know whether he is the father of a particular child or not, and his refusal to take the test may reflect nothing more than a fear of the financial consequences of being found to be the father.

All in all, the muddle at the heart of these cases shows just how inappropriate the 'fair, just and reasonable' test is. A test as vague as this whose meaning and applicability is in dispute at every turn can hardly be regarded as a positive contribution to the law.

# Epilogue

'The proper constitutional relationship of the executive with the courts is that the courts will respect all acts of the executive within its lawful province, and that the executive will respect all decisions of the courts as to what its lawful province is.'[1] At first sight this appears to represent an even-handed balance between executive and judiciary in keeping with the fashionable doctrine of the separation of powers. On closer examination, however, a very different picture emerges. According to this formulation the judges have an obligation to recognise all acts of the executive 'within its lawful province', but it is the judges who decide what that 'lawful province' is. Does this mean that it is for the judges to decide – and, presumably, therefore, also to change – the scope and content of executive authority, or in other words, what the executive is permitted or not permitted to do?[2]

If so, then what this does is blatantly to give the judges legislative power, which is supposedly the preserve of Parliament, while at the same time effectively placing the judiciary above the executive. Far from promoting the separation of powers, this would have the effect of allowing the judiciary to usurp the power of the other two branches of Government. The doctrine of the separation of powers aims at equality between executive, legislature and judiciary – a system of 'checks and balances'. In practice as well as in theory, the rights of the executive are in inverse proportion to those of the judiciary. The more power the judiciary exercises, the less power is left to the executive, and vice versa. So, if the judiciary is allowed to determine this balance, it will be deciding not only the rights of the executive but also its own rights – thus flying in the face of yet another fundamental principle, namely that nobody should be a judge in his own cause.[3]

To use a sporting analogy, a judge is essentially a referee or umpire. He decides whether a particular rule of the game has been broken, but he does not make the rules. Is it permissible for a football player to handle the ball? This will depend primarily on the type of football we are talking about. In association football, or soccer, handling of the ball is generally strictly forbidden except to goalkeepers, while in rugby and American football the rules permit it. In soccer it is for the referee to decide whether a particular player has broken this rule at a particular time in a particular game, but it is not for the referee to decide whether there should be a no-handling rule or not. That is a matter of legislation, or law-making, for the controlling body of the sport to decide. Whether a particular referee happens to agree or disagree with the rule is irrelevant. It is his duty to enforce it. There may be some borderline cases, such as, for example, where a player's hand accidentally brushes against the ball. Here the referee has to interpret the rule to determine whether the incident in question constitutes 'handling' the ball or not. This is an exercise very familiar to judges, and, as we have seen, the dividing line between interpretation and law-making is a narrow one.[4] But that is very different from the claim to judicial law-making that we find in the quoted passage.

The quotation in question comes from the judgement of Nolan LJ (as he then was) in the case of *M v Home Office*. But what is the authority for it? None is cited in the judgement, which is hardly surprising, as it is in keeping neither with the fundamental principle of the legislative supremacy of Parliament nor, as we have seen, with the doctrine of the separation of powers.[5] Yet it has commended itself to commentators and has been widely adopted as a statement of constitutional principle.[6]

*M v Home Office* itself represents the practical application of this doctrine. A unanimous House of Lords there decided that a court could issue an injunction against the Crown (i.e. against a minister in his official capacity) and that if the Crown disobeyed such an order the Crown could be held in contempt of court.[7] Both these propositions were unprecedented and flew in the face of the Crown Proceedings Act 1947. 'An established statute', it has aptly been remarked, was here 'virtually re-written' by the court.[8] So much so, indeed, that the Scottish Court of Session refused to follow the House of Lords decision.[9] *M v Home Office* is in fact nothing less than an example of judges arrogating to themselves the right to curtail the power of the executive and in so doing to subject the executive and the legislature in a significant sense to the judiciary. *M v Home Office* was a milestone, but it is no isolated case. There has been no shortage of instances of judicial activism – or indeed judicial supremacism – in the decade since it was decided.[10] And the planned establishment of a new 'Supreme Court', if it comes into being, will do nothing to abate this trend.

# Notes

## I. Principles, Rules and Policies

**1**. Lord Denning, *The Discipline of Law*, London, 1979, p. 292.

**2**. 'Principle': A.L. Goodhart, 'The Ratio Decidendi of a case' (1930) 40 Yale LJ 161. Cf. J. Stone, 'The Ratio of the Ratio Decidendi' (1959) 22 MLR 597. 'Rule of law': E.H. Levi, *An Introduction to Legal Reasoning*, Chicago, 1949.

**3**. Lord Denning, loc. cit.

**4**. *Burmah Oil v Lord Advocate* [1965] AC 75.

**5**. Sir William Blackstone, *Commentaries on the Laws of England*, 1765, I.68-69.

**6**. Ibid., 69.

**7**. Ibid., 70.

**8**. Lord Reid, 'The Judge as Lawmaker' (1972) 12 Journal of the Society of Public Teachers of Law, 22 at 27. See the discussion in Chapter V.1.

**9**. *Murphy v Brentwood District Council* [1990] 2 All ER 908 at 923, referring to *Anns v Merton* [1977] 2 All ER 492.

**10**. Ronald Dworkin, *Taking Rights Seriously*, London, 1977, p. 26f.

**11**. *Riggs v Palmer* (1889) 115 NY 506, 22 NE 188.

**12**. *Malcolm v Oxford University* [1990] Times Law Reports 240 (23 March 1990).

**13**. *Malcolm v Oxford University* [1990] Times Law Reports 789 (19 December 1990). See article by Michael Arnheim in Solicitor's Journal, 1990.

**14**. Sir Matthew Hale, *History of the Pleas of the Crown* 1 Hale PC (1736) 629.

**15**. *R v J – (rape: marital exemption)* [1991] 1 All ER 759.

**16**. *R v R – (rape: marital exemption)* [1991] 4 All ER 481.

**17**. Lord Keith: [1991] 4 All ER 489.

**18**. Lord Lane CJ: [1991] 2 All ER 257 at 266, [1991] 2 WLR 1065 at 1074.

**19**. *Nagle v Feilden* [1966] 2 QB 633.

**20**. Lord Denning, *The Discipline of Law*, London, 1979, p. 172f.

**21** *Donoghue v Stevenson* [1932] AC 562.

**22**. See Chapter VI.1.

**23**. See Chapter VIII.1.

**24**. Bracton, *On the Laws and Customs of England*, tr. S.E. Thorne, Cambridge, Mass., vol. II, p. 181f.

**25**. *Broom's Legal Maxims*, ed. Herbert Manisty and Herbert Chitty, 7th edn, London, 1900.

**26**. See the discussion on judge-made law in Chapter V.1.

## II. Law and Logic

**1**. Cicero, *de Re Publica* III.22.33.

**2**. *Coggs v Bernard* (1703) 92 ER 107; [1558-1774] All ER Rep 1.

**3**. *The Common Law*, Boston, 1881, p. 1.

**4**. *Collected Legal Papers*, New York, 1920, p. 50.
**5**. (1897) 10 Harv LR 457-478.
**6**. *Donoghue v Stevenson* [1932] AC 562.
**7**. *George v Skivington* (1869) LR 5 Exch 1.
**8**. *Lockett v Charles* [1938] 4 All ER 170.
**9**. *Marbury v Madison* 5 US 137 (1803).
**10**. *A, X, Y and Others v Secretary of State for the Home Department* [2002] EWCA Civ 1502.
**11**. *Liversidge v Anderson* [1941] 3 All ER 338.
**12**. Peter Robson and Paul Watchman (eds), *Justice, Lord Denning and the Constitution*, Aldershot, 1981, p. 27f.
**13**. *Central London Property Trust v High Trees House* [1947] KB 130.
**14**. *Hughes v Metropolitan Railway Co* (1877) 2 App Cas 239.
**15**. *Salisbury v Gilmore* [1942] 1 All ER 457.
**16**. *Birmingham & District Land Co v London & North Western Railway Co.* (1888) 40 ChD 268.
**17**. *Magor & St Mellons Rural District Council v Newport Corporation* [1950] 2 All ER 1226, [1951] 2 All ER 839.
**18**. Ibid. at 1235.
**19**. Ibid. at 1236.
**20**. *Seaford Court Estates Ltd v Asher* [1949] 2 All ER 155.
**21**. [1951] 2 All ER 839 at 841.
**22**. *Assam Railways v Inland Revenue Commissioners* [1935] AC 445.
**23**. *R v West Riding of Yorkshire County Council* [1906] 2 KB at 717, *per* Farwell LJ.
**24**. *Black-Clawson International Ltd v Papierwerke Waldhof-Aschaffenburg AG* [1975] 1 All ER 810.
**25**. *Pepper v Hart* [1993] 1 All ER 42 at 69d-e. Cf. *Re Parliamentary Privilege Act 1770* [1958] AC 331.
**26**. *Erskine May's Treatise on the Law, Privileges, Proceedings and Usage of Parliament*, 22nd edn, London, 1997, p. 153.
**27**. See for example two recent cases where the House of Lords reversed highly literal interpretations adopted by the Court of Appeal: *Mannai Investment Co v Eagle Star* [1997] 3 All ER 352 (HL) reversing [1996] 1 All ER 55 (CA); and *Allison v A.E. Limehouse* [1991] 4 All ER 500 (HL) reversing [1990] 2 All ER 723 (CA).
**28**. See for example Carol Harlow and Richard Rawlings, *Law and Administration*, 2nd edn, London, 1997, p. 602f, referring to the treatment of the Crown Proceedings Act 1947 by the House of Lords in *M v Home Office* [1994] 1 AC 377: 'An established statute was virtually re-written' by the judges.
**29**. See Chapter X and Excursus C to Chapter VIII.

### Excursus A. 'Ministers are no more elected than judges'

**1**. Lord Nolan and Sir Stephen Sedley, *The Making and Remaking of the British Constitution*, London, 1997.
**2**. Ibid., p. 25.
**3**. Ibid.
**4**. *X Ltd v Morgan-Grampian* [1991] 1 AC 1 at 48.
**5**. Nolan and Sedley, op. cit., p. 27.
**6**. *M v Home Office* [1994] 1 AC 377.
**7**. Carol Harlow and Richard Rawlings, *Law and Administration*, 2nd edn, London, 1997, p. 602f.
**8**. Gerald Kaufman, *How to be a Minister*, 2nd edn, London, 1997, p. 1.

**9**. Rodney Brazier, *Ministers of the Crown*, Oxford, 1997, p. 63.
**10**. Sir Stephen Sedley in Lord Nolan and Sir Stephen Sedley, op. cit., p. 27.
**11**. Brazier, op. cit., p. 65.
**12**. Harold Wilson, *The Labour Government 1964-1970*, London, 1971, p. 65.
**13**. Richard Crossman, *The Diaries of a Cabinet Minister*, vol. I, London, 1975, p. 134.
**14**. Ibid., p. 135.
**15**. Wilson, op. cit., p. 66.
**16**. Ibid., p. 65.
**17**. Ibid., p. 66.
**18**. Ibid.
**19**. Sedley and Nolan, loc. cit.

## III. Obedience to the Law

**1**. C.H. McIlwain, *Constitutionalism and the Changing World*, Cambridge, 1939, p. 55.
**2**. Ibid., p. 66.
**3**. *Salmond on Jurisprudence*, 11th edn by Glanville Williams,London, 1957, p. 155.
**4**. J. Austin, *The Province of Jurisprudence Determined*, ed. Hart, London, 1954, p. 9ff.
**5**. Ronald Dworkin, *Taking Rights Seriously*, London, 1977, p. 211.
**6**. Ibid.
**7**. Ibid., p. 208.
**8**. *Trials of War Criminals before the Nürnberg Military Tribunals under Control Council Law No. 10*, Nürnberg, October 1946 – April 1949, vol. V, US Government Printing Office, Washington DC, 1950, p. 992.
**9**. Ibid.
**10**. Ingo Müller, *Hitler's Justice: The Courts of the Third Reich*, Cambridge, Mass., 1991, p. 92.
**11**. Judgment of 27 July 1949, Oberlandesgericht, Bamberg, discussed in H.L.A. Hart, 'Positivism and the Separation of Law and Morals', (1958) 71 Harv LR, 593-629; Lon Fuller, 'Positivism and Fidelity to Law – a Reply to Professor Hart', (1958) 71 Harv LR, 630-672.
**12**. Xenophon, *Memorabilia* I.ii.41-46, translated by M. Arnheim.
**13**. *Re A (Children) (Conjoined Twins: Surgical Separation)* [2000] 4 All ER 961.

## IV. Higher Law

### IV.1. Does European law have higher law status?

**1**. *Stoke-on-Trent City Council v B&Q plc* [1991] 4 All ER 221, per Hoffmann J.
**2**. *Blackburn v Attorney-General* [1971] 2 All ER 1380 (CA), per Lord Denning MR.
**3**. *Macarthys v Smith* [1979] 3 All ER 325 at 329 c/d (CA), per Lord Denning MR.
**4**. *Garland v British Rail Engineering* [1983] 2 AC 751 (HL), per Lord Diplock.
**5**. *NV Algemene Transport en Expeditie Onderneming Van Gend en Loos v Nederlandse Administratie der Belastingen* Case 26/62: [1963] ECR 1; [1963] CMLR 105.
**6**. *Costa v ENEL* Case 6/64: [1964] ECR 585; [1964] CMLR 425.
**7**. *Amministrazione delle Finanze dello Stato v Simmenthal SpA* Case 106/77: [1978] ECR 629; [1978] 3 CMLR 263.
**8**. *Factortame Ltd v Secretary of State for Transport (No. 1)* [1990] 2 AC 85; [1989] 2 All ER 692 (HL); *(No. 2)*, Case C-213/89 [1991] 1 All ER 70 (ECJ & HL); [1991] 1 AC 603.
**9**. Case C-213/89 [1990] ECR I-2433; [1990] 3 CMLR 1; [1991] 1 All ER 70 (ECJ & HL).
**10**. [1991] 1 All ER 70 at 120.
**11**. *R v Secretary of State for Transport, ex parte Factortame Ltd* [1991] 3 All ER 769.
**12**. *Re Nationality of Fishermen: EC Commission v United Kingdom* [1991] 3 CMLR 706.
**13**. See n. 1 above.

**14**. *Internationale Handelsgesellschaft mbH v Einfuhr- und Vorratstelle für Getreide und Futtermittel (SOLANGE I)* Case 11/70: [1970] ECR 1125.
**15**. [1972] CMLR 177 at 181; 255.
**16**. [1974] 2 CMLR 540 (decided on 29 May 1974).
**17**. [1970] ECR 1125.
**18**. *Stoke-on-Trent City Council v B&Q plc* [1991] 4 All ER 221, per Hoffmann J.
**19**. *Wünsche Handelsgesellschaft Bundesverfassungsgericht* (Beschluß des Zweiten Senats vom 22. Oktober 1986), BVerfGE Band 73, S.339, [1987] 3 CMLR 225 at 251f.

### IV.2. Does human rights law have higher law status?

**1**. Paper kindly sent to the author by Lord Steyn, based on a lecture given by Lord Steyn at a conference organised and held by Justice and Sweet & Maxwell on 19 October 2000. In the interests of accuracy it is perhaps worth pointing out that only part of the European Convention on Human Rights has been incorporated into UK law. But this does not affect the discussion in this chapter.
**2**. Andrew Z. Drzemczewski, *European Human Rights Convention in Domestic Law: A Comparative Study*, Oxford, 1983, p. 281 (Germany), p. 286 (Italy), p 302 (Turkey).
**3**. *Rights Brought Home: the Human Rights Bill* (Cm 3782), Para 2.13.
**4**. Ibid.
**5**. See Excursus A to Chapter II.
**6**. See n. 1 above.
**7**. See Chapter V.1 and Excursus A to Chapter II.
**8**. *R v Secretary of State for the Home Department, ex parte Anthony Anderson* [2002] UKHL 46.
**9**. [2001] EWCA Civ 1698, para 23.
**10**. *Dennis Stafford v UK* (2002) 35 EHRR 32 at para 78.
**11**. Ibid. at para 89.
**12**. [2002] UKHL 46 at para 31.
**13**. Ibid. at para 9.
**14**. Ibid.
**15**. BBC News website, 21 October 2002.
**16**. *Ring v Arizona* Case No. 010-488, 24 June 2002. http://laws.findlaw.com/us/000/01-488.html.
**17**. *Duport Steels v Sirs* [1980] 1 All ER 529 at 541.
**18**. See the discussion in Chapter V.1.
**19**. Circuit judges may be removed by the Lord Chancellor for incapacity or misbehaviour: Courts Act 1971, s 17(4). High Court judges and above may be removed by the Crown on an address by both Houses of Parliament. But even a criminal conviction, for driving with more than the permitted level of alcohol in his blood, did not trigger any such consequences for a High Court judge in 1975. And a recent finding by the House of Lords that a law lord ought not to have been sitting on a particular case owing to his association with a pressure group involved in the case as an intervener did not result in the law lord's resignation nor in any action being taken against him. See the discussion in Chapter V.2.

## V. Constitutional Principles

### V.1. The rule of law

**1**. A.V. Dicey, *Introduction to the Study of the Law of the Constitution*, 10th edn, London, 1959, p. 188.
**2**. Ibid.

**3**. Neither of these examples is actually given by Dicey.
**4**. Dicey, op. cit., p. 193.
**5**. Ibid., p. 195f.
**6**. Ibid., p. 196.
**7**. A.V. Dicey, *Lectures on the Relation between Law and Public Opinion*, London, 1905, p. 481f.
**8**. Ibid., p. 482.
**9**. Lord Reid, 'The Judge as Lawmaker' (1972) 12 Journal of the Society of Public Teachers of Law, 22.
**10**. Ibid.
**11**. Ibid., p. 25.
**12**. Ibid.
**13**. Ibid., p. 26.
**14**. Ibid., p. 27.
**15**. Ibid., p. 23.
**16**. Ibid., p. 29.
**17**. Ibid., p. 26.
**18**. Ibid.
**19**. Erskine I, 147, quoted Reid, ibid., p. 24.
**20**. David M. Walker, *The Oxford Companion to Law*, Oxford, 1980, p. 1109.
**21**. Viscount Stair, *The Institutions of the Law of Scotland*, University Presses of Edinburgh and Glasgow, 1981.
**22**. Ibid., p. 1109.
**23**. *Burmah Oil v Lord Advocate* [1964] 2 All ER 348 (HL).
**24**. *Madzimbamuto v Lardner-Burke* [1969] 1 AC 645.
**25**. *British Railways Board v Pickin* [1974] AC 765, [1974] 1 All ER 609 (HL).
**26**. Sir John Laws, 'Law and Democracy' [1995] Public Law 72-93, at p. 73.
**27**. Lord Irvine, 'Judges and Decision-Makers: The Theory and Practice of Wednesbury Review' [1996] Public Law 59-78 at p. 77f.
**28**. Lord Irvine, 'Principle and Pragmatism: the Development of English Public Law under the Separation of Powers', 18 September 1998, Hong Kong. http://www.open.gov.uk/lcd/speeches/1998/hongkong.htm
**29**. See Lord Woolf, 'Droit Public – English Style' [1995] Public Law 57-71. See also: Laws LJ (e.g. 'Law and Democracy' [1995] Public Law 72-93) and Sedley LJ (e.g. 'Human Rights: a 21st Century Agenda' [1995] Public Law.
**30**. Lord Woolf cites his source as simply F.A. Mann, 3rd Blackstone Lecture, 1978, p. 91.
**31**. *Bonham's Case* (1610) 8 Co Rep 118. See the discussion on this case in Chapter V.2.
**32**. *Tregor's Case*, YB 8 Ed III 26 (1335). C.K. Allen, *Law in the Making*, 6th edn, London, 1958, p. 433. See also Theodore F.T. Plucknett, *Statutes and their Interpretation in the Fourteenth Century*, Cambridge, 1922, and T.F.T. Plucknett, 'Bonham's Case and Judicial Review' (1928) Harv LR xl, 30.
**33**. William Blackstone, *Commentaries on the Laws of England*, 1st ed, 1765, vol. I, p. 91.
**34**. *R v Williams* 1 W Bl 95.
**35**. *Brandling v Barrington* (1827) 6 B & C 467 at 475; *Miller v Salamons* (1852) 21 LJ (Ex) 161 at 197.
**36**. *Lee v Bude & Torrington Junction Railway Co* (1871) LR 6 CP 576 at 582.
**37**. Blackstone, *Commentaries*, I.178.
**38**. Ibid., p. 157.
**39**. A phrase originally applied to Charles X of France (reigned 1824-30).
**40**. Co 4 Inst 36.

**41**. Cited by Catherine Drinker Bowen, *The Lion and the Throne*, Boston, 1956, p. 440.

**42**. Lord Irvine, 'Judges and Decision-Makers: The Theory and Practice of Wednesbury Review' [1995] Public Law 59 at 61.

**43**. *British Railways Board v Pickin* [1974] AC 765 at 782.

**44**. *M v Home Office* [1994] 1 AC 377.

**45**. Carol Harlow and Richard Rawlings, *Law and Administration*, 2nd edn, 1997, p. 602f.

**46**. *McDonald v Secretary of State for Scotland* 1994 SLT 692 (Court of Session), per Lord Justice Clerk (Ross).

**47**. Cited by Justice Scalia in *Morrison v Olson* (1988) 487 US 654, 101 L Ed 2d 569 at 609, 108 S Ct 2597.

**48**. John Chipman Gray, *Nature and Sources of the Law*, 2nd ed, 1921, 102, 125, 172, as quoted by Felix Frankfurter, 'Reflections on Reading Statutes' in *The Supreme Court: Views from Inside*, ed. Alan F. Westin, New York, 1961, p. 80.

**49**. Ibid., p. 125.

**50**. *Magor and St Mellons Rural District Council v Newport Corporation* [1951] 2 All ER 839.

**51**. Daniel J Boorstin in Editor's Preface to Robert G. McCloskey, *The American Supreme Court*, Chicago, 1960, p. v.

**52**. Ibid., p. 56.

**53**. O.W. Holmes, 'The Path of the Law' (1897) 10 Harv LR 457-78.

**54**. Cited by W. Twining, 'The Bad Man Revisited' (1972-73) 58 Cornell LR 275.

**55**. Sir Frederick Pollock, *Essays on Jurisprudence and Ethics*, London, 1882, p. 238.

**56**. Ibid., p. 240.

**57**. Ibid., p. 246.

**58**. Ibid., p. 250.

**59**. Cited by Raoul Berger, *Impeachment: The Constitutional Problems*, Cambridge, Mass., 1973, p. 103n.

**60**. *West Coast Hotel Co v Parrish* 300 US 379 (1937).

**61**. *Morehead v New York ex rel Tipaldo* 298 US 587 (1936).

**62**. *Plessy v Ferguson* 163 US 537 (1896).

**63**. *Brown v Board of Education of Topeka* 347 US 483 (1954).

**64**. *Regents of the University of California v Bakke* 438 US 265 (1978).

**65**. *Furman v Georgia* 408 US 238 (1972).

**66**. *Gregg v Georgia* 428 US 153 (1976).

**67**. See Lief H Carter, 'Capital Punishment', *The Oxford Companion to the Supreme Court of the United States*, ed Kermit L. Hall, New York, 1992, p. 126.

**68**. Oliver Wendell Holmes, *The Common Law* (1881), Boston, Mass., 1990, p. 41.

**69**. Robert H Bork, *Slouching towards Gomorrah*, New York, 1996, p. 109.

**70**. Ibid., p. 98.

**71**. Ibid., p. 105.

**72**. Ibid., p. 107.

**73**. See E.J. Dionne Jr. and William Kristol (eds), *Bush v Gore: The Court Case and Commentary*, Brookings Institution, 2001, pp. 311-16; Alan M. Dershowitz, *Supreme Injustice: How the High Court Hijacked Election 2000*, New York, 2001.

**74**. James Madison, Alexander Hamilton and John Jay, *The Federalist Papers* (1788 ed.), Harmondsworth, 1987, p. 437.

**75**. Ibid., p. 438.

**76**. Ibid., p. 440.

**77**. *Marbury v Madison* 1 Cranch (5 US) 137 (1803).

**78**. *Donoghue v Stevenson* [1932] AC 562, [1932] All ER Rep 1.

**79**. [1932] All ER Rep 1 at p. 5.

**80**. Ibid. at p. 10.

**81**. Ibid.

**82**. *MacPherson v Buick Motor Co* 217 NY 382, 111 NE 1050 (1916).

**83**. *Glanzer v Shepard* 233 NY 236, 135 NE 275 (1922).

**84**. *Ultramares v Touche* 255 NY 170, 174 NE 441 (1931); *Hedley Byrne v Heller* [1963] 2 All ER 575.

**85**. *Jacob & Youngs Inc v Kent* 230 NY 239, 129 NE 889 (1921).

**86**. *Steward Machine Co v Davis* 301 US 548 (1937).

**87**. *Helvering v Davis* 301 US 619 (1937).

**88**. B. Cardozo, *The Nature of the Judicial Process*, New Haven, Conn., 1921, pp. 128-9 – cited in n. 12 to Stevens' judgment in *TWA v Franklin Mint* 466 US 243 (1984).

**89**. *West Coast Hotel Co v Parrish* 300 US 379 at 404 (1937).

**90**. *Brown v Board of Education* 346 US 483 (1954).

**91**. James F. Byrnes, 'The Supreme Court must be curbed', *US News & World Report*, 18 May 1956, pp. 50-58, as reprinted in: *The Supreme Court: Views from Inside*, ed. Alan F. Westin, New York, 1961, p. 113ff.

**92**. White, 'The Working Life of the Marshall Court, 1815-35', 70 Va LR 1, 49-50 (1984).

**93**. *TWA v Franklin Mint Corp* 466 US 243 (1984).

### V.2. 'No one should be a judge in his own cause'

**1**. 12 Co Rep 114.

**2**. Co Litt 141a.

**3**. *Day v Savadge* Hob 85 at 87; 80 ER at 237.

**4**. 8 Co Rep at 118a; 77 ER at 652

**5**. Blackstone, *Commentaries on the Laws of England*, 1st ed, 1765, I.157.

**6**. *Madzimbamuto v Lardner-Burke* [1969] 1 AC 645 at 723.

**7**. *Mersey Docks v Gibbs* LR 1 HL 93 at 110.

**8**. *Webb and Hay v The Queen* (1994) 181 CLR 41, (1994) 122 ALR 41.

**9**. *Dimes v Grand Junction Canal Co* (1852) 3 HL Cas 759, 10 ER 301

**10**. Ibid.

**11**. *R v Bow Street Metropolitan Stipendiary Magistrate, ex parte Pinochet Ugarte (No 2)* [1999] 1 All ER 577 at 589.

**12**. *R v Bow Street Metropolitan Stipendiary Magistrate, ex parte Pinochet Ugarte* [1998] 4 All ER 897.

**13**. After the first House of Lords judgment in *Pinochet*, so closely involved was Amnesty International in the case that it actually sought judicial review to forestall any attempt by the Home Secretary to block Senator Pinochet's extradition to Spain: *R v Secretary of State for the Home Department, ex parte Amnesty International* (Queen's Bench Divisional Court, 9 December 1998) – Lawtel 10/12/98.

**14**. *R v Bow Street Metropolitan Stipendiary Magistrate, ex parte Pinochet Ugarte (No 2)* [1999] 1 All ER 577.

**15**. Ibid. at 583.

**16**. Ibid. at 595f.

**17**. *Locabail v Bayfield Properties* [2000] 1 All ER 65 at 70f.

**18**. Ibid. at 71.

**19**. Ibid.

**20**. *R v Bow Street Metropolitan Stipendiary Magistrate, ex parte Pinochet Ugarte (No 2)* [1999] 1 All ER 577 at 589.

**21**. *Locabail v Bayfield Properties* [2000] 1 All ER 65 at 81.

**22**. Ibid. at 87.

**23**. Ibid. at 92.

**24**. *R v Gough* [1993] 2 All ER 724.
**25**. Ibid. at 737-738.
**26**. Ibid. at 740.
**27**. Ibid. at 735.
**28**. *R v Spencer* [1985] 1 All ER 673 (CA), [1986] 2 All ER 928 (HL).
**29**. *R v Sussex Justices, ex parte McCarthy* [1923] All ER Rep 233.
**30**. *R v Gough* [1993] 2 All ER 724 at 731.
**31**. *R v Sussex Justices, ex parte McCarthy* [1923] All ER Rep 233 at 234.
**32**. *Metropolitan Properties v Lannon* [1968] 3 All ER 304 at 309-310.
**33**. *R v Camborne Justices, ex parte Pearce* [1954] 2 All ER 850 at 855.
**34**. Lord Esher MR in *Eckersley v Mersey Docks* [1891] 4 All ER Rep 1130 at 1132, [1894] 2 QB 667.
**35**. *R v Gough* [1993] 2 All ER 724 at 737.
**36**. *R v Morris* (1991) 93 Cr App R 102.
**37**. *R v Gough* [1993] 2 All ER 724 at 736.
**38**. *R v Spencer* [1985] 1 All ER 673 (CA), [1986] 2 All ER 928 (HL).
**39**. [1985] 1 All ER 673 at 685.
**40**. [1986] 2 All ER 928 at 939.
**41**. *Webb and Hay v The Queen* (1994) 181 CLR 41, (1994) ALR 41.
**42**. See for example *Commonwealth v Murphy*, 295 **Ky** 466, 174 SW2d 681, *Hughes v Black*, 156 **Me** 69, 160 A2d 113.
**43**. See for example *Suttles v Northwestern Mut L Ins Co* 193 **Ga** 495, 19 SE2d 396, 21 SE2d 695, 143 ALR 343.
**44**. See *Lynip v Alturas School District* 29 **Cal** App 158 158, 155 P 109, and 30 **Cal** App 794, 160 P 175.
**45**. 28 United States Code 455(a).
**46**. See *R v Bow Street Metropolitan Stipendiary Magistrate, ex parte Pinochet Ugarte (No 2)* [1999] 1 All ER 577 at 593, *per* Lord Hope.
**47**. 28 USC 144.
**48**. See *Diehl v Crump*, 72 **Okla** 108, 179 P 4, 5 ALR 1272. 28 USC 144 – 46 Am Jur 2d §215, p. 237.
**49**. 47 Am Jur 2d §219ff., p. 808ff.
**50**. See *Alabama Fuel & Iron Co v Powaski*, 232 **Ala** 66, 166 So 782.
**51**. *Commonwealth v Webster*, 59 **Mass** (5 Cush) 295).
**52**. *Fugate v State*, 169 **Neb** 420, 99 NW2d 868.
**53**. *Gray v State*, 19 **Tex** Civ App 521, 49 SW 699.
**54**. *State v Giudice*, 170 **Iowa** 731, 153 NW 336; *Johnson v State*, 88 **Neb** 565, 130 NW 282.

## VI. Legal Rights and Obligations

### VI.1. 'Where there is a right there is a remedy'

**1**. *Ashby v White* (1703) 92 ER 126, 2 Raym Ld 938.
**2**. *Donoghue v Stevenson* [1932] AC 562.
**3**. *Anns v Merton* [1977] 2 All ER 492.
**4**. Ibid. at 503.
**5**. *East Suffolk Rivers Catchment Board v Kent* [1940] 4 All ER 527.
**6**. *Sheppard v Glossop Corporation* [1921] 3 KB 132 (CA).
**7**. Ibid. at 150.
**8**. *Murphy v Brentwood District Council* [1990] 2 All ER 908 (HL).
**9**. House of Lords Practice Statement: *Note* [1966] 3 All ER 77.
**10**. *Murphy v Brentwood District Council* [1990] 2 All ER 908 at 923.

**11**. *D & F Estates v Church Commissioners* [1988] 2 All ER 992.
**12**. *Murphy v Brentwood District Council* [1990] 2 All ER 908.
**13**. *Junior Books v Veitchi* [1982] 3 All ER 201 (HL).
**14**. *Hedley Byrne v Heller* [1963] 2 All ER 575.
**15**. *Gorris v Scott* (1874) LR 9 Exch 125.
**16**. *Phillips v Britannia Hygienic Laundry Co* [1923] All ER Rep 127; [1923] 2 KB 832.
**17**. [1923] All ER Rep 127 at 132.

### VI.2. 'Nobody shall profit from his own wrongdoing'

**1**. Co Littleton 148b.
**2**. *Riggs v Palmer* (1889) 115 NY 506, 22 NE 188 at 190. This case is cited by Ronald Dworkin as an example of a principle overriding the normally applicable legal rule: *Taking Rights Seriously*, London, 1977, p. 23ff.
**3**. *Davitt v Titcumb* [1989] 3 All ER 417.
**4**. *Re Crippen (decd)* [1911] P 108.
**5**. *Cleaver v Mutual Reserve Fund* [1892] 1 QB 147.
**6**. *Re Pollock* [1941] 1 All ER 360.
**7**. *Daily Telegraph*, 27 April 1998.
**8**. Ibid.
**9**. See www.scotcourts.gov.uk/opinions/PRO2007.html.

### VI.3. The presumption of regularity

**1**. Coke on Littleton 6b, 323b.
**2**. Ibid., p. 232.
**3**. *Gibson v Doeg* 2 H&N 615.
**4**. *Re Sandilands* LR 6 CO 411.
**5**. *Marine Investment Co v Haviside* LR 5 HL 624.
**6**. *Malpas v Clements* 19 LJ QB 435.
**7**. *Avery v Bowden* 6 E&B 953.
**8**. Ibid. at 973.
**9**. *Smith & Smith v Smith* (1866) LR 1 P&D 143; 35 LJP & M 65.
**10**. Ibid.
**11**. *Harris v Knight* (1890) 15 PD 170.
**12**. Ibid.
**13**. *In the Estate of Bercovitz* [1962] 1 All ER 552 applying the test set out in *Phipps v Hale* (1874) LR 3 P&D 166.
**14**. *Wood v Smith* [1991] 3 WLR 514; [1991] 2 All ER 939.
**15**. [1992] 3 All ER 556.
**16**. *Re Sandilands* LR 6 CP 411.
**17**. Coke on Littleton 36a.
**18**. *Fox's Case* 8 Co Rep 93b.
**19**. See n. 9 above.
**20**. *Ross v Helm* [1913] 3 KB 462.
**21**. *The Prince's Case* (1606) 8 Co Rep 1.
**22**. *Pickin v British Railways Board* [1974] All ER 609 at 618f.; [1974] AC 765.
**23**. *O'Reilly v Mackman* [1982] 3 All ER 1124 at 1133.
**24**. *Dillon v The Queen* [1982] 1 All ER 1017.
**25**. *Scott v Baker* [1968] 2 All ER 993.
**26**. *Boyd-Gibbins v Skinner* [1951] 1 All ER 1049.

## VII. Human Rights

### VII.1. Individual liberty

**1.** 5 Co Rep 92.

**2.** Coke's reference to the statute in question as 21 Henry VII c. 39 is probably incorrect. This citation uses the traditional form of dating by regnal year, which would place the Act in the 21st year of the reign of Henry VII, or 1506. But there was no Parliament sitting in that year. The precise date of the statute to which Coke was referring is not known, but it is unlikely that it was a figment of his imagination!

**3.** *R v Anthony Edward Martin* [2001] EWCA Crim 2245, [2002] 2 WLR 1.

**4.** *Beckford v R* [1987] 3 All ER 425.

**5.** Ibid. at 431.

**6.** *American Jurisprudence 2d* (40 AmJur 2d §174, 1968 as updated to 2000).

**7.** *R v Secretary of State ex parte Venables & Thompson* [1997] 3 All ER 97.

**8.** Ibid. at 137.

**9.** *T v United Kingdom; V v United Kingdom* 99/121-22 7 BHRC 659 (15/9/99 & 16/12/99).

**10.** See Chapter VII.2.

### VII.2. Freedom of expression

**1.** *Cassell v Broome* [1972] 1 All ER 801.

**2.** Ibid. at 876.

**3.** *Entick v Carrington*, State Trials xix, 1044.

**4.** *Wilkes v Wood*, State Trials xix, 1166.

**5.** *John Tutchin's* case, State Trials xiv, 1125.

**6.** *Entick v Carrington*, op. cit.

**7.** *Attorney General v Guardian Newspapers Ltd (No 2)* [1988] 3 All ER 545.

**8.** Ibid. at 660.

**9.** *Derbyshire County Council v Times Newspapers* [1993] 1 All ER 1011 at 1021 (summarising Lord Goff in *A-G v Guardian Newspapers*, quoted above).

**10.** *Reynolds v Times Newspapers* [1999] 4 All ER 609.

**11.** Ibid. at 629.

**12.** See Chapter IV.2.

**13.** *Totalise v The Motley Fool Ltd* (Lawtel, Owen J, 19 February 2001).

**14.** Based on *Norwich Pharmacal v Commissioners of Customs & Excise* [1974] AC 133.

**15.** At first instance the defendant website operators were not only ordered to disclose the identity of 'Z Dust' but were also subjected to a costs order, which is contrary to the normal rule in *Norwich Pharmacal* applications. The costs order was successfully appealed by one of the defendants: *Totalise v Motley Fool* [2001] EWCA Civ 1897. But there was no appeal against the *Norwich Pharmacal* order itself.

**16.** *Informationsverein Lentia v Austria* ECtHR 24/11/93, para 38.

**17.** 315 HC Official Report (6th series) col 536 (2 July 1998).

**18.** *American Cyanamid v Ethicon* [1975] 1 All ER 504.

**19.** *Imutran Ltd v Uncaged Campaigns Ltd* [2002] FSR 20.

**20.** *Naomi Campbell v Mirror Group Newspapers Ltd* [2002] EWHC 499 (QB).

**21.** 315 HC Official Report (6th series) cols 538-9 (2 July 1998).

**22.** 315 HC Official Report (6th series) col 536, (2 July 1998).

**23.** *R v Central Independent Television plc* [1994] 3 All ER 641 at 652, per Hoffmann LJ.

**24.** *X Ltd v Morgan-Grampian Ltd* [1990] 2 All ER 1 (HL).

**25.** *Goodwin v UK* (1996) 22 EHRR 123 96/15.

**26**. *Interbrew v Financial Times & others* [2002] EWCA Civ 274.

**27**. *Camelot Group v Centaur Ltd* [1998] 1 All ER 251 at 259.

**28**. *Naomi Campbell v Mirror Group Newspapers Ltd* [2002] EWHC 499 (QB).

**29**. *Naomi Campbell v Mirror Group Newspapers Ltd* [2002] EWCA Civ 1373.

**30**. *A v B & Another, sub nomine Garry Flitcroft v Mirror Group Newspapers Ltd* [2002] EWCA Civ 337.

**31**. *X Ltd v Morgan Grampian* [1990] 2 All ER 1.

**32**. *Goodwin v UK* (1996) 22 EHRR 123.

**33**. *Attorney-General v Guardian Newspapers* [1990] 1 AC 109, [1987] 3 All ER 316.

**34**. *The Observer & The Guardian v UK* (1991) 14 EHRR 153.

**35**. *Douglas v Hello!* (2000) 9 BHRC 543.

**36**. *Venables & Thompson v News Group Newspapers* [2001] 2 All ER 908.

**37**. *Daily Telegraph*, 4 December 2001.

**38**. The quotations are from *Venables & Thompson v News Group Newspapers* (2001) 9 BHRC, paras. 76 and 82 respectively.

**39**. The quotations are from *Venables & Thompson v News Group Newspapers* (2001) 9 BHRC, paras. 111 and 33 respectively.

**40**. *Attorney General v Guardian Newspapers (No 2)* [1990] 1 AC 109 at 281.

**41**. BBC radio interview as reported in the *Daily Telegraph*, 29 July 2002.

**42**. *Wilkinson v Downton* [1897] 2 QB 57.

**43**. *Schenk v United States* 249 US 47 (1919).

**44**. Alan Dershowitz, *Shouting Fire*, Boston, 2002, p. 147.

**45**. *Texas v Johnson* 491 US 397 (1989).

**46**. *Eichman v United States* 496 US 310 (1990).

**47**. *Brind v Secretary of State for the Home Department* [1991] 1 All ER 720.

**48**. *Brind v UK* Admissibility Application No. 18714/91 – http://hudoc.echr.coe.int.

**49**. *Attorney-General v Times Newspapers* [1991] 2 All ER 398.

**50**. *Attorney-General v Punch* [2001] EWCA Civ 403 (Lawtel – 23 March 2001).

**51**. *R v Shayler* [2002] UKHL 11, [2002] 2 All ER 477.

**52**. Tony Weir, *A Casebook on Tort*, 8th edn, 1996, p. 525.

**53**. Eric Barendt, Laurence Lustgarten, Kenneth Norrie and Hugh Stephenson, *Libel and the Media: The Chilling Effect*, Oxford, 1997.

**54**. Ibid., p. 196.

**55**. Ibid., p. 183.

**56**. *Hulton & Co Ltd v Jones* [1910] AC 20.

**57**. *Ward v James* [1965] 1 All ER 563 at 575.

**58**. *John v MGN Ltd* [1996] 2 All ER 35.

**59**. *Derbyshire County Council v Times Newspapers Ltd* [1993] 1 All ER 1011.

**60**. *City of Chicago v Tribune Co* (1923) 307 **Ill** 595.

**61**. *New York Times Co v Sullivan* (1964) 376 US 254 at 277.

**62**. *Reynolds v Times Newspapers Ltd* [1999] 4 All ER 609.

**63**. Ibid. at 629.

**64**. *Tolstoy Miloslavsky v United Kingdom* (1995) 20 EHRR 442 95/20.

**65**. *Janowski v Poland* (2000) 29 EHRR 705 99/3.

**66**. *Oberschlick v Austria* (1995) 19 EHRR 389 91/29; *Oberschlick (No 2) v Austria* (1998) 25 EHRR 357 97/41; *Prager and Oberschlick v Austria* (1996) 21 EHRR 1 95/11.

**67**. *De Haes & Gijsels v Belgium* (1998) 25 EHRR 1 97/7.

### Excursus B. Liberty and equality

**1**. Isaiah Berlin, *Four Essays on Liberty*, Oxford, 1969, p. 123.

**2**. Thomas Hobbes, *Leviathan* I.13.

**3**. Berlin, op. cit., p. 131.
**4**. Berlin, op. cit., p. 131f.
**5**. Berlin, op. cit., p. 162.
**6**. Rousseau, *Du Contrat Social* II, 3.
**7**. Rousseau, *Du Contrat Social* IV, 1.
**8**. See Richard A. Epstein, *Forbidden Grounds: The Case Against Employment Discrimination Laws*, Cambridge, Mass, 1992. This ambitious book seeks to show that anti-discrimination laws 'set one group against another, impose limits on freedom of choice, undermine standards of merit and achievement, unleash bureaucratic excesses, mandate inefficient employment practices, and cause far more invidious discrimination than they prevent'. The author, a leading American legal academic, urges instead 'a return to the common law principles of individual autonomy that permit all persons to improve their position through trade, contract, and bargain, free of government constraint'.
**9**. Joseph Joubert as quoted in Rudolf Flesch, *The Book of Unusual Quotations*, London, 1959, p. 170.

## VIII. The Administration of Justice

### VIII.1. Judicial review

**1**. For a discussion of the meaning of these terms see Michael Arnheim, *Handbook of Human Rights Law*, London, 2004, ch. I.
**2**. Civil Procedure Rules 1998 (CPR) 54.19.
**3**. *Chief Constable of North Wales v Evans* [1982] 3 All ER 141 at 154 (HL).
**4**. *Associated Provincial Picture Houses v Wednesbury Corp* [1948] 1 KB 223, per Lord Greene MR.
**5**. *R v Secretary of State for the Home Department, ex parte Daly* [2001] UKHL 26, [2001] 3 All ER 433 at 447, para 32, per Lord Cooke of Thorndon.
**6**. Lord Irvine of Lairg, 'Judges and Decision-Makers: The Theory and Practice of *Wednesbury* Review' [1996] PL 59 at 63.
**7**. Sir John Laws, 'Is the High Court the Guardian of Fundamental Constitutional Rights?' [1993] PL 59 at 69.
**8**. *R v Secretary of State for the Home Dept ex parte Brind* [1991] 1 AC 697.
**9**. Lord Irvine of Lairg, 'Judges and Decision-Makers: The Theory and Practice of *Wednesbury* Review' [1996] PL 59 at 65.
**10**. *R v Ministry of Defence, ex parte Smith* [1995] 4 All ER 427 at 447.
**11**. *R v Ministry of Defence, ex parte Smith* [1996] 1 All ER 257 (CA), per Bingham MR.
**12**. *Lustig-Prean and Beckett v UK* (1999) 29 EHRR 548 99/53.
**13**. Ibid. at §81.
**14**. *Smith and Grady v UK* (1999) 29 EHRR 493 at 543, para 138.
**15**. *R v Secretary of State for the Home Department, ex parte Daly* [2001] UKHL 26, [2001] 3 All ER 433 at 446, para 28, per Lord Steyn.
**16**. Quoted by Lord Bingham p. 444 para 21.
**17**. *R v Secretary of State for the Home Department, ex parte Daly* [2001] UKHL 26, [2001] 3 All ER 433 at 446, para 28, per Lord Steyn citing *R (Mahmood) v Secretary of State for the Home Dept* [2001] 1 WLR 840.
**18**. See the discussion in Arnheim, *Handbook of Human Rights Law*, ch. III.
**19**. *R (Alconbury) v Secretary of State for the Environment* [2001] UKHL 23, [2001] 2 All ER 929 at 980 para 69.
**20**. Ibid., para 70.
**21**. Lord Hoffmann at least recognises that, by contrast with both the legislature and

the executive, judges are not democratically accountable. Cf. the views of Sedley LJ, discussed in Excursus A to Chapter II.

**22**. *Council of Civil Service Unions v Minister for the Civil Service* [1984] 3 All ER 935 at 949ff.

**23**. *Council of Civil Service Unions v Minister for the Civil Service* [1984] 3 All ER 935 at 950j/951a.

**24**. *Anisminic Ltd v Foreign Compensation Commission* [1969] 2 AC 147.

**25**. See Chapter VIII.2 on ouster clauses.

**26**. *Council of Civil Service Unions v Minister for the Civil Service* [1984] 3 All ER 935 at 950j.

**27**. See *Duport Steels v Sirs* [1980] 1 All ER 529.

**28**. *R v Secretary of State for Home Affairs ex parte Jayaram Khadka, Evening Standard*, 7 November 1996.

**29**. *The Times*, 13 May 1997.

**30**. *R v Cambridge Health Authority, ex parte B* [1995] 2 All ER 129 at 138g.

**VIII.2. Ouster clauses**

**1**. *Anisminic Ltd v Foreign Compensation Commission* [1969] 2 AC 147, [1969] 1 All ER 208 (HL).

**2**. [1969] 1 All ER 208 at 215H.

**3**. Ibid. at 216C.

**4**. *R v Northumberland Compensation Appeal Tribunal, ex parte Shaw* [1952] 1 All ER 122 at 127, cited in *Anisminic* [1969] 1 All ER 208 at 245.

**5**. *O'Reilly v Mackman* [1983] 2 AC 237 at 278, [1982] 3 All ER 1124 at 1129c.

**6**. *Re Racal Communications Ltd* [1980] 2 All ER 634 at 638c.

**7**. [1969] 1 All ER 208 at 213-214.

**8**. [1969] 1 All ER 208 at 235.

**9**. *R v Northumberland Compensation Appeal Tribunal, ex parte Shaw* [1952] 1 All ER 122 (at 127).

**10**. *Pearlman v Keepers & Governors of Harrow School* [1979] 1 All ER 365; [1978] 3 WLR 736.

**11**. [1979] 1 All ER 365 at 371.

**12**. *Re Racal Communications Ltd* [1980] 2 All ER 634.

**13**. Christopher Forsyth, 'Lord Denning and Modern Administrative Law', Denning Symposium proceedings, University of Buckingham, 23 January 1999, p. 3.

**14**. *Pearlman v Keepers & Governors of Harrow School* [1979] 1 All ER 365 at 376.

**15**. *Re Racal Communications Ltd* [1980] 2 All ER 634 at 637b.

**16**. Ibid. at 645e.

**17**. Ibid. at 640b.

**18**. [1980] 1 All ER 284 at 286.

**19**. [1979] 1 All ER 365.

**20**. *Page v Hull University Visitor* [1993] 1 All ER 97.

**21**. See *R v Panel on Take-overs & Mergers ex parte Datafin Ltd* [1987] QB 815, [1987] 1 All ER 654 (CA).

**22**. *Thomas v University of Bradford* [1987] 1 All ER 834.

**23**. *Casson v University of Aston in Birmingham* [1983] 1 All ER 88 at 90-91.

**24**. [1987] 1 All ER 834 at 847j.

**25**. Ibid. at 852j.

**26**. Ibid. at 850b, glossed by remarks in *Page v Hull University Visitor* [1993] 1 All ER 97 at 100g.

**27**. [1993] 1 All ER 97 at 113j.

**28**. Ibid. at 114a-d.

**29**. Ibid. at 100j.

**30**. Ibid. at 108b.

**31**. *South East Asia Fire Bricks v Non-Metallic Mineral Products Manufacturing Employees Union* [1981] AC 363 at 370, [1980] 2 All ER 689 at 692.

**32**. [1993] 1 All ER 97 at 108g.

**33**. Ibid. at 109c.

**34**. Ibid. at 107d.

**35**. *Council of Civil Service Unions v Minister for the Civil Service* [1985] AC 374.

**36**. *M v Home Office* [1994] 2 AC 377.

**37**. *Thomas v University of Bradford* [1987] 1 All ER 834 at 849h.

**38**. [1993] 1 All ER 97 at 101c.

**39**. [1969] 1 All ER 208 at 236H-237A.

**40**. *Ex parte Bradlaugh* (1878) 3 QBD 509 at 513, cited in *Anisminic Ltd v Foreign Compensation Commission* [1969] 1 All ER 208 at 238D.

**41**. [1969] 1 All ER 208 at 256I.

**42**. 9 *Halsbury's Laws of England* (2nd edn) p. 888 (= vol. 11, 3rd edn, p. 62).

**43**. *R v Minister of Health, ex p Committee of Visitors of Glamorgan County Mental Hospital* [1938] 4 All ER 32 at 36.

**44**. [1969] 1 All ER 208 at 226I.

**45**. [1968] 2 QB 862, [1967] 2 All ER 986.

**46**. [1969] 1 All ER 208 at 232I-233A.

**47**. *R v Northumberland Compensation Appeal Tribunal, ex parte Shaw* [1952] 1 All ER 122 at 127.

**48**. [1969] 1 All ER 208 at 233I-234B.

**49**. [1969] 1 All ER 208 at 216D.

**50**. [1969] 1 All ER 208 at 235E-H.

**51**. *Ridge v Baldwin* [1963] 2 All ER 66 at 71D.

**52**. Lord Woolf, 'Droit Public – English Style' [1995] Public Law 57 at 69.

**53**. *Griffiths v Secretary of State for the Environment* [1983] 1 All ER 439.

**54**. Lord Irvine LC, 'Principle and Pragmatism: The Development of English Public Law under the Separation of Powers' (18 September 1998), Lecture at the Hong Kong High Court, p. 8 – http://www.open.gov.uk?lcd/speeches/1998/hongkong.htm.

## Excursus C. Pollock on the common law

**1**. Sir Stephen Sedley, 'The Common Law and the Constitution' in Nolan and Sedley, *The Making and Remaking of the British Constitution*, London, 1997, p. 15.

**2**. F.E. Pollock, *Essays on Jurisprudence and Ethics*, 1882, p. 85.

**3**. Ibid., p. 71f.

**4**. Ibid., p. 73.

**5**. Ibid.

**6**. Ibid., p. 84.

**7**. Ibid.

**8**. Ibid. p. 85.

**9**. Ibid.

**10**. Ibid., p. 86.

**11**. Ibid., p. 90.

**12**. Sedley, loc. cit.

**13**. Pollock, op. cit., p. 240. See the discussion in Chapter V.1.

# *Notes to pages 240-265*

## IX. Contract

### IX.1. Contract as agreement

**1**. P.S. Atiyah, *Essays on Contract*, Oxford, 1986, p. 18f.
**2**. *Pharmaceutical Society v Boots* [1953] 1 All ER 482.
**3**. *White & Carter v McGregor* [1961] 3 All ER 1178 (HL).
**4**. Atiyah, op. cit., p. 28f.
**5**. *Anglo-Cyprian Trade Agencies v Paphos Wine Industries* [1951] 1 All ER 873.
**6**. *Thompson Ltd v Robinson* [1955] 1 All ER 154.
**7**. *Charter v Sullivan* [1957] 1 All ER 809 (CA).
**8**. Atiyah, op. cit., p. 19.
**9**. Ibid., p. 23.
**10**. *Luxor (Eastbourne) Ltd (in liquidation) v Cooper* [1941] 1 All ER 33.
**11**. *Trollope v Martyn Bros* [1934] 2 KB 436.
**12**. [1941] 1 All ER 33 at 43.
**13**. *Jaques v Lloyd D. George* [1968] 2 All ER 187.
**14**. Atiyah, op. cit., p. 203.

### IX.2. Strict contractual liability

**1**. *Photo Production v Securicor* [1980] AC 827, per Lord Diplock.
**2**. *Beswick v Beswick* [1967] 2 All ER 1197 (HL).
**3**. *Paradine v Jane* (1647) 82 ER 897, [1558-1774] All ER Rep 172.
**4**. *Tatem v Gamboa* [1938] 3 All ER 135 at 143f, per Goddard J.
**5**. *Taylor v Caldwell* (1863) 122 ER 309, [1861-73] All ER Rep 24.
**6**. *Digest* XLV title 1, art. 33.
**7**. Pothier, *Traité des Obligations* part 3, ch. 6, art. 632 (vol. II, p. 131).
**8**. The quotations are from [1861-73] All ER Rep 24 at 28 and 29 respectively.
**9**. *Krell v Henry* [1903] 2 KB 740.
**10**. *Chandler v Webster* [1904] 1 KB 493 (CA).
**11**. *Blakeley v Muller* [1903] 2 KB 760 (Note) at 762, per Channell J.
**12**. *Fibrosa Spolka Akcyjna v Fairbairn* [1942] 2 All ER 122.
**13**. Ibid. at 130.
**14**. Ibid. at 132.
**15**. *Readhead v Midland Rail Co* (1868) [1861-73] All ER Rep 30.
**16**. [1861-73] All ER Rep 30 at 33.
**17**. *Crofts v Waterhouse* (1825) 130 ER 536.
**18**. *Coggs v Bernard* (1703) 92 ER 107, [1558-1774] All ER Rep 1.
**19**. See *'The Albazero'* [1976] 3 All ER 129 at 133 (Lord Diplock).
**20**. See *Ludditt v Ginger Coote Airways* [1947] 1 All ER 328 (PC).
**21**. *Donoghue v Stevenson* [1932] AC 562; [1932] All ER Rep 1.
**22**. *Lockett v Charles* [1938] 4 All ER 170.
**23**. *Jacob & Youngs Inc v Kent* (Court of Appeals of New York, 1921) 230 NY 239, 129 NE 889.
**24**. Thomas D. Crandall and Douglas J. Whaley, *Cases, Problems and Materials on Contracts*, Boston, 1987, p. 37.
**25**. E. Farnsworth, *Contracts*, New York, 1982, §8.15 – cited by Crandall, op. cit., p. 836.
**26**. Samuel Williston, *Treatise on the Law of Contracts*, 3rd edn, ed. W. Jaeger, London, 1957.
**27**. *Ruxley Electronics v Forsyth* [1995] 3 All ER 268.

## X. New Principles?

### X.1. Legitimate expectation

**1**. *R v Brent Council ex p Gunning* (1985) 84 LGR 168.
**2**. *Re Westminster City Council* [1986] AC 668.
**3**. Case 289/81 *Mavridis v Parliament* [1983] ECR 1731.
**4**. *Schmidt v Secretary of State for Home Affairs* [1969] 1 All ER 904.
**5**. Ibid. at 907
**6**. Ibid. at 909B.
**7**. *McInnes v Onslow Fane* [1978] 3 All ER 211.
**8**. *R v Secretary of State for Foreign and Commonwealth Affairs, ex parte Everett* [1989] 1 All ER 655 (CA).
**9**. *Lloyd v McMahon* [1987] 1 All ER 1118 (HL).
**10**. Ibid. at 1170a.
**11**. Ibid. at 1161c.
**12**. *R v Devon County Council, ex parte Baker* [1995] 1 All ER 73.
**13**. *R v Home Secretary ex parte Ruddock* [1987] 2 All ER 518.
**14**. *R v Secretary of State for the Home Department, ex parte Khan* [1985] 1 All ER 40 (CA).
**15**. *R v Secretary of State for the Home Department, ex parte Pierson* [1998] AC 539.
**16**. Ibid. at 590G-591A.
**17**. *Schmidt v Secretary of State for Home Affairs* [1969] 1 All ER 904, *O'Reilly v Mackman* [1982] 3 All ER 1124 and *R v Rochdale Metropolitan BC, ex parte Schemet* [1993] 1 FCR 306.
**18**. *Re Liverpool Taxi Owners' Association* [1972] 2 All ER 589.
**19**. *Attorney General of Hong Kong v NG Yuen Shiu* [1983] 2 All ER 346, [1983] 2 AC 629.
**20**. *Council of Civil Service Unions v Minister for the Civil Service* [1984] 3 All ER 935 (HL).
**21**. *R v Secretary of State for the Environment, ex parte National & Local Government Officers' Association* (1993) 5 Admin LR 785 at 804E.
**22**. *R v Commissioners of Customs and Excise, ex parte F & I Services Ltd* [2001] EWCA Civ 762.
**23**. *O'Reilly v Mackman* [1982] 3 All ER 1124.
**24**. *R v Department for Education and Employment, ex parte Begbie* [2000] 1 WLR 1115 at 1133E (Sedley LJ).
**25**. *Canada & Dominion Sugar Co Ltd v Canadian National (West Indies) Steamships Ltd* [1946] 3 WWR 759 at 764.
**26**. *Dillwyn v Llewelyn* (1862) 4 De GF & J 517.
**27**. *Central London Property Trust Ltd v High Trees House* [1947] KB 130.

### X.2. 'Fair, just and reasonable?'

**1**. *Caparo v Dickman* [1990] 2 AC 605.
**2**. *Mohammed Khalif Farah v British Airways* CCRTI 1999/0917/B1 – Court of Appeal – Lawtel 6/12/99 (unreported), para 11.
**3**. *Marc Rich v Bishop Rock Marine ('The Nicholas H')* [1995] 3 All ER 307.
**4**. Ibid. at 326.
**5**. *Home Office v Dorset Yacht Co Ltd* [1970] 2 All ER 294.
**6**. *Marc Rich v Bishop Rock Marine ('The Nicholas H')* [1994] 3 All ER 686 at 692-3.
**7**. *Marc Rich v Bishop Rock Marine ('The Nicholas H')* [1995] 3 All ER 307 at 321.
**8**. Ibid. at 322.

**9**. *Child Support Agency v Rust* Lawtel Document No. C9400023, 2/12/99.

**10**. *Child Support Agency v G (Refusal of Paternity Test)* Lawtel Document No. C8000408, 16/6/97.

## Epilogue

**1**. *M v Home Office* [1992] 4 All ER 97 (Court of Appeal) at 146, *per* Nolan LJ.

**2**. Could the passage possibly mean only that the courts are to determine whether a decision of the executive is or is not within its lawful province – i.e. whether it is ultra vires or not – without actually deciding what that lawful province is (except insofar as interpreting the scope of that province as already laid down by time-honoured law or convention)? That would be a much more accurate statement of the true constitutional role of the judiciary, similar to that of a sports referee, deciding whether a particular action is in breach of the rules but without the right to make or change the rules. But it is hard to see how the quoted passage could have this more restricted meaning.

**3**. Discussed in Chapter V.2.

**4**. See Chapter V.1.

**5**. In his wildest judicial supremacist phase Sir Edward Coke CJ remarked that 'the King cannot change any part of the common law, nor create any offence by his proclamation which was not an offence before, without Parliament': Case of Proclamations, 1610, Coke's Reports, Part XII, p. 74. Coke ends his report with the remark that 'it was resolved [viz by the assembled judges] that the King hath no prerogative but that which the law of the land allows him.' Is this a veiled claim for the right of the judiciary to determine the nature and extent of executive authority? The phrase 'the law of the land' means the common law. But, while denying the right of the King (i.e. the executive) to change the common law, Coke makes no attempt to claim this right for the judiciary. So, even this case, which is perhaps the most promising possible authority for Lord Nolan's formulation (though none is cited), does not actually support it.

**6**. It was even endorsed by Lord Irvine of Lairg as Lord Chancellor, who commended the passage with the words: 'Lord Nolan expressed the true position in terms that I doubt can be improved.' After quoting the passage, Lord Irvine remarks: 'The present administration [i.e. the Blair Government] recognises that this is how a mature, democratic government should relate to the courts.' 'Principle and Pragmatism: The Development of English Public Law under the Separation of Powers', Lecture delivered 18 September 1998, Hong Kong. (From the website of the Department of Constitutional Affairs.) Lord Irvine's strictures on judicial supremacism are discussed in Chapter V.1.

**7**. *M v Home Office* [1993] 3 All ER 537 (House of Lords). It is important to note that government ministers had long been personally legally liable for their actions. There was no problem about finding 'Kenneth William Baker' (i.e. the Home Secretary in his own name) in contempt of court, which was the result in the Court of Appeal. What the House of Lords did was to substitute 'the Secretary of State for the Home Department' as the person who was in contempt of court. What difference did this make? On the face of it, very little. But the substitution signified the court's claim of jurisdiction over the Crown.

**8**. Carol Harlow and Richard Rawlings, *Law and Administration*, 2nd ed., London, 1997, p. 602f. See p. 104 above.

**9**. See p. 104 above.

**10**. See in particular Chapters V and VIII.

# Index

# Index